KU-652-460

CONTENTS

FIGURES

TABLES

ACKNOWLEDGEMENTS

The editors are extremely grateful to their colleagues who have contributed chapters to the book and have provided support and encouragement for the project over several months.

Most of the chapters are based on data from the *Growing Up in Ireland* study, Ireland's national longitudinal study of children. Ireland is extremely fortunate to have this major, long-term project focusing on children and childhood. The project is funded by the Department of Children and Youth Affairs (DCYA) and is overseen by the DCYA in association with the Central Statistics Office. It also receives a contribution in Phase 2 from the Atlantic Philanthropies. The study is implemented by a consortium of researchers led by the Economic and Social Research Institute (ESRI) and Trinity College Dublin (TCD). The research infrastructure provided by the *Growing Up in Ireland* study is helping to improve our collective understanding of children and young people in Ireland today and provides a unique scientific framework for the development of evidence-informed practice and policy in this area. We would like to thank all of those involved in the funding, managing and implementation of the project since it began in 2006.

We are extremely grateful to our colleagues in the ESRI and Trinity College for their support and assistance throughout the project.

The biggest word of thanks goes, of course, to almost 20,000 children, young people and their families who participate in the *Growing Up in Ireland* project, along with their teachers and school Principals, all of whom have given so generously of their time to participate in the study since its inception in 2006. *Growing Up in Ireland* and the research emerging from it (including outputs such as this book) would simply not have been possible without the time, commitment and assistance that they have so readily given to the study over almost a decade.

The editors and authors accept full responsibility for the content of the book and for any errors or omissions.

James Williams
Elizabeth Nixon
Emer Smyth
Dorothy Watson

CONTRIBUTORS

Joanne Banks is a Research Officer at the Economic and Social Research Institute. Her research interests include special educational needs, inclusion and student engagement. She has published work on special educational needs prevalence and identification, special class provision and the everyday school experiences for students with different types of needs.

Megan A. Curran is an Irish Research Council Postgraduate Scholar and doctoral student in social policy in University College Dublin's School of Social Policy, Social Work and Social Justice, as well as an independent researcher and consultant focusing on issues of economic and social inclusion. With degrees from Fordham University, the University of Edinburgh, and University College Dublin, she has legislative, policy development, and advocacy experience in the United States and Europe, and expertise in child and family policy, anti-poverty strategies, public benefits, and women's equality issues.

Merike Darmody is a Research Officer at the Economic and Social Research Institute and an Adjunct Assistant Professor at the Department of Sociology, Trinity College Dublin. Her key area of interest lies in ethnic, cultural linguistic and religious diversity in contemporary societies and education systems. She has been involved as a national expert in a European Commission-funded international comparative study on the educational needs of newly-arrived migrant children and a comparative project on the provision of religious education in multicultural societies.

Tony Fahey has been Professor of Social Policy in University College Dublin since 2007 and previously worked in the Economic and Social

Research Institute. His main research interests are in family demography, family policy and various aspects of social policy, particularly housing and social inequality. His current main focus is on family patterns in Ireland in the early 21st century.

Sheila Greene is a Fellow Emeritus at Trinity College Dublin and a former Professor of Childhood Research. She is a co-founder and former Director of the Children's Research Centre and was one of the authors of the *Design Brief* for **Growing Up in Ireland** and its Co-Director from 2006-2011. Her publications include *The Psychological Development of Girls and Women* (Routledge, 2003/2015), *Researching Children's Experience* (Greene & Hogan, Sage, 2005), and *Key Thinkers in Childhood Studies* (Smith & Greene, Policy Press, 2014), as well as journal articles and commissioned reports.

Gillian Kingston is a former a Research Assistant at the Economic and Social Research Institute. She worked on a number of migration- and equality-related projects, including discrimination in Ireland, people with disability in the labour market, the equality impact on the unemployment crises, the annual monitoring report on integration and many others.

Richard Layte is Professor of Sociology at Trinity College Dublin and a Research Professor at the Economic and Social Research Institute. Much of his work stems from a core interest in the structure of social and economic stratification in modern societies and its impact on individual life-chances, health and wellbeing. He has a particular interest in improving understanding of how family background influences child health and development and the impact this has on the child's educational outcomes, adult health and life expectancy. He also has a keen interest in Irish healthcare and the role that healthcare can play in improving health and wellbeing.

Bertrand Maître is a Senior Research Officer at the Economic and Social Research Institute. His main research interests include poverty and inequality, social exclusion and income distribution. His latest publications have been in areas related to the role of disability and parental expectations on child wellbeing, family economic stress and its effect on children's socio-emotional outcomes and household joblessness.

Selina McCoy is an Associate Research Professor at the Economic and Social Research Institute, Dublin and Adjunct Professor at Trinity College Dublin. Her research interests focus on social inequality in educational participation and outcomes, including a particular focus on the wellbeing and development of young people with disabilities. She has published widely in peer-reviewed journals, most recently *Child Indicators Research, European Journal of Special Needs Education, The Economic and Social Review* and *International Journal of Inclusive Education*. She is the Irish national expert at the European Commission Independent Experts on Education and Training.

Cathal McCrory is a Psychologist and Senior Research Fellow with the Irish Longitudinal Study on Ageing (TILDA) at Trinity College Dublin. His expertise is in the field of human development and ageing and his research explores the pathways, processes, and mechanisms through which socially-mediated variation in exposure to risk and protective factors over the life course precipitates earlier biological ageing among the more socially disadvantaged. A major focus of his work has been to estimate the impact of early life factors on the risk of disease and mortality in later life.

Frances McGinnity is an Associate Research Professor at the Economic and Social Research Institute and Adjunct Professor of Sociology at Trinity College Dublin. She received her doctorate from Nuffield College, Oxford in 2001 and came to the ESRI in 2004 from the Max Planck Institute for Human Development in Berlin, Germany. Her research focuses on labour market inequality, work-life balance, childcare, discrimination and migrant integration, in Ireland and from a comparative perspective. She is currently an associate editor of *Work, Employment and Society* and a member of the International Panel on Social Progress.

Aisling Murray is a Research Officer at the Economic and Social Research Institute and a member of the **Growing Up in Ireland** study team since the project started in 2006. A psychologist, her main research interests are cognitive development and influences on development in early childhood. She is a member of the Royal Irish Academy's Social Sciences Committee and co-ordinator of the Policy Group in the Society for Longitudinal and Life-course Studies. Her recent publications have been on the effect of childcare, home learning environment and breastfeeding on cognitive and social development from infancy to five years.

Elizabeth Nixon is an Assistant Professor in Developmental Psychology at the School of Psychology and Senior Research Fellow at the Children's Research Centre, Trinity College Dublin. She is a Co-Investigator on *Growing Up in Ireland* (Phases 1 and 2) and is Co-Director of the Infant and Child Research Laboratory within the School of Psychology at TCD. Her research interests include parenting, child development within diverse family structures and children's agency.

Anne Nolan is a Senior Research Officer at the Economic and Social Research Institute. She is also a Research Affiliate at the Irish Longitudinal Study on Ageing (TILDA) at Trinity College Dublin, and on the Study Team Management Group of *Growing Up in Ireland*. Her main research interest is health economics, with a particular focus on healthcare financing and access, socio-economic inequalities in health and Irish health policy.

Jean Quigley is a Lecturer and Researcher, Director of Postgraduate Teaching & Learning and Co-Director of the Infant and Child Research Laboratory in the School of Psychology at Trinity College Dublin. Her research expertise is in language development, with particular reference to early first language acquisition and to neurodevelopmental disorders, including Autism Spectrum Disorders. She is also using the *Growing Up in Ireland* study data to investigate risk and protective factors for early language development. Her work currently focuses on the identification and analysis of important interpersonal interactional variables for language acquisition and for overall optimal development.

Helen Russell is an Associate Research Professor at the Economic and Social Research Institute. She is also Adjunct Professor of Sociology at Trinity College Dublin. Her research interests include gender, equality, social exclusion and the intersection between work and family life, including the effects of childcare on child outcomes. Recent publications examine work-life balance across Europe, the effects of unemployment on wellbeing, and household joblessness. She is the co-author of the

Growing Up in Ireland study *Non-Parental Childcare and Child Cognitive Outcomes at Age 5*, published in 2015.

Michael Shevlin is Professor in Inclusive Education in the School of Education at Trinity College Dublin. His main research interests include school and educational experiences of children with disabilities and developmental delays and ensuring that the voice of the child is heard in developing the education system. Michael sits on numerous expert advisory groups and editorial boards.

Emer Smyth is a Research Professor at the Economic and Social Research Institute and Adjunct Professor in the School of Sociology at Trinity College Dublin. Her main research interests centre on education, school to work transitions, gender and comparative methodology. She has conducted a number of studies on the effects of schooling contexts on student outcomes, emphasising the importance of taking account of student voice in policy development. She is on the management team of the *Growing Up in Ireland* study and has conducted a number of studies based on *Growing Up in Ireland* data on topics such as school experiences and wellbeing, geographical variation in child outcomes and the factors influencing transition to second-level education.

Lorraine Swords is an Assistant Professor in Child and Adolescent Psychology at the School of Psychology, Trinity College Dublin. She teaches in the area of developmental psychology, with particular focus on topics relating to child health and wellbeing. Her research interests lie in understanding peer interactions in the context of physical or mental health conditions in childhood and adolescence, focusing on help-seeking, help-giving and stigmatising responses. Her recent work in this area appears in *Psychiatry Research* (2016), the *Journal of Adolescent Research* (2015), and *Mental Health Review Journal* (2015).

Maeve Thornton is a Research Fellow at the Economic and Social Research Institute and a member of the *Growing Up in Ireland* study team since the project started in 2006. Before working on the *Growing Up in Ireland* study, she spent five years working as a researcher in both the University of Ulster (UU) and Queen's University Belfast (QUB), where she worked on the Youth Development Study, a longitudinal study of adolescent drug use, as well as the Youth Development Study Family

Survey. Her main area of interest lies in exploring the risk and protective factors that are associated with social, emotional and behavioural outcomes for children and young people.

Dorothy Watson is a sociologist and Associate Research Professor at the Economic and Social Research Institute and Adjunct Professor at the Department of Sociology in Trinity College Dublin. Her main research focus has been on social exclusion and equality, both in Ireland and in a comparative European context. Recent publications include work on childhood economic vulnerability in the recession, household joblessness transitions in Ireland, educational and work circumstances of people with a disability, a comparative European analysis of exposure to workplace risks and developing a multidimensional indicator of quality of life in Europe. She jointly co-ordinates Social Inclusion and Equality research at the ESRI and is a member of the management team of the *Growing Up in Ireland* survey.

Christopher T. Whelan is an Emeritus Professor in the School of Sociology and the Geary Institute for Public Policy, University College Dublin, an Associate Member of Nuffield College, Oxford, a Research Affiliate at the Economic and Social Research Institute and a Member of the Royal Irish Academy. He was formerly Professor of Sociology in the School of Sociology, Social Policy and Social Work at Queen's University Belfast, Chair of the Standing Committee of the Social Sciences of the European Science Foundation and the European Consortium for Sociological Research.

James Williams is a Research Professor at the Economic and Social Research Institute and Adjunct Professor at the Children's Research Centre in Trinity College Dublin. He has been Principal Investigator of the *Growing Up in Ireland* project since it began in 2006. His research interests include child development, poverty, deprivation and income distribution and the application of statistical methodologies to the collection of social and economic data. He has published in areas including child development and childcare, poverty, the labour market and methodology. From 1996 to 2006 he was Director of the ESRI's Survey Division.

FOREWORD

As Minister for Children and Youth Affairs, I am delighted to have been invited in this 10th anniversary year of the *Growing Up in Ireland* project to prepare the *Foreword* to this most exciting book, which is largely based on data from the study. Not only is it appropriate to mark 10 years of the *Growing Up in Ireland* project with the publication of this book on child outcomes, but also to consider the extent to which the theme of equality, which ran throughout the *Proclamation of Independence* read at the GPO 100 years ago this year, is reflected in the lives of children in 21st century Ireland.

The authors of the book note that our founding fathers, when referring to '... *cherishing all of the children of the nation equally*' were speaking in a more metaphorical than literal sense. It is, nonetheless, most important at this juncture in our history to consider how children and young people are faring and whether they are each being afforded equitable life chances. This is all the more important in view of our recent history of rapid economic buoyancy, followed by a period of unprecedented recession.

The past century has brought significant improvements in educational opportunities, health outcomes, and in child and family supports. Nonetheless, despite such progress, the chapters in this book, drawing on data from *Growing Up in Ireland*, underline the extent to which those from more disadvantaged backgrounds continue to fare less well across a range of outcomes. As the book notes, there is still much to be done to ensure that we cherish all of the nation's children equally.

The well-being of children and young people has assumed centre stage in government policy across recent years. The publication of the

National Children's Strategy in 2000 and (more recently) *Better Outcomes, Brighter Futures* clearly established an integrated, cross-government approach to ensuring that the lives of children, young people and their families are fully supported and that all children have as good a start in life as possible. Only in doing so will we be able to reach the goal set out in *Better Outcomes* of ensuring that Ireland becomes:

> *... one of the best small countries in the world in which to grow up and raise a family, and where the rights of all children and young people are respected, protected and fulfilled; where their voices are heard and where they are supported to reach their maximum potential now and in the future.*

This focus on children and child-based policy has also been reflected in substantial State funding in one of the largest and most complex studies ever undertaken in Ireland – the *Growing Up in Ireland* study. This longitudinal study of almost 20,000 children, young people, their families and main caregivers has been carried out since 2006. The study touches on all of the key domains of the life of a child in modern Ireland: their family life, their education, their socio-emotional and behavioural well-being and their physical growth and development. I am delighted to say that the project puts Ireland at the international vanguard of children's research. Although the range of topics included in the book is really very substantial, this represents only a small proportion of the research potential offered by the *Growing Up in Ireland* project. This potential will grow as the data from successive rounds of interviews accumulate and the longitudinal nature of the project can be exploited to the full. *Growing Up in Ireland* provides us with a remarkable window on our most important national asset – our children. They are our future and we must, as in this book, strive to further understand how best we can help them to optimise that future to the full.

The authors of the book come from a range of backgrounds and disciplines, including sociology, psychology, geography and economics – each bringing their particular disciplinary perspective to bear on the analysis presented. While each chapter individually provides valuable insights into particular aspects of children's development, taken together they provide a very broad and holistic view of child well-being that has not previously been presented in Ireland. I would like to congratulate all the authors on this welcome contribution.

I would also like to take this opportunity, on behalf of all those responsible for the *Growing Up in Ireland* project, to thank the huge number of people who have participated in it and given so generously of their time to the study – in particular, the children and young people, their families, their school principals and teachers. They collectively make *Growing Up in Ireland* possible and thus help to improve our understanding of how we can best make the lives of all children growing up in Ireland as full and rewarding as possible.

Dr Katherine Zappone TD
Minister for Children and Youth Affairs

Comhairle Contae
Átha Cliath Theas
South Dublin County Council

1: INTRODUCTION

James Williams, Elizabeth Nixon,
Emer Smyth & Dorothy Watson

Background

Ireland has experienced many critical moments in its often tumultuous history. None was more significant or defining than the Easter Rising of 1916. Central to the Rising was the reading of the *Proclamation of Independence* on the steps of the General Post Office by Pádraig Pearse on 24 April of that year. In the words of the *Proclamation*:

> *... The Republic guarantees religious and civil liberty, equal rights and equal opportunities to all its citizens, and declares its resolve to pursue the happiness and prosperity of the whole nation and of all its parts, cherishing all of the children of the nation equally, and oblivious of the differences carefully fostered by an alien Government, which have divided a minority from the majority in the past.* (Pearse & Dolmen Press, 1975)

Although Pearse used 'children' in a metaphorical sense to refer to all the citizens of 'Mother Ireland', it is worth asking whether 100 years on from that momentous April afternoon in 1916, Ireland does, in fact, cherish all of its children equally.

The Easter Rising and the State itself were born out of a protest against unequal treatment of its citizens, at that time by our colonial neighbour. Equality was a theme that was stressed at several points in the *Proclamation*. It is also at the core of this book, in which we bring together contributions from a range of disciplines to shed light on the processes of child development and to investigate how that development is influenced by a variety of demographic, family and socio-economic factors. The book considers the supports necessary for some children to ensure that they can participate in all aspects of society on an equal footing with their peers, regardless of their family circumstances, physical health, ethnic origins or other background characteristics. It puts a firm focus on children themselves and their outcomes, regardless of any context or environment in which they may be growing up, with a view to assessing the extent to which they are treated equally in 21st century Ireland.

In the early decades of the State, policy was often slow to directly recognise the status of children in their own right, and to adopt a rights-based approach to their development, in the terms set out, for example, in the *Convention on the Rights of the Child* (United Nations, 1989). The main policy focus in the early years of the State was on the family, the view (perhaps more implicitly than explicitly stated at the time) being that the benefits provided to support families would benefit children. The government's main policy statement on children and families in contemporary Ireland is set out in *Better Outcomes, Brighter Futures* (Department of Children and Youth Affairs, 2014). This document recognises the status of children in their own right and clearly establishes the importance of equality in all aspects of childhood as being central to government policy:

> *The diversity of children's experiences, abilities, identities and cultures is acknowledged and reducing inequalities is promoted through* Better Outcomes, Brighter Futures *as a means of improving outcomes and achieving greater social inclusion.* (Department of Children and Youth Affairs, 2014, p.20).

Further, one of the main outcomes aspired to in the policy is that:

> *Inequalities* [should be] *addressed across all sectors, including health, education and justice. Children and their parents* [should not] *face discrimination of any kind, irrespective of membership of the Traveller Community, race, gender, sexual orientation, gender identity, civil status, disability, birth or other status. All children in need* [should] *have equality of access to, and participation in, a range of public services.*

The needs of children and young people [should be] *placed at the centre of Government decision-making. Policies and services for children, young people and their families* [should be] *based on identified need; informed by evidence from knowledge, practice and research* ... (Department of Children and Youth Affairs, 2014, pp.20-21).

Current government policy on children clearly shares the principles of equality that were set out in the 1916 *Proclamation*. This book explores the extent to which these principles are, in fact, reflected in the outcomes and wellbeing of all groups of children in Ireland in 2016.

The *Growing Up in Ireland* Project

As noted by Greene *et al.* (2010a) there has been a relative scarcity of large-scale, in-depth studies directly focusing on children or the family in Ireland, partly due to a lack of good quality quantitative data. Exceptions to this include Hannan's work on the family in the 1970s (Hannan & Katsiaouni, 1977; Hannan, 1979) and Humphrey's research on urban family life in the late 1940s (Humphreys, 1966). There has been a rich tradition of ethnographic research on the family, much of which derives from Arensberg & Kimball's work in the 1930s (Arensberg & Kimball, 1940, cited in Greene *et al.*, 2010a, p.8).

Throughout the book we make extensive use of research and data that have emerged over recent years from the *Growing Up in Ireland* study. This is a major longitudinal study of children and young people, along with their families and other key caregivers such as teachers and child minders. It is funded by the Department of Children and Youth Affairs, and is overseen by the Department in association with the Central Statistics Office. It receives a contribution in phase 2 from The Atlantic Philanthropies. The remainder of this book draws on data from this study to explore the themes of diversity, equality, inequality and access to the resources and services that are necessary for child development to ensure that all children in the State can equitably achieve their maximum potential.

Growing Up in Ireland follows the fortunes of almost 20,000 children and their families over time. The main objectives of the study are to describe the lives of children, to establish what is typical and normal, as well as what is atypical and problematic. The study provides a very strong statistical evidence-base for researchers, policy-makers, practitioners and everyone with an interest in understanding all facets and dimensions of child development. Over recent years it has been increasingly used as an important input to the formation of effective and responsive policies and services for children and their families, not least in *Better Outcomes, Brighter Futures* (Department of Children and Youth Affairs, 2014).

Growing Up in Ireland has two cohorts of children. The first is referred to as the **Infant Cohort** and is based on just over 11,100 children and their families. The families in this cohort were first interviewed between September 2008 and April 2009, when the Study Children were 9 months old, with a second interview taking place between December 2010 and June 2011, when they were aged 3. This cohort was further interviewed on an intensive face-to-face basis when the children were aged 5 and had just made the transition to primary school. At that time their school principal and teacher also played an immensely important role in the study by completing a number of questionnaires about themselves, their schools and, most importantly, about the Study Children whom they teach. More information was collected through postal questionnaires from the children's main caregiver (mostly their mother) when the child was aged 7. The children and their families, school principal and teacher will be further interviewed on an intensive face-to-face basis when the children are aged 9, in 2017.

The second cohort in the *Growing Up in Ireland* project is made of older children and young people, and is referred to as the **Child Cohort**. This is based on just over 8,500 children, their families and their teachers. Interviews first took place with the Child Cohort when the children were aged 9, with follow-up interviews when they were aged 13 and subsequently aged 17. It is planned to re-interview the young adults in this cohort in 2018 when they are aged 20.

Growing Up in Ireland is the most ambitious and complex research project ever to have been undertaken in the social sciences in Ireland and signifies a major public investment in our children and young people. The project reflects the recognition by government of the importance of understanding the processes and interrelationships involved in child development and the influence that these have on the quality of life (immediate and long-term) for all children growing up in 21st century Ireland. The wealth of data from the *Growing Up in Ireland* study provides researchers, policy analysts and others with the information necessary to investigate the numerous interrelated dimensions of a child's life, with a view to improving child outcomes and wellbeing.

Growing Up in Ireland focuses on child outcomes in three main areas of their lives:

- Physical health and development
- Socio-emotional and behavioural wellbeing
- Educational achievement and intellectual capacity.

As discussed in detail in *Greene et al.* (2010b, p.13), the underlying conceptual framework adopted by *Growing Up in Ireland* emphasises the importance of the environments and contexts within which children live. This framework has evolved from the bioecological approach developed by, for example, Bronfenbrenner (1979, 2001) and Bronfenbrenner & Morris (2006). It sees the child's world as consisting of a series of nested multi-layered systems, all of which exert an influence on the child's development, to greater or lesser degrees. The family has the most immediate influence on the child. The school, neighbourhood and other contexts also directly influence the child and his / her outcomes. Equally, the relationships that the children themselves or their parents have outside the home (for example, in school or in the workplace) also affect the dynamic within the home and, ultimately, the child's outcomes and wellbeing. At a somewhat higher level, the structures and institutions of society, as well as government policies and service provision also impact directly and indirectly on children – for example, through health, welfare or education policies. At the broadest macro-level, cultural ideologies, attitudes, beliefs and social mores also affect the growing child.

Each of these systems and contexts, working independently of each other and in combination, all influence children and determine their experiences, wellbeing and ultimate outcomes – physical, cognitive and emotional. The *Growing Up in Ireland* project records a wealth of information that can be used to unpick the influences and interactions of these factors on the life of the child. The study allows cross-cutting analysis from one area of the child's life to another. It facilitates, for example, a consideration of how characteristics and circumstances in the child's family affect their educational outcomes, or how peer relationships may be associated with academic performance or engagement with school, or how children's physical health may affect their socio-emotional wellbeing. Being longitudinal, the *Growing Up in Ireland* study also allows researchers and analysts to track changes over time, to assess the extent to which factors impact on the child at the micro-level as he / she develops and grows. In particular, it facilitates a consideration of how early life experiences are reflected in outcomes throughout the later life-course.

Changing Ireland

There is little in the Ireland of 2016 that would have been recognisable in 1916. The social, economic and demographic structures of the country have completely changed over the last century, with the pace of change accelerating dramatically from the early 1980s.

Figure 1.1: Total Population in Ireland, 1926-2011

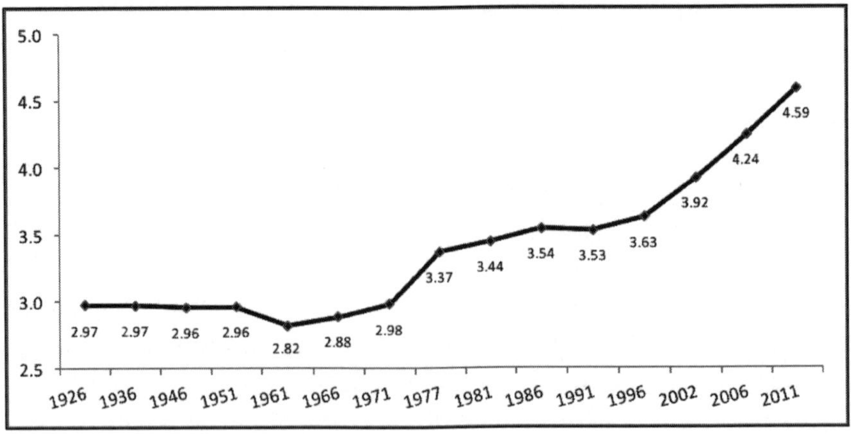

Source: Central Statistics Office.

Figure 1.1 shows that the total population in the Republic of Ireland grew from 2.97 million in the first *Census of Population* held in the new State in 1926 to 4.59 million in 2011, a growth of over 54 per cent.

Demographic and family structures have experienced major transformations over the period. Figure 1.2, for example, summarises the percentage of the total population aged less than 15 years as recorded in selected Censuses from 1926. It indicates that children represented a relatively stable proportion of the total population (with some fluctuation), in the region of 30 to 33 per cent from 1926 until the early 1980s. From then on we experienced a general overall decline in the proportion of children in the total population over successive censuses. By 2011 only 22.6 per cent of the population was below 15 years of age, reflecting a fall in fertility rates and family size over the period.

Figure 1.2: Proportion of Total Population Under Age 15, 1926-2011

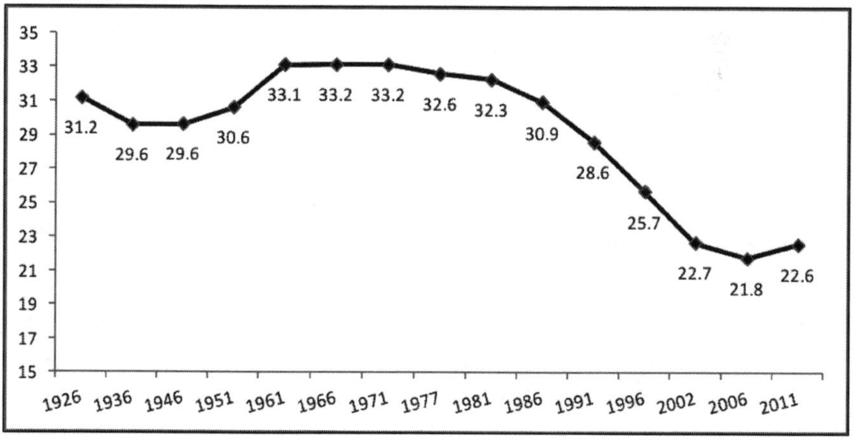

Source: Central Statistics Office.

The annual number of births has also fluctuated since the 1926 *Census of Population* (Department of Industry and Commerce, 1926) (**Figure 1.3**). Trends follow patterns of economic prosperity and decline and related migration flows. The chart shows low levels of births from the 1930s, gradually rising (with annual fluctuations) to a peak of 72,000 before the recession of the 1980s.

That recession and associated emigration resulted in a sharp decline in annual births, reaching a low of just under 51,000 in 1996, rising thereafter to 74,000 in 2011. The sharp rise in the early 2000s reflected the general economic buoyancy of the so-called 'Celtic Tiger' years and associated high levels of immigration, particularly of younger persons in the prime family formation phases of the lifecycle – a large proportion of whom came from Eastern European countries following those countries' accession to the European Union and the completion of the European internal market in 2004.

Figure 1.3: Total Births in Ireland, 1926-2015

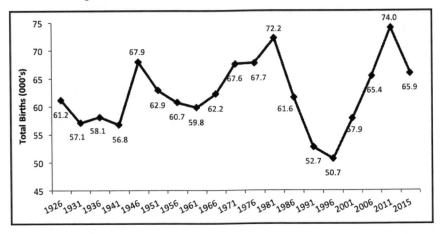

Source: Central Statistics Office.

An important aspect of changing trends in the composition of live births was the percentage of mothers who recorded their nationality as being other than Irish. In 2004 18 per cent of live births were to mothers who recorded their nationality as non-Irish. By 2013 this figure had risen to 23 per cent (Healthcare Pricing Office, 2014). This clearly reflects trends in net immigration over the boom years of the early 2000s and illustrates the degree to which young parents and their families in Ireland were increasingly multicultural, with all this brings in terms of new and different approaches to child-rearing practices, many of which are significantly different from the traditional models that existed in Ireland throughout the early decades of the 20th century.

As an indicator of change in family structures, **Figure 1.4** summarises trends in the percentage of births outside marriage. The chart clearly illustrates that the proportion of all live births outside marriage remained below 5 per cent until 1980 when it began to increase quite sharply each year until 2000, when the figure stood at 31.5 per cent. It began to level out in broad terms thereafter, increasing to 35.1 per cent by 2011. This is generally in line with Western European trends, with rates of live births outside marriage being 35 per cent in Germany in 2014, 47.6 per cent in the UK (2012) and 54.9 per cent in Norway (2012). The rate in Ireland is higher than some Eastern European countries – Poland at 24.2 per cent (2014) and Lithuania at 29.0 per cent (2014).

Figure 1.4: Live Births outside Marriage as a Percentage of All Births, 1960-2012

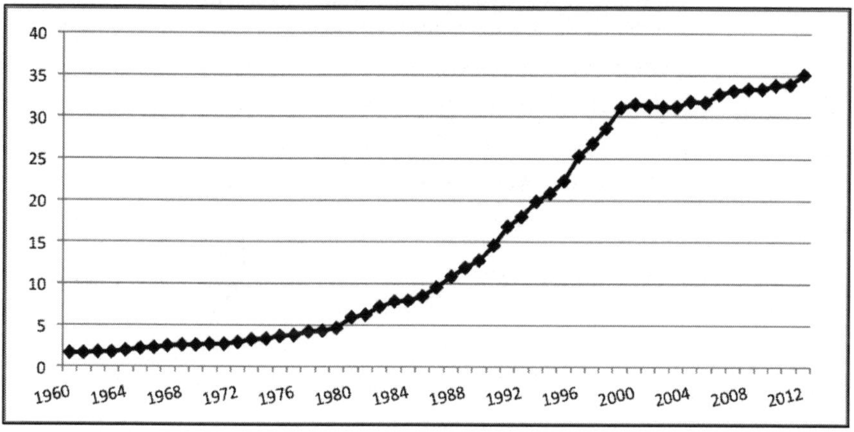

Source: Eurostat (http://ec.europa.eu/eurostat/web/population-demography-migration-projections/births-fertitily-data/database).

This increase in the proportion of live births outside marriage in Ireland was clearly very significant. It should be noted, however, that not all of the children in question were born into one-parent families. Many of the children born outside marriage are, in fact, born into two-parent, non-marital families. As outlined in **Table 1.1**, in 2011 5 per cent of all family units were cohabiting couples with children. Lunn & Fahey (2011) note, for example, that cohabitation in general has seen a marked increase in recent years, with a four-fold increase in cohabitation between 1996 and 2006.

These trends reflect the relatively recent introduction of new legislation in the area of marriage and relationships. Divorce was introduced to Ireland in June 1996. A total of 87,770 people were recorded as being divorced in the 2011 *Census of Population* (Central

Statistics Office, 2012). In 2014 there were 22,045 marriages, 2,632 of
which involved the bride and / or groom entering into a second union.
In that same year there were 392 Civil Partnerships. Same-sex marriage
was introduced in November 2015. To the end of 2015 there were 91
same-sex marriages (Central Statistics Office, 2016a).

**Table 1.1: Family Units in Private Households in
Ireland, 2011**

	Per cent
Husband and wife without children	22.2
Cohabiting couple without children	7.1
Husband and wife with children	47.4
Cohabiting couple with children	5.1
Lone mother with children	15.8
Lone father with children	2.5
All family units	**100.00**
All family units – number	1,179,210

Source: Central Statistics Office (http://www.cso.ie/px/pxeirestat/Statire/
SelectVarVal/Define.asp?maintable=CD507&PLanguage=0).

Changes between 1916 and 2016 have been evident not only in
changing family and related structures. Very radical changes are evident
in the social and economic structure of the nation as we moved from a
largely agricultural base in a very closed and protectionist economy
throughout the 1930s to the gradual opening of trade in the 1960s. The
changes in the economic structure of the country are reflected in **Table
1.2**, which gives a breakdown of persons at work by broad occupation,
in 1911 and 2011.

The table shows that we have moved from a position of having
almost half of those at work involved in the agricultural or primary
sector in 1911 to less than 5 per cent a century later. Similarly, the
industrial sector has substantially reduced in relative importance over
the period. The commensurate increases in service sector activity are
marked, especially in professional services activity, where we can see an
almost five-fold increase in relative importance in employment terms
over the period in question.

Table 1.2: Occupational Breakdown of Those at Work, 1911 and 2011

1911	Per Cent	2011	Per Cent
Agricultural Class	48.4	Farming, fishing and forestry workers	4.9
Industrial Class	26.8	Manufacturing and building	12.8
Professional Class	8.8	Clerical, Managing & govt. Workers + Professional, technical & health workers	40.3
Commercial Class	5.6	Sales & Commerce workers; Communications, warehouse, transport workers	21.5
Domestic Class	10.4	Personal service & childcare workers; Other gainful occupations (incl. n.e.s.)	20.5
Total	**100.0**		**100**

Source: Central Statistics Office (2016b), Table 2 (http://www.cso.ie/en/ releasesandpublications/ep/p-1916/1916irl/society/livingconditions/#d.en.96138).

Note: Breakdown for 1911 refers to the island of Ireland.

Changes in the characteristics of society, especially in the aggregate wellbeing of its citizens, can be seen right across the board. In 1911, life expectancy was 53.6 years among males and 54.1 among females. By 2011 this had risen to 78.3 and 82.7 years respectively (Central Statistics Office, 2016, pp.13-14).

Equally, there have been clear improvements in participation in education among children over the century. The 1911 *Census of Population* recorded that only 30 per cent of 14- to 15-year-olds and 10 per cent of 15- to 18-year-olds were in full-time education (Central Statistics Office, 2012). Children aged 6 to 14 were required to attend school for 75 days a year, though those from farming or related backgrounds were excused from attending due to 'domestic necessity ... husbandry and the ingathering of crops, or giving assistance in the fisheries, or other work requiring to be done at a particular time or season ...' (Central Statistics Office, 2016). The number of children sitting State examinations has increased dramatically over the century. In 1916, on the island of Ireland, 6,971 students sat the 'Junior' examinations (the lowest of a three-level State examinations system); 2,785 sat the 'Middle' level exams and 1,420 sat the 'Senior' exams. In the Republic of Ireland in 2015, 59,522 students sat the Junior Certificate and 55,007 sat the Leaving Certificate exams (Central Statistics Office, 2016).

An Outline of the Book

Clearly the Ireland of 2016 and the circumstances of children and their families living here are very different to those of 1916. The central question that we address in the book is whether social and other opportunities are distributed equally among our children. Are some groups of children in the Ireland of 2016 substantially and systematically disadvantaged relative to others? Do we as a nation fulfil the aspirations set out in the *Proclamation* of 1916 and cherish all of our children equally, or do we find that the Ireland of 2016 still has (in Pearse's terminology) minorities divided from the majority – albeit, perhaps, along different lines to those evident in 1916?

The remainder of the book presents 13 chapters to address this question. **Chapters 2** and **3** set the historical context for the book. **Chapter 2** begins by providing an overview of the way in which childhood has been conceptualised in Ireland over the last 100 years and the extent to which the rights and personhood of children have been advanced.

Chapter 3 addresses in detail some of the major changes that have taken place in family size and structures since 1916 and considers whether these have universally worked to the advantage of all children. The chapter examines issues around family size and number of siblings, death among children and family stability / instability.

Chapter 4 considers the role of family structure and process in children's development and asks whether these represent a source of inequality in children's lives, placing children in certain types of family at risk of relatively poorer developmental outcomes.

Chapter 5 explores the ways in which family socio-economic status may influence cognitive and learning outcomes for children. The chapter considers whether the inequalities in question which are associated with lower levels of financial and other resources in the home can be remediated, at least in part, through parental support of their children in other ways.

Chapter 6 provides a detailed discussion of the history of childcare provision in Ireland throughout the 20th century before investigating trends in non-parental childcare for infants in the first few years of life. The role of the Free Pre-school Year, a major policy shift in the Irish context, is also discussed.

Chapter 7 changes the focus to education and investigates the extent to which social inequalities are evident in children's experiences of integration into primary education. In particular, the chapter examines the nature of social differentiation in the transition process to the primary education system and begins to unpack the extent to which any such social differentiation reflects inequalities in relation to a number of factors, including the home learning environment, early cognitive development and previous experience of formal care settings.

Chapter 8 examines aspects of provision for children with special educational needs and considers their inclusion within Irish mainstream education in recent years. It considers how much of the education and care of children with special needs in the early decades of the 20th century was provided by religious orders before going on to discuss how, since the early 1990s, there has been a substantial shift in focus from segregated educational provision towards a more inclusive view of special education, principally delivered within mainstream schools. In particular, the chapter considers the proportion of children with special educational needs and variations in levels according to the background characteristics of the children in question.

Chapter 9 discusses a number of aspects of the social engagement and integration of the increasing proportions of migrant children in Ireland, particularly their integration within the education system. It highlights important differences between different migrant groups in their educational and social outcomes, as well as differences in outcomes between migrant and non-migrant children.

Chapter 10 focuses on aspects of social disadvantage and trends in children's health and development. Issues including social profiling of low birth weight, maternal-reported health status of their children, the effects of smoking during pregnancy on the child's development, as well as aspects of overweight and obesity among children, are examined.

Chapter 11 discusses healthcare use among children and the extent to which the current system of healthcare financing in Ireland leads, in particular, to differences in patterns of the use of GP services by children that are not predicted by their need for healthcare. The analysis investigates not only variations in use levels but also considers the demand implications of future policy proposals around extending free GP care to further cohorts of children.

Chapter 12 considers the prevalence of anti-social behaviour in the early teenage years in Ireland, the nature of this behaviour and the extent to which anti-social behaviour is associated with socio-economic characteristics of the family, family structure and other factors such as parenting style, the adolescent's self-esteem and peer influences.

Chapter 13 examines the economic vulnerability of families with children in Ireland, focusing, in particular, on the effects that the post-2007 recession has had on the material circumstances of children and the relationship between economic vulnerability and socio-emotional outcomes for children.

Finally, **Chapter 14** provides an overview of the findings presented throughout the book. In doing so, it attempts to answer the core question that we posed in the opening paragraphs: notwithstanding the undoubted improvements between 1916 and 2016 in the circumstances and living conditions facing children, can we identify groups of children within contemporary Irish society who are particularly disadvantaged and whom we possibly do not cherish as we should?

References

Arensberg, C. & Kimball, S.T. (1940). *Family and Community in Ireland*, Cambridge, MA: Harvard University Press.

Bronfenbrenner, U. (1979). *The Ecology of Human Development: Experiment by Nature and Design*, Cambridge, MA: Harvard University Press.

Bronfenbrenner, U. (2001). The bioecological theory of human development, in Smelser, N.J. & Baltes, P.B. (eds.), *International Encyclopedia of the Social and Behavioural Sciences* (Vol. 10, pp.6963-70), New York: Elsevier.

Bronfenbrenner, U. & Morris, P.A. (2006). The bioecological model of human development, in Damon, W. & Lerner, R.M. (series eds.) & Lerner, R.M. (vol. ed.), *Handbook of Child Psychology: Vol. 1. Theoretical Models of Human Development* (6th ed., pp.793-828), New York: Wiley.

Central Statistics Office (2012). *This is Ireland: Highlights from Census 2011*, Dublin: Stationery Office.

Central Statistics Office (2016a). *Marriages and Civil Partnerships, 2015*, Statistical Release, 15 April, Dublin: Stationery Office, available at http://www.cso.ie/en/releasesandpublications/er/mcp/ marriagesandcivilpartnerships2015/.

Central Statistics Office (2016b). *Life in 1916 Ireland: Stories from Statistics*, Dublin: Stationery Office.

Department of Children and Youth Affairs (2014). *Better Outcomes, Brighter Future: The National Policy Framework for Children and Young People*, Dublin: Stationery Office.

Department of Industry and Commerce, Statistics Branch (1926). *Census of Population*, Dublin: Stationery Office.

Greene, S., Williams, J., Doyle, E., Harris, E., McCrory, C., Murray, A., Quail, A., Swords, L., Thornton, M., Layte, R., O'Dowd, T. & Whelan, C.T. (2010b). *Growing Up in Ireland: Review of the Literature Pertaining to the First Wave of Data Collection with the Child Cohort at 9 years*, Dublin: Department of Health and Children.

Greene, S., Williams, J., Layte, R. Doyle, E., Harris, E., McCrory, C., Murray, A., O'Dowd, T., Quail, A., Swords, L., Thornton, M. & Whelan, C.T. (2010a). *Growing Up in Ireland: Background and Conceptual Framework*, Dublin: Department of Health and Children.

Hannan, D.F. (1979). *Displacement and Development: Class, Kinship and Social Change in Irish Rural Communities*, Dublin: Economic and Social Research Institute.

Hannan, D.F. & Katsiaouni, L.A. (1977). *Traditional Families? From Culturally-prescribed Roles to Negotiated Roles in Farm Families*, Dublin: Economic and Social Research Institute.

Healthcare Pricing Office (2014). *Perinatal Statistics Report 2013*, Dublin: Health Service Executive.

Humphreys, A.J. (1966). *New Dubliners*, London: Routledge.

Lunn, P. & Fahey, T. (2011). *Households and Family Structures in Ireland: A Detailed Statistical Analysis of Census 2006*, Dublin: Family Support Agency / Economic and Social Research Institute.

Pearse, P., Ireland (Provisional Government, 1916) & Dolmen Press (1975). *The Easter Proclamation of the Irish Republic, 1916*, Dublin: Dolmen Press.

United Nations (1989). *Convention on the Rights of the Child*, Geneva: United Nations.

2: CHANGING PERCEPTIONS & EXPERIENCES OF CHILDHOOD, 1916-2016

Sheila Greene

Introduction

This chapter examines the way that Irish ideas about childhood, official responses to children and knowledge about children and children's experiences have changed between 1916 and 2016. Since it is impossible to offer a convincing and complete history encompassing the changes that have taken place over the last 100 years in a short book chapter, the task is approached by contrasting attitudes to childhood and children and the reality of children's lives in and around 1916 and now.

There is a dearth of information on children in 1916 in comparison to 2016. As Luddy & Smith noted, with reference to Ireland, 'there is considerable historical work to be completed on the understanding of children and childhood in the 19th and early 20th century' (2014, p.19). Forty children died in the Easter Rising in 1916 but, tellingly, it was only in 2012 that a complete list of their names and ages was compiled. The list was drawn up, not by an historian but by the broadcaster, Joe Duffy (2015). One can conclude that children occupied a marginal position in Irish historical scholarship throughout much of the 20th century. However, in recent years, there has been a new interest in the history of childhood in Ireland, which has resulted in the excavation of knowledge on children and childhood. This upsurge of interest has led to a flurry of historical publications and the establishment, in 2014, of the Irish History of Childhood Research Network.

In creating a picture of the way childhood was understood in 1916, this chapter refers to scholarship on the history of childhood that has a focus on Britain, since in 1916 Ireland was still under British rule and subject to the laws of the then United Kingdom of Great Britain and Ireland. In 1916 very few scholars in Ireland, or indeed internationally, would have had a formal interest in childhood or children. When one turns to 2016, however, one can reference the multiple, rich sources of information that are now available.

Irish scholars, from a range of disciplines in the humanities and social sciences, started to write about children as a topic of interest in their own right in the 1960s, but the amount and quality of scholarship has increased dramatically in the last two decades. There is also a comparatively recent commitment on the part of the State to collect data on children. The *2000 National Children's Strategy* had as one of its three overarching goals 'that children's lives be better understood' (Department of Health and Children, 2000, p.11). As a result, investment was made in a number of research and data-collecting initiatives, including a series of reports, *The State of the Nation's Children* (Department of Children and Youth Affairs, 2006-2014) and in the national longitudinal study of children in Ireland, **Growing Up in Ireland (www.growingup.ie)**, which started in 2006.

This chapter focuses also on the experiences of children themselves, highlighting the diversity of their experiences and the impact of social inequalities in particular. There are striking differences between 1916 and 2016 in the positioning of children in Irish society. These changes confirm both the changing nature of childhood and how children are understood and the impact of the wider context on children's daily lives and psychological welfare.

Perceptions of Childhood and Children

Children have always been with us and adults have always been concerned that children should survive and flourish, but the concept of childhood as a distinctly different stage from adulthood is a relatively recent phenomenon (Aries, 1960; Hendrick, 2009). Also, over historical time and in different geographical and cultural spaces, there is evidence of many diverse conceptions of what childhood entails and how children should be seen, understood and managed. Thus the view of childhood held by most people in the island of Ireland in 1916 differs from that held in Ireland today. Childhood seems to have been extended, since many references to children at the turn of the 20th century count as children those under the age of 14, judging by expectation of school attendance, or under 16 years old in legal matters, as enshrined in the *Children Act, 1908*. It is now common for the definition of childhood to refer to those aged 0 to 18, as defined in the *Convention of the Rights of the Child* (United Nations, 1989).

In 1900 the Swedish social reformer, Ellen Key, argued that the 20th century should become 'the century of the child'. Key had a questionable interest in eugenics, but in her perspective on children she exemplified a new and progressive recognition of children's status as persons, a respect for their lived experience and their capacity to think and act and make decisions. She says:

> *Our age cries for personality; but it will ask in vain, until we let*
> *our children live and learn as personalities, until we allow them*
> *to have their own will, think their own thoughts, work out their*
> *own knowledge, form their own judgements ...* (Key, 1900/1909,
> p.232)

Gillis, a contemporary historian of childhood, confirms Key's aspiration and identifies the dawn of the 20th century as the start of a new view of childhood in the Western world.

> *It is generally agreed that the idea of childhood as a special time*
> *deserving its own special space is itself an artefact of modernity.*
> *The idea that every child should be afforded such a childhood is a*
> *very recent thing, an aspiration of the privileged few that was*
> *democratized in Western countries only in the 20th century and*
> *has yet to gain acceptance in many parts of the world.* (Gillis,
> 2009, p.114)

One might assume that in Ireland in 1916 some forward-thinking adults embraced the modernist view of children as little persons with the right to be considered as such, while many others continued to see children as their parents' possessions, who should be 'seen and not heard' and whose role was to do what adults wanted them to do.

In the public or official arena, the view of childhood that was dominant at the turn of the 19th century in Ireland was undoubtedly similar in many ways to that which prevailed in the British Isles as a whole. Writing on England, Hendrick comments that 'in the last quarter of the 19th century school played a pivotal role in the making of a new kind of childhood' (1997, p.46). Education for all children was seen as the solution to the problems of delinquency, youthful moral depravity and indeed poverty, which had preoccupied many reformers and social commentators in the 18th and 19th centuries. Hendrick comments further that, between the 1880s and 1914, children and child welfare achieved a new social and political identity as children came to be seen as being 'of the Nation' – citizens in the making who are central to the nation's future wellbeing. Hendrick notes 'a shift of emphasis from the mid-19th century concern with rescue, reform and reclamation to the involvement of children in a consciously designed pursuit of the national interest' (1997, p.49).

Childhood became a focus of State intervention, shaped by the notion that this action was a necessary investment in the future. According to Nikolas Rose, childhood in the 20th century became 'the most intensively governed sector of personal existence' (1989, p.121). Thus the 20th century saw a marked intensification of society's focus on children, not just on their education and management but on their wellbeing and psychological health.

Part of this new focus on childhood was expressed in adults' interest in the formative role of childhood. This interest was fostered by the work of Freud and the new science of psychoanalysis. Child psychology had also emerged at the turn of the century. The 20th century is identified by many commentators as the era of the 'psychological child'. Many educated people started to reflect on their own childhood experiences and wonder about the effect of their behaviour as parents on their own children's developing psyches.

Children's literature flourished in the late 19th century, evolving from a didactic endeavour to one that recognised the separate world of childhood and the need to feed children's imaginations. Literature for

Irish children at the start of the 20th century was dominated by British publications. A small number of Irish writers, such as Kathleen Tynan and Edith Somerville, wrote for children as well as for adults and explored Irish themes or settings (Epplé, 2007; Stevens, 2007) but they were exceptions. In adult literature this new fascination with childhood was evident in a number of novels and memoirs. 1916 saw the publication of one of the most famous novels of this genre, James Joyce's *Portrait of the Artist as a Young Man*.

The turn of the last century appears to be a time when childhood was increasingly valued and the role of childhood in shaping future citizens and ensuring the vitality and identity of the Irish nation was the subject of increased attention and concern. As the century unfolded, it became clear that not all children were to benefit from the new level of recognition of the importance of positive childhood experiences. For example, it took many years for the levels of hidden child abuse and neglect in homes and institutions to be uncovered and addressed (Raftery & O'Sullivan, 1999; Commission to Inquire into Child Abuse, 2009).

Children and the Formal Institutions of Society and the State

The general perspective on children and their place in society can be inferred to some extent by examining legislation and State policies pertinent to children. Prior to the late 19th century, children of the upper and middle classes seem to have been seen as the responsibility of their parents: the State paid them little attention. The 18th and 19th centuries in Ireland saw a number of initiatives that had an impact on poor and needy children, some prompted by charitable impulses, others prompted by the dangers such children posed to public order and safety. The Dublin Society for Prevention of Cruelty to Children was established in 1890. Crossman points out that 'fear of the spread of immorality was as powerful a motivating force as empathy for victims of child poverty' and that this attitude was discernible well into the 20th century (2009, p.60). In the late 19th century children who were orphaned, abandoned or seen as out of control were housed in workhouses, industrial schools and reformatories, funded by the State but managed by religious institutions. In the 1901 *Census* the number of children in institutions of this kind was 11,200, amounting to 4.5 per cent of the population of children under the age of 14 (Luddy, 2014). Workhouses ceased to function in the early 1920s when Ireland became independent, but orphanages, industrial schools and reformatories continued to exist until the late 20th century. Unlike the UK, Ireland did not move away from caring for needy children in large institutions for many decades.

Writing about Ireland, Luddy states that 'the period between 1880 and 1914 is widely recognised as an era in which the "rights" of children became a focus of attention and concern for philanthropists, activists and, in turn, legislators' (2014, p.102). She notes that an article in *The Irish Times*, published in 1892, expressed the view that Ireland was 'far better' than England in its care of children and that 'this was the result ... of the beautiful and affective picture of the Virgin Mother holding the Divine Child in her arms (which) was always familiar to the Irish peasant and this intense belief in the Divine Infancy must cast its sanctity over all childhood' (2014, p.111). This romantic view of childhood innocence was very much part of the Victorian sensibility, but in the light of later revelations, the Catholic version of it might not have served to nurture and protect all Irish children.

School attendance for 6- to 14-year-olds was made compulsory in 1892, but many children stopped going to school by age 10. The 1918 Killanin Committee estimated that this applied to as much as half of the school population (Fahey, 1992). In 1900 a Revised Programme for primary education was introduced that was clearly influenced by a child-centred ideology, albeit one that saw children as in need of instruction in good values and behaviours. Bennett reports that the *New National Readers*, for use in schools, aimed to encourage 'the child's imagination but also focussed on the development of "little altruisms to counteract the self-centred and self-regarding instinct of childhood"' (2007, p.171). In fact, the main preoccupation for pre-1916 nationalists and the post-1916 State seemed to be pedagogy and moral instruction. As Kiberd notes, 'there was no fully developed imaginative literature specifically for children in Ireland until the mid-20th century' (2007, pp.21-22).

The *Children Act, 1908* crystallised the State's new sense of responsibility for children's welfare. It strengthened the 1889 legislation on child protection, introducing a raft of new regulations, some of which reached into the home to protect children against parental neglect and abuse. In Ireland this Act was not updated until the introduction of the *Children Act, 2001*, a shameful lapse in attention to juvenile justice, child welfare and protection.

Irish nationalism has deep roots and erupted in many different manifestations over centuries. By the end of the 19th century the nationalistic movement, strengthened by anger over the way Ireland fared during the famine, was popular and widespread. Irish patriots began to focus on the influences that were shaping children's attitudes and loyalties. Organisations such as the Irish Fireside Club, which operated between 1887 and 1924, were established to promote Irish history, culture and values among children. The adults involved were forthright about their goal of 'de-anglicizing and re-gaelicizing' their child members, who numbered more than 50,000 in 1894 (Nic Congáil, 2009). A priest at Castleknock College wrote in 1909 about his concerns that 'Irish boys during their plastic years are being West-Britonized' (Sheehy, 1909, p.185). The Christian Brothers founded a magazine, *Our Boys*, in 1914 to promote an Irish idea of manliness to counterbalance that promoted in British publications (increasingly preoccupied by war in Europe and the jingoistic sentiments associated with it). Cúchulainn, the boy-warrior, was proposed as a more fitting role model. Early accounts of the exploits of Cúchulainn's life might have made him a questionable role model for any young boy but the more romanticized version promoted by writers like Lady Gregory highlighted his prowess with the hurley stick as much as his aptitude as a fighter and did not mention his more bloodthirsty exploits or his philandering (Gregory, 1910). Pádraig Pearse, one of the leaders of the Easter Rising, also hailed Cúchulainn (or Setanta) as a role model and founded bi-lingual schools for boys (in 1908) and girls (in 1910) to educate children as Irish-speaking patriots and leaders.

Kennedy (2001) notes that the first Dáil got off to a good start in relation to children by asserting in its 1919 Democratic Programme that:

It shall be the first duty of the Republic to make provision for the physical, mental and spiritual wellbeing of the children, to secure that no child shall suffer hunger or cold from lack of food, clothing or shelter, that all shall be provided with the means and

facilities for their proper education and training as citizens of a
free and Gaelic Ireland.

However, by the time the *Constitution* of 1937 was written, the emphasis
had shifted from the rights of the child to the rights of the family. As the
Report on the Kilkenny Incest Investigation noted in 1993:

The very high emphasis in the Constitution *may consciously or*
unconsciously be interpreted as giving a higher value to the rights
of parents than to the rights of children. (South Eastern Health
Board, 1993)

The report recommends an amendment to the *Constitution* that would
include:

A specific and overt declaration of the rights of born children.
(South Eastern Health Board, 1993, p.326)

The *Constitution* framed Irish legislation relating to children
throughout the 20th century and it was only in 2012, when a
referendum on children's rights was held, that a new article was
inserted to read:

The State recognises and affirms the natural and imprescriptible
rights of all children and shall, as far as possible, by its laws
protect and vindicate those rights. (Government of Ireland,
1937/2012)

A number of other associated amendments to the *Constitution* were
made and the *Thirty-First Amendment of the Constitution (Children)
Act* was signed into law in 2015. This legislative change reflected a
changed attitude to children in Ireland, which had been a long time in
gestation. A significant step along the road to the Referendum came in
1993 when Ireland ratified the *Convention on the Rights of the Child*
(United Nations, 1989), which enshrines many important facets of
children's rights. As a ratifying State the government has had to be
regularly assessed in its treatment of the nation's children by the UN's
Committee on the Rights of the Child. Numerous failings have been
identified and some, but not all, have been rectified. In this process the
Children's Rights Alliance, a grouping of many children's organisations
and organisations concerned about children's rights, has been a forceful

voice for change and has held the government to account in its yearly
Report Cards (2016).

To mark the turn of the current century the Irish Government
invested in the development and publication by the then National
Children's Office of *Our Children – Their Lives: National Children's
Strategy* (Department of Health and Children, 2000), a visionary
document, very much influenced by the current international *zeitgeist* in
relation to child rights (2000). More government investment in research
on children followed, as noted earlier, plus a variety of specific
initiatives and sub-strategies designed to provide support to children
and youth, including the establishment of the Office of the Ombudsman
for Children, and eventually, in 2011, of a full Department for Children
and Youth Affairs with its own cabinet Minister.

One area that has remained problematic is child poverty. Of course
what we mean by child poverty has changed over the century. It is
essentially a relative concept. Today it is measured in terms of falling
below the median household income by a specified percentage and
lacking items or amenities deemed essential by today's standards.

In 2013 Eurostat reported that Ireland ranked 23rd out of 27 EU
countries in tackling child poverty. In Ireland, 38 per cent of children
were deemed to be at risk of poverty or social exclusion, against an
average for the EU of 27 per cent. During the period of austerity
following the financial crash of 2008, child poverty increased. This may
be seen as inevitable but in fact other states, also suffering from the
effects of the crash, were better able to protect children from its impact.
A study published by UNICEF in 2014 placed Ireland 37th out of 41
developed countries in the protection of children from poverty during
the financial crash (Fanjul, 2014). The child poverty rate in Ireland rose
by over 10 per cent between 2008 and 2012, while 18 other states
recorded a reduction. In Ireland in 2008, 6.8 per cent of children were
living in consistent poverty, assessed in terms of both low income and
the household's access to basic resources such as warm clothes and high
protein meals (Central Statistics Office, 2010). In 2013, 11.7 per cent of
children (138,000) were living in consistent poverty (Central Statistics
Office, 2015). One can conclude that the welfare of the most vulnerable
children is not a government or societal priority, and it is difficult not to
be pessimistic about the likely success of the commitment made in 2014

in the new national policy framework for children and young people *Better Outcomes, Brighter Futures* to 'lift 70,000 children out of consistent poverty by 2020' (Department of Children and Youth Affairs, 2014, p.93).

At a scholarly level the 1990s saw the establishment of the 'new sociology of childhood', soon to become the 'social studies of childhood' (Smith & Greene, 2014). This movement initiated a focus on the immediate experience of the child and a respect for the child's own perspective on his or her life. It highlighted the variety to be found among children in their experience of childhood and the constructed, rather than natural, status of childhood. Researchers and child advocates united in their promotion of children's voices. This interest echoes and elaborates on Article 12 of the *Convention on the Rights of the Child*, which enshrines children's right to a voice on matters of concern to them (United Nations, 1989). Ireland has seen a recent upsurge in studies of children in all the social sciences, health sciences and humanities. By contrast, even as recently as 1973, the important anthropological study *Inishkillane: Change and Decline in the West of Ireland* had no separate entry in its index for children. It notes under 'children': 'see family life; father; marriage; mother' (Brody, 1973).

Children's Daily Experience

It is possible from this distance to capture only glimpses of what childhood was like for Irish children in and around 1916. With very few exceptions this was a life without radio, cinema, cars, plane travel, telephones, holidays and antibiotics (Kennedy, 2001). In contrast, the average child of 2016 has access to instant entertainment *via* TV and the Internet, a family car, foreign travel, smart phones and the benefits of modern medicine. Taking just one specific example, in 1911 there were 9,800 cars registered in Ireland; in 2014 there were 1.9 million (Central Statistics Office, 2016).

The population of Ireland (26 counties) was 3.14 million in 1911 when a census was conducted; in the *2011 Census* it was 4.58 million. The average family size was larger than today, although one quarter of all women did not have any children. In 1911 married women had an average of almost six children (Daly, 2006). Today the average completed family size is 1.99 children, high in European terms but below replacement rate (Central Statistics Office, 2012). The *1911 Census* records that there were 920,377 children between the ages of 0 to 14 and in 2011 there was a similar number (979,590) but proportionately there were many more children in the population in 1911 than there are now (Central Statistics Office, 2016). Family size in 1911 varied by religion and by class, with poor Catholic families having the largest number of children. Family diversity has increased, with many children in 2016 living in single parent families, with unmarried parents and parents who have divorced or separated. Immigration has meant that 23.2 per cent of births in 2011 were to mothers of non-Irish nationality (Central Statistics Office, 2012).

Children today are much healthier, although there are threats to this good health from rising levels of obesity and inactivity (Williams *et al.*, 2009). The infant mortality rate fell from 99 to 3.6 *per* 1000 live births between 1900 and 2011. According to Kennedy, in the first decade of the century 6,500 children under the age of one died every year, the main cause of death being 'malnutrition and weakness' (Kennedy, 2001; Central Statistics Office, 2016).

Proportionately more children in 1916 were living in rural areas. As Kennedy notes, 'Ireland was predominantly an agrarian society' at this time (2001, p.1). Half of the workforce was engaged in agricultural work compared to 5 per cent today (Central Statistics Office, 2016). A major demographic change, with direct implications for children's way of life, has been the shift in population from West to East and the accompanying urbanisation. Children of farm labourers and small farmers were expected to help out on the land and with daily farm chores. This was also true of poor children in urban settings, who needed to find work from an early age to help their families survive. The *Employment of Children Act, 1909* was meant to combat the high levels of child labour and associated poor school attendance but was not properly implemented and soon judged to be 'a melancholy failure' (Luddy & Smith, 2014).

Ireland in 1916 was an exception to the general trend in Europe towards a rapid decline in family size. It remained out of step with the rest of Europe for most of the 20th century. This was in all probability influenced by the Roman Catholic Church and its attitude to contraception but may also have been influenced by a comparative lack of economic development. Children in 1916 were, therefore, often reared in large families, with all the advantages and disadvantages of having many siblings. For the poor, large families meant a continuous struggle for existence, with high levels of infant mortality, childhood sickness and failure to thrive. The tenements of Dublin were full of children and were noted as representing the worst housing conditions in the British Isles (Kennedy, 2001). There were 24,000 one-bed tenement apartments in Dublin in 1916 (Central Statistics Office, 2016). Farmar comments that, in Dublin in 1907, 'the constant items of a working-class diet were bread, usually without butter, and well-stewed tea with sugar' (1995, p.19). In contrast, children today have a high probability of surviving infancy and remaining in good health throughout their childhood and beyond.

Undoubtedly there was a lot of diversity in 1916 in how children were treated at home and in their comfort and resources. For example, photographs from this time show a marked discrepancy in appearance between the children of the middle and upper classes and those of the poor. While privileged children have beautifully-embroidered and carefully-pressed dresses and suits, the children of the poor are often dirty, ragged and without shoes (O'Connor, 2012). The contrast in appearance between children of different classes would be far less obvious today. While sex role stereotyping is still with us, boys and girls are less restricted today in terms of their choices and opportunities (Greene, in press). In the 1916 home, mothers dealt with children; fathers were distant figures. As O'Dannachair noted, in the early 20th century, 'a man never attended to small children. Should the wife be ill or die another woman must come at once to take care of the children' (1962, p.188).

By the end of the 20th century Ireland had become more affluent and global in its influences, with resulting impact on children's daily lives (Greene & Moane, 2000). A wave of immigrants introduced diversity into the previously homogeneous population. The influence of foreign media and entertainment reached into every child's home, diluting what was previously a cosy and somewhat insular culture. Inglis (2011) interviewed a number of children in 2005 and concluded that there is little left of a specifically Irish culture or lifestyle for Irish children, other than the widespread involvement with the Gaelic Athletic Association. Pearse would have been sorely disappointed.

Children's time at school has been extended, upwards and downwards, with many engaged in school-like activities from age 3 until their early 20s. A much larger percentage of children will go on to post-secondary education in a wide variety of institutions – almost 60 per cent compared to a privileged few attending the four universities in 1916. Kennedy comments that 'the biggest change in regard to children has come about as a result of their changing economic status' (2001, p.124). Where the majority of children and youth in 1916 were expected to work and contribute to the household economy, they are now expected to stay in education and thus remain financially dependent on their parents, often well into their 20s.

One area where change has been dramatic has been in corporal punishment. It was expected in the early 20th century that children would be chastised physically at school and at home. In a paper that traces the history of the use of corporal punishment in Ireland in the 20th century, Maguire & O'Cinneide assert that 'The physical chastisement of children was widely tolerated for much of the 20th century even to extremes that by today's standards would be regarded as abuse' (2005, p.635). Corporal punishment in schools was banned in 1982. Ireland has been criticised by the United Nations Committee of the Rights of the Child in this century for not banning corporal punishment in the home – most European countries have done so – but nonetheless parents use corporal punishment much less frequently today than they did in the last century (Nixon *et al.*, 2009).

In general, children in 2016 are treated with more kindness than they were 100 years ago. Children are given more say within the home and are less likely to be fearful of their parents, the large majority of whom report that they adopt an authoritative (firm but warm) parenting style (Nixon, 2012).

Another area where change has been significant is in engagement with religious practice. For Roman Catholic children and those of Protestant denominations, attendance at Mass and religious observance would have been a central part of life in 1916. A 2008 survey found that 51.6 per cent of Roman Catholics (who represent 90 per cent of the total population) attended Mass weekly or more often but that only

18.6 per cent of 18- to 24-year-olds did so (O'Mahony, 2011). Although many children still participate in rites of passage such as the First Communion, church attendance amongst young people of a Christian background is small and declining. Children who are non-Christian or non-religious are growing in number with increased immigration and the spread of atheism and agnosticism.

As a consequence of the failure to eliminate child poverty, as currently defined, there is a social divide between children that affects their daily life experience and future expectations. Equality is still an ideal, not a reality, for Irish children. One of the most striking general findings of *Growing Up in Ireland* is the socio-economic gradient, which can be found in just about any outcome measure employed in the study (Williams *et al.*, 2009). This means that children's outcomes vary by class, with children from higher income households consistently faring better than children from lower income households.

Food poverty is still an issue for a significant minority of children, both in terms of amount and quality of food. In 2015 a study by Kelloggs on the 'food divide' surveyed 408 teachers: 77 per cent of the teachers reported that the number of children coming to school hungry had increased in the past year. They claimed that 17 per cent of children in their classes came to school at least once a week without having had enough to eat that morning, while 22 per cent of children in disadvantaged schools were arriving at school without having breakfast or enough to eat. Breakfast clubs are commonplace in such schools. In contrast, 25,000 children benefit from private secondary schooling in institutions part-subsidised by the State.

Several categories of children aside from the poor suffer extra levels of disadvantage. Traveller children are more likely to suffer from ill-health and are more likely to leave school early. The *2006 Census* found that 63.2 per cent of children from the Travelling community had left school by 15 compared to 13.3 per cent nationally. Infant mortality is much higher, with 10 per cent of Traveller children dying before age 2 compared to 1 per cent in the general population (Kelleher, 2010). Children in one-parent families are twice as likely to live in poverty (One Family, 2015). The welfare of the children of adults in direct provision is also a matter of serious concern. A Health Information and Quality Authority report in 2015 found that young people in these settings, of whom there were 1,600 at that time, were nine times more likely to be the subject of a child protection or welfare concern than the wider child population. In May 2016 there was also a peak in the number of homeless children, with 2,177 children living in temporary accommodation (Department of the Environment, 2016), a situation that causes them considerable distress and impedes their education and welfare (Halpenny *et al.*, 2001).

Conclusion

Undoubtedly life for the generality of children in Ireland has improved over the last 100 years, particularly in relation to their survival, health and access to resources such as good housing, warm clothes and schooling. The children of 2016 have less to fear from the adults around them in terms of intentional or unintentional neglect, exploitation or cruelty than had their counterparts in 1916.

The marked disparity between children in life circumstances seen in 1916 has diminished. But it has not gone away. Child poverty is still a feature of today's Ireland. Class and family income still influence children's health, educational achievement and eventual employment (Nolan *et al.*, 2006).

There may be some ways in which the average child in 1916 may have had a more enjoyable childhood. They had more freedom to roam, whether on the streets or in the fields. They were more likely to provide their own entertainment, without the presence of televisions, computers, electronic games and devices that provide ready-made amusement for children today. Manufactured toys and board games were available to the more affluent child – for example, Monopoly was first produced in 1903 – but children spent a lot of time playing indoor and outdoor games such as hide and seek and hopscotch or games of their own invention. Obesity would have been rare in 1916, whereas one quarter of 9-year-olds in 2007 were assessed as overweight or obese (Williams *et al.*, 2009). No one would wish to return to a time when some poor children were undoubtedly on the edge of starvation, but the daily diet and level of activity of the average child in 1916 may well have been healthier than that of children today.

The modern child may have more pressure in his or her life in terms of achievement at school and in a social world increasingly dominated by celebrity culture, preoccupation with appearance and the need to successfully negotiate social media. Inglis comments on the 'new individualism that is based on self-expression and self-fulfilment' in which Irish children today are acculturated, which contrasts with the traditional focus on self-denial and humility that characterised childhood for most of the 20th century (2011, p.64). Inglis emphasises the influence of 'the methods and demands of the market' on children, to which we have to add the impact of modern technology and social media. Children are engaged in new means of presenting the self and new ways of forming relationships. The ultimate effect of these changes in social behaviour on their wellbeing are yet to unfold.

Several international scholars have commented on the negative conditions that are associated with affluence and the modern lifestyle. The eminent child psychologist, Urie Bronfennbrenner, and his colleagues sounded an alarm in 1996, saying that 'the forces of disarray, increasingly being generated in the broader society, have been producing growing chaos in the lives of children and youth' (Bronfennbrenner *et al.*, 1996, pp.*ix*). Around that time he also commented on 'a progressive decline in American society of conditions that research increasingly indicates may be critical for developing and sustaining human competence throughout the life course' (1995, p.643). His concerns included increased family instability, adults spending less time with their children and increasing materialism. The British psychiatrist Michael Rutter expressed similar concerns, highlighting the substantial body of literature indicating '... there has been a considerable rise in the level of psychosocial disturbances in young people over the last half-century' (Rutter & Smith, 1995, p.62).

The idea that affluence does not necessarily bring increased child wellbeing has been termed 'modernity's paradox', which has been defined as 'the decline in indicators of human development linked to rising social inequalities despite post-modern society's unprecedented economic prosperity' (Li *et al.*, 2008, p.64.) The term 'modernity's paradox' is accredited to Keating & Hertzman, who published a book chapter with that title in 1999. Aside from their worries about the conditions associated with modern life in privileged societies that are linked to negative outcomes for children, Keating & Hertzman expressed concern about the impact of inequality on child health and pointed to the differences in child wellbeing between relatively equal, mainly Scandinavian, and relatively unequal, mainly English-speaking, rich countries. Unfortunately Irish social and economic policies have served to place us in the ranks of the more unequal wealthy societies, with children at the bottom of the heap suffering the consequences most acutely.

It is important for us in Ireland to ask whether the factors supporting child wellbeing are being undermined or supported. While many children seem to do well, we need both to attend to the children not doing well and to continue to interrogate, on behalf of all children, what we mean by doing well.

In June 2015 the Minister for Children and Youth Affairs launched a new *National Strategy on Children and Young People's Participation in Decision-making 2015-2020* (Department of Children and Youth Affairs, 2015) and stated:

> *Key to this strategy is the recognition that children and young people are not 'beings in becoming' but 'citizens of today' with the right to be respected during childhood, their teenage years and their transition to adulthood.*

It remains to be seen whether these fine words translate into respect and support for all children in Ireland, regardless of the family they come from.

As part of the official Centenary Commemoration, a major children's event was held in June 2016 in Áras an Uachtaráin 'to honour the children of the past and the children of the present.' In 100 years public awareness of children's justifiable claim to have their own rights and personhood has advanced beyond recognition. In this regard alone, the children of 1916 would have been amazed.

References

Aries, P. (1960). *Centuries of Childhood: A Social History of Family Life*, New York: Vintage.

Bennett, J. (2007). Values and primary school textbooks in Ireland 1900-1999, in Shine Thompson, M. & Coghlan, V. (eds.), *Studies in Children's Literature: Divided Worlds* (pp.170-85), Dublin: Four Courts Press.

Brody, H. (1973). *Inishkillane: Change and Decline in the West of Ireland*, London: Faber & Faber.

Bronfenbrenner, U. (1995). Developmental ecology through space and time: A future perspective, in Moen, P., Elder, G.H. & Luscher, K. (eds.), *Examining Lives in Context: Perspectives on the Ecology of Human Development* (pp.619-47), Washington DC: American Psychological Association.

Bronfenbrenner, U., McClelland, P., Wetherington, E., Moen, P. & Ceci, S.J. (1996). *The State of Americans: This Generation and the Next*, New York: The Free Press.

Central Statistics Office (2010). *Survey on Income and Living Conditions, 2009*, Dublin: Stationery Office.

Central Statistics Office (2012). *Statistical Yearbook of Ireland, 2012*, Dublin: Stationery Office.

Central Statistics Office (2015). *Survey on Income and Living Conditions, 2013*, Dublin: Stationery Office.

Central Statistics Office (2016). *Life in 1916 Ireland: Stories from Statistics*, retrieved from http://www.cso.ie/en/statistics/lifein1916irelandstoriesfromstatistics/

Children's Rights Alliance (2016). *Report Card 2016*, Dublin: Children's Rights Alliance, available at http://www.childrensrights.ie/content/report-card-2016.

Commission to Inquire into Child Abuse (2009). *Report of the Commission to Inquire into Child Abuse, vols. I-V*, Dublin: Stationery Office.

Crossman, V. (2009). Cribbed, contained and confined? The care of children under the Irish Poor Law, 1850-1920, *Eire-Ireland*, 44, 1 & 2, 37-61.

Daly, M. E. (2006). Marriage, fertility and women's lives in 20th century Ireland, *Women's History Review, 15*, 571-85.

Department of Children and Youth Affairs (2006-2014). *State of the Nation's Children*, biennial reports, available at http://www.dcya.gov.ie/viewdoc.asp?fn=/documents/Research/StateoftheNationReport.htm.

Department of Children and Youth Affairs (2014). *Better Outcomes, Brighter Future: The National Policy Framework for Children and Young People*, Dublin: Stationery Office.

Department of Children and Youth Affairs (2015). *National Strategy on Children's and Young People's Participation in Decision-making, 2015-2020*, Dublin: Stationery Office.

Department of Health and Children, National Children's Office (2000). *Our Children, Their Lives: National Children's Strategy*, Dublin: Stationery Office.

Department of the Environment, Community and Local Government (2016). *Homelessness Report January 2016*, retrieved from http://www.environ.ie/sites/default/files/publications/files/homelessness_report_january_2016_0.pdf.

Duffy, J. (2015). *Children of the Rising: The Untold Story of the Young Lives Lost during Easter 1916*, Dublin: Hachette Books Ireland.

Epplé, C. (2007). 'Wild Irish with a vengeance': Definitions of Irishness in Kathleen Tynan's children's literature, in Shine Thompson, M. and Coghlan, V. (eds.), *Studies in Children's Literature: Divided Worlds* (pp.32-40), Dublin: Four Courts Press.

Fahey, T. (1992). State, family and compulsory schooling in Ireland, *Economic and Social Review*, 23, 369-96.

Fanjul, G. (2014). *Children of the Recession: The Impact of the Economic Crisis on Child Wellbeing in Rich Countries, Report Card 12*, Florence: UNICEF Innocenti Research Centre.

Farmar, T. (1995). *Ordinary Lives*, Dublin: A & A Farmar.

Gillis, J. (2009). Transitions to modernity, in Qvortrup, J., Corsaro, W.A. & Honig, M.S. (eds.), *The Palgrave Handbook of Childhood Studies* (pp.114-26), Basingstoke: Palgrave Macmillan.

Government of Ireland (2012). *Bunreacht na hÉireann (Irish Constitution)*, Dublin: Stationery Office.

Greene, S. (in press). Nine-year-old boys and girls: On different paths?, in Ryan-Flood, R. (ed.), *Gender, Intimacy and Contemporary Ireland*, London: Routledge.

Greene, S. & Moane, G. (2000). Growing up Irish: Changing children in a changing society, *Irish Journal of Psychology*, 21, 122-37.

Gregory, Lady A. (1910/1999). *Irish Myths and Legends*, Philadelphia, PA: Running Press.

Halpenny, A.M., Greene, S., Hogan, D. & McGee, H. (2001). *Homeless Mothers and Their Children*, Dublin: Children's Research Centre / Royal College of Surgeons in Ireland.

Health Information and Quality Authority (2015). *Report on Inspection of the Child Protection and Welfare Services Provided to Children Living in Direct Provision Accommodation under the National Standards for the Protection and Welfare of Children, and Section 8(1)(c) of the Health Act 2007*, Dublin, Health Information and Quality Authority.

Hendrick, H. (1997). *Children, Childhood and English Society*, Cambridge: Cambridge University Press.

Hendrick, H. (2009). The evolution of childhood in Western Europe c.1400-1750, in Qvortrup, J., Corsaro, W.A. & Honig, M.S. (eds.), *The Palgrave Handbook of Childhood Studies* (pp.99-113), Basingstoke: Palgrave Macmillan.

Inglis, T. (2011). Mapping changes in Irish childhood, *Eire-Ireland*, 46 (Fall/Winter), 63-83.

Keating, D.P. & Hertzman, C. (1999). Modernity's Paradox, in Keating, D.P. & Hertzman, C. (eds.), *Developmental Health and the Wealth of Nations*, New York: Guilford Press.

Kelleher, C. (2010). *All-Ireland Traveller Health Survey: Our Geels. Summary of Findings*, Dublin: School of Public Health, Physiotherapy and Population Science, University College Dublin.

Kelloggs (2015). *Is the Food Divide Getting Bigger?*, May, retrieved from http://www.kelloggs.ie/en_IE/news-center.html.

Kennedy, F. (2001). *Cottage to Crèche: Family Change in Ireland*, Dublin: Institute of Public Administration.

Key, E. (1900/1909). *The Century of the Child*, London & New York: G.P. Putnam's Sons.

Kiberd, D. (2007). Literature, childhood and Ireland, in Bradford, C. & Coghlan, V. (eds.), *Expectations and Experience: Children, Childhood and Children's Literature* (pp.13-28), Lichfield: Pied Piper Publishing Ltd.

Li, J., McMurray, A. & Stanley, F. (2008). Modernity's paradox and the structural determinants of child health and wellbeing, *Health Sociology Review, 17*, 64-77.

Luddy, M. (2014). The early years of the NSPCC in Ireland, in Luddy, M. & Smith, J. (eds.), *Children, Childhood and Irish Society, 1500 to the Present* (pp.100-20), Dublin: Four Courts Press.

Luddy, M. & Smith, J. (eds.) (2014). *Children, Childhood and Irish Society, 1500 to the Present*, Dublin: Four Courts Press.

Maguire, M. & O'Cinneide, S. (2005). 'A good beating never hurt anyone': The punishment and abuse of children in 20th century Ireland, *Journal of Social History, 38*, 635-52.

Nic Congáil, R. (2009). 'Fiction, amusement, instruction': The Irish Fireside Club and the educational ideology of the Gaelic League, in Luddy, M. & Smith, J. (eds.), *Children, Childhood and Irish Society, 1500 to the Present* (pp.164-83), Dublin: Four Courts Press.

Nixon, E. (2012). *How Families Matter for Social and Emotional Outcomes of Nine-year-old Children*, Dublin: Office of the Minister for Children and Youth Affairs.

Nixon, E., Halpenny, A.M. & Watson, D. (2009). *Parents' and Children's Perspectives on Parenting Styles and Discipline in Ireland*, Dublin: Stationery Office.

Nolan, B., Layte, R., Whelan, C.T. & Maître, B. (2006). *Day In, Day Out: Understanding the Dynamics of Child Poverty in Ireland*, Dublin: Institute of Public Administration / Combat Poverty Agency.

O'Connor, A. (2012). *Small Lives 1860-1970*, Dublin: Gill and Macmillan.

O'Dannachair, C. (1962). The family in Irish tradition, *Christus Rex, XVI(3)*, 185-96.

O'Mahony, E. (2011). *Practice and Belief among Catholics in the Republic of Ireland*, Dublin: Irish Catholic Bishops Conference.

One Family (2015). *One Family Pre-Budget Submission 2015*, retrieved from http://www.onefamily.ie/policy/one-family-pre-budget-submission-2015.

Raftery, M. & O'Sullivan, E. (1999). *Suffer the Little Children: The Inside Story of Ireland's Industrial Schools*, Dublin: New Island.

Rose, N. (1989). *Governing the Soul*, London: Routledge.

Rutter, M. & Smith, D.J. (1995). *Psychosocial Disorders in Young People: Time Trends and Their Causes*, Chichester: Wiley.

Sheehy, J.S. (1909). The need of an Irish 'boys' paper, *The College Chronicle, Castleknock 24*, 32.

Smith, C. & Greene, S. (2014). *Key Thinkers in Childhood Studies*, Bristol: Policy Press.

South Eastern Health Board (1993). *Kilkenny Incest Investigation,* Dublin: Stationery Office.

Stevens, J.A. (2007). The little big house: Somerville and Ross's works for children, in Shine Thompson, M. & Coghlan, V. (eds.), *Studies in Children's Literature: Divided Worlds* (pp.41-49), Dublin: Four Courts Press.

United Nations (1989). *Convention on the Rights of the Child*, Geneva: United Nations.

Williams, J., Greene, S., Doyle, E., Harris, E., Layte, R., McCoy, S., McCrory, C., Murray, A., Nixon, E., O'Dowd, T., O'Moore, M., Quail, A., Smyth, E., Swords, L. & Thornton, M. (2009). *Growing Up in Ireland: The Lives of Nine-year-olds*, Dublin: Office of the Minister for Children and Youth Affairs.

3: CHILDREN & FAMILIES, THEN & NOW

Tony Fahey & Megan Curran

Introduction

That the lives of children in Ireland have improved greatly since 1916 is undeniable. Children today are healthier, better nourished, better housed and better educated than their predecessors of 100 years ago. Equally important is the greater dignity and respect shown to children. For example, routine beatings in the home or school that were once thought good for children (Maguire & Ó Cinnéide, 2005) are today illegal, and it would be unconscionable now to ostracise or neglect children because of accidents of birth – for example, because they were born outside marriage or had a disability. Nonetheless, the picture is not entirely positive: adequate supports for vulnerable children and equality of treatment for all children are still far from being achieved. The ways society fails children are still many, as other chapters in this volume show. Nevertheless, it seems clear that when the 1916 *Proclamation* spoke of cherishing all the children of the nation equally, notions at the time of what 'cherishing' meant in regard to actual children (if not the metaphorical children of Mother Ireland) would fall short if judged by the standards of what is routinely expected for children today.

The family circumstances of children are one domain where improvements in children's lives can be examined but where many would argue that, contrary to the general trend for children, change has not always worked to children's advantage. From the welter of detail that one could track in this domain, this chapter picks out two major movements that go to the heart of how children's family contexts have evolved since the early 20th century:

- Decline in family size
- Change in patterns and levels of family disruption.

The fall in family size started in Ireland about 100 years ago, moved ahead quite slowly and was part of a global shift towards small-family norms that is fundamental to modern family life (for a general overview, see Reher, 2011). Changes in family disruption are more difficult to sum up since they take different forms and move in different directions over time. Some forces that disrupted family life in the past, such as the premature death of parents and the early departure of children from the family home, declined in the first half of the 20th century. But new forms of disruption in the shape of divorce, childbearing outside marriage, unstable cohabitation and serial family formation grew in the closing decades of the century (Lesthaeghe, 2010). While the precise effects of the latter departures from traditional marital models of family life are unclear (Chapple, 2009; Hannan *et al.*, 2013), they are rarely said to be benign on balance and belong to a category of developments where downsides for children are possible. A picture that encompasses both the long-term fall in family size and changing patterns of family disruption thus has the advantage that it gets at fundamental aspects of family change affecting children over the past century but is also is open to both positive and negative sides of what change has meant for children.

This chapter outlines the broad contours of these trends over the past century and, in light of the focus of this volume on social inequalities between children, examines how change spread unevenly in society and led to shifting social disparities in children's family circumstances at various points in time.

From Large to Small Families

Completed family size is usually measured as the average number of children born to women in an age-group by the time they have reached the end of their child-bearing span (usually taken to be age 45). However, that measure does not capture what is most important for children, namely, the number of siblings they have (which we will refer here to as 'sibsize', where an only child is counted having a sibsize of one). We tend to assume that if women on average have, say, four children, their children on average are in four-sibling families but in fact mean sibsize in populations of children is usually greater than the mean family size of their mothers since children's sibsize is influenced by how unevenly children are distributed among mothers (for a technical analysis, see Preston, 1976). Take, for example, two women who together have six children and thus have a mean family size of three. Their mean of three is unaffected by how the six children are distributed between them: whether the divide is three and three, four and two, five and one or six and zero, the mean for the two women remains at three. Matters are different for sibsize among the children since the more they are bunched into one of the two families, the larger their mean sibsize. If, for example, the children were divided three and three between the two women, their mean sibsize would be 3, but if the divide were four and two, mean sibsize would rise to 3.33, and it would rise progressively to 4.33 and 6.0 if the divide shifted to five / one or six / zero. The implication of this illustration is that if we want to trace the emergence of small families in any population over time, we have to recognise that the story will differ depending on whether we examine the question from the perspective of women's completed fertility or children's sibsize.

To see what this difference in perspective means in the Irish case, **Figure 3.1** takes a century-long view and shows mean completed family size for women with completed families and mean sibsize for their children in 1911, 1961 and 2011 (data are available only for married women in 1911 and 1961 and cover all women in 2011).

Figure 3.1: Family Size among Women with Completed Families and Sibsize among Their Children, 1911, 1961 and 2011

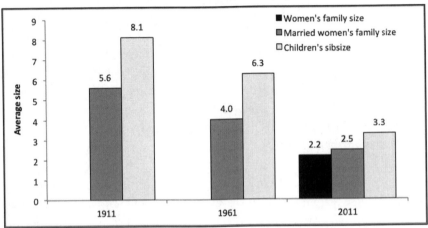

Sources: Authors' calculations from Registrar of Births, Deaths and Marriages (1911), General Report, Table 165; Central Statistics Office (1961), Vol 8, Table 17; Central Statistics Office (2012), Profile 5, CD549.

Note: 'Women with completed families' refers to women aged 45 to 54 in 1911 and aged 45 to 49 in 1961 and 2011.

Figure 3.2: Percentage Distribution of Children in Completed Families in 1911, 1961 & 2011, by Sibsize

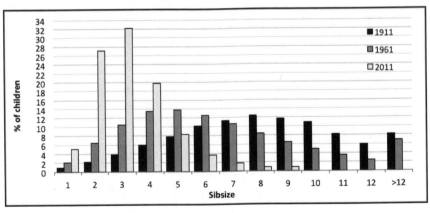

Sources: Authors' calculations from Registrar of Births, Deaths and Marriages (1911), General Report, Table 165; Central Statistics Office (1961), Vol 8, Table 17; Central Statistics Office (2012), Profile 5, CD549.

Figure 3.2 extends that picture by showing the distribution of children by sibsize for the same years. Note that the term 'children' here refers to women's offspring of any age rather than to young people below an age threshold. Children of women aged 45 to 54 would range in age from infancy up to the early 30s, with most in their teens or early 20s.

Taken together, these graphs show the large sibsize of children in 1911 and the great drop that has occurred in the 100 years since then. In 1911, an average family size of 5.6 among married women translated into an average sibsize of 8.1 among their children. Although the range of sibsize in 1911 was wide and flat (as **Figure 3.2** shows), families of very many siblings were the norm – 45 per cent of the children belonged to families of nine or more siblings while only 7 per cent were in families of three siblings or less. By 1961, sibsizes had declined but were still exceptionally large by Western standards of the time. The most common sibsizes were 4, 5 and 6 rather than 7, 8 or 9, but there was still a wide spread at the higher end: sibsizes of 9 or more still accounted for 22 per cent of children and the mean sibsize was over 6.

By 2011, we are into the modern era of the small family. This era brings a concentration of sibsize around a lower mean so that there is now less diversity in this aspect of children's lives. But it is also notable that 'small' in this context is not as small as we might think. This was the era in which women's cohort fertility rates in Ireland and many other countries had fallen to replacement level or below – that is, to around two children per woman (or in some countries much less than that). In Ireland in *Census 2011* (Central Statistics Office, 2012), the mean fertility of women who had just reached the end of their childbearing years was 2.18 (see **Table 3.2** in the **Appendix** to this chapter). However, this was the average of what remained a quite uneven distribution of fertility – Ireland continued to have both a high level of childlessness (OECD, 2016) and a high incidence of families of four or more children (Shkolnikov *et al.*, 2007). In consequence, sibsize remained relatively high: the mean sibsize for children of women aged 45 to 49 in 2011 was 3.3, over one-third of children (35 per cent) belonged to families of four or more siblings, and the one-child family accounted for only one child in 20. This pattern placed Ireland at the top of sibsize table among rich countries, among which the United States came closest to Ireland with a sibsize of 2.98 and 27 per cent of children in families of four or more children (Fahey, 2015; Shkolnikov *et al.*, 2007). The surprise from these data is that the present time, which might rightly be called the era of the small family from an adult point of view, would better be called the era of the moderately-sized family from their children's perspective.

Coping with Large Families

Going back to 1911, one might wonder how children could flourish in such large families, given that typical incomes and dwellings were small and the quantum of time and attention that parents could give to their children was as limited by the 24-hour day as it is today. This large question goes beyond the scope of the present chapter but a couple of factors that affected how families coped can be mentioned here.

Figure 3.3: Deaths among Children of Women aged 45 to 54, by Children's Sibsize, 1911

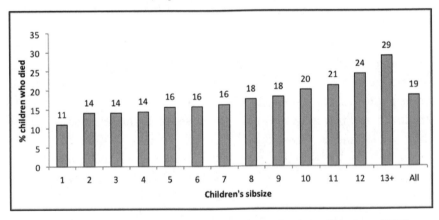

Source: Authors' calculations from Registrar of Births, Deaths and Marriages (1911), General Report, Table 165.

One was that some children died young, a tragic fact in itself but one that eased the pressure on resources for surviving siblings. The 1911 Census (Registrar General of Births, Deaths and Marriages, 1911) gives us some information on this factor, since married women were asked to record not only how many children they had given birth to but also how many had died by the census date. As **Figure 3.3** shows, among married women aged 45 to 54 in 1911, 19 per cent of their children had died. Death was most likely for children in larger families but the link with family size was not strong. Going from the two-sibling to the seven-sibling family, for example, the risk of death for children rose only from 14 per cent to 16 per cent, though it rose more sharply for very large families, reaching 29 per cent among those with 13 or more siblings. At the other end, it was 11 per cent among one-child families, which meant that over one in 10 mothers who had an only child saw that child die by the time the mother had reached her 50s. Moving on 100 years to the present, infant and childhood deaths have not disappeared but they have fallen to low levels and have become rare as a source of disturbance in family life: the survival rate of children to age 20 is now 99.23 per cent among males and 99.42 per cent among females (Central Statistics Office, 2015).

A second coping pattern that was widely used among families in early 20th century Ireland was the early exit of children from the family home, either to be fostered by relatives or to work for non-relatives as household or farm servants. Mobility of teenagers between households as a stage in young people's lives was a common part of growing up in pre-industrial Europe (Hajnal, 1982). Informal fosterage among relatives helped even out the distribution of children between those who had too many children and those who had too few (see, for example, Jane Gray's account of the 'circulation of children' in early 20th century Ireland, based on oral history recollections from present-day older people – Gray, 2014). These practices survived well into the 20th century in Ireland, though patterns of informal fosterage have not been quantified and we have only limited information on child servanthood.

A bleak version of what such servanthood could involve was captured in Patrick MacGill's autobiographical novel, *Children of the Dead End: Autobiography of a Navvy*, published in 1914. As a 12-year old in the Glenties area in Donegal, he was despatched by his impoverished parents to the hiring fair in Strabane in Co Tyrone (what he terms a 'slave market' for children), where he was taken on by a local tenant farmer. A little over a year later, following a well-trodden path for teenagers of his background, he ran away to a semi-vagabond life of potato-picking and navvying in Scotland. How typical is MacGill's account cannot easily be judged but it echoes many of the

themes highlighted in Richard Breen's research on farm servanthood in
Kerry in the same era (Breen, 1983). Few of the children Breen wrote
about were quite as young as MacGill when they were sent to the hiring
fairs but there are other accounts of children as young as age 8 or 9
being sent out to farm service (Guinnane, 1997, p.171). Guinnane's
estimates from the *1911 Census* suggest that up to one-third of 15- to
19-year-olds then living in better-off counties in Ireland were farm or
domestic live-in servants, though in poorer countries like Mayo, where
children moved to other parts of the country to find work, the
proportion in this category living within the county dropped below one
in 10 (Guinnane, 1997, pp.179-80). Teenage emigration accounted for
almost one-fifth of male and one-third of female emigration in the
decade after 1911, with a substantial proportion occurring before age
15 (Guinnane, 1997, p.182).

Social Inequalities in Family Size

The advent of long-term fertility decline in Western countries in the late
19th century caused families to become smaller on average but also
opened a widening gap in family size between the large lower class
family on the one hand and the newly-shrinking middle and upper class
families on the other (Ramsden, 2008; van Bavel, 2010). This pattern
was less marked in Ireland since the precipitous drop in fertility that
was common in Western countries in the early decades of the 20th
century was slower to occur in Ireland. Nevertheless, wide variation in
family size did occur: as we saw in **Figure 3.2** above, children's sibsizes
in both 1911 and 1961 ranged over the full spectrum from one or two
at one extreme to 13 or more at the other. One source of this diversity
was the age at which mothers married – in general, as **Figure 3.4** shows,
children's sibsize in both 1911 and 1961 became steadily smaller the
older their mother's age at marriage. **Figure 3.4** also shows that
children's sibsizes were lower in 1961 than in 1911 for mothers at all
ages of marriage, with the largest drop for those who had married in
their 20s and the smallest for those who had married as teenagers. Here
we see the impact of a rising incidence of fertility limitation within
marriage by the 1960s.

Figure 3.4: Sibsize among Children in Completed Families, by Mother's Age at Marriage, 1911 and 1961

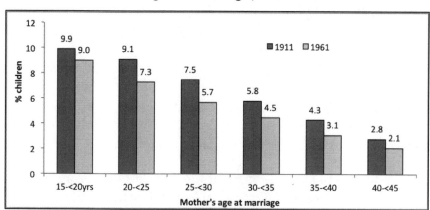

Sources: Authors' calculations from Registrar of Births, Deaths and Marriages (1911), General Report, Table 165; Central Statistics Office (1961), Vol 8, Table 17.

In addition, in both 1911 and 1961, great variation in sibsize occurred even among children whose mothers had married at around the same age. In 1911, for example, we calculate that, among mothers who had married in the age-range 25 to 29, one-fifth of their children had sibsizes of five or less, one-fifth had sibsizes of 10 or more, with the rest ranged in between. The causes of this variation are hard to pin down and remind us of the wealth of factors that could impinge on the sexual and childbearing behaviour of couples, even in the days before modern birth control became common.

This still leaves the question of how much of the variation in children's sibsize was structured by their family's position on the social scale – that is, to what extent a social gradient in family size existed. We cannot answer that question for 1911 as census data for that year provides no occupational or social class breakdowns, though there seems little evidence of marked social gradients in family patterns (Guinnane, 1997, pp.193-209, pp.241-71). The picture becomes clearer from the 1940s onwards when census returns classified fertility outcomes by occupational group. Glass (1968) examined this aspect of the 1961 Irish census data and concluded that social differentials in fertility outcomes were narrow in Ireland by European standards but also that this was so for the unusual reason that middle and upper classes had not yet adopted small-family norms (1968, pp.118-19; see also Hannan, 2015, p.48). The remarkable feature in Ireland around the mid-20th century, then, was not just the high average family size but the persistence of relatively large families among middle and upper class families, a pattern that by then was gone in most of the Western world.

We can get a picture of social class variations in children's sibsize in recent decades from census samples for 1971 and 2011 that are available through the Integrated Public Use Microdata Series in the University of Minnesota (Minnesota Population Center, 2015). These data confirm a picture of relative social equality in children's sibsize (**Figure 3.5**).

Figure 3.5: Mean Sibsize among Children of Women Aged 45 to 49, by Social Group

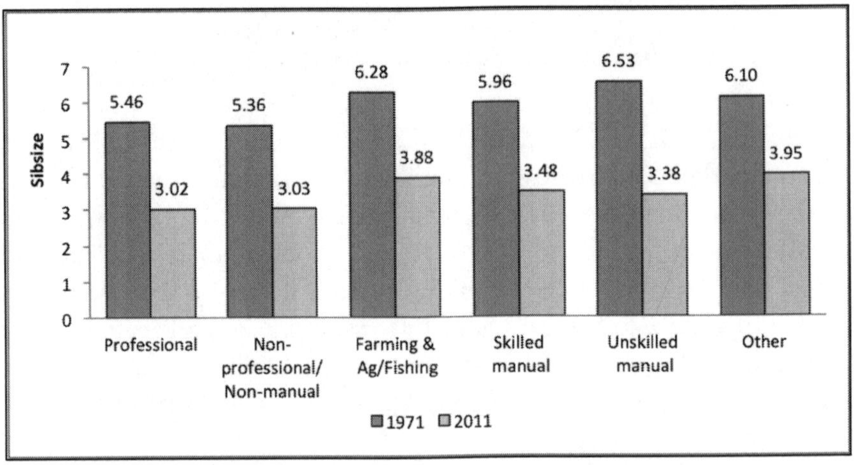

Source: Authors' calculations from 10 per cent Census sample, Central Statistics Office (1971, 2011) (IPUMS International).

In his analysis in 1968, Glass had identified a fertility ratio between the bottom and top of the social class scale of 1.2 to 1 or 1.3 to 1 as indicating relatively low social inequality (1968, pp.118-19). Applying that rough metric here, we find that none of the high-to-low class ratios in sibsize in Ireland had exceeded 1.22 to 1 in 1971 or 1.30 to 1 in 2011. In other words, while social class differences along expected lines did exist, they were at the modest end of the range. Furthermore, confirming Glass's (1968) judgement, the striking feature in 1971 was the large sibsizes in the professional and non-manual social classes, lying in the range 5.36 to 5.46. By 2011, sibsizes had fallen by around 2.5 for children in most social classes and by over 3 for those in the unskilled manual group. This too is a significant pattern, since it indicates that, over this period of substantial decline in fertility, the social class gradient in family sizes did not get any steeper but rather retained its historical relatively flat character. This pattern may have been a consequence of a 'Catholic effect' on middle and upper class fertility in Ireland but, if so, it was a distinctively *Irish* Catholic effect since it had no consistent parallel in other Catholic countries in Europe.

Figure 3.6: Mean Sibsize among 9-year-olds in Ireland with Primary-educated and Tertiary-educated mothers, 1971 and 2011

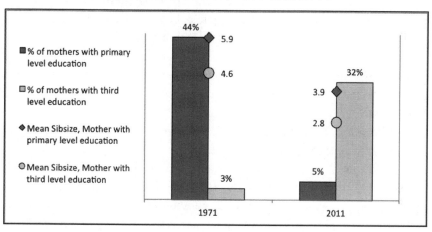

Source: Authors' calculations from 10 per cent Census sample, Central Statistics Office (1971, 2011) (IPUMS International).

The data for 1971 and 2011 also enable us to look at social inequalities in sibsize by maternal education. **Figure 3.6** selects 9-year-old children from the 1971 and 2011 census micro-data and contrasts the sibsizes of those whose mothers were at the two ends of the educational range – primary *versus* tertiary education. The results show first the sharp rise in mothers' education that occurred over the period, itself an important influence on children's family contexts. Mothers with primary education only dropped from 44 per cent of all mothers in 1971 to 5 per cent in 2011, while those with tertiary education rose from 3 per cent to 32 per cent. While mean sibsize among children of the less-educated mothers was higher than that of tertiary-educated mothers in both years, a large decline had occurred for both groups in the period. This suggests that smaller families emerged not simply because the share of well-educated mothers in the population had risen but also because mothers at the lowest end of the educational range kept pace with the overall trend towards smaller family sizes.

Family Disruption

We now turn to the second major strand of change in children's family contexts that we wish to examine in this chapter: trends in the form and incidence of family disruption. It over-simplifies matters to apply the term 'family disruption' only to various forms of departure from the traditional ideal of the intact nuclear family of father, mother and children. Yet it is useful as a shorthand for the element of structural vulnerability typically present in families when children and their two parents do not live together on a more or less continuous basis in a family home.

Looking back to the early 20th century, a devastating form of disruption was that caused by the death of parents, leaving children as semi-orphans or full orphans depending on whether one or both parents died. In the *Censuses* of 1926, 1936 and 1946, information was collected on children up to age 14 as to whether their father and mother were alive. As **Figure 3.7** shows, 22 per cent of 14-year-olds in 1926 had lost a parent and 7.4 per cent of 5-year-olds had done so, with a small proportion of these having lost both parents. By 1946, the incidence of orphanhood had dropped but was still substantial at 15 per cent for 14-year-olds and 5.3 per cent of for 5-year-olds.

These figures indicate, then, that the death of parents was a real risk facing children in the first half of the 20th century. When combined with other risks of separation of children from parents outlined earlier, it is likely that 100 years ago disruption of children's co-residence with the father-mother couple in childhood or the early adolescent years occurred for at least one in four and possibly a considerably higher proportion of children.

Figure 3.7: Orphanhood among Children at Selected Ages, 1926 and 1946

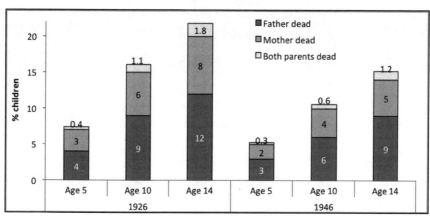

Sources: Department of Industry and Commerce (1926), Vol 5, Table 11A;
Department of Industry and Commerce (1946), Vol 5, Table 13A.

The period around the mid-20th century can be regarded as a golden age of the marital family in Western countries (Therborn, 2004, pp.162-90). The effects of poverty and high death rates that had ravaged the family in previous decades had abated by then and the new disturbances caused by marital breakdown, unstable cohabitation and childbearing outside marriage had not yet become common. This apogee of the marital family was well reflected in the 1971 Census returns in Ireland, where as **Table 3.1** suggests, some 91 per cent of children aged under 15 years were living with two married parents, with a further 3 per cent accounted for by a widowed parent. The small proportions with a married father or mother who was not present on Census night may have been due to temporary absence rather than marital breakup but even at that its incidence was small (a study in the early 1970s estimated that between 3,000 and 8,000 husbands had deserted their wives, which was a mere fraction of 1 per cent of all married couples – O'Higgins, 1974, pp.1-2). The level of inclusion of children under the umbrella of the marital family that these figures reflect is unlikely to have been exceeded in a substantial way for any sustained period in Ireland outside of the middle decades of the 20th century.

Table 3.1: Distribution of Children under Age 15, by Parenting Situation, 1971

	Two married parents	Married mother, father absent	Married father, mother absent	Widowed parent	Other	Total
%	91.4	1.9	1.0	3.0	2.6	100

Source: 10 per cent Census sample, Central Statistics Office (1971) (IPUMS International).

Figure 3.8: Births outside Marriage as a Percentage of Total Births, Ireland, 1960-2015

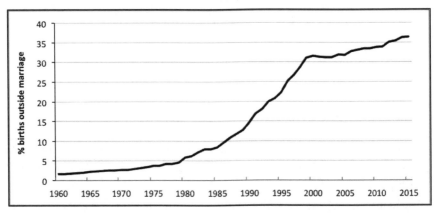

Source: Eurostat (n.d.) and Central Statistics Office, Vital Statistics.

From that point on, we can identify three major movements away from the overwhelmingly marriage-centred pattern of children's family contexts in the 1960s and 1970s.

The first was the silent revolution in the treatment of unmarried mothers and their children that took place in the 1970s and 1980s and was followed by rapid growth in childbearing outside marriage (Fahey, 2015). A welfare payment for unmarried mothers and their children introduced in 1973 (the Unmarried Mothers Allowance) represented a critical change in the normative climate. This was added to by the *Status of Children Act, 1987*, which removed the concept of 'illegitimacy' from Irish law. The behavioural consequences became evident mainly from the early 1980s to the late 1990s, during which time the share of births taking place outside marriage soared from one in 20 to one in three (**Figure 3.8**). Since the late 1990s, the pace of increase in this type of family formation has slowed and, in 2015, 36 per cent of births took place outside marriage. It should be noted, however, that births outside marriage do not necessarily indicate lone-parenthood: in 2014, over half (58 per cent) of births outside marriage were to parents who were living together at the time of birth (as evidenced by the recording of the same address for both parents on the birth registration form – Central Statistics Office, 2014, Table 6).

The second movement concerns marital breakdown (for details, see Fahey, 2012, 2014). As we have seen, marital breakdown was almost unknown in Ireland early in the early 1970s. Various forms of legal and informal separation began to become extensive around the mid-1980s and grew for almost two decades. Divorce became available in 1996 but had only limited impact: divorce rates spurted upwards for a decade or so but then peaked at a low level and fell by some 25 per cent between 2007 and 2013. By then the marital breakdown rate (combining all forms of legal and *de facto* separation, as well as divorce) was about double the divorce rate on its own but even at that it remained low by international standards. Rates of remarriage following exit from a previous marriage also seem to be low, in part because the pool of divorced people is still relatively small but also because of what appears to be a slowness among those who have come out of one marriage to enter another (Lunn & Fahey, 2011, pp.71-72). Thus while marital breakdown and divorce have become an accepted part of the landscape, they have not yet become a dominant feature.

The third recent movement that affects family stability is the rise of cohabitation. The number of cohabiting couples has been growing steadily since the 1990s, having increased from 31,300 in 1996 to 140,857 in 2011. Cohabitation is primarily a stepping-stone to marriage and is widely accepted as such in the population: a survey of attitudes to family formation in 2011 found that 84 per cent of respondents felt that it was better to live with someone before marrying while three-quarters of those who were cohabiting said that they were very likely to eventually marry their partner (Fine-Davis, 2011, p.60, p.69). In *Census 2011*, cohabiting couples represented about one in seven of all couples, married and cohabiting, and almost 10 per cent of couples with children. Age patterns of cohabitation in the past suggested that a transition either to marriage or to break-up of the relationship eventually occurred among the majority, with only a small proportion continuing in the arrangement for the long-term (Lunn & Fahey, 2011, pp.33-51).

The growth of childbearing outside marriage, marital breakdown and cohabitation has created new family contexts for children and reduced the dominance of the stable marital family of the 1970s noted earlier. However, the latter model is still by far the most common experience for children. Data on 9-year-olds from the *Growing Up in Ireland* study, the large-scale tracking survey of children and their families that commenced in 2007-2008, shows that almost eight out of 10 lived with both of their biological parents (for a more detailed analysis, see Fahey *et al.*, 2012, pp.20-21). Step-families accounted for only 3.3 per cent of 9-year-olds, a low figure by international standards (Lunn & Fahey, 2011, pp.70-72). This suggests that serial family formation, often thought of as one of the great sources of diversity and complexity in family life in the modern Western world, is still relatively unusual among families with dependent children in Ireland. Alongside the traditional two-parent family, the lone-parent family is really the only other family type that accounts for a substantial number of children, with close to one in five 9-year-olds in that category (Fahey *et al.*, 2012, p.22). One factor that tends to push up the incidence of lone-parenthood in Ireland is the low rate of entry into second unions already mentioned, a form of exit from lone-parenthood that is more common in other countries.

Social Inequalities in Family Instability

We have seen earlier that social inequalities in family size are limited in Ireland. The situation is somewhat different in regard to family instability where stratification by socio-economic status is evident and is tied in with other sources of difference in how family formation occurs, particularly the age at which child-bearing begins. Broadly speaking, the evidence on this question is that better-educated adults wait until their late 20s before starting their families and then do so after they marry, or at least after they form relatively stable relationships (many of which lead to marriage). Solo parenthood and parenthood within unstable cohabitation, on the other hand, are more likely to occur among less advantaged mothers and especially among those who have a first birth at a young age, though we should not overstate the differentials involved. For example, among the 9-year-olds studied in the *Growing Up in Ireland* survey, 85 per cent of those whose mothers had third-level education had lived with both of their biological parents since birth, which compares with 74 per cent of those whose mothers had not finished second-level education. Even so, more than half of early-start mothers formed ongoing and stable partnerships (usually through marriage) and so had 'standard' family trajectories (Fahey *et al.*, 2012, pp.29-30). The underlying reality here is that the stable two-parent family is the dominant family form across all major categories of the population and what differentiates those of lower socio-economic status is a somewhat greater *relative* risk of more unstable family trajectories rather than a very high *absolute* risk of that outcome.

Conclusion

The look back over the past century of change in children's family circumstances presented in this chapter has first shown the sharp decline in the average size of children's sibling group, which has fallen from over 8 in 1911 to 3.3 today. Almost half (45 per cent) of children of 100 years ago were in families of nine or more siblings, a family type that is almost unknown today. Yet, since women today on average have only two children, an average sibsize of 3.3 for children today is surprisingly large – it means that one-third of Irish children now grow up in families of four or more siblings. One lesson here is that we need to pay attention to family size looked at from a children's, rather than from an adult's, point of view since one is by no means a direct counterpart of the other. We have also seen that over the past century Ireland has never had an extended period of steep social gradients in family size. Some social disparities in family size were always present, but these never emerged as a major social divide the way they did in other Western countries.

Family instability is often thought of as a late 20th century invention, and in regard to unmarried childbearing, cohabitation and marital breakdown there is truth in that view. However, early in the 20th century, we find that other forms of disruption were common because of the ravages of economic hardship and disease on family life and the sometimes desperate adaptations that parents and children had to devise in response. About one in five of children had died by the time their mothers had finished childbearing and parents also died while their children were still young, with consequences that are now hard to recapture but were undoubtedly devastating. It is likely that a child of 100 years ago was as much exposed to family disruption of these kinds as a child is to the kinds of break-up of adult unions that give rise to lone parenthood today. The over-riding pattern is of the wide range of survival strategies that families and their children had to adopt 100 years ago and the highly varied, unpredictable and insecure paths to adulthood that children experienced as a result, in contrast to which paths through childhood today seem generally more standardised, structured and secure.

Appendix

Table 3.2: A Century of Family Size among Women with Completed Fertility and of Sibsize among Their Children

	Family size among women with completed fertility[a]				Sibsize among children of women with completed fertility		
	1911	1961	2011		1911	1961	2011
	Married[b]	Married[b]	All	Ever-married[c]			
Family size / sibsize	%	%	%	%	%	%	%
0	13.9	12.8	17.6	7.1			
1	5.1	8.6	11.2	8.7	1.0	2.2	5.1
2	5.8	12.9	29.6	28.1	2.2	6.5	27.1
3	7.0	14.0	23.4	22.7	3.9	10.5	32.2
4	8.2	13.5	10.8	10.5	5.9	13.5	19.8
5	8.8	11.1	3.7	3.5	7.9	13.8	8.4
6	9.5	8.4	1.4	1.3	10.2	12.6	3.7

	Family size among women with completed fertility[a]				Sibsize among children of women with completed fertility		
	1911	1961	2011		1911	1961	2011
	Married[b]	Married[b]	All	Ever-married[c]	1911	1961	2011
7	9.1	6.1	0.6	0.5	11.4	10.6	1.8
8	8.8	4.2	0.2	0.2	12.5	8.4	0.9
9	7.3	2.9	0.2[d]	0.2	11.7	6.5	0.9
10	6.1	2.0			10.9	5.0	
11	4.2	1.3			8.3	3.6	
12	2.8	0.8			6.0	2.5	
13+	3.4	1.3			8.2	6.9	
Total	100	100	98.8[e]	98.5[e]	100	100	100
Mean family size	5.6	4.01	2.18	2.48	8.12	6.27	3.27
% with family size of 7+	42	19	1.0	0.9	69	41	3.5
% with family size of 3 or less	32	48	82	67	7	19	65

Sources: Authors' calculations from Registrar of Births, Deaths and Marriages (1911), General Report, Table 165; Central Statistics Office (1962), Vol 8, Table 17; Central Statistics Office (2012), Profile 5, CD549.

[a] 1911: Ages 45 to 54; 1961 & 2011: Ages 45 to 49; [b] Excluding singles and widows; [c] Currently married, divorced / separated & widowed; [d] 9 or more; [e] Excluding 'not stated'.

References

Breen, R. (1983). Farm servanthood in Ireland, 1900-1940, Economic History Review 36, 87-102.

Central Statistics Office (1961). Census, Dublin: Stationery Office.

Central Statistics Office (2012). Census 2011, Dublin: Stationery Office.

Central Statistics Office (2014). Vital Statistics: Yearly Summary 2014, Dublin: Stationery Office.

Central Statistics Office (2015). *Irish Life Tables No. 16, 2010-12*, Dublin: Stationery Office.

Chapple, S. (2009). *Child Wellbeing and Sole Parent Family Structure in the OECD: An Analysis*, OECD Social, Employment and Migration Working Papers No. 82, Paris: Organization for Economic Cooperation and Development.

Department of Industry and Commerce, Statistics Branch (1926). *Census of Population*, Dublin: Stationery Office.

Department of Industry and Commerce, Statistics Branch (1946). *Census of Population*, Dublin: Stationery Office.

Fahey, T. (2012). Small bang? The impact of divorce legislation on marital breakdown in Ireland, *International Journal of Law, Policy and the Family* 26, 242-58.

Fahey, T. (2014). Divorce patterns and trends: An overview, in Eekelaar, J. & George, R. (eds.), *Routledge Handbook of Family Law and Policy* (pp.96-110), London: Routledge.

Fahey, T. (2015). The family in Ireland in the new millennium, in Connolly, L. (ed.), *The 'Irish' Family* (pp.54-69), London: Routledge.

Fahey, T., Keilthy, P. & Polek, E. (2012). *Family Relationships and Family Wellbeing: A Study of the Families of Nine-year-olds in Ireland*, Dublin: University College Dublin / Family Support Agency.

Fine-Davis, M. (2011). *Attitudes to Family Formation in Ireland: Findings from the Nationwide Study*, Dublin: Family Support Agency.

Glass, D.V. (1968). Fertility trends in Europe since the Second World War, *Population Studies 22*, 103-46.

Gray, J. (2014). The circulation of children in rural Ireland during the first half of the 20th century, *Continuity and Change 29*, 399-421.

Guinnane, T.W. (1997). *The Vanishing Irish: Households, Migration and the Rural Economy in Ireland*, Princeton: Princeton University Press.

Hajnal, J. (1982). Two kinds of pre-industrial household formation system, *Population and Development Review, 8,* 449-94.

Hannan, C. (2015). Marriage, fertility and social class in 20th century Ireland, in Connolly, L. (ed.), *The 'Irish' Family* (pp.39-53), London: Routledge.

Hannan, C., Halpin, B. & Coleman, C. (2013). *Growing Up in a One-parent Family: Family Structure and Child Outcomes*, Dublin: Family Support Agency.

Lesthaeghe, R. (2010). The unfolding story of the second demographic transition, *Population and Development Review, 36,* 211-51.

Lunn, P. & Fahey, T. (2011). *Households and Family Structures in Ireland: A Detailed Statistical Analysis of Census 2006*, Dublin: Economic and Social Research Institute / Family Support Agency.

MacGill, P. (1914). *Children of the Dead End: Autobiography of a Navvy*, London: Herbert Jenkins Limited.

Maguire, M. & Ó Cinnéide, S. (2005). 'A good beating never hurt anyone': The punishment and abuse of children in 20th century Ireland, *Journal of Social History*, 38, 635-52.

Minnesota Population Center (2015). *Integrated Public Use Microdata Series, International: Version 6.4* [machine-readable database], Minneapolis: University of Minnesota.

O'Higgins, K. (1974). *Marital Desertion in Dublin: An Exploratory Study*, Broadsheet No. 9, Dublin: Economic and Social Research Institute.

OECD (2016). *Family Database* (Table SF2, 5A), Paris: Organization for Economic Cooperation and Development.

Preston, S. (1976). Family sizes of children and family sizes of women, *Demography, 13,* 105-14.

Ramsden, E. (2008). Eugenics from the New Deal to the Great Society: Genetics, demography and population quality, *Studies in History and Philosophy of Biological and Biomedical Sciences* 39(4), 391-406.

Registrar General of Births, Deaths and Marriages (1911). *Census of Population*, Dublin: Stationery Office.

Reher, D.S. (2011). Economic and social implications of demographic transition, *Population and Development Review, 37 (Supplement)*, 11-33.

Shkolnikov, V.M., Andreev, E.M., Houle, R. & Vaupel, J.W. (2007). The concentration of reproduction in cohorts of women in Europe and the United States, *Population and Development Review, 33,* 67-99.

Therborn, G. (2004). *Between Sex and Power: Family in the World, 1900-2000*, London: Routledge.

van Bavel, J. (2010). Subreplacement fertility in the West before the baby boom: Past and current perspectives, *Population Studies, 64,* 1-18.

4: IS FAMILY STRUCTURE A SOURCE OF INEQUALITY IN CHILDREN'S LIVES?

Elizabeth Nixon & Lorraine Swords

Much early research in the field of divorce and single-parenthood indicated that growing up with a single or divorced parent conferred a risk of poorer developmental outcomes on children, including higher levels of emotional and behaviour problems and lower academic achievement (Amato, 2001; Pryor & Rodgers, 2001). However, research adhering to this model of comparing children's outcomes across family structures has been limited by its failure to take account of the processes or mechanisms that underlie inequalities in children's outcomes, according to family structure. Furthermore, single-parent households are not a homogeneous group and there is much variability in outcomes within these families. Contemporary research now pays attention to this variability in order to identify those characteristics of families that may counteract the negative effects of being in a household headed by a single parent.

The analyses presented in this chapter use data from the first two waves of the Child Cohort of *Growing Up in Ireland* (ages 9 and 13). The chapter broadly seeks to understand how children in single-parent households in *Growing Up in Ireland* are faring and what family characteristics underlie positive and negative outcomes for children. In the first part of the chapter, the extent to which family structure represents a risk factor or a source of inequality in children's lives will be examined. Children living in single-parent households and their counterparts from two-parent households will be compared in an effort to understand whether living in a single-parent household is associated with more negative outcomes for children. In the second part of the chapter, the extent to which single-parent households are characterised by lower levels of economic resources, relative to those living in households headed by a couple, will be examined. In the third part, the analysis will focus on interpersonal relationships and processes (or what goes on within families) and whether or how they differ according to family structure. In the final part of the chapter, the relative role of family structure and family resources and processes will be considered. This analysis will show that some – but not all – of the differences between single-parent and two-parent households can be accounted for by lower levels of social and economic resources available to those in single-parent households. The merit of focusing on what goes on *within* these families, as opposed to what these families *look like structurally*, will be illustrated. Through demonstrating how resources within families – regardless of family structure – are the key drivers of positive developmental outcomes for children, we will argue that growing up in a single-parent family is not an inevitable source of disadvantage for children.

The Changing Landscape of the Family in Ireland

The demography of the family in Ireland, as in many Western societies, has changed significantly over the past number of decades. Marriage and childbearing is being delayed, while rates of cohabitation, births outside marriage and divorce have increased, and single-parent and step-parent families have become a relatively common feature of our social landscape. In addition to rising levels of single-parent families, patterns of single-parenthood have also shifted dramatically over the past few decades. Thus, the premature death of a spouse / parent has now been replaced as the main source of single-parenthood by new routes of entry *via* marital breakdown and non-marital childbearing (Fahey & Russell, 2001; Canavan, 2012). For example, between the mid-1980s and 2006, there was a five-fold increase in the number of people whose marriages broke down, and in the same intervening period, lone-parenthood has a little more than doubled (Lunn *et al.*, 2009). The proportion of births outside marriage increased from less than 10 per cent in 1986 to approximately one-third in 2006, a rate that has remained stable for the past decade. Much of this increase reflects children born to cohabiting rather than married couples, and the proportion of children born to women not in a relationship remains low. However, international research indicates that cohabiting relationships tend to be less stable than marriage and children born to cohabiting rather than married couples are significantly more likely to experience a transition to a lone-parent family (Kiernan & Mensah, 2010; Bumpass & Lu, 2000).

Figures from the 2006 *Census* suggest that 18 per cent of children live with lone parents, and 2.5 per cent of children live in step-families, of whom just over half (1.3 per cent of all children) were themselves step-children (the offspring of one partner in the couple) (Lunn & Fahey, 2011). Figures from the 2011 *Census* reveal that a similar proportion of children – approximately 19 per cent – live with lone parents (Central Statistics Office, 2012). Thus, one-parent families represent a significant minority of families in Ireland.

Alongside the changing demographic profile of families in Ireland, policy and legislative shifts have also occurred – though the pace of these shifts has been slow. Cumulatively, these changes reflect a greater acceptance of diverse family forms and a gradual de-stigmatisation of families not conforming to the traditional nuclear family form of two married parents with biological children. Historically, as a consequence of the strong influence of Catholic teaching and the enmeshed relationship of the State and Church, 'the family' that was afforded protection by the *Constitution* was the family based on marriage. Unmarried motherhood in Ireland carried a stigma that was difficult to shake (Luddy, 2011). Children born to these women were considered 'illegitimate' and were not afforded the same legal rights as children born to married parents. As noted by Fahey, 'the legal down-grading of children born outside of marriage, however harsh on the innocent children involved, was an acceptable price to pay for safeguarding the institution of marriage' (1998, p.393).

With the enactment of the *Status of Children Act, 1987*, discrimination against children born outside marriage in relation to succession rights was abolished and unmarried fathers could – for the first time – establish guardianship rights of their children. Divorce was finally introduced into Ireland, following a very narrowly-won referendum in 1996, and although provisions for dealing with legal separation had already been developed within family law, the introduction of divorce dealt with the right of separated individuals to remarry, thus placing remarried families on an equal footing with first-married families (Fahey & Nixon, 2013). Other significant changes since 2010 have afforded certain legal rights to cohabiting couples and the legalisation of same-sex marriage. In particular in relation to children, the *Children and Family Relationships Act*, signed into law in 2015, represents a significant step forward in the evolution of child-centred family law. Specifically the Act recognises the diverse reality of contemporary family forms in Ireland and seeks to address discrimination currently faced by children in non-traditional families. For example, the Act ensures that children can enjoy a legal relationship with the person who provides care to them on a day-to-day basis, regardless of the marital and, to some extent, cohabiting status of parents, and it includes provisions for children being parented by same-sex couples or conceived through donor-assisted human reproduction (Children's Rights Alliance, 2015). Thus, the State has come some way in acknowledging the various family structures in which children in Ireland today are being reared, although further work is needed to ensure that all family forms are valued and recognised as equal.

Family Structure and Children's Outcomes

In response to rising rates of non-marital birth and parental separation and concern about the 'break-up' of the family, a strong interest has developed in understanding how growing up in diverse family forms impacts upon children's wellbeing. Much of this research began with the assumption that children living in one-parent families would fare worse than children living in two-parent families. For the most part, this expectation has been borne out consistently in the research. Hundreds of studies that have compared children in single-parent and two-parent families have found small but significant differences between the two groups. For example, children from divorced families tend to display higher levels of social, emotional and behavioural problems in childhood, have poorer school grades, are more likely to drop out of school, be suspended or expelled from school, have contact with the law, and use illicit substances. Children from single-parent families typically have one-and-a-half to two times the risk of an adverse outcome in comparison with children from two-parent, first-married families (intact families) (Pryor & Rodgers, 2001; Amato, 2001; Simons & Associates, 1996). The size of differences in outcomes between children based on their family structure varies somewhat depending on the outcome under consideration. For example, where approximately 10 per cent of children from intact families have behaviour problems, studies typically find a higher proportion of children from separated families have behaviour problems, but this proportion has ranged from 13 per cent to 33 per cent, depending upon the study (Pryor & Rodgers, 2001).

Pryor & Rodgers reported that differences in academic and educational outcomes between children from intact and separated families tended to be larger than the difference for behaviour problems. In this case, where approximately 10 per cent of children from intact families display poor educational and academic outcomes, the majority of studies reported poorer outcomes for between 17 per cent and 34 per cent of children from separated families. Amato & Keith (1991) and later Amato (2001) reported on an analysis of a combined pool of data from 159 published studies. They found that children from intact families consistently tended to do better academically than children from divorced households. They concluded that, although the size of the difference between children from intact and divorced families tended to be small, the gulf between the two groups was growing larger over time.

The conclusion that can be drawn from the extensive body of research conducted thus far is that family structure does make a difference to children's outcomes. The evidence suggests that, within both groups of one-parent and two-parent family children, some children do very well and some children do poorly. However, overall, the likelihood of having a poor outcome is higher among children from single-parent families.

In the rest of this section, attention is turned to children in Ireland. The key questions to be addressed are:

- How well are children in single-parent and two-parent families faring in Ireland?

- Does living in a single-parent family confer a risk for poorer wellbeing and development?

In order to address these questions, children from *Growing Up in Ireland* at age 9 and at age 13 in couple-headed *versus* single-parent households were compared in terms of emotional and behavioural problems, self-esteem and academic competencies. At Wave 1, when the children were age 9, 8,568 children and their families participated. When the children were age 13, 7,525 families re-participated at Wave 2, representing 88 per cent of the sample who participated at Wave 1.

A number of authors have previously considered how children in single-parent *versus* two-parent households have fared, based upon data collected in *Growing Up in Ireland*. Family structure in the study was determined based on responses to questions asked of the primary caregiver (in 99 per cent of cases, this was the child's mother) regarding marital status and whether they were currently living with a partner. Hannan & Halpin (2014) reported that, at age 9, approximately 82.5 per cent of children were living in couple-headed households and 17.5 per cent of children in a one-parent family. This latter figure closely resembles the 19 per cent of single-parent households reported in the 2011 *Census* (Central Statistics Office, 2012). Within these two broad groups, there is some diversity in terms of the marital status of the parents, and for the single-parent households, diversity in the routes into lone-parenthood. Within the 17.5 per cent of single-parent households, 8.1 per cent of mothers had previously been married and were now separated, while 9.4 per cent of mothers had never married (Hannan & Halpin, 2014). Within the 13-year-old sample, 19.1 per cent of the families were classified as single-parent households.

Nixon (2012) reported that at age 9, children in single-parent families had higher scores than children in families headed by a couple on a screening measure of emotional and behavioural problems (the Strengths and Difficulties Questionnaire [SDQ], Goodman, 1997). Extending this analysis to those children at age 13, information collected from mothers on the SDQ was considered. The SDQ assesses emotional problems (for example, *Child has many fears, is easily scared*), hyperactivity and inattention (for example, *Child is constantly fidgeting and squirming*), conduct problems (for example, *Child often fights with other children or bullies them*) and peer relationship problems (for example, *Child is rather solitary, tends to play alone*). Responses to 20 items on the scale are summed into a total 'difficulties' score. Using the cut-off score of 13 determined by the scale authors (Goodman, 1997), children can be classified as having 'no difficulties' or being 'problematic' (incorporating the 'borderline' and 'abnormal' categories). **Figure 4.1** below illustrates that at both ages 9 and 13, the children in single-parent households were more likely to be classified as 'problematic' on the SDQ scale than children in couple-headed households.

Figure 4.1: Percentage of Children Classified as 'Problematic' on the SDQ at Age 9 and 13, According to Family Structure

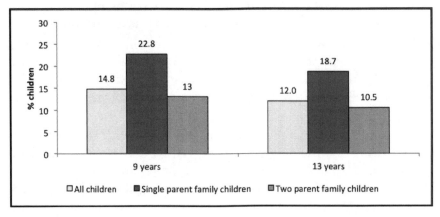

At both ages, the proportion of children classified as problematic was nearly one-third to almost double in the single-parent *versus* two-parent family groups, indicating that there is a higher risk of poorer developmental outcomes associated with growing up in a single-parent family.

A similar pattern can be observed when examining verbal and numerical abilities for the *Growing Up in Ireland* children at both age 9 and 13. As noted in **Figure 4.2** below, based on tests of reading and mathematics at age 9, and tests of verbal and numerical abilities at age 13, children from single-parent families scored lower than two-parent-family children. On average, at age 9, single-parent-family children scored 6.2 and 7.8 percentage points lower than children from two-parent families, on reading and mathematical tests respectively. Similarly, at age 13, single-parent-family children scored on average 6.5 and 7.6 percentage points lower than two-parent family children, on verbal and numerical ability tests respectively.

Figure 4.2: Percentage of Correct Responses on Ability Tests at Age 9 and 13, According to Family Structure

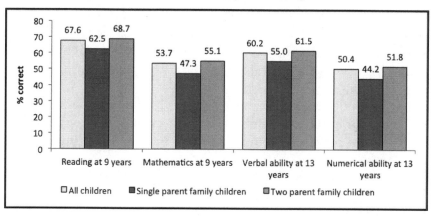

Similar patterns can be observed when considering how the children and young people themselves feel. This analysis is based on two measures. First, children at age 13 completed the Short Moods and Feelings Questionnaire (SMFQ, Angold *et al.*, 1995). This is a brief screening measure (non-clinical assessment) of depressive symptoms and scores above a cut-off of 12 may signify that the child is suffering from depression. Second, children at both age 9 and 13 completed the Piers-Harris Scale (Piers & Herzberg, 2002), which is a standardised measure of a person's perception of themselves (known as self-concept). The scale covers six different aspects of one's sense of self and being in the world, measuring: physical appearance and attributes, freedom from anxiety, intellectual and school status, behavioural adjustment, happiness and satisfaction, and popularity. A total score reflects how the individual perceives himself or herself overall.

In terms of the SMFQ, the analyses revealed that 7.2 per cent of the sample of 13-year-olds achieved a score greater than 12, indicating levels of symptomology above the cut-off for depression. Of particular note is that the proportion of children scoring greater than 12 was one-third higher among the single-parent-family children: 10.2 per cent of children from the single-parent-family group were above this cut-off for depression, in comparison with 6.5 per cent of the children from the two-parent households. Thus, the risk of depression is greater among the single-parent family children.

In terms of the children and young people's self-concept, similar distinctions emerged between the two groups of children based on their family structure. As illustrated in **Figure 4.3**, at both age 9 and 13, children from the single-parent households received significantly lower scores across all domains of self-concept than children from the two-parent households (selected domains shown only, but this pattern was true for all domains measured).

Figure 4.3: Average Scores on Self-concept Sub-scales at Age 9 and 13, According to Family Structure

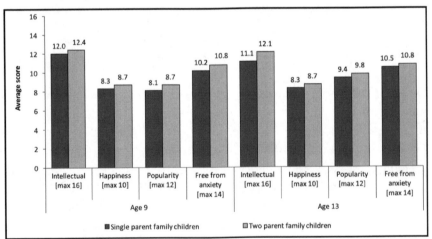

The key conclusions that can be drawn from these analyses of the Child Cohort data at ages 9 and 13 are that children from single-parent households are at a relative disadvantage on a range of outcomes in comparison with their counterparts from households headed by two parents. The magnitude of the difference between groups of children based upon family structure varies, depending upon the outcome under consideration. For example, in relation to the domains of self-concept considered above, single-parent-family children on average scored no less than one unit below children from two-parent families on the self-concept scale. However, in relation to literacy and numeracy abilities, these differences extended to between 6 and 8 percentage points lower for children from single-parent households. Similarly the proportion of children classified as 'problematic' in terms of their emotional and behavioural problems at age 9, and as 'depressed' at age 13, was of the order of one-third higher for children from single-parent households. Thus, while these differences may seem small at first glance, they are not insignificant and small occurrences of disadvantage across multiple domains of functioning may cumulatively accrue to reflect higher overall levels of disadvantage. In addition, as noted by Pryor & Rodgers (2001), even modest differences between children from single-parent and two-parent households can be of huge importance at population level, when implications for services and the financial and societal costs of poor outcomes are taken into account. Furthermore, the impact of these small differences becomes even greater as increasing proportions of children are spending at least part of their childhood living in a single-parent household. In the following section, attention is turned to understanding what might underlie this modest but robust association between family structure and children's outcomes.

Family Structure and Economic Resources

A variety of explanations have been proposed in an attempt to understand why it might be that children from single-parent households are at higher risk of poorer outcomes than children from two-parent households. One such explanation pertains to the resources that are available to the household. To put it simply, two parents in a household have more resources, in terms of time, energy and money, to invest in their children than has one parent. Amato (1995) argues that the disadvantage that accrues to children in single-parent households can be accounted for by considering how household structure affects children's access to resources. One type of resource that has known significant consequences for children's development is that of economic resources (Duncan & Brooks-Gunn, 1997; McLoyd, 1998). Having fewer economic resources is associated with a range of negative outcomes for children, in terms of their physical and mental health, language and cognitive development, academic achievement and educational attainment (Yoshikawa *et al.*, 2012).

Across many countries, single-parent families tend to be over-represented among the less-well-educated and lower socio-economic classes and this pattern holds true in Ireland also (Fahey & Russell, 2001). For example, based on *Census 2006* figures, Lunn *et al.* (2009) reported that the likelihood of lone-parenthood as a result of a non-marital birth (as opposed to following parental separation) is 10 times less likely among graduates than among those who did not complete secondary schooling. They also reported a higher risk of marital breakdown among women in lower social classes – specifically, the proportion of separated women in semi-skilled or unskilled manual occupations is approximately double the corresponding proportion among women in professional, managerial and technical occupations. In 2006, more than one-quarter of lone-parent households (27.6 per cent) were living in consistent poverty (Fahey & Field, 2008). In 2014, the consistent poverty rate within single-parent households was 22.1 per cent, in comparison with 7.9 per cent within two-parent households (Central Statistics Office, 2015).

In order to establish whether this link between economic resources and family structure is echoed among families in *Growing Up in Ireland*, income and maternal education levels were analysed, according to family structure. Equivalised household income was used, which is an adjusted measure of income that takes account of the number of adults and children in a household, thus making comparisons across different family structures more meaningful. The average equivalised household income for single-parent households was €14,600 and €13,000 when children were aged 9 and 13, respectively. The corresponding figures for two-parent households were €20,000 and €16,700, at child age 9 and 13, respectively. Thus, single-parent households have significantly lower levels of income than two-parent households. Further evidence of the income discrepancies between single-parent and two-parent households comes from examining families in the highest and lowest income groups or quintiles (the highest income quintile represents the one-fifth of families with the highest earnings, the lowest income quintile represents the one-fifth of families with the lowest earnings). Analyses showed that 39 per cent of single-parent households were in the lowest income quintile at Wave 1 (9 years) and 27 per cent at Wave 2 (13 years); in comparison, 16 per cent and 20 per cent of two-parent households were in the lowest income quintile at Waves 1 (9 years) and 2 (13 years), respectively.

Stark differences in the extent to which single-parent *versus* couple-headed households were reliant upon social welfare payments were also apparent. At Wave 1 (9 years) and Wave 2 (13 years), 21 per cent and 20 per cent of single-parent households received all of their household income through social welfare, respectively. This compares with 4 per cent and 7 per cent of two-parent households that are wholly reliant on social welfare, at Wave 1 (9 years) and Wave 2 (13 years) respectively.

Figure 4.4: Percentage of Mothers Who Achieved Primary School or Lower Secondary School Education and Primary or Postgraduate Degree, at Wave 1, According to Family Structure

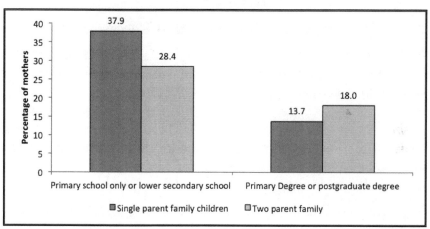

Finally, maternal education, a key indicator of socio-economic status, was compared across single-parent and two-parent households. As illustrated in **Figure 4.4**, mothers from single-parent households were more likely to have left secondary school prior to completing their Leaving Certificate; and mothers from two-parent households were more likely than single mothers to have attained a primary or post-graduate degree [data for Wave 1 only are shown, as minimal change in highest levels of maternal education is expected between Waves 1 and 2].

Based on these analyses of *Growing Up in Ireland* data, it appears that there is a clear association between family structure and socio-economic status. As reflected in the international literature and previous research based in Ireland, a higher proportion of single-parent families than couple-headed families are wholly dependent on social welfare and are found in the lowest income quintile. Furthermore, a higher proportion of mothers in single-parent families have lower levels of education than mothers in two-parent households. In light of these findings, it is plausible to suggest that some of the difficulties experienced by children living in single-parent family structures, as outlined in the first section of the chapter, may be explained by the position of relative economic disadvantage in which many of these families live. An additional explanation may lie in the interpersonal resources and family processes within these families.

Family Structure and Interpersonal Resources

As noted in the previous section, Amato (1995) suggested that access to limited resources may underlie the poorer outcomes often found among children from single-parent households. While economic resources may represent one such category of resources, interpersonal resources are no less significant. Interpersonal resources cover a myriad of factors, including the amount of contact time children have with parents, access to appropriate role models, sensitive parenting, being disciplined and monitored, as well as parental wellbeing. Amato has noted that:

> ... *as a general principle, the greater the number of adults who provide economic resources, support, regulation and positive role models to children, the more positive is children's development.* (1995, p.25)

Several studies have reported that single parents spend less time with their children than those parenting in a couple (Kendig & Bianchi, 2008) and that their parenting is characterised by less discipline and supervision (Hetherington, 1989). Perhaps owing to their relative lack of resources, single parents display poorer psychological wellbeing and experience higher levels of stress than those parenting as part of a couple (Meadows *et al.*, 2008; Tein *et al.*, 2000). Based upon research such as this, variations in child adjustment according to family structure have been attributed to variations in parenting practices and parental wellbeing, a perspective known as the family process perspective. This view suggests that what goes on *within* the family (processes) are more significant drivers of child wellbeing than what a family *looks like* (structure) (Acock & Demo, 1994).

One of the key avenues by which family structure may influence child outcomes is through its effect on parenting and parental wellbeing (Simons & Associates, 1996). In the analyses of *Growing Up in Ireland* data that follows, maternal wellbeing and quality of parenting and the parent-child relationship is considered, according to family structure. Mothers completed the Centre for Epidemiological Studies Depression Scale (CES-D, Radloff, 1977), which is a short eight-item measure for screening for symptoms of depression. Total scores on the scale can range from 0 to 24, and respondents who score 7 or above on the scale are considered to have elevated levels of depressive symptoms and to be at risk for depression. Based on this cut-off, 19.3 per cent of single mothers and 7.3 per cent of two-parent-family mothers were at risk for depression at Wave 1. The corresponding percentages for Wave 2 were 21.2 per cent of single mothers and 9.4 per cent of two-parent-family mothers. While this is not a clinical diagnosis of depression *per se*, these figures reveal that over twice as many single mothers exhibit significantly higher levels of depressive symptoms than mothers in two-parent households.

In terms of parenting and quality of the parent-child relationship, data were collected from both children and mothers. At both waves, mothers completed the Pianta Child-Parent Relationship Scale (Pianta, 1992), which yields a measure of 'closeness and conflict' in the parent-child relationship. At Wave 2, children completed the Inventory of Parent and Peer Attachment (IPPA, Armsden & Greenberg, 1987) and mothers completed the Monitoring and Supervision Scale (Stattin & Kerr, 2000). The IPPA yields a measure of 'trust' (defined as parental understanding and respect and mutual trust) and 'alienation' (defined as feelings of alienation and isolation) in the parent-child relationship. The Monitoring and Supervision Scale taps into parents' knowledge of their child's whereabouts, activities and associations (Monitoring sub-scale) and the extent to which parents believe children are open with them about their activities and what is going on in their lives (Disclosure sub-scale). For each of these dimensions of parenting and the parent-child relationship, scores were compared for those in single-parent and two-parent households. **Table 4.1** illustrates the findings from this analysis.

Table 4.1: Comparison of Dimensions of Parenting and the Parent-child Relationship, According to Family Structure

Dimension	Reporter	Wave	Age	Family Structure Comparison
Closeness	Mother	1	9	No difference
	Mother	2	13	SP lower than TP, negligible effect size (d = 0.09)
Conflict	Mother	1	9	SP higher than TP, small effect size (d = 0.27)
	Mother	2	13	SP higher than TP, small effect size (d = 0.20)
Trust	Child	2	13	SP lower than TP, negligible effect size (d = 0.07)
Alienation	Child	2	13	No difference
Monitoring	Mother	2	13	SP lower than TP, negligible effect size (d = 0.11)
Disclosure	Mother	2	13	No difference

Note: SP – Single-parent household, TP – Two-parent household; effect sizes are measured by Cohen's d, a way of interpreting the size or magnitude of differences between the average scores of two groups (negligible effects range from 0 < 0.15 and small effects range from > 0.15 to < 0.40).

Some small differences did emerge on these measures on parenting and parent-child relationships between single-parent and two-parent households. Specifically, conflict was higher at both time points in the single-parent households, and mothers in single-parent households reported less monitoring. However, where differences did exist, they tended to be small in magnitude, and there were no differences in ratings of closeness and alienation in the mother-child relationship. Thus, these findings provide tentative support for the idea that quality of relationships may be somewhat compromised in single-parent households.

Family Structure, Economic Resources and Family Processes

Having previously considered associations between family structure and children's outcomes and between family structure and economic and family resources, the question that remains is whether family structure or other characteristics reliably associated with family structure can explain why children in single-parent families fare less well (on average) than children in two-parent families. Using social and emotional difficulties as an outcome of interest, a logistic regression model was run to predict whether children would be classified as having 'no difficulties' or as having difficulties (termed 'problematic') on the SDQ at age 13, based on a range of predictor variables from Wave 1 at age 9. Family structure (single-parent *versus* two-parent household) was the first predictor, followed by economic variables (specifically household income and highest level of maternal education), and then followed by interpersonal variables (maternal depression and conflict in the parent-child relationship). As illustrated in **Table 4.2**, the odds of children from single-parent households being classified as having an emotional / behavioural difficulty was greater than 1 and statistically significant, which means that these children had a greater likelihood of being classified as 'difficult' when compared with children from two-parent households. In the first step of the analysis, family structure was entered into the model alone – the odds ratio of 2.153 indicates that the odds of children from single-parent households being classified as 'problematic' are 2.15 times higher than the odds of a child from a two-parent household being classified as 'problematic'. When economic variables (income and maternal education) are entered into the model next, the odds of being classified as 'problematic' based on family structure reduced from 2.15 to 1.69.

In terms of income, those in the lowest and second income quintiles had greater odds of being classified as 'problematic', in comparison with those from the highest income quintile, as did those children whose mothers did not proceed to third-level education. In the final step of the model, children from single-parent households were 1.38 times more likely to be classified as 'problematic' in comparison with children from two-parent households, when economic and interpersonal resources (maternal depression and parent-child conflict) were also accounted for. Here, children whose mothers were depressed were 1.63 times more likely to be 'problematic' and children were 1.1 times more likely to be classified as 'problematic' for every unit change in levels of mother-child conflict.

These findings suggest that family structure was a significant predictor of emotional and behavioural difficulties. Family structure remained a significant predictor, even after controlling for household income, maternal education, maternal depression and parent-child conflict.

Table 4.2: Model of Being Classified as 'Having Emotional and Behavioural Difficulties' (at Age 13)

Predictor Variable (All at age 9)	Odds Ratio		
Family Structure [Ref. Two-parent household]	2.153***	1.693***	1.381**
Income Quintile [Ref. Highest (5th) income quintile]			
Lowest (1st)		1.906***	1.856***
Second		1.512**	1.542**
Middle (3rd)		1.144NS	1.105NS
Fourth		1.109NS	1.062NS
Highest Level of Mothers' Education [Ref. postgraduate]			
None or primary		4.491***	4.256***
Lower Secondary		2.547***	2.522***
Higher Secondary		1.881**	1.960**
Third Level Non-Degree		1.522NS	1.517NS
Primary Degree		1.164NS	1.436NS
Maternal Depression [Ref. Not Depressed]			1.634***
Parent-Child Conflict			1.105***

*Levels of significance are indicated as follows: *** $p < 0.001$; ** $p < 0.01$, * $p < 0.05$, NS – non-significant. An odds ratio of 1 means that a child in a particular group has an equal likelihood of being classified as having emotional/behavioural difficulties in comparison with a child in the reference group. Where an odds ratio is greater than 1, the odds of being classified as having a difficulty is increased, relative to those in the reference group.*

Conclusion

In this chapter, the role of family structure in children's development has been considered. Drawing upon data from the Child Cohort of *Growing Up in Ireland*, at ages 9 and 13, the findings revealed a consistent pattern of disadvantage for children living in single-parent households, in comparison with their peers from two-parent households, across all of the outcomes considered and at both time points. In terms of emotional and behavioural problems, the proportion of children classified as having difficulties was at least one-third greater in single-parent households, based on both children's and mothers' reports. On verbal and numerical reasoning tests, single-parent family children scored on average 6 or 7 percentage points lower. Overall, these patterns of difference tended to be small but were consistent over time. Thus, in keeping with international research on this topic, the findings indicated that growing up in a single-parent family structure does represent a source of inequality in children's lives.

In an attempt to explain why family structure represents a risk factor in children's development, the analysis moved to focus upon both economic and interpersonal resources within different family structures. The findings revealed a stronger likelihood of welfare dependence, lower maternal education and lower income among single-parent households than two-parent households. Of course, given this strong overlap between family structure and socio-economic status, there is a challenge in attributing negative outcomes of children living in single-parent families to family structure *per se* and not to socio-economic status. The selection argument suggests that childbearing outside of marriage and / or marital separation is more likely to occur among those who are socio-economically disadvantaged, and it is this disadvantage rather than lone-parenthood that compromises children's development (Hannan & Halpin, 2014). Consistent with this perspective, many studies find that, after controlling for income (or other indices of socio-economic status), the relationship between family structure and children's outcomes diminishes somewhat, suggesting that at least part of the reason that single-parent family children do less well is due to their relative lack of economic resources. This perspective was partly borne out in the current analysis: when modelling emotional and behavioural difficulties, family structure effects decreased, but remained significant, even after controlling for income and maternal education.

A focus upon interpersonal resources and family processes also revealed some differences between single-parent families and couple-headed households. Over twice as many single mothers than mothers in two-parent families scored above the cut-off for depression on the screening instrument, indicating significantly higher levels of depressive symptoms among single mothers. Levels of conflict in mother-child relationships were higher and levels of parental monitoring were lower in single-parent *versus* two-parent households – overall, however, these differences were small in magnitude. The family process and strain perspectives suggest that family structure differences can be accounted for by these elevated levels of psychological distress and poorer quality of parent-child relationships, which tend to characterise single-parent households more than two-parent households. Again, this perspective was partly supported by the analysis explaining emotional and behavioural outcomes. Maternal depression and mother-child conflict, both of which were higher in single-parent households, represented significant drivers of emotional and behavioural outcomes, although family structure itself still remained significant.

This analysis is not without limitations. A focus on overall group differences according to household structure conceals the wide variability in outcomes within groups. Children from two-parent, as well as single-parent, families develop difficulties, while the substantial majority of children from single-parent families grow up to be successful and well-adjusted. The categories of family structure used – single-parent *versus* couple-headed households – were crude and no doubt obscured considerable heterogeneity within each type of household. For example, no account was taken of the route into being in a single-parent household (one parent continuously absent, parental separation) or a couple-headed household (traditional 'nuclear' family, step-family), or of the number and timing of family structure transitions that children had experienced, all of which are known to be important factors in understanding children's development in diverse families (McLanahan & Sandefur, 1994; Raley & Wildsmith, 2004).

Notwithstanding these limitations, our findings suggest that family structure does indeed represent a source of inequality in children's lives, and places children in single-parent households at risk of poorer developmental outcomes. In order to buffer children against this risk, greater understanding of the mechanisms underpinning the risk associated with single-parent families is needed. Our analysis points to the important role that socio-economic disadvantage and family processes play in this link between family structure and children's outcomes, and highlights important targets for intervention and prevention efforts. Striving to improve parental wellbeing and support good quality family relationships may buffer children from negative outcomes, regardless of family structure or socio-economic disadvantage.

References

Acock, A. & Demo, D.H. (1994). *Family Diversity and Wellbeing*, Thousand Oaks, CA: Sage.

Amato, P.R. (1995). Single-parent households as settings for children's development, wellbeing and attainment: A social network / resources perspective, *Sociological Studies of Children, 7*, 19-47.

Amato, P.R. (2001). Children of divorce in the 1990s: An update of the Amato & Keith (1991) meta-analysis, *Journal of Family Psychology, 15*, 355-70.

Amato, P.R. & Keith, B. (1991). Parental divorce and the wellbeing of children: A meta-analysis, *Psychological Bulletin, 110*, 26-46.

Angold, A., Costello, E.J., Messer, S.C., Pickles, A., Winder, F. & Silver, D. (1995). The development of a short questionnaire for use in epidemiological studies of depression in children and adolescents, *International Journal of Methods in Psychiatric Research, 5*, 237-49.

Armsden, G.C. & Greenberg, M.T. (1987). The inventory of parent and peer attachment: Relationships to wellbeing in adolescence, *Journal of Youth & Adolescence, 16*, 427-54.

Bumpass, L. & Lu, H. (2000). Trends in cohabitation and implications for children's family contexts in the United States, *Population Studies, 54*, 29-41.

Canavan, J. (2012). Family and family change in Ireland, *Journal of Family Issues, 33*, 10-28.

Central Statistics Office (2012). *Statistical Yearbook of Ireland, 2012*, Dublin: Stationery Office.

Central Statistics Office (2015). *Survey of Income and Living Conditions 2014*, Dublin: Stationery Office.

Children's Rights Alliance (2015). *Briefing Note on the Children and Family Relationships Bill, 2015*, Dublin: Children's Rights Alliance.

Duncan, G.J. & Brooks-Gunn, J. (eds.) (1997). *Consequences of Growing Up Poor*, New York: Russell Sage Foundation.

Fahey, T. (1998). Family policy in Ireland: A strategic overview, in Commission on the Family, *Strengthening Families for Life: Final Report of the Commission on the Family* (pp.384-403), Dublin: Stationery Office.

Fahey, T. & Field, C.A. (2008). *Families in Ireland: An Analysis of Patterns and Trends*, Dublin: Stationery Office.

Fahey, T. & Nixon, E. (2013). Family policy in Ireland, in Robila, M. (ed.), *Family Policies across the Globe* (pp.125-36), New York: Springer.

Fahey, T. & Russell, H. (2001). *Family Formation in Ireland*, Dublin: Economic and Social Research Institute.

Goodman, R. (1997). The strengths and difficulties questionnaire: A research note, *Journal of Child Psychology and Psychiatry, 38*, 581-86.

Hannan, C. & Halpin, B. (2014). The influence of family structure on child outcomes: Evidence for Ireland, *The Economic and Social Review, 45*, 1-24.

Hetherington, E.M. (1989). Coping with family transitions: Winners, losers and survivors, *Child Development, 60*, 1-14.

Kendig, S.M. & Bianchi, S.M. (2008). Single, cohabiting and married mothers' time with children, *Journal of Marriage and Family, 70*, 1228-40.

Kiernan, K. & Mensah, F. (2010). Partnership trajectories, parent and child wellbeing, in Hansen, K., Joshi, H. & Dex, S. (eds.), *Children of the 21st Century: The First Five Years* (pp.77-94), Bristol: Policy Press.

Luddy, M. (2011). Unmarried mothers in Ireland, *Women's History Review, 20*, 109-26.

Lunn, P. & Fahey, T. (2011). *Households and Family Structures in Ireland: A Detailed Statistical Analysis of Census 2006*, Dublin: Family Support Agency / Economic and Social Research Institute.

Lunn, P., Fahey, T. & Hannan, C. (2009). *Family Figures: Family Dynamics and Family Types in Ireland, 1986-2006*, Dublin: Family Support Agency / Economic and Social Research Institute.

McLanahan, S. & Sandefur, G. (1994). *Growing Up with a Single Parent: What Hurts, What Helps,* Cambridge, MA: Harvard University Press.

McLoyd, V.C. (1998). Socio-economic disadvantage and child development, *American Psychologist, 53*, 185-204.

Meadows, S.O., McLanahan, S.S. & Brooks-Gunn, J. (2008). Stability and change in family structure and mental health trajectories, *American Sociological Review, 73*, 314-34.

Nixon, E. (2012). *How Families Matter for Social and Emotional Outcomes of Nine-year-old Children*, Dublin: Department of Children and Youth Affairs.

Pianta, R.C. (1992). *Child-parent Relationship Scale*, Virginia: University of Virginia.

Piers, E.V. & Herzberg, D.S. (2002). *Piers-Harris Children's Self-Concept Scale – Second Edition Manual,* Los Angeles, CA: Western Psychological Services.

Pryor, J. & Rodgers, B. (2001). *Children in Changing Families*, Oxford: Blackwell.

Radloff, L.S. (1977). The CES-D scale: A self-report depression scale for research in the general population, *Applied Psychological Measurement, 1*, 385-401.

Raley, R.K. & Wildsmith, E. (2004). Cohabitation and children's family instability, *Journal of Marriage and the Family, 66,* 210-19.

Simons, R.L. & Associates (1996). *Understanding the Differences between Divorced and Intact Families: Stress, Interaction and Child Outcome,* Thousand Oaks, CA: Sage.

Stattin, H. & Kerr, M. (2000). Parental monitoring: A reinterpretation, *Child Development, 71,* 1072-85.

Tein, J., Sandler, I.N. & Zautra, A.J. (2000). Stressful life events, psychological distress, coping and parenting of divorced mothers: A longitudinal study, *Journal of Family Psychology, 14,* 27-41.

Yoshikawa, H., Aber, J.L. & Beardslee, W.R. (2012). The effects of poverty on the mental, emotional and behavioural health of children and youth: Implications for prevention, *American Psychologist, 67,* 272-84.

5: PARENTAL INVESTMENT & CHILD DEVELOPMENT

Jean Quigley & Elizabeth Nixon

Introduction

The family environment represents a significant site for early learning and development and family socio-economic status (SES) is an important predictor of children's cognitive, language and academic outcomes. Substantial research attests to the links between indicators of family SES, such as parents' education, occupation and income levels, and a range of child outcomes, including literacy and numeracy skills, language proficiency, IQ, and school achievement. SES-related inequalities emerge prior to the initiation of formal schooling, and extend beyond the school years. A number of pathways have been proposed to account for how family SES influences children's outcomes. The family investment perspective posits that higher income, occupational status and parental education result in families having the financial and social resources to invest in their children's education and learning. For example, families with more money can purchase goods, materials, experiences and services, which can promote children's academic competencies. Another pathway by which advantage is conferred is *via* parental expectations, aspirations and practices in which parents routinely engage. For example, providing a high-quality home literacy environment and active communication and engagement with the child promotes optimal cognitive and language outcomes.

Our goal in this chapter is to evaluate potential pathways through which family SES may influence cognitive and learning outcomes for children in Ireland. First, our analyses will examine the extent to which inequalities in family SES from the earliest period predict children's later outcomes. Second, our analyses will consider whether or how family SES is associated with the investments parents are enabled to make for their children, and how these investments relate to children's outcomes. The chapter will argue that the inequalities in children's cognitive and learning outcomes based on family SES can be partially remediated through parental provision of particular resources to support children's learning and development. In the chapter, we use data collected in the *Growing Up in Ireland* study on 11,100 9-month-old infants, followed up when they were age 3; and on 8,568 9-year-old children, followed up when they were age 13.

Family Socio-economic Status and Child Development Outcomes

Inequality is pervasive in the lives of children in Ireland today and family socio-economic status (SES) is one of the major sources of this inequality. According to the most recent data available (2013), 12 per cent of children in Ireland live in poverty, a further 18 per cent are at risk of poverty, and children are 1.4 times more likely than adults to live in consistent poverty (Department of Social Protection, 2015). SES is a multi-faceted construct, comprising both an economic position as well as a social one. SES can be broadly conceptualised as the *capital* (resources / assets / status) available to an individual. Capital incorporates financial capital (which can be denoted by income or access to material resources), human capital (non-material resources such as maternal education), and cultural capital (resources accrued through social status and connections providing access to educational and career opportunities) (Bradley & Corwyn, 2002; Guo & Harris, 2000). The measurement of SES in *Growing Up in Ireland* broadly maps onto these aspects of capital. Data were collected on *financial capital* (denoted by household income), *cultural capital* (indexed by parental occupational status), and *human capital* (measured by level of maternal education).

There is considerable international evidence that children from low SES backgrounds are at risk of poorer outcomes compared to their more advantaged peers. On average, these children tend to do less well in school and to complete fewer years in education, have lower levels of IQ, and do less well on specific indices of mathematics, reading, language and vocabulary (Bradley & Corwyn, 2002; McLoyd, 1998; Tucker-Drob, 2013; Petrill *et al.*, 2004). These discrepancies emerge early; for example, SES-related differences in children's vocabulary are already evident by age 2 (Hoff, 2003), and continue throughout childhood and adolescence. Further, disparities in cognitive, language and academic outcomes outweigh SES-related disparities in physical health, and contribute to the transmission of poverty across generations (Duncan *et al.*, 1998).

Two main pathways have been proposed by which SES might effect disparities in child development, both of which focus primarily on financial capital: the Family Stress Model (FSM) (Conger & Conger, 2002) and the Family Investment Model (FIM) (Bradley *et al.*, 2001; Yeung *et al.*, 2002). The Family Stress Model proposes that poverty or financial hardship is associated with conditions that stress parents, disrupt family and parent-child relationships, and lead to diminished quality of parenting. The Family Investment Model, on the other hand, theorises that reduced access to financial and cultural capital to 'invest' in children leads to reduced opportunity and diminished quality of the home learning environment. Several studies have found that the causal pathways proposed by the FIM primarily predict the cognitive development of young children and that the causal pathways proposed by the FSM primarily predict their social and emotional development (Conger & Conger, 2002; Yeung *et al.*, 2002). That is, family stress processes are better predictors of behavioural problems, whereas parental investments are better predictors of cognitive performance disparities. In this chapter, we focus upon the Family Investment Model and the mechanisms by which various forms of capital can be translated into advantage for the child's cognitive development.

The Family Investment Model

According to the Family Investment Model (FIM), parental investment explains the very strong association between family SES and the outcomes for the children of that family. The focus of this economically-based model is on family income but, increasingly, other forms of capital generated by familial SES are being explored in this context. Higher SES parents have greater access than lower SES parents to financial and human capital. Parents with these greater resources are likely to invest their capital in ways that facilitate their children's development, while more disadvantaged families must invest in more immediate family needs (Bradley & Corwyn, 2002; Duncan & Magnuson, 2003; Linver et al., 2002; Mayer, 1997). This investment perspective argues that the pathways through which SES and income affect children's outcomes are those associated with money and time. Higher SES, incorporating income and education, especially maternal education, means being able to buy more toys, games and especially books, to buy educational and extracurricular activities and experiences for the child, to pay for high quality childcare and later schools, to afford to live in a safe neighbourhood, and importantly having more time to spend interacting, talking and reading with their child and engaging in leisure activities. Thus, according to this model, parental investments will explain the association between SES and child development.

Obviously an economic investment model of family resources has financial resources at its core. Money is, of course, critically important for a family with children. Although the findings are complex and contingent on a number of factors, such as the age or gender of the child, there is evidence to suggest that improvements in family income may have beneficial effects for parents and children (Huston et al., 2005; Leventhal et al., 2005; Morris et al., 2005). Even a small increase in a disadvantaged family's earnings in the first two years of a child's life can lead to significant improvements in that child's adult circumstances (Noble, 2014). However, on its own, increased income is unlikely to be sufficient to counter the disadvantage associated with lower SES. Ultimately, raw income has small, if significant, effects, and income alone is unlikely to close the gap between children from low-income and higher-income families.

The translation of resources into child outcomes does not depend only on the available financial resources but also on characteristics of the household, such as parents' educational level and parenting abilities. Arguably the social and human capital in the home is as important as the financial capital. It is becoming increasingly evident that poverty exerts much of its influence through its effects on the proximal parenting process, *via* the key mechanisms associated with forms of human capital.

Human capital in the form of maternal education is the component of SES most consistently and strongly associated with children's achievement (Bornstein *et al.*, 2003). It is generally found to have a larger effect than paternal education on children's educational outcomes (Haveman & Wolfe, 1995) and has long been used as a measure of human capital in a child's home (Entwisle & Astone, 1994). Maternal education is more stable than income, which tends to fluctuate over time and is more sensitive to public policies, and is more robustly associated with parenting practices and children's outcomes than family income (Bornstein & Bradley, 2003; Ginsborg, 2006; Liberatos *et al.*, 1988). Over and above her employment status and her income, a mother's level of education is arguably the most important form of capital available in the family and can impact directly on the child under the general rubric of cognitive stimulation and *via* the provision of enriching literacy environments and experiences. Maternal education level ought to be conceptualised not simply as a proxy for family resources or socio-economic standing, but rather 'as an important determinant of the quality of the child's learning environment' (Magnuson *et al.*, 2009, p.312), with implications for children's developmental outcomes.

Family Socio-economic Status, Parental Investment and Children's Outcomes

The goal of these analyses is to investigate the key tenets of the Family Investment Model, using data from both the Infant and Child Cohorts of *Growing Up in Ireland*. Specifically three research questions were addressed:

- Does a family's financial (family income) and human capital (maternal education) matter for children's outcomes?

- Do parents from different SES households invest differently in their children?

- Do these investments make a difference to children's outcomes?

The focus of the analyses is on children's verbal and language outcomes, measured at age 3 and 13. At age 3, a naming vocabulary test (from the British Abilities Scales) was administered. In this test, the child is shown a series of pictures of objects and is asked to name them. Their test score reflects their expressive verbal ability. At age 13, the Drumcondra Reasoning Test – Verbal sub-test was administered. This test assesses the child's ability to understand, think and reason in and with words.

We chose to focus on language outcomes because family SES is an important environmental predictor of language (Küntay, 2013) and language is very vulnerable to the effects of low SES (Noble et al., 2005). Environmental influences are more influential on language in the early years and for lower SES groups than genetic factors (Tucker-Drob et al., 2011; Turkheimer et al., 2003). In addition, language skills are protective in child development (Blanden, 2006; Pianta et al., 1990), play a key role in social-emotional, behavioural and academic outcomes (Conti-Ramsden & Botting, 2004; Harrison et al., 2009), and are highly predictive of individual success, especially academic success (Snow et al., 1998).

Taking an interactionist perspective, it is important to look at the interactions between an individual's innate ability and environmental influences. Natural ability alone cannot provide infants with all they need to successfully acquire language; interactional experiences with the adults in their environment are necessary. One aspect of the experience provided to the child, the quantity and quality of their mother's child-directed speech, which varies as a function of her education level, is strongly associated with their language outcomes. SES differences have been found as early as age 9 months in children's cognitive ability (Halle et al., 2009) and in their language skills (McNally & Quigley, 2014) and this gap widens until we observe the language ability of 4-year-old children from low SES backgrounds lagging almost one full year behind their more privileged counterparts (Taylor *et al.*, 2013). Even within low-SES cohorts, clear gradients of language ability are observed in accordance with SES and any improvement in education, however small, matters (Mirowsky & Ross, 2003; Moore & Schmidt, 2004). One study, for instance, found improved outcomes for the children of mothers who had received on average just 1.34 years of schooling when compared with those whose mothers had no education at all (Andrabi *et al.*, 2011).

Language input is a particularly powerful mediator of SES effects (Thomas *et al.*, 2013) and these effects have been shown to drastically reduce when differences in parental input are controlled for with middle- and high-SES families (Hoff, 2003; Huttenlocher *et al.*, 2002; Huttenlocher *et al.*, 2010). Higher maternal education is strongly associated with the type of language input and maternal investment behaviour during the crucial early period, from birth to age 3, have been identified as most conducive to children's language development. Vocabulary growth is positively correlated with the quantity and quality of speech to which a child is exposed (Hart & Risley, 1995; Huttenlocher *et al.*, 1991). Mothers with a higher level of education talk more to their children (Hart & Risley, 1995; Hoff-Ginsberg, 1991), are more likely to read to them (Bianchi & Robinson, 1997; Hofferth, 2006; Sandberg & Hofferth, 2001; Whitehurst *et al.*, 1994) and to actively engage them in conversations that tend to be more complex and to elicit feedback (Hoff-Ginsberg, 1991; Purcell-Gates, 2000; Shonkoff & Phillips, 2000) than less educated parents. Higher-educated mothers are more likely to use questions and praise compared with lower-educated mothers who use more directives and commands (Laosa, 1980; Richman *et al.*, 1992; Tracey & Young, 2002). On average, children from low-SES families have smaller vocabularies and slower vocabulary growth than children from middle- and high-SES families (Arriaga *et al.*, 1998; Fenson *et al.*, 1994). In a study with an exclusively low-income sample, Pan *et al.* (2005) found that child vocabulary was associated with diversity of maternal linguistic input and with maternal language and literacy skills.

As language, especially vocabulary size, is one of the domains most affected by, and most sensitive to, SES effects, and as language ability is very strongly associated with later school readiness and academic success, we have chosen to focus our analysis upon language development and the mechanisms by which human and financial capital, and parental investments affects language development in different age cohorts.

Does a family's financial (family income) and human capital (maternal education) matter for children's language outcomes?

In this section we consider whether a family's financial and human capital are associated with children's language outcomes. First, we used data from the first two waves of the Infant Cohort of *Growing Up in Ireland*, collected when the children were aged 9 months and aged 3. Children's verbal abilities at age 3 were measured using the naming vocabulary test of the British Abilities Scale. The findings show a clear gradient among children's verbal abilities at age 3, according to maternal education and income level of families (both measured when the infants were aged 9 months). For example, as illustrated in **Figure 5.1**, there was already a 15-point difference in the average verbal ability score of 3-year-old children whose mothers had no secondary level education, in comparison with children whose mothers had a postgraduate education.

Figure 5.1: Average Total Scores on Naming Vocabulary Test at Age 3, According to Mothers' Highest Level of Education

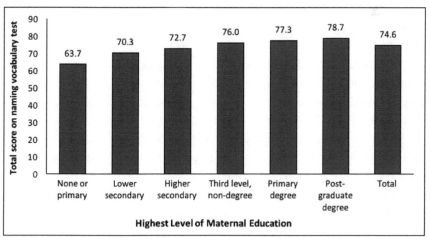

Similarly, children from the families in the first income quintile (the one-fifth of families who had the lowest income) displayed significantly lower verbal scores at age 3 (average score 68.4) than children in the middle (third) quintile group (average score 74.8), who in turn also had lower scores than those in the highest (fifth) income quintile group, whose average score was 78.7. Thus these findings suggest that, even by the time children are age 3, the human and financial capital available within their household is reliably associated with language outcomes.

Figure 5.2: Average Percentage of Correct Responses on the DVRT at Age 13, According to Mothers' Highest Level of Education

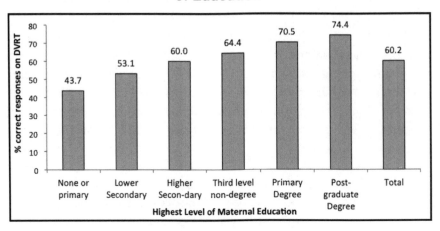

Next, we examined data from the first two waves of the Child Cohort of *Growing Up in Ireland,* collected when the children were aged 9 and 13. Here, children's outcomes were tested using the Verbal sub-test of the Drumcondra Reasoning Test (hereafter referred to as the DVRT). The findings from this analysis also highlight that children's verbal reasoning at age 13 was clearly patterned according to the income level of the household and the highest level of maternal education when the children were age 9. For example, the percentage of correct responses on the DVRT ranged from 51 per cent for those in the lowest income quintile to 60 per cent for those in the middle (third) income group to 68 per cent for those in the highest income quintile group. Similarly, comparing groups according to mothers' highest level of education, the percentage of correct responses increased in line with mothers' highest level of education. As illustrated in **Figure 5.2**, children whose mothers had a postgraduate degree achieved a mean of 74 per cent correct responses in comparison to a mean of 44 per cent correct responses where mothers had no secondary level education.

Together these findings concur with those that have emerged from the *Growing Up in Ireland* Infant Cohort data, and also suggest that children from families with higher levels of income and maternal education exhibit a clear advantage in terms of their verbal abilities at age 13.

Do parents from different SES households invest differently in their children?

Our main interest is in understanding *how* the human capital generated in higher SES contexts, predominantly *via* the pathway of higher levels of maternal education, is leveraged to bestow educational and academic advantage on the children in these families, who are then better placed to make use of the educational system. This happens not just as children progress through the school system but has already begun to play out before children even start school and has ensured their school readiness (Reardon, 2013). Higher levels of maternal education have consistently been associated with a body of skills, knowledge, and resources that the mother can bestow on the child, even independently of her income or employment status / potential. Maternal education captures a range of factors linked to social class position and beliefs regarding early development and schooling (Fuller *et al.*, 1996) and the social network and infrastructure they can create for their children. Augustine *et al.* (2009) propose three mechanisms according to which maternal educational attainment works to influence their child's development:

- Through type, quality and quantity of childcare arrangements
- Through participation in school activities, cultivation of maternal standards and values around attainment and indirectly engendering aspirations in the children
- Directly, under the general rubric of cognitive stimulation, through the more complex language environment, the increased learning

opportunities and intellectual activities mothers with more
education are more likely to provide.

Both interpersonal and material investments will lead to more positive
developmental outcomes.

Different SES groups engage in different investment behaviours. For
example, time spent with children engaged in developmentally-
appropriate input (directly interacting with, engaged in shared activities,
reading to, talking to) is an investment behaviour that can promote
children's future human capital (Guryan *et al.*, 2008). Mothers with
higher levels of education spend more time directly interacting with
their children, even though they may spend more time working outside
the home, and, further, they spend that time together differently. Higher
SES mothers tend to adjust their activities with their child to be more
developmentally-appropriate more effectively than lower-SES mothers
(Kalil *et al.*, 2012). With young infants and toddlers, Kalil *et al.* found
that middle-class mothers focussed largely on reading and problem-
solving, learning activities that promote school readiness and prepare a
child for an academic environment. In middle childhood, more time and
money is spent resourcing and managing the child's life and
extracurricular activities outside the home.

With respect to *Growing Up in Ireland* data, mothers reported on
the extent to which they talked to their babies (at age 9 months), while
they were engaged in other activities. Overall the proportion of mothers
who reported talking to their baby 'often' or 'always' was high and
there was little difference across groups of mothers, based on their
highest level of education. For example, 88 per cent of mothers who
had not completed secondary education reported talking to their babies
'often' or 'always'; the corresponding percentages for mothers with a
primary degree and a postgraduate degree were 91 per cent and 89 per
cent respectively. Thus, parental investment in terms of talking to their
infants did not differ according to maternal education at age 9 months.

Information about the child's access to books in the home was also
recorded at age 3. Overall, 29 per cent of children whose mother had
no secondary level education had access to just 10 or fewer books in the
home. This figure decreased to 11 per cent in households where
mothers had completed secondary school and to 3 per cent where
mothers had a postgraduate degree. In contrast, 72 per cent of children

in households where mother had a postgraduate degree had access to 30 or more books in the home. This decreased to 45 per cent in households where mothers had completed secondary school and to 23 per cent in households where mothers had no secondary level education. These reflect stark differences in the availability of reading materials across households, based on mothers' level of education.

At age 3, parents were asked to report upon the extent to which they engaged in a range of activities with their children, including reading to them, saying the alphabet and numbers, singing songs / nursery rhymes, playing board / card games, doing art work, and playing active games. Mothers reported how many times a week they did each of these activities, and responses were added to yield a total score. A maximum score of 42 could be achieved, if mothers completed all of the activities every day of the week. The data revealed that mothers from the highest education group engaged in an average of 35 activities per week, while mothers from the lowest education group engaged in an average of 33 activities per week. Small, though statistically significant, differences in the number of activities engaged in per week emerged but only between mothers with the highest levels of education (degree and postgraduate degree) and mothers who had not completed secondary school. In looking specifically at the frequency with which mothers engaged in book-reading with their 3-year-old children, **Figure 5.3** illustrates the number of days per week mothers read to their children, according to their education level.

A clear pattern is evident – a substantially higher proportion of children whose mothers had a primary or a postgraduate degree were read to every day than children whose mothers had a lower educational attainment. The frequency with which children were read to every day increased according to mother's education level. Thus, the evidence suggests that mothers' education level is associated with their investment in promoting their pre-school-aged children's developing literacy skills.

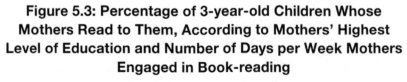

Figure 5.3: Percentage of 3-year-old Children Whose Mothers Read to Them, According to Mothers' Highest Level of Education and Number of Days per Week Mothers Engaged in Book-reading

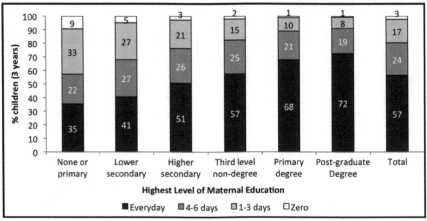

In terms of the provision of cognitive stimulation or an environment that promotes verbal skills among older children, information was collected from the *Growing Up in Ireland* Child Cohort at age 9 on children's access to a computer at home, the use of the public library, and the number of children's books to which the child has access. Here a consistent pattern emerged: children from households with a higher level of maternal education were more likely to have access to a computer, a greater number of books in the home, and were more likely to use the public library (**Figure 5.4**). For example, 59 per cent of children whose mother had no secondary level education had access to a computer at home, in comparison with over 90 per cent of children whose mothers had any form of third-level education. Approximately 57 per cent of children whose mothers did not complete their Leaving Certificate used the public library with their child, in comparison with 71 per cent of mothers who had at least a primary degree. Over one-third of children whose mothers had not entered secondary school had access to fewer than 10 books at home; the comparable figure for children whose mothers had a postgraduate degree was less than 2 per cent.

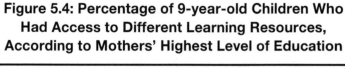

**Figure 5.4: Percentage of 9-year-old Children Who
Had Access to Different Learning Resources,
According to Mothers' Highest Level of Education**

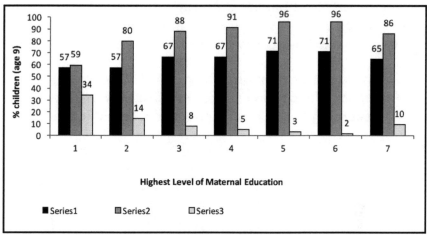

Expectations for children's education were also patterned according to maternal education. Mothers were asked to indicate how far they expected their children to go in education – the majority of mothers who themselves had completed third-level expected their children to do the same, whereas mothers who had left school early or who did not have third-level education were less likely to expect their children to do so. For example, 43 per cent of mothers who had not gone to secondary school expected their children to progress to either the Junior Certificate, the Leaving Certificate or to complete an apprenticeship. In contrast, 5 per cent of mothers with a degree and 2 per cent of mothers with a postgraduate degree expressed these educational expectations for their children. Only 11 per cent of mothers who had not progressed beyond primary school expected their children to attain a postgraduate degree, while 52 per cent of mothers with postgraduate qualifications expected their children to achieve the same.

Having 9-year-old children involved in extracurricular activities and sharing activities with children also differed by maternal levels of education. Children reported on whether or not they had engaged in any of a series of activities with their parents in the past week. Activities were categorised as either indoor activities (reading together at home or playing games at home) or outdoor activities (going swimming, playing games outside or going to the park). **Figure 5.5** illustrates the patterns of indoor and outdoor shared activities (based on children's reports), according to maternal education. As maternal education increased, the proportion of children who engaged in both indoor and outdoor activities with their parents also increased.

Figure 5.5: Percentage of 9-year-old Children Who Engaged in Indoor and Outdoor Activities with Parents, According to Mothers' Highest Level of Education

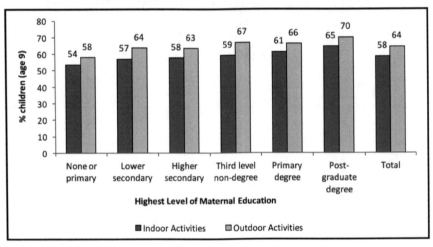

In terms of the children's engagement in extracurricular activities, the patterns were similar – children whose mothers had higher levels of education were substantially more likely to be enrolled in an arts activity (such as dance, art, drama or music classes), and to be in a sports club (such as Gaelic or soccer). Just over one-third of children (34 per cent) whose mothers had not attended secondary school were enrolled in an activity such as dance or music classes. This compares with almost 50 per cent of children whose parents had completed second-level education, and 70 per cent of children whose parents had a postgraduate degree. Participation in extracurricular sports activities also varied considerably by maternal education: here, 56 per cent of children whose mothers had the lowest level of education participated, in comparison with 78 per cent of children whose parents had completed second-level education and 87 per cent of parents with a postgraduate degree. One potential barrier to having a child enrolled in extracurricular activities is the lack of financial resources to pay for these activities. For example, the majority of parents whose children attended arts-related activities were required to pay for these activities (94 per cent). Of the children whose parents did not have to pay for the activity (6 per cent of the total), 41 per cent came from households where mothers had not completed secondary school. This compares with just 12 per cent of households where mothers had at least a primary degree. Similarly, 83 per cent of parents paid for their children to participate in a sports club, and of those who did not pay, 33 per cent came from households where mothers had not completed secondary school, in comparison with 14 per cent of families where mothers had at least a primary degree. These findings suggest that, where activities are available that do not require payment, children from households with lower levels of income or where mothers have lower levels of education will take up these activities.

Taken together, the findings presented on both the Infant Cohort and the Child Cohort provide compelling evidence that parents, and especially mothers, invest differentially in experiences and resources for their children, depending upon their own level of education. It is not the case that mothers who have lower levels of education never read or play with their children, or that their children do not participate in extracurricular activities, and have no access to resources such as books and computers in their home. However, the findings do point to a lower likelihood of them having such resources and experiences in comparison with children whose mothers have higher levels of education. The Family Investment Model suggests that it is through parental investments such as those reported on above that human capital is passed from parent to child. Thus, the question as to whether these parental investments translate into improved child outcomes is a crucial one to consider.

Do parental investments make a difference to children's outcomes?

The extent to which parental investment matters for children's outcomes was tested using analysis whereby indicators of investment were modelled onto children's verbal ability scores, while also controlling for indicators of household financial and human capital.

The first analysis, focusing upon the Infant Cohort, considered the association between 'investment behaviours' on the part of parents, such as how often mothers reported talking to their baby while doing other things (at 9 months), and how often they read and did other activities with their toddler (at age 3), and children's verbal ability scores at age 3. In the first step of the model, these parenting behaviours, along with access to books at home, were considered alone (without controlling for maternal education and household income level). Together, these predictors explained 9 per cent of the variance in children's verbal ability scores. Three-year-olds whose mothers reported talking more frequently to them at age 9 months, reading to them more frequently at age 3, and who had access to a greater number of books at home had higher scores. In addition, the more often parents reported engaging in certain activities per day with their child, the higher the child's scores. In the final step of the model illustrated in **Table 5.1**, maternal education, income and the child's communication score at age 9 months were included, and these explained an additional 2 per cent of the variance in children's verbal ability scores, yielding a total of 11 per cent variance explained. With the inclusion of these variables, the frequency with which mothers spoke to their babies at age 9 months became insignificant, although access to books in the home, number of days a week that parents read to their child, and the total number of activities parents engaged in with their child at age 3 remained significant predictors of children's verbal ability scores.

Next, we considered how parental investments and financial and human capital in a household at age 9 were associated with children's verbal reasoning ability, measured by the DVRT at age 13. The first set of variables entered into the model were having access to a computer at home, using the public library, and the number of books to which the child has access at home. Together these three variables explained 8 per cent of variance in children's outcomes, and all were significant predictors of the child's score.

Table 5.1: Model of Children's Verbal Ability at Age 3

Predictor Variables	Standardised Coefficient	Significance level
Frequency of talking to baby while doing other things (age 9 months) [Ref. 'Always talk to baby']		
Never talk	-.019	NS
Rarely talk	-.012	NS
Sometimes talk	-.023	*
Often talk	-.012	NS
Access to books (age 3 years) Ref. access to more than 30 books]		
No books	-.065	***
Less than 10 books	-.143	***
10-20 books	-.116	***
21-30 books	-.039	***
Total number and frequency of activities engaged in with child (age 3 years)	.028	*
Number of days a week parents read to their child (age 3 years)	.106	***
Income Quintile [Ref. Highest (5th) income quintile]		
Lowest (1st)	-.092	***
Second	-.063	***
Middle (3rd)	-.030	*
Fourth	.026	*
Highest Level of Maternal Education [Ref. postgraduate degree]		
None or Primary	-.050	***
Lower Secondary	-.040	**
Higher Secondary	-.042	**
Third Level Non-Degree	-.023	NS
Primary Degree	-.014	NS
Total Communication Score at 9 months	.111	***

*** p < 0.001; ** p< 0.01; * p < 0.05; NS – non-significant.

Table 5.2: Model of Children's Verbal Reasoning at Age 13

Predictor Variable (All at age 9)	Standardised Coefficient	Significance level
Access to a Computer at Home	.015	NS
Access to Books [Ref. Access to more than 30 books]		
No books	-.019	*
Less than 10 books	-.042	***
10 to 20 books	-.048	***
21 to 30 books	-.045	***
Use of Public Library	.008	NS
Indoor activities with parents (reading, board games)	-.010	NS
Outdoor activities with parents (going to park, games)	-.041	***
Arts-based extracurricular activities	-.036	***
Sport-based extracurricular activities	.012	NS
Educational expectations [Ref. postgraduate degree]		
Junior Cert only	-.022	*
Leaving Certificate	-.067	***
Apprenticeship	-.035	**
Diploma / Certificate	-.070	***
Primary Degree	.004	NS
Income Quintile [Ref. Highest (5th) income quintile]		
Lowest (1st)	-.047	***
Second	-.028	*
Middle (3rd)	-.012	NS
Fourth	-.010	NS
Highest level of maternal education [Ref. postgraduate degree]		
None or Primary	-.082	***
Lower Secondary	-.114	***
Higher Secondary	-.103	***
Third Level Non-Degree	-.056	***
Primary Degree	-.021	NS
Reading test score	.574	***

*** $p < 0.001$; ** $p < 0.01$; * $p < 0.05$; NS – non-significant.

However, in the final model, presented in **Table 5.2**, controlling for the other variables, only the number of books to which the child had access remained significant, with higher scores being associated with having more books available. The second set of variables entered into the model included shared activities with parents and attendance at sports and arts-based extracurricular activities. The inclusion of these variables explained an additional 2 per cent of variance in children's outcomes. Interestingly, participating in shared activities with parents was associated with lower DVRT scores, but being enrolled in arts-based or sports-based activities was associated with higher scores, perhaps reflecting more developmentally-beneficial activities and experiences for this age group. A US-based study found that the amount of time college-educated parents are spending with their children is increasing faster than for less-educated parents (Duncan & Murnane, 2011), but also that they spend more time and money facilitating the child's socialisation and extracurricular activities.

In the third step of the model, a variable on mothers' expectations for how far their child would progress within the educational system was included, and explained an additional 7 per cent of variance in DVRT scores; children's scores were lower when mothers had lower expectations of their child's educational progression. It is important to note, in the context of the interactional model being proposed here, a child's future academic attainment is also likely to reflect, at least in part, the child's own academic ability, where the parents of a child who is not performing very well academically will likely adjust expectations accordingly. It would be interesting to have data on earlier parental expectations, before the confound of knowing the child's actual ability in middle childhood begins to take effect.

In the fourth step of the model, highest maternal education level and household income were included and an additional 4 per cent of variance in DVRT scores was explained. Generally, higher income levels and higher levels of maternal education were associated with higher scores. However, DVRT scores did not differ between children from the fourth and fifth (highest) income quintile groups or for children of mothers who had either a primary or a postgraduate degree. Thus, there is no evidence in this data of a widening achievement gap according to income, for the top income groups, with an achievement gap evident just for the lower and higher earning groups. However, it is possible that we may see a trend emerging in the future, similar to the one that has been documented in the United States (Reardon, 2013), where the achievement gap has widened between middle-income and high-income groups, possibly related to growing income inequality.

The final model, presented in **Table 5.2**, controlled for the child's verbal score at age 9 and a total of 46 per cent of variance in children's outcomes was explained. The weighty contribution of the child's earlier language ability underscores how early language ability and learning drive later language and academic success. Among the other most significant predictors of the child's DVRT scores at age 13 were:

- Having access to a greater number of books in the home
- Engaging in outdoor activities with parents
- Being enrolled in arts-based extracurricular activities
- Mothers having expectations that their child will receive either a primary or a postgraduate degree
- Coming from the third, fourth or highest income quintile families
- Having a mother with at least a primary or postgraduate degree.

Conclusion

In this chapter, we have identified several important sources of resilience and protective factors pertaining to maternal pathways of influence on children's cognitive and language development. Environment matters for language development for all children and is especially protective for children typically at greater risk of poorer cognitive outcomes. The key message arising from these findings is that literacy in the home, engaged parenting, reading and speaking to the child, and having high expectations for the child are important protective factors for language development, in particular where well-known risk factors are present (low levels of maternal education and low levels of family income). It is important to note that the investments we have discussed are not necessarily universal and may vary by ethnicity and by parental beliefs around the importance of certain types of activities (Iruka *et al.*, 2014). It is also important to investigate the relationship between family SES and child outcomes in the context of

Ireland and its particular set of 'unobservable characteristics' – for example, policy practices and public opinion. For example, research has shown that the relationship between spending on education and intergenerational social mobility varies between countries, both in the size and strength of the association (for example, Bradbury *et al.*, 2012; Burton *et al.*, 2012), and Ireland has one of the lowest rates of intergenerational social mobility in the OECD and one of the lowest rates of spending on education (OECD, 2010a; 2010b).

Large cohort studies like *Growing Up in Ireland* have the potential to explore the child and environmental characteristics that influence development of language and the point at which they impact. If the ultimate goal is to provide information to support parents and to provide earlier intervention and prevention, the message that arises here is that what you do as a parent is more important than who you are and what you have, and that effective parenting support can ameliorate some of the negative impacts of intergenerational poverty. By understanding these factors, interventions may be targeted at critical junctures throughout childhood. This work can identify parental and familial factors and practices impacting on parenting capacity and family functioning and can provide solid evidence to assist with policy and practice.

While some of the known risk factors associated with poorer child outcomes are not amenable to intervention (in the case of language development, for instance, infant's gender, mother's age, infant temperament), many can be targeted on foot of evidence-based data and are highly susceptible to interventions (for example, reading to the child). Environmental influences have been shown to be more influential on language in the early years and for lower SES groups than genetic factors. Thus, intergenerational transmission of disadvantage can be addressed in part by publicising the message that parents have a very important role to play in their child's lives, beyond that of provision of material resources.

References

Andrabi, T., Das, J. & Khwaja, A.I. (2011). What did you do all day?' Maternal education and child outcomes, *The Journal of Human Resources, 47*, 873-912.

Arriaga, R.J., Fenson, L., Cronan, T. & Pethick, S.J. (1998). Scores on the MacArthur Communicative Development: Inventory of children from low- and middle-income families, *Applied Psycholinguistics, 19*, 209-23.

Augustine, J.M., Cavanagh, S.E. & Crosnoe, R. (2009). Maternal education, early childcare and the reproduction of advantage, *Social Forces, 88*, 1-29.

Bianchi, S.M. & Robinson, J.P. (1997). 'What did you do today?' Children's use of time, family composition, and the acquisition of social capital, *Journal of Marriage and the Family, 59*, 332-44.

Blanden, J. (2006). *Bucking the Trend – What Enables Those Who Are Disadvantaged in Childhood to Succeed Later in Life?*, London: Department for Work and Pensions.

Bornstein, M.H. & Bradley, R.H. (eds.) (2003). *Socio-economic Status, Parenting, and Child Development*, Mahwah, NJ: Erlbaum.

Bornstein, M.H., Hahn, C.S., Suwalsky, J. & Haynes, O.M. (2003). Socio-economic status, parenting, and child development: The Hollingshead Four-Factor Index of Social Status and The Socio-economic Index of Occupations, in Bornstein, M.H. & Bradley, R.H. (eds.), *Socio-economic Status, Parenting, and Child Development* (pp.29-82), Mahwah, NJ: Erlbaum.

Bradbury, B., Corak, M., Waldfogel, J. & Washbrook, E. (2012). Inequality in early childhood outcomes, in Ermisch, J., Jantti, M. & Smeeding, T. (eds.), *From Parents to Children: The Intergenerational Transmission of Advantage* (pp.87-119), New York: Russell Sage Foundation.

Bradley, R.H. & Corwyn, R.F. (2002). Socio-economic status and child development, *Annual Review of Psychology, 53*, 371-99.

Bradley, R.H., Corwyn, R.F., McAdoo, H.P. & Garcia Coll, C. (2001). The home environments of children in the United States Part I: Variations by age, ethnicity, and poverty status, *Child Development, 72*, 1844-67.

Burton, P., Phipps, S. & Zhang, L. (2012). From parent to child: Emerging inequality in outcomes for children in Canada and the US, *Child Indicators Research, 6*, 1-38.

Conger, R.D. & Conger, K.J. (2002). Resilience in Midwestern families: Selected findings from the first decade of a prospective, longitudinal study, *Journal of Marriage and Family, 64*, 361-73.

Conti-Ramsden, G. & Botting, N. (2004). Social difficulties and victimisation in children with SLI at 11 years of age, *Journal of Speech, Language and Hearing Research, 47*, 145-61.

Department of Social Protection (2015). *Social Inclusion Monitor 2013*, Dublin: Stationery Office.

Duncan, G.J. & Magnuson, K. (2003). Off with Hollingshead: Socio-economic resources, parenting and child development, in Bornstein, M.H. & Bradley, R.H. (eds.), *Socio-economic Status, Parenting, and Child Development* (pp.83-106), Mahwah, NJ: Erlbaum.

Duncan, G.J. & Murnane, R.J. (2011). The American dream: Then and now, in Duncan, G.J. & Murnane, R.J. (eds.), *Whither Opportunity? Rising Inequality, Schools and Children's Life Chances* (pp.3-23), New York, NY: Russell Sage Foundation / Spencer Foundation.

Duncan, G.J., Brooks-Gunn, J., Yeung, J. & Smith, J. (1998). How much does childhood poverty affect the life chances of children?, *American Sociological Review, 63*, 406-23.

Entwisle, D.R. & Astone, N.M. (1994). Some practical guidelines for measuring youth's race / ethnicity and socio-economic status, *Child Development, 65*, 1521-40.

Fenson, L., Dale, P., Reznick, J., Bates, E., Thal, D. & Pethick, J. (1994). Variability in early communication development, *Monographs of the Society for Research in Child Development, 59*(5), Ann Arbor, MI: Society for Research in Child Development.

Fuller, B., Holloway, S. & Liang, X. (1996). Family selection of childcare centers: The influence of household support, ethnicity, and parental practices, *Child Development, 67*, 3320-37.

Ginsborg, J. (2006). The effects of socio-economic status on children's language acquisition and use, in Clegg, J. & Ginsborg, J. (eds.), *Language and Social Disadvantage: Theory into Practice* (pp.9-27), London: Wiley.

Guo, G. & Harris, K.M. (2000). The mechanisms mediating the effects of poverty on children's intellectual development, *Demography, 37*, 431-47.

Guryan, J., Hurst, E. & Kearney, M. (2008). Parental education and parental time with children, *Journal of Economic Perspectives, 22*, 23-46.

Halle, T., Forry, N., Hair, E., Perper, K., Wandner, L., Wessel, J. & Vick, J. (2009). *Disparities in early learning and development: Lessons from the early childhood longitudinal study – Birth Cohort (ECLS)*, Washington, DC: Child Trends.

Harrison, L.J., McLeod, S., Berthelsen, D. & Walker, S. (2009). Literacy, numeracy, and learning in school-aged children identified as having speech and language impairment in early childhood, *International Journal of Speech-Language Pathology, 11*, 392-403.

Hart, B. & Risley, T. (1995). *Meaningful Differences in the Everyday Experience of Young American Children*, Baltimore, MD: Paul H. Brookes.

Haveman, R. & Wolfe, B. (1995). The determinants of children's attainments: A review of methods and findings, *Journal of Economic Literature, 33*, 1829-78.

Hoff-Ginsberg, E. (1991). Mother-child conversation in different social classes and communicative settings, *Child Development, 62*, 782-96.

Hoff, E. (2003). The specificity of environmental influence: Socio-economic status affects early vocabulary development *via* maternal speech, *Child Development, 74*, 1368-78.

Hofferth, S.L. (2006). Residential father family type and child wellbeing: Investment *versus* selection, *Demography, 43*, 53-77.

Huston, A.C., Duncan, G.J., McLoyd, V.C., Crosby, D.A., Ripke, M.N., Weisner, T.S. & Eldred, C.A. (2005). Impacts on children of a policy to promote employment and reduce poverty for low-income parents: New Hope after 5 years, *Developmental Psychology, 41*, 902-18.

Huttenlocher, J., Haight, W., Bryk, A., Seltzer, M. & Lyons, T. (1991). Vocabulary growth: Relation to language input and gender, *Developmental Psychology, 27*, 236-48.

Huttenlocher, J., Vasilyeva, M., Cymerman, E. & Levine, S.C. (2002). Language input at home and at school: Relation to syntax, *Cognitive Psychology, 45*(3), 337-74.

Huttenlocher, J., Waterfall, H., Vasilyeva, M., Vevea, J. & Hedges, L. (2010). Sources of variability in children's language growth, *Cognitive Psychology, 61*, 343-65.

Iruka, I., Dotterer, A.M., & Pungello, E. (2014). Ethnic variations of pathways linking socio-economic status, parenting, and pre-academic skills in a national representative sample, *Early Education and Development, 25*, 973-94.

Kalil, A., Ryan, R. & Corey, M. (2012). Diverging destinies: Maternal education and the developmental gradient in time with children, *Demography, 49*, 1361-83.

Küntay, A. (2013). Learning to Talk about Chairs (and Other Things: Emergence and Development of Language-and-Communication in Children), Inaugural address 22 May, University of Utrecht.

Laosa, L.H. (1980). Parent education, cultural pluralism, and public policy: The uncertain connections, *Research Report Series, 1*, 1-22.

Leventhal, T., Fauth, R.C. & Brooks-Gunn, J. (2005). Neighborhood poverty and public policy: A 5-year follow-up of children's educational outcomes in the New York City Moving to Opportunity Demonstration, *Developmental Psychology, 41*, 933-52.

Liberatos, P., Link, B.G. & Kelsey, J.L. (1988). The measurement of social class in epidemiology, *Epidemiological Review, 10*, 87-121.

Linver, M.R., Brooks-Gunn, J. & Kohen, D.E. (2002). Family processes as pathways from income to young children's development, *Developmental Psychology, 38*, 719-34.

Magnuson, K.A., Sexton, H.R., Davis-Kean, P.E. & Huston, A.C. (2009). Increases in maternal education and young children's language skills, *Merrill-Palmer Quarterly, 55*, 319-50.

Mayer, S. (1997). *What Money Can't Buy: Family Income and Children's Life Chances*, Cambridge, MA: Harvard University Press.

McLoyd, V.C. (1998). Socio-economic disadvantage and child development, *American Psychologist, 53*, 185-204.

McNally, S. & Quigley, J. (2014). An Irish cohort study of risk and protective factors for infant language development at 9 months, *Infant and Child Development, 23*, 634-49.

Mirowsky, J. & Ross, C.E. (2003). *Education, Social Status and Health*, NJ: Aldine Transaction.

Moore, Q. & Schmidt, L. (2004). *Do Maternal Investments in Human Capital Affect Children's' Academic Achievement?*, Department of Economics Working Papers 13, Williamstown, MA: Department of Economics, Williams College.

Morris, P., Duncan, G. & Clark-Kauffman, E. (2005). Child wellbeing in an era of welfare reform: The sensitivity of transitions in development to policy change, *Developmental Psychology, 41*, 919-32.

Noble, K.G. (2014). Rich man, poor man: Socio-economic adversity and brain development, *Cerebrum*, May, retrieved from http://www.dana.org/Cerebrum/ 2014/Rich_Man,_Poor_Man__ Socioeconomic_Adversity_and_Brain_Development/.

Noble, K.G., Norman, M.F. & Farah, M.J. (2005). The neurocognitive correlates of socio-economic status in kindergarten children, *Developmental Science, 8*, 74-87.

OECD (2010a). *Doing Better for Children*, Paris: Organization for Economic Cooperation and Development.

OECD (2010b). *A Family Affair: Intergenerational Social Mobility across OECD Countries*, Paris: Organization for Economic Cooperation and Development.

Pan, B.A., Rowe, M.L., Singer, J.D. & Snow, C.E. (2005). Maternal correlates of growth in toddler vocabulary production in low-income families, *Child Development, 76*, 763-82.

Petrill, S.A., Pike, A., Price, T. & Plomin, R. (2004). Chaos in the home and socio-economic status are associated with cognitive development in early childhood: Environmental mediators identified in a genetic design, *Intelligence, 32*, 445-60.

Pianta, R., Egeland, B. & Sroufe, L.A. (1990). Maternal stress and children's development: Prediction of school outcomes and identification of protective factors, in Rolf, J.E., Masten, A., Cicchetti, D., Nuechterlein, K. & Weintraub, S. (eds.), *Risk and Protective Factors in the Development of Psychopathology* (pp.215-35), Cambridge, MA: Cambridge University Press.

Purcell-Gates, V. (2000). *Now We Read, Now We Speak*, Hillsdale, NJ: Erlbaum.

Reardon, S.F. (2013). The widening income achievement gap, *Educational Leadership, 70*, 10-16.

Richman, A.L., Miller, P.M. & LeVine, R.A. (1992). Cultural and educational variations in maternal responsiveness, *Developmental Psychology, 28*, 614-21.

Sandberg, J.F., & Hofferth, S.L. (2001). Changes in children's time with parents, U.S. 1981-1997, *Demography, 38*, 423-36.

Shonkoff, J.P. & Phillips, D.A. (2000) (eds.). *From Neurons to Neighbourhoods: The Science of Early Childhood Development*, National Academy Press: Washington, DC.

Snow, C., Burns, S. & Griffin, P. (eds.). (1998). *Preventing Reading Difficulties in Young Children,* Washington, DC: National Academy Press.

Taylor, C.L., Christensen, D., Lawrence, D., Mitrou, F. & Zubrick, S.R. (2013). Risk factors for children's receptive vocabulary development from four to eight years in the Longitudinal Study of Australian Children, *PLoS ONE* 8(9): e73046.

Thomas, M.S., Forrester, N.A. & Ronald, A. (2013). Modeling socio-economic status effects on language development, *Developmental Psychology, 49,* 2325-43.

Tracey, D.H. & Young, J.W. (2002). Mothers' helping behaviours during children's at-home oral-reading practice: Effects of children's reading ability, children's gender, and mothers' educational level, *Journal of Educational Psychology, 94,* 729-37.

Tucker-Drob, E.M, Rhemtulla, M., Harden, K.P, Turkheimer, E. & Fask, D. (2011). Emergence of a gene X socio-economic status interaction on infant mental ability between 10 months and 2 years, *Psychological Science, 22,* 125-33.

Tucker-Drob, E.M. (2013). How many pathways underlie socio-economic differences in the development of cognition and achievement?, *Learning and Individual Differences, 25,* 12-20.

Turkheimer, E., Haley, A., Waldron, M., D'Onofrio, B. & Gottesman, I.I. (2003). Socio-economic status modifies heritability of IQ in young children, *Psychological Science, 14,* 623-28.

Whitehurst, G.J., Arnold, D.S., Epstein, J.N., Angell, A.L., Smith, M. & Fischel, J.E. (1994). A picture book reading intervention in day-care and home for children from low-income families, *Developmental Psychology, 30,* 679-89.

Yeung, W.J., Linver, M.R. & Brooks-Gunn, J. (2002). How money matters for young children's development: Parental investment and family processes, *Child Development, 73,* 1861-79.

6: INEQUALITIES IN ACCESS TO EARLY CARE & EDUCATION IN IRELAND

Aisling Murray, Frances McGinnity & Helen Russell

Introduction

Infants and pre-school children require constant supervision and hence the question as to who looks after a young child when the parents are temporarily unavailable is one that has been faced by families for generations. As more parents, particularly mothers, seek to combine parenting duties with paid work outside the home, the issue of childcare becomes even more key to everyday family life. Many parents, however, also hope that the hours their young children spend in someone else's care will go beyond meeting their basic needs and provide some positive input to their development. In addition, as the young child starts to walk, talk and explore the physical and social environment, parents may seek out some form of early childhood education specifically in order to promote the child's development.

So the question of equality of access to quality early care and education is pertinent to at least two areas of debate. First, non-parental care facilitates parental work outside the home and, from the child's perspective, increases the family income and its ability to afford a range of goods and services that ultimately benefit the child. Second, young children would be expected – particularly from age 3 to 5 – to benefit from a learning environment that fosters early educational development. Parents are therefore likely to consider the benefits of different types of care settings for their children's development when making decisions about care arrangements. Other considerations are also relevant for parents – in Ireland cost, in particular, is a major issue – but there is also a question of availability of alternatives (for example, not everyone has a granny to call on or a suitable childcare centre in the local area) and childcare arrangements for other children in the family.

In this chapter, we review the historical background to the current childcare situation in Ireland since 1916 – this being particularly tied in with the nature of women's work outside the home. Then we draw on the *Growing Up in Ireland* survey to look at the childcare experiences of children at age 9 months, and especially at age 3, before finishing with a short review of the same children at age 5 and their use of a new universal pre-school scheme and the start of formal schooling.

A Historical Perspective on Childcare in the 20th Century

The history of childcare in the early to mid-20th century and the early years of the Republic are very much entwined with the nature of work, particularly women's work, the structure of families in Ireland and the nature of primary school provision. The 1937 *Constitution* firmly put woman's place in the home. Article 41.2 states:

> ... *in particular, the State recognises that by her life within the home, woman gives to the State a support without which the common good cannot be achieved. The State shall, therefore, endeavour to ensure that mothers shall not be obliged by economic necessity to engage in labour to the neglect of their duties in the home.* (Government of Ireland, 1937)

In the 1930s a marriage bar came into force, whereby most women in public sector jobs, and many in the private sector (including in banks), were forced to resign when they got married. The number of mothers recorded in paid employment for the first half of the century was low and therefore the 'necessity' for non-parental childcare was relatively low. Census estimates from 1926 through to 1971 suggest that around

5 per cent to 6 per cent of all married women were gainfully employed, rising to 7 per cent in the 1971 *Census* (Fahey, 1990). However, as Fahey (1990) cogently argues, this is likely to have been an underestimate, particularly for married women, given women's involvement in farm labour and part-time work in industry. Yet the nature of subsistence farm work, where many mothers were present in the home even if working, combined with more multigenerational living arrangements and the presence of other adults in the household (Geraghty *et al.*, 2015), meant that demand for non-familial childcare was low. In addition, the Irish fertility pattern of low marriage rates and high fertility within marriage until the 1960s (Coleman, 1992), resulting in very large families (Hannan, 2015), meant that at least some children could be looked after by older siblings, if not by grandparents or other relatives. An additional contributing factor to the lack of, and perhaps low demand for, formal non-familial childcare arrangements was the early age at which children could start school. In 1916, children could enrol in the infant classes of national schools from age 3 (O'Connor, 2010). The *Annual Statistical Report* for 1926 (Department of Education, 1928) shows that there were 171,431 children enrolled in infant classes within the national school system on 30 June that year, which when compared to the number of children recorded in the 1926 *Census* suggests that most children aged 3 to 5 were at school. The age of national school enrolment increased to age 4 in 1934.

In the early part of the 20th century then, we can assume that the vast majority of children were looked after by their parents and most non-parental childcare and education in the early years was provided by co-resident family members, occasionally in-home family employees or – in terms of education – infant classes at national (primary) school. Two categories of in-home employee that are either unheard of now, or have substantially evolved, were the 'governess' and 'nursery maid'. A search of the 'occupation' field in the 1911 *Census* returns 1,437 governesses (down from 2,053 in the 1901 *Census*) and 306 individuals with occupations such as 'nursery maid', 'children's maid', 'children's nurse', and 'nursemaid'; presumably these were employed by upper and middle class families. Apart from these more specialised occupations, live-in servants generally were more common in this period than today: a search of the 1911 *Census* shows that there were over 160,000 individuals living in households (all households, not just those with children) where their relationship to the head of household was listed as 'servant', with around 58 per cent of these being women or girls. Crèches were unusual, although not unheard of, with at least two in Dublin city: Rathmines and Meath Street – the latter building still hosting a crèche and kindergarten today. There appears to be little documented evidence of the type of arrangement now usually termed 'childminder', although it would seem likely that more casual arrangements between friends and neighbours existed.

An important development in the 1960s was the setting up of the first early childhood intervention for children in a disadvantaged area of Dublin. Earlier in the decade the Commission of Inquiry on Mental Handicap, cited by Kelleghan (1977), had recommended the setting up of pre-schools to counter the dearth of learning opportunities for children growing up in areas with concentrations of low income families. The Rutland Street Project in 1969, set up in a deprived area of Dublin city, comprised a pre-school centre staffed with teachers, social workers and a nurse (Kelleghan, 1977), and was followed by a new junior school two years later. According to Fallon (n.d.), this initiative was the only State pre-school intervention programme until the Early Start pre-school initiative in a limited number of disadvantaged schools in the 1990s.

By the early 1970s female labour market participation had begun to rise, partly related to decreasing family size, increasing educational attainment of girls and young women, changes in legislation, such as the lifting of the marriage bar in the 1970s and changes in the nature of labour demand, such as the growth in clerical and service sector jobs (Fahey *et al.*, 2000). By 1983, total female labour market participation was estimated to be around 40 per cent, with married women's participation around 27 per cent (Fahey *et al.*, 2000). By the early 1980s the rise in the need for non-parental childcare had become of sufficient concern to merit the establishment of a 'working party on childcare facilities for working parents' and its subsequent report in 1983. This report commissioned a survey of mothers (employed and not-employed), which found very low usage of centre-based care among employed mothers with pre-school children (less than 5 per cent) but quite high rates of home-based, non-relative care – as well as high rates of relative care (Working Party on Child Care Facilities for Working Parents, 1983). This 1983 survey also recorded some interesting socio-economic (SES) trends, similar to more recent findings from the *Growing Up in Ireland* survey, where children in higher SES groups were the most likely to experience care by non-relatives, and low SES families the least likely. The latter part of the mid-century period also saw the establishment of a number of representative, voluntary and professional bodies related to childcare, indicative of the increasing frequency of non-parental care on a regular and more formalised basis – for example, The Irish Preschool Play Association was founded in 1969, St. Nicholas Montessori Teachers' Association in 1975, Comhchoiste Réamhscolaíochta (for Irish-language playgroups and pre-schools) in 1978, Childminding Ireland in 1983 and the National Children's Nurseries Association in 1988.

By the 1990s, the pace quickened in relation to the regulation of, and demand for, the provision of childcare, against a backdrop of a remarkable growth in female employment during the recent economic boom in Ireland (McGinnity *et al.*, 2013). In the 1980s female labour market participation was rising, but still low by European standards (Fahey *et al.*, 2000). Women's participation in Ireland rose from 42 per cent in 1990 to 63 per cent in 2007, when it converged with the EU average (Russell *et al.*, 2009). The participation of mothers of young children (under age 5) rose from 54 per cent in 1998 to a peak of 60 per cent in 2007 (Russell *et al.*, 2009), which was significant but less than for mothers of older children (aged 5 to 15) that had risen from 52 per cent to 65 per cent in the same time period. A census of childcare services in 1999-2000 (that mainly comprised centres and excluded childminders) reported that playgroups / pre-schools were the most common sessional (part-time) service (53.8 per cent) and crèches / day-care services were the most frequent full-day service (36.8 per cent) (Area Development Management, 2002). As a percentage of all children nationally, the report estimated that 4.8 per cent of infants aged under 1 attended (centre-based) childcare facilities, rising to 12.8 per cent of 1-year-olds to 3-year-olds and peaking at 23.6 per cent of children aged 3 to 6.

A broader range of childcare arrangements was covered by an ESRI survey in 1997 (Williams & Collins, 1998). The survey sampled over 1,000 households with a child under age 12 as a supplement to the EU

Consumer Survey. The study found that between 9.00am and 1.00pm three-quarters of infants (aged 1 and under) were cared for in their own home by a parent or another relative. Of the remaining quarter, a childminder's home was the most frequent location (12 per cent); only 3 per cent were in a childcare centre and the remainder were in another type of home care. However, toddlers (aged 2 to 3) were much more likely to be in a crèche – at least in the morning (20 per cent) – and somewhat less likely to be cared for in their own home by a parent or other relative (64 per cent). Usage of centre-based care increased again for children aged 4 (26 per cent) but perhaps of even greater interest was the finding that nearly 50 per cent of this group were in (primary) school, and only 18 per cent were at home. Later in this chapter we examine the trend for school starting age in 2012-2013 using the *Growing Up in Ireland* survey.

Provision of Early Childhood Care and Education in Ireland

The national policy context – how childcare is funded and organised – determines the cost and availability of early childhood care and education to parents (Smeeding, 2013). This may have a profound effect on childcare arrangements for children from different backgrounds (Gambaro *et al.*, 2014). Fahey & Russell (2006) argue that government support for childcare in Ireland had been guided by a number of competing objectives – supporting child development, female employment (and gender equality), social inclusion, and support for high birth rates. Significantly, the government tried to steer a course that was neutral between providing support for care in the home (by parents) and care outside the home. Raising child benefit was a key element of the 'childcare strategy': child benefit in Ireland increased threefold between 1999 and 2003 (Wolfe *et al.*, 2013).

The very end of the 20th century saw the publication of the *National Childcare Strategy* (Department of Health and Children, 2000) and the setting up of a national coordinating committee to implement it. This was followed by the allocation of significant State funds to develop the childcare sector and the setting up of County Childcare Committees (Hayes & Bradley, 2006). Yet another important element of policy was that, in Ireland, when the demand for childcare rose during the boom, much financial support was indirectly provided in the form of capital grants to encourage private and community sector provision, in contrast to other Northern European countries and continental Europe where there was more emphasis on State provision of services (Fahey & Russell, 2006). There was a very significant expansion of childcare places between 2000 and 2010 (McGinnity *et al.*, 2015). Provision of maternity (and parental) leave is also an important element of policy in relation to the care of very young children. All female employees who become pregnant while in employment in Ireland are entitled to take maternity leave after the birth of their child, and all but a few receive payment during this period. The duration of paid maternity leave in Ireland is currently 26 weeks, and unpaid leave 16 weeks (see McGinnity *et al.*, 2015 for more details). Unpaid parental leave for mothers and fathers was introduced in Ireland in 1998. From September 2016, fathers will be entitled to two weeks paid paternity leave on the birth of a child.

Regarding non-parental childcare of children aged 3 and under, the private sector dominates provision, with low State intervention and very low government investment. An influential report by UNICEF rated 25 affluent countries on 10 benchmarks relating to the provision of early childhood education and care (ECCE) (Adamson, 2008). Ireland came in joint last, achieving only one benchmark. There has been progress on some of these policy indicators since this report (see McGinnity *et al.*, 2015), but State financial support for and investment in non-parental childcare in Ireland is still very low in a comparative context. Public investment in Ireland's pre-school services amounts to less than 0.2 per cent GDP (Start Strong, 2014a).[1] The average investment in OECD countries has recently increased to 0.8 per cent GDP (OECD, 2016). Childcare is expensive: OECD estimates of childcare costs to parents in Ireland are among the highest in Europe (McGinnity *et al.*, 2015). For most parents there is no financial support for childcare: an important exception is for disadvantaged children in community crèches.

---

[1]   OECD (2016). The published OECD figure for Ireland (0.5%) includes the infant classes of primary schools (nearly 0.4% GDP). Excluding this, pre-school spending in Ireland is 0.16% GDP.

These community crèches are, in fact, an important exception to private provision of childcare in Ireland. Significant government funding of community crèches was initially provided in the form of staffing grants provided under the Equal Opportunities Childcare programme 2000-2006 in 1990, which replaced earlier *ad hoc* sources of funding though these often did not suffice, so staff from community employment schemes were used (Wolfe *et al.*, 2013). In 2008 the funding scheme for delivering community childcare was changed, with funding of community childcare schemes now being linked to social welfare receipt by the parents. Community sector services currently make up around 25 per cent of centre-based services and typically serve disadvantaged communities (Pobal, 2015). The Community Childcare Subvention (CCS) scheme subsidises approximately 25,000 places in participating community-based providers, out of an estimated 130,000 children attending centre-based care (including the Free Pre-school Year, see below) (Pobal, 2015) – and a total cohort of approximately 356,000 children aged 0 to 4. The maximum subsidy is €95 per week, significantly lower than the costs of delivery. One problem with this scheme is that in some areas there are no community providers and therefore no access to this support for disadvantaged children (Start Strong, 2014b). Another smaller scheme, the Childcare Education and Training Support (CETS) programme, offers some financial support for childcare to facilitate parents' participation in education or training schemes.

The introduction of the Free Pre-school Year in January 2010, which is available in the academic year preceding school entry, represents the main policy initiative in the area in recent years. It replaced a universal cash supplement (Early Childcare Supplement) with an early care and education service for all children, albeit for a limited number of hours. When introduced, the scheme was open to children aged between 3 years 2 months and 4 years 7 months, and estimates since then put take-up in the region of 94 to 95 per cent of eligible children (McGinnity *et al.*, 2015; Oireachtas Library & Research Service, 2012).

The compulsory school starting age is 6 in Ireland, which was initially introduced in 1892 (O'Connor, 2010). In 1985, the Minister for Education announced that children could not enter the year known as 'First Class' (which is typically preceded by two years of Infant Classes) *until* they were age 6 – but affirmed that enrolment to Infant

Classes was possible from age 4. In practice, although Irish children do not have to start school until age 6, around 40 per cent of 4-year-olds and nearly all 5-year-olds attend State-funded primary schools (Department of Education and Science, 2004) and are taught by teachers with graduate-level qualifications. The early age of school start in Ireland is unusual in comparative perspective, and some commentators have categorised Irish provision of early care and education as a 'mixed' system: in many other European countries children do not start school until age 6 or 7, and under 6s are in pre-school settings (Kaga *et al.*, 2010).

Childcare in Ireland at Age 9 months in 2008-2009

In this section we draw on the *Growing Up in Ireland* study to examine trends in non-parental childcare for infants in the first year of life, a time when children are completely dependent on adult care. The first interview with the *Growing Up in Ireland* Infant Cohort took place when the study child was 9 months old in 2008-2009, around the time that the combination of statutory paid and unpaid maternity leave available for working mothers comes to an end. At that stage, 39 per cent of the infants were reported to be in some form of regular non-parental childcare (of any duration). Whether the infant was experiencing non-parental care was heavily influenced by the employment status of the mother, which in itself showed marked socio-economic trends: McGinnity *et al.* (2013) found that highly-educated mothers, and those with a resident partner, were more likely to return to work at the end of statutory maternity leave. Lone mothers were both more likely to be among the group of 'early returners', at one end of the spectrum, and among those who were not in employment when the child was age 9 months old at the other end. In addition to maternal employment status, other significant determinants of childcare use in infancy were income (greater income, more likely) and family size (more children, less likely). The most frequent reason given for returning to work by 9 months was financial, suggesting that at this early age the use of non-parental childcare was seen as a necessity rather than a more pro-active choice (although not all infants in regular childcare had mothers in employment).

Figure 6.1: Main Type of Regular Non-parental Childcare in the *Growing Up in Ireland* Infant Cohort at Age 9 months

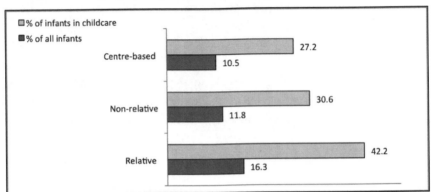

*Source: **Growing Up in Ireland** Infant Cohort at 9 months, 2008-2009, adapted from McGinnity et al. (2013), weighted.*

Figure 6.1 (adapted from McGinnity *et al.*, 2013) shows that care by a relative was the most common form of non-parental childcare for children at age 9 months: 42.2 per cent of children in childcare, which equates to just over 16 per cent of all infants. The majority of relatives looking after infants were grandparents. The next most common type of care was provided by non-relatives (11.8 per cent of all infants) – the majority of whom were childminders – followed by centres such as crèches (10.5 per cent).

Further analysis by McGinnity *et al.* (2013) suggested that socio-economic advantage, measured by income and education, was associated not just with patterns in overall use of non-parental care but also type of care. Care by non-relatives, which was almost always paid for, was more common for infants from socio-economically advantaged backgrounds. In contrast, care by relatives dominated in families with lower income and education. In general, centre-based care was associated with socio-economic advantage although this trend was not as linear as for non-relative care – possibly due to the availability of places in community crèches in some disadvantaged areas.

Childcare at Age 3 in 2010-2011

Childcare arrangements by social class and parental employment

At age 3 in 2010-2011, half of all children in *Growing Up in Ireland* were in some form of regular non-parental childcare for at least 8 hours per week. Over half of these (27 per cent of the total) were in centre-based care, with the remainder split evenly between relative and non-relative care (**Table 6.1**). There were clear gradients in terms of social class (LHS of **Table 6.1**) with the most advantaged 'professional / managerial' groups more likely to use non-parental childcare overall (63 per cent) and having the highest percentage of centre-based care. The other social class groups made less use of non-parental care but where it was used, centre-based care was the most frequent of the three options (relative, non-relative or centre).

An even greater contrast is observed in relation to the employment status of the mother (right area of **Table 6.1**): where she was in regular employment, three-quarters of 3-year-olds had non-parental care. About one-third were in centre-based care, and one-fifth each in relative and non-relative care. Conversely, the majority of children with mothers on home duties had no regular non-parental childcare. However, interestingly, when they did, it was nearly always centre-based. In keeping with findings from other Irish surveys in previous decades (Fine-Davis, 1983; Williams & Collins, 1998), this pattern is suggestive of a more active choice for care related to early education around age 3 that is not entirely driven by a necessity for 'supervision' of the child in the parent's absence. Even within the *Growing Up in Ireland* Infant Cohort, it can be seen that, in contrast to Wave 1 when the children were only age 9 months (see previous section), use of centre-based care has risen from 11 per cent to 27 per cent by age 3. Additionally, we shall see (in a later section) that there was near-universal take-up of the Free Pre-school Year scheme when the children were aged around 4.

Table 6.1: Main Childcare Arrangements at Age 3, by Social Class and Mother's Employment

	Household Social Class[a]				Mother		
	Professional / Managerial	Non-manual	Skilled Manual Semi- / Unskilled	Never worked / unclassified	Employed	Not employed	Total
Parental care	37%	45%	72%	70%	26%	77%	50%
A relative in your home or their home	12%	18%	8%	4%	20%	2%	11%
A non-relative in your home or their home	17%	11%	5%	1%	21%	1%	12%
Centre-based caregiver	34%	26%	16%	24%	33%	19%	27%
N	4,621	1,844	2,738	582	4,424	5,357	9,781

a: Social class is measured principally in terms of occupation. In **Growing Up in Ireland**, the social class of both resident parents (where relevant) was recorded and the higher of the two was selected as the 'household social class'.

Modelling childcare use at age 3

Table 6.2 presents results of a series of statistical models of how non-parental childcare at age 3 is associated with social class, parental employment, other characteristics and income. The purpose of the statistical model is to disentangle the different influences on use of non-parental childcare. For instance, we saw that social class is associated with parental employment and that both are associated with use of childcare. The statistical model allows us to ask whether there are any additional differences in the use of non-parental childcare by social class, apart from those linked to parental employment. An odds ratio of more than 1 implies that a child with these characteristics is more likely to be in non-parental childcare.

Table 6.2: Models for Any Regular Non-parental Care at Age 3

		Model 1		Model 2		Model 3	
		OR		OR		OR	
Social Class (Ref. Managerial / Technical)	Professional	1.33	↑	1.63	↑	1.37	↑
	Non-manual	.77	↓	.74	↓	n.s.	
	Skilled	.23	↓	.49	↓	.69	↓
	Semi/unskilled	.25	↓	.48	↓	.67	↓
	Never worked	.29	↓	.74	↓	n.s.	
	Class missing	.24	↓	.65	↓	n.s.	
PCG employment (Ref. No hours / not employed)	Hrs 15 or less			2.91	↑	2.79	↑
	Hrs 16-29			7.31	↑	6.50	↑
	Hrs 30-39			10.38	↑	8.13	↑
	Hrs 40 plus			12.24	↑	9.16	↑
Child chronic condition (Ref. No condition)	Activities not hampered			1.34	↑	1.38	↑
	Activities hampered			1.24	↑	1.26	↑
PCG ethnicity (Ref. Irish)	Non-Irish			.64	↓	.73	↓
Number of siblings (Ref. None)	One sibling			.71	↓	.73	↓
	Two siblings			.47	↓	.53	↓
	Three siblings (or more)			.44	↓	.52	↓
Couple (Ref. One-parent family)	Resident partner			.55	↓	.46	↓
Income (Ref. Highest income quintile)	Lowest					.25	↓
	Second					.27	↓
	Third					.33	↓
	Fourth					.55	↓
	Income missing					.43	↓
	Constant	1.66		1.04		2.63	

Source: **Growing Up in Ireland** Infant Cohort at age 3, own calculations.

Models unweighted. OR=Odds Ratio. Arrows indicate whether a particular group were more or less likely to use childcare at 3 years compared to the reference group. n.s. = not statistically significant at p<.01.

Turning first to the social class pattern, in Model 1, we can see that families with higher social class are more likely to use regular non-parental childcare: the odds were 1.3 times higher for 'Professionals' than those in the 'Managerial / Technical' reference group but all the other social class groups were less likely to use childcare when the child was aged 3 (their odds ratios are less than 1, see **Table 6.2**).

The second model controls for a selection of other parental and family level variables linked to social class and the requirement for childcare. Not surprisingly, chief among these is the employment status of the mother. From **Table 6.2**, it is clear that where the mother works outside the home, even part-time, there is a sharp increase in the use of regular non-parental childcare – and furthermore that this increases with the number of hours worked. The odds ratio for use of non-parental childcare where the mother works 40 hours or more per week relative to no hours is just over 12, whereas the odds ratio compared to working for 15 hours per week or less is a more modest 2.9.

This model (2) also shows that the use of non-parental childcare is more likely where the child has a chronic health problem or disability, where the parents are Irish nationals, and where the child has no, or fewer, brothers or sisters. A three-year-old in a two-parent household was also less likely to experience non-parental care (OR = 0.55). Of particular note is the fact that differences in social class remain significant (with the exception of the 'never worked' group), even with the control for the mother's employment status.

The final model on non-parental care adds what is, given costs in the Irish context, a potentially major determinant of childcare use – income. As expected, families in the highest income group were more likely to use non-parental childcare for their 3-year-old; with the odds ratio for the lowest income quintile only 0.25 that of the highest (see **Table 6.2**). This relationship between income and childcare use is significant even when social class and mother's employment are taken into account, as they are in Model 3. The inclusion of income into the model impacts on the relationship between childcare use and social class, in particular the difference between the 'Non-manual' and 'Managerial / Technical' reference is reduced to almost zero (OR =.97). These findings are consistent with those of Byrne & O'Toole (2015) on non-parental childcare at age 3.

Overall, then, we can say that 3-year-olds are more likely to experience non-parental care on a regular basis when they come from two-parent families of higher social class and income; where the mother is in full-time employment and Irish; and the child has few or no siblings but does have a health condition (even if not hampered in their daily activities by it). This last observation on the effect of a health condition is intriguing and counter-intuitive to an extent, as one might have expected the healthiest children to be the most likely to get non-parental childcare. One possibility is that parents are more likely to become aware of a condition with less obvious symptoms because of feedback received from a childcare worker; alternatively it may be that children with some health conditions need a level of care that requires extra assistance either informally or from specialised carers.

Choosing centre-based over other care type

Given that maternal employment is such a strong driver of childcare usage, the following model on the choice between home-based and centre-based care focuses on mothers who are employed and who use any non-parental care (with a control for number of hours worked). Earlier studies on a smaller scale (for example, Williams & Collins, 1998; Fine-Davis, 1983) suggested that there may be an increase in preference for centre-based care when a child gets to age 2 to 3 compared to an infant. Centre-based care is also of particular interest as it has been the main focus of policy development for pre-school age children (age 3 to 5). The model presented in **Table 6.3** examines whether social class, and other factors, is associated with a change in the likelihood of a 3-year-old being in regular centre-based care. We look at the influence of household, family and child characteristics as above, but also include region (rural / urban) and presence of a resident grandparent. In addition, hours of employment is now considered as a continuous variable.

Table 6.3: Use of Centre-based Care at Age 3 for Employed Mothers Only

		Model 1 OR		Model 2 OR	
Social Class (Ref. Managerial / Technical)	Professional	1.46	↑	1.37	↑
	Non-manual	.78	↓	n.s.	
	Skilled	.60	↓	.65	↓
	Semi/unskilled	.66	↓	.72	↓
Child has health condition (Ref. None)	Not hampered	1.36	↑	1.35	↑
	Hampered	n.s.		n.s.	
PCG ethnicity (Ref. Irish)	Non-Irish	1.66	↑	1.72	↑
Number of siblings (Ref. None)	One sibling	.87	↓	n.s.	
	Two siblings	.65	↓	.67	↓
	Three siblings (or more)	.47	↓	.50	↓
Couple (Ref. One-parent family)	Resident partner	n.s.		n.s.	
Resident grandparent (Ref. None)	Resident grandparent	.75	↓	.75	↓
Region (Ref. Urban)	Rural area	.47	↓	.49	↓
Hours of PCG employment	Hours	.99	↓	.99	↓
Income (Ref: Highest income quintile)	Lowest			n.s.	
	Second			.74	↓
	Third			.70	↓
	Fourth			.72	↓
	Income missing			n.s.	
	Constant	1.77		2.26	
N=4,065	Pseudo R	.09		.10	

*Source: **Growing Up in Ireland** Infant Cohort at age 3, own calculations.*

PCG = Primary caregiver, most of whom were mothers. Excludes mothers who are not employed and excludes mothers in employment but not using any non-parental care. Models unweighted. OR=Odds Ratio. Arrows indicate whether a particular group were more or less likely to use centre-based childcare at age 3 compared to the reference group. n.s. = not statistically significant at p<.01.

Model 1 includes all of these factors except income. The results show that, as with overall use of non-parental childcare, higher social class groups were more likely to use centre-based care. Likewise, an increasing number of siblings reduced the likelihood of centre-based care (although the effect of just one sibling was only marginally significant). The child having a health condition tended to be associated with higher odds of using centre-based care, but this only applies to children with less severe conditions that do not influence the child's daily activities. However, for some factors, the influence on centre-based care differed from more general use: non-Irish working mothers were more likely to use centre-based care (OR = 1.66) and the presence of a resident partner had no effect among working mothers. Longer working hours were associated with a reduced likelihood of centre-based care. Among the new variables, children in rural areas were much less likely to be in a centre (OR = 0.47), as were those who lived with a grandparent, although the effect for the latter was considerably weaker (closer to 1 or 'no difference'; OR = 0.75).

The addition of income in Model 2 has an interesting effect. Although the general trend remains for higher income to be associated with a greater chance of using centre-based care, in this instance those in the highest income group do not differ significantly from those in the lowest (OR = 0.81, p = .216). This is most likely due to the availability of free or heavily-subsidised places to families in disadvantaged areas *via* a limited number of State schemes – with the effect that the middle income groups are actually the lowest users of centre-based care. We note that there is potentially a greater selection effect for mothers in the lowest income households, whereby employment for this group is more conditional on the availability of subsidised childcare.

In this second model, there is also evidence that income accounts for part of the class difference in use of centre-based care: the reference 'Managerial / Technical' group is no longer significantly different (at the 5 per cent level) from the 'Non-manual' and 'Semi- / Unskilled' groups. Most of the other trends remain relatively unchanged, apart from a further attenuation of the effect of a single sibling.

Children at Age 5 in 2012-2013 – Free Pre-school Year Experience and School Start

Use of the Free Pre-school Year scheme

The children in the *Growing Up in Ireland* Infant Cohort were among the first to have the option of availing of a new universal scheme giving free access to an academic year in an approved centre. **Figure 6.2** shows that there was very high uptake of the free pre-school year (95.6 per cent) across all social class groups but it was highest among the most advantaged groups: 98 per cent among 'Professionals' and just 85 per cent for the 'Never worked' group. **Figure 6.2** also illustrates the extent to which the free pre-school year 'makes up' for the reduced access to centre-based care (with, presumably, a greater focus on education) seen among the low-middle social class groups at age 3. For example, only 14 per cent of children from 'Skilled manual' backgrounds were in a centre as their main care type at age 3 but over 94 per cent attended the Free Pre-school Year (FPSY). Furthermore, most families in the higher socio-economic groups would have sent the study child to a pre-school even if the FPSY scheme had not been in place (89 per cent of 'Professional' families) but this percentage declined as socio-economic disadvantage increased. This means that, in the case of 5-year-olds whose families were in the 'Non-manual' social class group for example, it is estimated that an extra 22 per cent of these children attended pre-school because of the scheme (96 per cent who did attend less 74 per cent who would have gone anyway).

Parents who did not avail of the scheme were asked why this was the case. There was diversity in the reasons given, with the most common (about one-third of non-attendees) being that the child was already settled into another childcare or pre-school arrangement that was not part of the FPSY scheme or that was funded under another scheme (for example, Early Start); 18 per cent did not avail of the scheme because their child had special needs; about 12 per cent reported that the hours did not suit or no places were available locally; and still others chose not to avail of the scheme for a variety of personal reasons (for example, child did not settle, preferred not to send) (McGinnity *et al.*, 2015).

Figure 6.2: Social Class Differences in Enrolment in Free Pre-school Year (FPSY) at Age 5, Percentage Who Would Have Attended a Pre-school even in the Absence of the FPSY Scheme and Use of Centre-based Care at Age 3

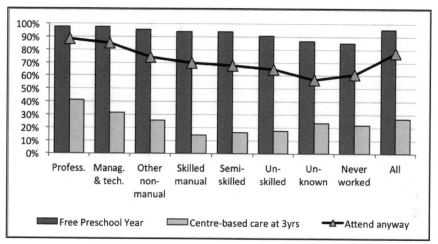

*Source: **Growing Up in Ireland** Infant Cohort at age 5, own calculations, weighted.*

Figures for care at age 3 are confined to those who were re-interviewed at age 5.

School start

The other major player in early childhood care and education is the national (primary) school system. In an age of increasing need for childcare, the question inevitably arises as to whether parents might wish to start their children at school earlier than they otherwise would because of childcare difficulties. As was discussed in **Section 1**, Irish children have traditionally had an early start to formal schooling with an age of enrolment as young as age 2 in the 19th century but currently between age 4 to 6. There has been a more recent move towards starting children at age 5 rather than age 4, presumably in the belief that a later start is better for the child although possibly also related to an increase in pre-school participation. According to official statistics[2] 48 per cent of children in Junior Infants were aged 4 or under for the

---

[2]   *Annual Reports* available online from the Department of Education and Skills (http://www.education.ie/en/Publications/Statistics/Statistical-Reports/).

1995-1996 school year but by the 2013-2014 academic year this percentage had decreased to 36 per cent. In 2009, before the introduction of the Free Pre-school Year Scheme, 41.2 per cent of enrolled children were aged 4 and under.

Table 6.4: Percentage of Children Starting School in September 2012, by Family Income Quintile and Month of Birth

Month of birth	Dec-07	Jan-08	Feb-08	Mar-08	Apr-08	May-08	Jun-08
Approx. Age of child in Sept 2012	4y 9m	4y 8m	4y 7m	4y 6m	4y 5m	4y 4m	4y 3m
Started School Sept 2012	98%	93%	91%	80%	70%	47%	34%
Family Income	Percentage of children who had started school						
Quintile One (Low)	98%	95%	94%	77%	76%	62%	52%
Quintile Two	99%	93%	92%	84%	76%	49%	37%
Quintile Three	99%	88%	94%	83%	69%	44%	29%
Quintile Four	99%	95%	93%	76%	61%	45%	32%
Quintile Five (High)	97%	97%	86%	84%	64%	38%	23%

*Source: **Growing Up in Ireland** Infant Cohort at age 5, Key Findings, No.1 (2013).*

Analysis of the *Growing Up in Ireland* Infant Cohort at age 5 reveals interesting interactions between income and child age in relation to timing of school-start. Fieldwork at age 5 took place in late spring / early summer of 2013 and 72 per cent of the cohort had already started school (nearly all the previous September). **Table 6.4** shows how many children in each birth month commenced school in September 2012 according to their family's income bracket. From the first column it is apparent that nearly all children born in December 2007, and who would have been aged 4 years, 9 months by 1 September 2012 started school at that time regardless of family income. For the next few months, there is a gentle decrease in the overall number of children starting school but the trends are broadly similar across all income groups. Clear differences emerge, however, for the youngest children – those born in June 2008, who would have been aged only 4 years and a few months in September 2012: at this point fewer than a quarter of children in the highest income bracket started school that year in contrast to about half of the youngest children from the lowest income families. In other words, there is evidence of an earlier school-start among children from lower socio-economic backgrounds.

Conclusion

This chapter examined social class differences in early care and education at age 9 months, age 3 and age 5, using evidence from the *Growing Up in Ireland* Infant Cohort. The data were presented after a brief consideration of how care and education has developed for children over the past century. Evidence is limited, but it does suggest that rates of non-parental care for infants were very low until recent decades, though participation in infant classes in schools was high. The past 25 years has seen substantial growth in early care and education for children aged 3 and under as mothers' employment increased rapidly during the recent economic boom in Ireland.

State investment in early care and education for children aged 3 and under in Ireland is, and has been, very low by international standards; the private sector dominates provision and costs to most parents are very expensive. There are some subsidised places in centre-based care for disadvantaged children, but not all disadvantaged children can avail of them. The recent introduction of the Free Pre-school Year, a universal scheme, is an important exception to this lack of investment and uptake has been very high.

Drawing on earlier work (McGinnity *et al.*, 2013) the chapter showed how for 9-month-old infants, relative care, typically by grandparents, is the most common form of non-parental childcare. This is followed by care by childminders and nannies, with centre-based care being the least common of these three types. Socio-economic advantage, measured by income and education, was associated not just with higher overall use of non-parental care, but also with type of care. Care by non-relatives, which was almost always paid for, was more common for infants from socio-economically advantaged backgrounds. In contrast, relative care dominated in families with lower income and education. In general, centre-based care was associated with socio-economic advantage although this trend was not as clear as for non-relative care, which we suggest is due to the availability of places in community crèches in some disadvantaged areas.

At age 3, children from managerial and professional backgrounds were more likely to experience non-parental care on a regular basis than children from other class backgrounds. The models showed that mothers' employment is important in understanding class differences in care, as is family income: class differences are smaller when we account for these. Regarding care type, centre-based care is more common at age 3 than it was at age 9 months. Similar factors are associated with centre-based care for those whose mothers are employed, with income contributing to class differences in care type, though the role of subsidised centre-based care for disadvantaged children is also evident.

The *Growing Up in Ireland* data shows that the Free Pre-school Year, while for a limited number of hours per week, made a very big difference to the proportion of children attending centre-based care settings. Participation in the Free Pre-school Year was high among all social groups, though slightly higher among advantaged groups. School start by age of interview at age 5, by contrast, was highest among disadvantaged class groups. While almost all *Growing Up in Ireland* children aged 4 years and 9 months in September 2012 had started school by the interview at age 5, children who had only turned age 4 the previous June were much more likely to start that September if they were from lower income groups; while younger children with parents in higher income brackets tended to have school-start postponed until the following September.

Class differences in access to care and education are marked in the early years in Ireland, partly linked to the relatively high cost of childcare for parents. The general pattern of disadvantaged children being more likely to be in the sole care of their mother than children from professional and managerial backgrounds, although tempered slightly by the provision of centre-based care for disadvantaged children in community crèches, still remains. The class differences in participation in the Free Pre-school Year are much smaller and overall participation in this scheme is very high. In terms of entry into school, the pattern of class participation in early care and education is reversed, with disadvantaged children more likely to be at school at age 5 than the children of higher social class backgrounds, though factors contributing to this require further investigation. And, of course, in keeping with the lively policy and academic debates on the consequences of non-parental care for children's development and wellbeing, further research would be required to explore the implications of these care patterns for social inequality, a task that the *Growing Up in Ireland* data are excellently suited to. In the meantime, initial indications that show a certain levelling of access to pre-school care and education within regulated centres as a result of the Free Pre-school Year are to be welcomed.

References

Adamson, P. (2008). *The Childcare Transition: A League Table of Early Childhood Education and Care in Economically Advanced Countries*, Report Card 8, Florence: UNICEF Innocenti Research Centre.

Area Development Management. (2002). *National Childcare Census Report: Baseline Data 1999-2000*, Dublin: Area Development Management / Department of Justice, Equality and Law Reform.

Byrne, D. & O'Toole, C. (2015). *The influence of childcare arrangements on child wellbeing from infancy to middle childhood. A report for TUSLA*, Maynooth: Maynooth University.

Coleman, D.A. (1992). The demographic transition in Ireland in international context, *Proceedings of the British Academy*, 79, 53-77.

Department of Education (1928). *Report of the Department of Education for the School Years 1925-26-27 and the Financial and Administrative Year 1926-27*, Dublin: Stationery Office, available at http://www.education.ie/en/Publications/Statistics/stats_statistical_report_1926_1927.pdf.

Department of Education and Science (2004). *A Brief Description of the Irish Education System*. Dublin: Communications Unit, Department of Education and Science, available https://www.education.ie/en/Publications/Education-Reports/A-Brief-Description-of-the-Irish-Education-System.pdf.

Department of Health and Children, National Children's Office (2000). *Our Children, Their Lives: National Children's Strategy*, Dublin: Stationery Office.

Department of Industry and Commerce, Statistics Branch (1926). *Census of Population*, Dublin: Stationery Office.

Fahey, T. (1990). Measuring the female labour supply: Conceptual and procedural problems in Irish official statistics, *The Economic and Social Review*, 21, 163-91.

Fahey, T. & Russell, H. (2006). Childcare, in Morgenroth, E. & Fitzgerald, J. (eds.), *Ex-ante Evaluation of the Investment Priorities for the National*

Development Plan 2007-2013 (pp.290-303), Dublin: Economic and Social Research Institute.

Fahey, T., Russell, H. & Smyth, E. (2000). Gender equality, fertility decline and labour market patterns among women in Ireland, in Nolan, B., O'Connell, J. & Whelan, C.T. (eds.), *Bust to Boom? The Irish Experience of Growth and Inequality* (pp.244-67), Dublin: Institute of Public Administration.

Fallon, J. (ed.) (n.d.). *Early Childhood in Ireland: Evidence and Perspectives,* Dublin: Centre for Early Childhood Development and Education, retrieved from http://siolta.ie/media/pdfs/03_early_childhood_in_ireland.pdf.

Fine-Davis, M. (1983). Annex 1: Complete Report of Nationwide Survey of Mothers' Attitudes toward Child Care and Employment, in Working Party on Childcare Facilities for Working Parents (1983), *Report to the Minister for Labour*, Dublin: Stationery Office.

Gambaro, L., Stewart, K. & Waldfogel, J. (eds.) (2014). *An Equal Start? Providing Quality Early Education and Care for Disadvantaged Children,* Bristol: Policy Press.

Geraghty, R., Gray, J. & Ralph, D. (2015). 'One of the best members of the family': Continuity and change in young children's relationships with their grandparents, in Connelly, L. (ed.), *The Irish Family*, Oxford: Routledge.

Government of Ireland (1937/2012). *Bunreacht na hÉireann (Irish Constitution),* Dublin: Stationery Office.

Growing Up in Ireland Study Team (2013). Transition to school among five-year-olds, *Key Finding No. 1, Infant Cohort at Five Years,* Dublin: Economic and Social Research Institute / Department of Children and Youth Affairs.

Hannan, C. (2015). Marriage, fertility and social class in 20th-century Ireland, in Connelly, L. (ed.), *The Irish Family* (pp.39-53), Oxford: Routledge.

Hayes, N. & Bradley, S. (2006). A decade of reflection: Early childhood care and education in Ireland 1996-2006, *Proceedings of Centre for Social and Educational Research Early Childhood Care and Education Seminar Series, Dublin,* November, retrieved from http://arrow.dit.ie/csercon/1/.

Kaga, Y., Bennett, J. & Moss, P. (2010). *Caring and Learning Together: A Cross-national Study on the Integration of Early Childhood Care and Education within Education*, Paris: UNESCO.

Kelleghan, T. (1977). *The Evaluation of an Intervention Programme for Disadvantaged Children*, Windsor: NFER Publishing Co.

McGinnity, F., Murray, A. & McNally, S. (2013). *Mothers' Return to Work and Childcare Choices for Infants in Ireland,* Dublin: Department of Children and Youth Affairs.

McGinnity, F., Murray, A. & Russell H. (2015). *Non-parental Childcare and Child Cognitive Outcomes at Age 5: Results from the Growing Up in Ireland Infant Cohort,* Dublin: Department of Children and Youth Affairs.

O'Connor, M. (2010). *The Development of Infant Education in Ireland, 1838-1948: Epochs and Eras,* Oxford / Bern: Peter Lang.

OECD (2016). *Family Database,* retrieved from http://www.oecd.org/els/family/database.htm.

Oireachtas Library & Research Service (2012). *Early Childhood Education and Care,* Spotlight Series, No. 4, April 2012. Retrieved from https://www.oireachtas.ie/parliament/media/housesoftheoireachtas/libraryresearch/spotlights/spotEarlyEd180412.pdf, 22 August 2016.

Pobal (2015). *Annual Early Years Sector Survey Report 2014,* Dublin: Pobal / Department of Children and Youth Affairs.

Registrar General of Births, Deaths and Marriages (1901). *Census of Population,* Dublin: Stationery Office.

Registrar General of Births, Deaths and Marriages (1911). *Census of Population,* Dublin: Stationery Office.

Russell, H., McGinnity, F., Callan, T. & Keane, C. (2009). *A Woman's Place? Female Participation in the Paid Labour Market,* Dublin: Equality Authority / Economic and Social Research Institute.

Smeeding, T. (2013). *On the Relationship between Income Inequality and Intergenerational Mobility,* AIAS, GINI Discussion Paper 89.

Start Strong (2014a). *The Double Dividend: Childcare That's Affordable and High Quality,* Dublin: Start Strong.

Start Strong (2014b). *'Childcare'. Business or Profession?,* Dublin: Start Strong.

Williams, J. & Collins, C. (1998). Childcare arrangements in Ireland: A report to the Commission on the Family, in Commission on the Family (eds.), *Strengthening Families for Life* (pp.460-504), Dublin: Stationery Office.

Wolfe, T., O'Donoghue-Hynes, B. & Hayes, N. (2013). Rapid change without transformation: The dominance of a national policy paradigm over international influences on ECEC development in Ireland 1995-2012, *International Journal of Early Childhood,* 45,191-205.

Working Party on Childcare Facilities for Working Parents (1983). *Report to the Minister for Labour,* Dublin: Stationery Office.

7: INEQUALITIES FROM THE START? CHILDREN'S INTEGRATION INTO PRIMARY SCHOOL

Emer Smyth

Introduction

At the beginning of the 20th century, primary education was free but attending second-level education required the payment of fees or the receipt of a scholarship. As a result, according the *1911 Census*, only 30 per cent of 14- to 15-year-olds and 10 per cent of 15- to 18-year-olds were in full-time education (Registrar General of Births, Deaths and Marriages, 1911). While no data are available on the social profile of these students, it is likely that attendance among older teenagers was largely confined to those from more privileged backgrounds. It took 50 more years before social inequalities in the Irish educational system received policy attention, with the production of the *Investment in Education* report (OECD / Department of Education, 1966). This report presented new analyses, indicating significant variation in full-time educational participation by social class background and geographical location. The report findings provided the impetus for the introduction of free secondary education for all, a move that resulted in the large-scale expansion of educational participation.

In the years that followed, a sizeable body of research emerged documenting inequality in educational participation and outcomes at secondary and post-secondary level; an overview of this research is provided in the following section. The focus of policy responses within primary and second-level education has been on the provision of additional support for children and young people attending schools, with a concentration of disadvantaged students rather than addressing inequalities across the broader school-going population. In addition, there has been an information gap on social differentiation in school completion and academic performance, especially in the last decade.

Until the *Growing Up in Ireland* study, there has been a lack of systematic information on the educational experiences and outcomes of those in primary education. Data from Wave 1 of the Child Cohort study indicate that achievement in reading and mathematics among 9-year-olds varies significantly by parental social class, mother's education, household income and family structure (Smyth *et al.*, 2010). Data on the Infant Cohort provide a unique opportunity to explore whether such inequalities date back to the period of school entry. Information on early educational experiences is all the more important, given the debate on the relative importance of the early years to later outcomes. Thus, some commentators (such as Heckman, 2002) emphasise the crucial, if not definitive, impact of cognitive development in the early years on adolescent and adult outcomes. In contrast, other observers have criticised the overemphasis on critical periods to the exclusion of considering learning as a process that occurs throughout school and into adult life (Rutter, 2002). In addition, there is a large body of work that highlights the way in which school processes can reproduce (or counter) social inequalities (see, for example, Teddlie & Reynolds, 2000), suggesting the importance of taking a life-course perspective on inequalities.

This chapter investigates the extent to which social inequalities are evident in children's experiences of integration into primary education. The analyses focus on three main outcomes:

- The primary caregiver's (hereafter referred to as the mother's) report of the child's ease of transition to primary school
- Teachers' perceptions of the child's disposition and attitudes (for example, interest in classroom activities, maintaining concentration)

- Teachers' rating of the child's use of language for communication and understanding (as a measure of the child's readiness to engage with the formal curriculum).

Analyses exploit the rich set of measures of children's social background, looking at the impact of social class, parental education, household income and family structure on these outcomes. The chapter seeks to document the nature of social differentiation in the transition process but, more importantly, to unpack the extent to which any such social differentiation reflects inequalities in relation to a number of explanatory processes, including the home learning environment, early cognitive development and previous experience of formal care settings.

Educational Inequality in Ireland

Much of what we know about educational inequality in Ireland relates to second-level and higher education. Later sections of the chapter will present new analyses of social differences in the early years of primary education but it is worthwhile placing these findings in the context of previous research on the scale and patterning of educational inequality. Virtually all growth in participation in primary education occurred prior to the formation of the Irish State (Tussing, 1978). Over three-quarters of children aged 6 to 14 were in full-time education at the beginning of the 20th century, but, as noted above, this was the case for only 30 per cent of 14- to 15-year-olds and 10 per cent of 15- to 18-year-olds (Registrar General of Births, Deaths and Marriages, 1911). There was no coherent policy on (equality of) educational opportunity until the 1960s (Ó Buachalla, 1988). In 1966 the joint OECD / Department of Education *Investment in Education* report presented new analyses indicating that the full-time educational participation of 15- to 19-year-olds varied from 47 per cent among those from higher professional backgrounds to only 10 per cent among those from semi- and unskilled manual backgrounds. The report also highlighted the way in which many older students remained in primary school because of financial barriers to transferring to secondary education. The report findings provided the impetus for the introduction of free second-level education in 1967, though a number of schools remained outside the free scheme and continued to charge fees. The period following the introduction of free education saw a rapid growth in educational participation among 14- to 17-year-olds (Tussing, 1978). The minimum school leaving age was raised to 14 in 1972 but much of the growth in participation among this age group had already occurred by this point (Tussing, 1978).

Second-level participation rates continued to grow in the 1980s, plateauing somewhat in the 1990s, before beginning to climb again in the 2000s. By 2013-2014, upper secondary completion rates had reached a high of 91 per cent of those entering second-level education (Department of Education and Skills, 2015). Information from the *School Leavers' Survey*, a nationally representative survey of those leaving full-time second-level education conducted from 1980 to 2007, allows us to examine the extent to which participation varied by social background over this period. The categories used are based on the Central Statistics Office's social class grouping; farmers are presented as a separate category because of their distinctive profile in relation to educational participation. At the beginning of the 1980s, Leaving Certificate completion varied markedly by parental social class, with the vast majority (four-fifths) of those from higher professional backgrounds staying in school to the end of Senior Cycle compared with a third of those from unskilled manual backgrounds. At this stage, farmers resembled the intermediate / other non-manual groups in their rates of school completion. By 2006-2007, Leaving Certificate completion rates had increased significantly across all social classes, with the exception of the higher professional group who had already reached near-saturation in participation levels by 1980-1981. Increased participation was greatest among those from working-class (manual) backgrounds but farm family participation also increased dramatically, matching the levels of the higher professional group by 2006-2007. Given on-going improvements in school retention levels to 2014-2015, it is likely that the social gap in Leaving Certificate completion has narrowed further. However, this cannot be systematically assessed because of the lack of data on the social background of school leavers.

Having a Leaving Certificate qualification acts as an important gateway into post-school education / training and employment, with early school leavers experiencing high levels of unemployment (Smyth & McCoy, 2009). Furthermore, the grades achieved within second-level

Cherishing All the Children Equally?

education play an additional role in accessing higher education (because of the use of 'points' calculated on the basis of Leaving Certificate subject grades and levels) and in influencing employment chances, especially in times of recession (Hannan *et al.*, 1996; Smyth, 2008).

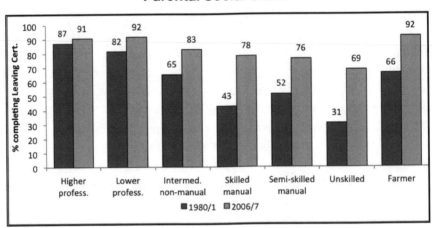

Figure 7.1: Leaving Certificate Completion, by Parental Social Class

Social class differentiation is evident in performance in the first State exam taken, the Junior Certificate exam (**Figure 7.2**). A grade point average was calculated taking account of the grades received and the levels taken, with values ranging from 0 (an 'E', 'F' or 'NG' grade in all subjects) to 10 (a higher level 'A' grade in all subjects). Using data from the *Post-Primary Longitudinal Study*, students from higher professional backgrounds were found to achieve grade point average scores of 7.9, relative to just 6.7 for young people from skilled manual backgrounds, 6.2 among the semi- and unskilled manual class and just 5.9 for the non-employed group (McCoy *et al.*, 2014a). Hence young people from higher professional backgrounds achieved, on average, 2 grades higher per subject taken in the Junior Certificate exam compared to those from non-employed backgrounds.

Although there has been some narrowing of the social gap in Leaving Certificate completion (see **Figure 7.1**), significant differences remain in achievement levels at this stage. **Figure 7.3** shows the proportion of Leaving Certificate leavers who achieved four or more 'honours' (that is, at least a C grade on a higher level paper). Over half of young people from higher professional backgrounds achieved this level but this was the case for only one-fifth of those from skilled or semi-skilled backgrounds and fewer than one in six from unskilled backgrounds.

Figure 7.2: Junior Certificate Grade Point Average, by Social Class

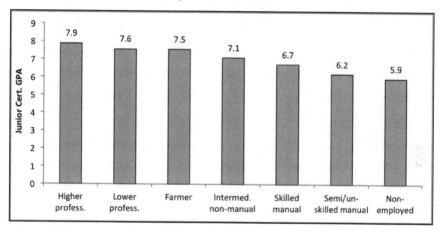

Source: McCoy et al. (2014) (author's analysis).

Junior Certificate results for students in the 12 case-study schools relate to 2005.

Figure 7.3: Proportion of Leaving Certificate Leavers Who Achieved Four or More C Grades or Higher at Higher Level, 2006-2007

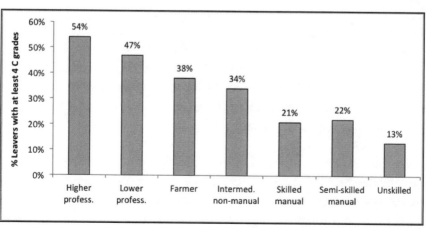

As indicated above, much less is known about inequality at primary level or even prior to school entry. There have been no formal examinations at primary level since the abolition in 1966 of the Primary Certificate, taken at the end of primary education. However, information from standardised tests of student achievement provides some insights into social differentiation at this stage of education. National assessments of reading and mathematics among Second and Sixth Class students have shown significant variation in achievement level by family socio-economic status (Eivers *et al.*, 2010). Similarly, analyses of reading, mathematics and science test results among Fourth Class students show significant variation by mother's education and home educational resources (such as books) (Cosgrove & Creaven, 2013). These analyses suggest that educational inequality within second-level education is, at least to some extent, rooted in the skills and dispositions acquired at primary level. However, until the *Growing Up in Ireland* data became available, we have been unable to trace potential differences back to the early stages of primary education.

In looking at educational inequality, it is crucial to explore specific aspects of Irish educational policy and practice that may ameliorate, or indeed exacerbate, social differentiation. Two features are worth highlighting here: the impact of school choice and the influence of school organisation and process. There has been a good deal of discussion of the 'market model' of education in the English context with the emergence of different types of schools and increasing competition evident between schools. In contrast, the degree of competition between schools in the Irish context has not received the same attention from policy-makers or indeed researchers. Almost half of Junior Cycle students do not attend their nearest or most accessible school (Hannan *et al.*, 1996; Smyth *et al.*, 2004), reflecting quite a remarkable degree of active selection of schools on the part of families. As found in other countries, parental choice of school in Ireland is closely related to social class, with those from higher professional groups making more active selections than those from other groups. School selection processes, therefore, accentuate differences between individual schools in their social class mix. The resulting social segregation between school sectors and among individual schools has important implications for the persistence of social class inequalities in educational outcomes. Students who attend schools with a high intake of young people from disadvantaged backgrounds are more likely to drop out of school before the Leaving Certificate, and tend to underperform in the Junior and Leaving Certificate examinations, compared to those in other schools, an effect that operates over and above that of individual social background (Smyth, 1999). This so-called 'multiplier effect' has been the focus of educational policy since the 1990s, with a succession of schemes designed to target additional resources towards schools serving more disadvantaged populations. While evaluation indicates some positive outcomes of these schemes, it should be noted that no such assistance is in place for the majority of working-class students who attend non-designated disadvantaged (DEIS) schools. This is a sizable group, with *Growing Up in Ireland* data on 13-year-olds indicating that over two-thirds (69 per cent) of those from semi- / unskilled and non-employed backgrounds attend non-DEIS schools.

A second salient feature of the Irish educational system is the degree of discretion afforded to schools over important aspects of organisation and process, albeit within the context of a highly-centralised curriculum and assessment system. Such variation in policy and practice at the school level may result in very different educational experiences for young people. Schools vary significantly in their approach to ability grouping, degree of subject choice, level of student and parental involvement, disciplinary climate, the nature of student-teacher interaction and academic climate (Smyth, 1999; Smyth *et al.*, 2011). All of these aspects of school policy and practice have important consequences for educational participation and attainment and thus for potential inequalities in educational outcomes.

Inequalities on Starting Primary School

The previous section has documented the nature of inequalities in educational outcomes among children and young people. Until the *Growing Up in Ireland* study, there has been a lack of information on the extent to which children start school with different skills and different levels of preparedness for the transition. Based on interviews conducted with the main caregivers (mostly mothers) and surveys of the teachers of 5-year-olds in the *Growing Up in Ireland* study, the analysis here focuses on three aspects of children's integration into primary school. Two dimensions are based on teachers' reports:

- The study child's attitudes and dispositions towards school (including whether they are interested in classroom activities, maintain attention, etc.)
- The study child's language for communication and thinking (how they listen and speak, and take turns in interacting with others).

The third dimension captures the ease of transition to primary school, as reported by their mother. This takes account of the frequency with which the child looks forward to school, says good things about school, complains about school and has been upset or reluctant to go to school.

Figure 7.4: Distribution of Positive Attitudes / Dispositions towards School and Language Skills among 5-year-olds, as Reported by Their Teachers

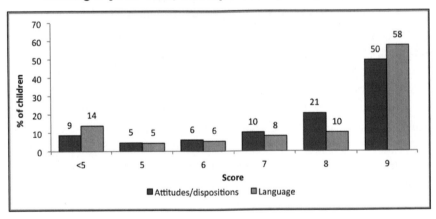

*Source: **Growing Up in Ireland**, Wave 3 of the Infant Cohort.*

Figure 7.4 shows teachers' reports of (a) attitudes and dispositions towards school and (b) language skills for communication / thinking among 5-year-olds. The measures have a maximum score of 9, with higher scores indicating more positive attitudes and better language skills. The figure shows that a significant proportion of children obtain the highest rating possible on both dimensions, though with a good deal of variation in the scores of other children. The average scores among 5-

year-olds in Ireland are broadly similar to those found among children in Northern Ireland, Scotland and Wales (Hansen & Jones, 2008).

Mothers tend to report a positive experience of school among their 5-year-old children (**Figure 7.5**). Four-fifths of children were described as frequently saying good things about school and looking forward to going to school. Between a fifth and a quarter of children complained about school or were upset or reluctant to go to school, though this was generally on an occasional ('once a week or less') rather than a regular basis ('more than once a week'). The remainder of the chapter looks at the factors that influence these perceptions of school, as well as children's dispositions and language skills.

Figure 7.5: Ease of Transition to Primary School, as Reported by Mothers

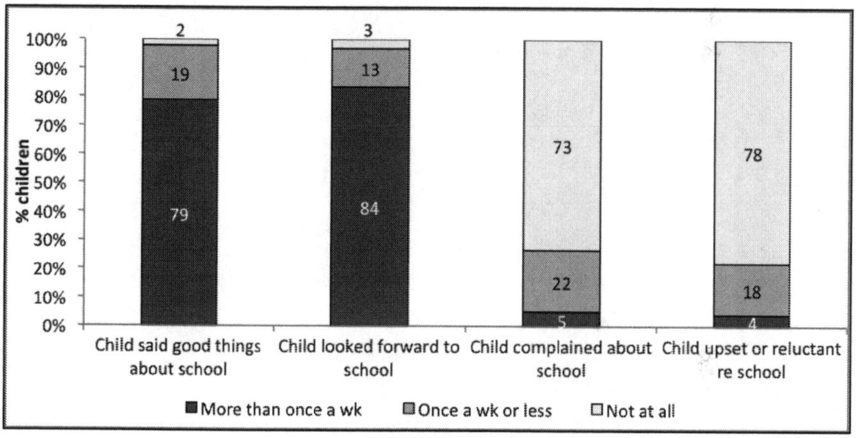

Source: **Growing Up in Ireland**, Wave 3 of the Infant Cohort.

Previous research on educational inequalities in Ireland has generally relied on measures of social class and, sometimes, parental education. An advantage of the *Growing Up in Ireland* data is the rich set of measures on different aspects of family background, including social class, mother's education, household structure (whether a one- or two-parent family), migrant status and household income (equivalised to take account of the number of adults and children in the household). We examine the relative influence of these factors in the following sections. Because of well-documented gender differences in educational experiences and outcomes in Ireland as elsewhere, gender is also taken into account in the analyses.

Important Influences on Early School Experiences

Figure 7.6: Influence of Social Background Characteristics on Attitudes to School, Language Skills, and Perceived Ease of Settling into School among 5-year-olds

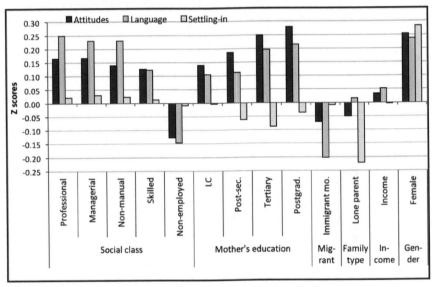

Source: **Growing Up in Ireland**, Wave 3 of the Infant Cohort.

Note: Results of a series of multivariate models. The outcomes have been standardised to have a mean of zero and a standard deviation of one to allow comparison across influences and outcomes. Reference categories: Social class: semi/unskilled; Mother's education: JC or less; Migrant status: not a migrant; Family type: couple; Income: average (income is standardised); Gender: male.

In **Figure 7.6** we present the results of a statistical analysis designed to identify the influence of family background factors on these three aspects of early school experiences:

- Child attitudes
- Child language skills
- Ease of transition to primary education.

Taking account of different dimensions of family background allows us to determine the relative impact of social, cultural and economic resources in shaping children's early outcomes.

Attitudes to school and language skills are significantly structured by both social class and education. Children from middle-class backgrounds (professional, managerial and other non-manual) have significantly more positive attitudes to school and better language skills than those from working-class groups (semi- / unskilled), with the lowest scores found among the children of non-employed families. Even taking account of social class, mother's education has an additional influence, with higher skills and more positive dispositions among 5-year-olds with graduate mothers. Household income when the child was age 9 months old is significantly related to later school preparedness, but the size of the effect is much smaller than for parental education or social class, reflecting the fact that income levels are likely to be less stable than education or class. Children from one-parent families do not differ significantly in skills or school attitudes from their peers, once household income, class and mother's education are taken into account. Children with immigrant mothers have lower levels of language skills at school entry, though this pattern potentially disguises important differences between nationality and language groups (see **Chapter 9**), and slightly less positive attitudes to school.

In contrast to the skills needed for engaging with school-based learning (language and attitudes), mothers' perceptions of their children's ease of transition to primary school vary remarkably little by social background. Only two dimensions emerge as having a significant influence. First, children from one-parent families have more difficulties settling into primary education than those from two-parent homes, even taking account of other socio-economic differences between these two groups. Second, mothers with tertiary degrees report slightly lower scores regarding ease of transition than other education groups. This pattern is only evident when other factors are taken into account, which suggests that these 5-year-olds do not have quite as easy a transition as might be expected given their more advantaged profile rather than that they experience significant difficulties *per se*.

Sizeable gender differences are evident in relation to all three outcomes – girls have more developed language skills, are more engaged with school and have fewer difficulties adapting to primary school. These gender differences are sizeable, being on a par with the impact of having a graduate mother. Further analyses were carried out to examine whether the effects of social background varied by gender. While there is some tendency for girls from skilled manual backgrounds to have more positive outcomes than their male counterparts, social background influences are broadly similar for girls and boys.

What Explains Differences in School Integration?

The previous section has documented clear social background differences in the attitudes and skills children bring with them to the school setting. However, there is a long-running debate about the relative size of such differences compared with other aspects of children's experiences within and outside school (see, for example, Rutter, 2002; Downey & Condron, 2016). In **Figure 7.7** we examine the relative contribution of seven sets of factors:

- Socio-economic background – social class, mother's education, family structure, migrant status and household income
- Gender of the child
- Whether the child has a disability or long-standing illness, as reported by their mother, or special educational need, as reported by their teacher
- The home environment, including the quality of the parent-child relationship, the home learning environment (that is, the frequency with which parents engage in activities such as reading with their child), whether the parent seeks to actively prepare the child for primary school and whether the child had experienced non-parental care prior to school entry
- Cognitive skills prior to school entry
- Cognitive skills and socio-emotional difficulties at age 5, typically assessed three to four months before teachers recorded their assessment of the child

- School characteristics, including whether the school is designated disadvantaged and the class level of the child (Junior or Senior Infants).

In doing so, we use a statistic known as R^2, which shows the proportion of variation in, say, attitudes that is accounted for by each group of factors. Later analyses will focus on whether these other groups of factors help *explain* how social background shapes child outcomes. Taken together, all of these factors explain 19 per cent of the variation found in attitudes to school, 25 per cent of the variation in language skills but only 9 per cent of the variation in ease of transition to school. The first 'block' within the chart shows the proportion of variation explained in attitudes to school, language skills and ease of transition by social class, mother's education, family structure, migrant status and household income. While these effects are statistically significant, they are not very large – in the order of 4 per cent to 5 per cent for attitudes and skills, and less than 1 per cent for settling into school. Thus, while social inequalities are evident on school entry, they are only partly explained by the financial and educational resources of the families into which children were born. Gender explains a further 1 per cent to 2 per cent of the differences found in these early school outcomes.

Figure 7.7: Proportion of Variation in Outcomes Explained by Different Sets of Factors

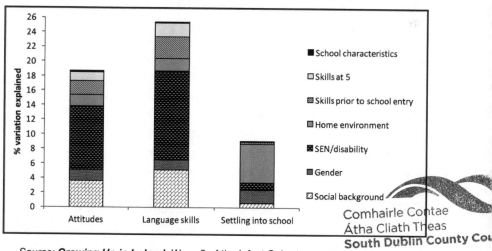

Source: Growing Up in Ireland, Wave 3 of the Infant Cohort.

Having a special educational need or disability explains a sizeable proportion (9 per cent to 12 per cent) of the differences found in early school-related skills. This is a broad definition, taking account of physical, intellectual, emotional-behavioural and specific learning difficulties as well as long-term chronic illness. Five-year-olds with a SEN are found to have much poorer language skills and less engagement in school. Having a SEN or disability also has a moderate influence on the ease of transition to primary school.

The next set of variables relate to the home environment. A large body of literature points to the importance of the home learning environment in shaping child academic outcomes (see, for example, Sylva *et al.*, 2010). The *Growing Up in Ireland* study had a number of different measures of home learning environment, reflecting the stage of child development, and also collected information on the quality of the parent-child relationship and the use of non-parental childcare. The analyses point to a significant but moderate (*c.* 2 per cent) influence of these home factors on attitudes and language skills. Home factors have a stronger effect on the ease of transition to primary education than any other factors. Thus, the development of language skills and integration into primary school are facilitated by more general educational activities in the home and by closer relationships between mothers and children. International research has suggested that having experience of formal, especially centre-based, childcare is likely to ease the transition to primary school because of the familiarity with routines and experience of interacting with other children (Magnusson & Waldfogel, 2005). However, there is considerable debate about the influence of non-parental childcare on cognitive and non-cognitive skills (see, for example, Jacob, 2009; Burger, 2010). Children who were cared for by a relative (other than their parents) at age 9 months or age 3 have slightly more positive attitudes to school at age 5, all else being equal. However, contrary to expectations, having experienced centre-based care does not seem to foster the kinds of dispositions (concentration, engagement) that help children engage in school. Language skills are more developed among children who had been in non-parental care, especially centre-based care, at age 9 months and / or were being cared for by relatives at age 3 (see McGinnity *et al.*, 2015, for similar findings in relation to verbal test scores for 3-year-olds). Children cared for by a non-relative at age 9 months have fewer transition difficulties, while those cared for by a relative have somewhat greater adjustment problems. Being in centre-based care at age 3 also eases the transition to primary school.

The next set of factors relates to the cognitive and non-cognitive skills that children have at age 9 months, age 3 and age 5. These skills are predictive of language skills and positive attitudes to school at age 5 so early skill development better equips children for the early years of primary education. However, better pre-entry cognitive skills have little appreciable influence on the ease of settling into school. The influence of pre-school skills on language skills and attitudes held, even controlling for test scores at age 5, indicating the persisting influence of early skill development.

School factors have a strong influence on the transition to second-level education and beyond, so it would be expected that they would also make a difference to children's integration into primary school. A control is included for the class group that children are in, as those in Senior Infants are more likely to be fully settled into school at that stage. This is partially confirmed with the Junior Infants group described as less settled by their mothers. Interestingly, however, Junior Infants are reported by teachers as having more positive dispositions to school, a pattern that holds even when other factors are taken into account. Previous research has shown the impact of school social mix on student outcomes (see, for example, McCoy *et al.*, 2014b). Children attending DEIS schools (those serving more disadvantaged populations) differ from their counterparts in other schools. Contrary to expectations, however, those in the most disadvantaged schools (those in urban areas) are found to have better school adjustment and language skills, all else being equal. Before taking account of social background and other factors, children in these schools have poorer outcomes. However, the findings indicate that they have better outcomes than might be expected given their disadvantaged background, thus suggesting that DEIS schools may be helping to bridge the gap in school adjustment.

What Explains Social Background Differences?

The previous section looked at the range of factors that influence integration into primary school. This section goes further by examining the extent to which these sets of factors may explain, or mediate, the influence of social background factors. These analyses allow us to distinguish between the direct and indirect effects of social background, while acknowledging that the background effects found among the 5-year-olds are relatively modest in scale. In other words, children from professional families may adjust better to primary school because they have a home learning environment that supports their development (an indirect effect) or they may settle in more readily, even taking account of the home learning environment (a direct effect).

Figure 7.8: Net Effect of Social Class and Maternal Education on Child Attitudes and Language Skills, Taking Account of SEN / Disability, Home Environment, Prior Skills and School Characteristics

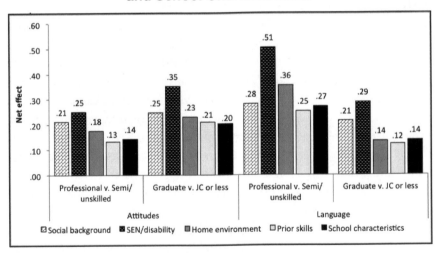

*Source: **Growing Up in Ireland**, Wave 3 of the Infant Cohort.*

Note: Analyses also control for family structure, household income and migrant status.

Figure 7.8 shows whether two dimensions of social background – social class and maternal education – continue to have a significant (direct) effect on child attitudes and language skills when the other sets of factors are taken into account. Ease of transition to primary school is not discussed here because of the absence of systematic variation by social class or parental education (see above).

Turning first to the child's attitudes towards school, the first column of **Figure 7.8** shows the net difference between children from middle-class (professional) and working-class (semi- / unskilled manual) families. Thus, middle-class children are more likely to come to school with the dispositions that will help them engage with learning. The second column suggests that the social class gap is even wider when SEN and disability are taken into account. In other words, the prevalence of SEN / disability across social groups obscures some of the achievement gap in the early years. Columns 3 and 4 show the gap reducing in size; thus, home environment and early cognitive and non-cognitive skill development help explain much of the advantage experienced by middle-class children. In fact, social class differences in attitudes are no longer significant when home environment and prior skills are taken into account. A broadly similar pattern is found when we consider the difference between the children of graduate mothers and those whose mothers have lower secondary education or less. The education gap becomes wider when we take account of the effects of SEN / disability and is partly explained by home factors, especially the home learning environment. Thus, graduate mothers foster school readiness among their children by engaging in educational activities with them from an early age. In contrast to social class, having a graduate mother continues to have a direct effect on child dispositions towards school and so is not explained by the array of processes considered here.

The social class gap in language skills is wider than is found for attitudes to school. Like school attitudes, the gap is wider when SEN and disability are taken into account. A good deal of the gap is explained by home environment and prior skill development, indicating that middle-class families foster language skills through early educational activities. Home environment also explains much of the gap in skills between the children of graduate mothers and those whose mothers have the lowest levels of education.

In sum, the social differentiation found in children's dispositions towards school and in their language development is, in part, related to the presence of books and educational activities in the home and exposure to formal childcare. However, the educational and social resources possessed by the family continue to have a direct effect on the skills children bring with them to the school context.

Conclusion

Some dimensions of educational inequality have declined significantly in the century since 1916, principally because of the dramatic growth in educational participation. However, young people's achievement levels at the end of second-level education continue to reflect their social background, a pattern that serves to limit the life-chances of many working-class young people. This chapter explores whether these differences in educational outcomes reflect variation in the skills and dispositions young children bring to the school context. It examines three aspects of child development at school entry:

- The attitudes and dispositions they hold towards school (including crucial factors such as concentration skills)
- Their language skills
- Their ease of settling into the school context.

The analyses show that the attitudes and language skills possessed by 5-year-olds differ significantly according to their social class background, their mother's education and household income. At the same time, background factors explain relatively little of the variation found in these skills; typically only 4 per cent to 5 per cent of the variation in attitudes and skills is accounted for family background. What is noteworthy too is that these social background factors explain less of the social gap in outcomes than SEN / disability, home environment and early skill development. Furthermore, the ease of settling into primary school does not vary markedly by social class, maternal education or income. The social differentiation that is found is, in part, related to the presence of books and educational activities in the home as well as exposure to non-parental childcare. However, the educational and social resources possessed by the family continue to have a direct effect on the skills children bring with them to the school context.

The findings presented in this chapter have important implications from a policy perspective. While the analyses show the importance of early skill development for school readiness, they do not support the assumption that early childhood is a critical period that sets social inequalities in stone for the remainder of the educational career. In fact, the findings suggest a good deal of variation within, as well as between, social groups in child skills and dispositions on starting school. The social inequalities we find in second-level completion and achievement rates therefore appear to reflect the continuing influence of family economic, educational and social resources throughout the school career, with more advantaged parents engaging in active school choice, possessing greater knowledge of the system to help their children make the choices that will ensure their educational success, and paying for the kinds of out-of-school activities that foster academic development.

References

Burger, K. (2010). How does early childhood care and education affect cognitive development?, *Early Childhood Research Quarterly*, 25, 140-65.

Cosgrove, J. & Creaven, A.M. (2013). Understanding achievement in PIRLS and TIMSS 2011, in Eivers, E. & Clerkin, A. (eds.), *National Schools, International Contexts: Beyond the PIRLS and TIMSS Test Results* (pp.201-239), Dublin: Educational Research Centre.

Department of Education and Skills (2015). *Retention Rates of Pupils in Second-level Schools: 2008 Entry Cohort*. Dublin: Stationery Office.

Downey, D.B. & Condron, D.J. (2016). Fifty years since the Coleman Report: Rethinking the relationship between schools and inequality, *Sociology of Education*, 89, 207-20.

Eivers, E., Clerkin, A., Millar, D. & Close, S. (2010). *The 2009 National Assessments Technical Report*, Dublin: Educational Research Centre.

Hannan, D.F., Smyth, E., McCullagh, J., O'Leary, R. & McMahon, D. (1996). *Coeducation and Gender Equality*, Dublin: Oak Tree Press.

Hansen, K. & Jones, E.M. (2008). Foundation stage profile and devolved teacher administration survey, in Hansen, K. & Joshi, H. (eds.), *Millennium Cohort Study Third Survey: A User's Guide to Initial Findings* (pp.98-117), London: Institute of Education.

Heckman, J.J. (2002). Skill formation and the economics of investing in disadvantaged children, *Science, 312*, 1900-02.

Jacob, J.I. (2009). The socio-emotional effects of non-maternal childcare on children in the USA: A critical review of recent studies, *Early Childhood Development and Care, 179,* 559-70.

Magnusson, K.A. & Waldfogel, J. (2005). Early childhood care and education: Effects on ethnic and racial gaps in school readiness, *The Future of Children, 15*(1), 169-96.

McCoy, S., Quail, A. & Smyth, E. (2014b). The effects of school social mix: Unpacking the differences, *Irish Educational Studies, 33,* 307-30.

McCoy, S., Smyth, E., Watson, D. & Darmody, M. (2014a). *Leaving School in Ireland: A Longitudinal Study of Post-School Transitions,* Research Series 36, August, Dublin: Economic and Social Research Institute.

McGinnity, F., Russell, H. & Murray, A. (2015). *Non-parental Childcare and Child Cognitive Outcomes at Age 5,* Dublin: Department of Children and Youth Affairs.

Ó Buachalla, S. (1988). *Education Policy in 20th Century Ireland,* Dublin: Wolfhound Press.

OECD / Department of Education (1966). *Investment in Education,* Dublin: Stationery Office.

Registrar General of Births, Deaths and Marriages (1911). *Census of Population,* Dublin: Stationery Office.

Rutter, M. (2002). Nature, nurture and development: From evangelism through science toward policy and practice, *Child Development, 73,* 1-21.

Smyth, E. (1999). *Do Schools Differ?,* Dublin: Oak Tree Press.

Smyth, E. (2008). Just a phase? Youth unemployment in the Republic of Ireland, *Journal of Youth Studies,* 11, 313-329.

Smyth, E. & McCoy, S. (2009). *Investing in Education: Combating Educational Disadvantage,* Dublin: Barnardo's / Economic and Social Research Institute.

Smyth, E., Banks, J. & Calvert, E. (2011). *From Leaving Certificate to Leaving School: A Longitudinal Study of Sixth Year Students,* Dublin: Liffey Press.

Smyth, E., McCoy, S. & Darmody, M. (2004). *Moving Up: The Experiences of First Year Students in Post-primary Education,* Dublin: Liffey Press.

Smyth, E., Whelan, C.T., McCoy, S., Quail, A. & Doyle, E. (2010). Understanding parental influence on educational outcomes among 9-year-old children in Ireland, *Child Indicators Research,* 3, 85-104.

Sylva, K., Melhuish, E., Sammons, P., Siraj-Blatchford, I. & Taggart, B. (2010). *Early Childhood Matters,* London: Routledge.

Teddlie, C. & Reynolds, D. (eds.) (2000). *The International Handbook of School Effectiveness Research,* London: Falmer Press.

Tussing, D. (1978). *Irish Educational Expenditure – Past, Present and Future,* Dublin: Economic and Social Research Institute.

8: INSIGHTS INTO THE PREVALENCE OF SPECIAL EDUCATIONAL NEEDS

Selina McCoy, Joanne Banks & Michael Shevlin

Historical Context

Special education has become an important feature of Irish mainstream education in recent years. Since the early 1990s there has been a real shift in focus from segregated educational provision towards a more inclusive view of special education mainly delivered within mainstream schools (Griffin & Shevlin, 2008).

During the 20th century, Irish special education can be described as having three phases:

- The era of neglect and denial
- The era of the special school
- The era of integration or inclusion (Swan, 2000).

The era of denial was characterised by very little government policy or legislation regarding special needs provision in Ireland. From the foundation of the State in 1919 to the early 1990s, much of the education and care, including the education and care of children with special needs (particularly outside of special schools), was carried out by the religious orders (Flood, 2013). The approach of the Irish government during this time was cautious and pragmatic as it tried to balance economic considerations with educational principles (MacGiolla Phádraig, 2007).

The 'era of the special school' began in the mid-20th century, where it was slowly recognised that children with special needs required education (Flood, 2013). In 1947 St Vincent's Home for Mentally Defective Children (founded in 1926) was recognised by the State as an official school. The establishment of this school, along with other similar schools that followed, reflected the belief at the time that children with special needs should not be educated alongside their peers, as this was considered to be detrimental to the education of 'normal' children and their teachers (Commission of Inquiry into the Reformatory and Industrial School System Assisting Children with Special Needs, cited in Flood, 2013). By 1960 official interest in special education was signalled by the government white paper, *The Problem of the Mentally Handicapped*. This paper recommended that a commission of inquiry on mental handicap be established and led to the publication of the *Report of the Commission of Inquiry on Mental Handicap* in 1965 (Coolahan, 2007). For the first time, a range of policy measures around curriculum, duration of programmes, school and class sizes, and teacher training, which were all aimed at improving the education of children who were mentally handicapped, was available. The report led to the expansion of new special schools around the country throughout the 1960s, 1970s and until the mid-1980s, to cater for children with physical, mental and sensory impairments. These special schools were designated as special national schools and operated under the rules for national schools (Department of Education and Science, 2007).

Since the early 1990s, there have been significant changes to Irish policy and legislation around special education. This policy evolution occurred through the interplay of a variety of factors at both national and international levels (Griffin & Shevlin, 2008). At this point Irish policy began to be influenced by international policy developments, where human rights-based (instead of needs-based) principles were being endorsed. In particular the *Convention on the Rights of the Child* (United Nations, 1989) created obligations for governments that ratified it in relation to the rights of all children, including those with disabilities (Stevens & O'Moore, 2009).

Over the years, Irish special education and general education, while connected, had developed separately and appeared to run along parallel lines. Special education had little presence in general education decision-making and policy development, and often appeared to be fragmented and lacking coordination (Griffin & Shevlin, 2008). A real shift towards an inclusive education policy was, however, most evident in the publication of the *Report of the Special Education Review Committee* (Department of Education, 1993). For the first time, it was recommended that students with a disability should be integrated in mainstream schools and participate in school activities with other students where possible (Department of Education, 1993). The report not only highlighted the conspicuous lack of legislation governing students with SEN but provided, for the first time, a definition of special needs beyond traditional medical disability categories. The new definition included those with severe and profound difficulties through to those who were exceptionally able and it included both physical and mental disabilities. In addition to student integration, the report also emphasised the importance of a continuum of provision and highlighted the inadequacy of teacher training in the area of special education.

The 1990s was also marked by a series of court cases against the State that had a significant impact on SEN provision in Ireland. In 1993, the State refused to educate certain groups of children who it claimed were 'ineducable' within the meaning of Article 42 of the *Constitution* (Glendenning, 1999). The case of *O'Donoghue v. Minister for Health* (1993) related to provision for a 9-year-old boy with severe disabilities. The High Court found the State had failed to provide Paul O'Donoghue with his constitutional right to 'free primary education' under Article 42. The State was obliged to make the necessary modifications to the curriculum and teaching to ensure that children with disabilities could make the best use of their inherent capacities (Stevens & O'Moore, 2009, p.23).

Another milestone was reached in 2004 when the *Education for Persons with Special Educational Needs Act* (EPSEN) was published. This signalled a further shift in thinking around children with special educational needs from segregation to integration to meaningful inclusion and participation in mainstream schools. Based on the *EPSEN Act*, the term SEN / disability now includes a broad range of difficulties ranging from physical, sensory, mental health or learning disabilities or 'any other condition which results in a person learning differently from a person without that condition'. The Act also established the National Council for Special Education, which was given overall responsibility for special needs provision in Irish schools, assessing applications for support and co-ordinating services throughout the country. Prior to the establishment of the National Council for Special Education, the Department of Education and Skills administered provision for special educational needs from a centralised structure. With the rapid growth of demand for provision for special educational needs in the late 1990s, the Department of Education and Skills was overwhelmed with applications for support as a result of the automatic response procedure (1998) (an administrative mechanism to allocate resources in a speedy fashion). It had been evident for some time that a more localised, flexible structure was necessary to respond appropriately to the complexities involved in special educational needs provision (Griffin & Shevlin, 2008).

Inclusion in Ireland: A Decade after EPSEN

Not surprisingly, changes in SEN policy and provision over the last two decades have had a significant impact on the educational experiences of children with SEN and their peers in mainstream settings. With some exceptions (Carr-Fanning *et al.*, 2013; Shevlin, 2010; Shevlin *et al.*, 2005), researchers have had little opportunity to examine school experiences for this group and compare their experiences to their peers without any disabilities or impairments. With the availability of *Growing Up in Ireland* data on 8,578 9-year-old children, however, this has begun to change (Banks & McCoy, 2011; Banks *et al.*, 2012; McCoy & Banks, 2012; McCoy *et al.*, 2012a; McCoy *et al.*, 2012b; McCoy *et al.*, 2014; Cosgrove *et al.*, 2014). For the first time, the *Growing Up in Ireland* study has provided a unique opportunity to combine data from three sets of key informants (children, their parents and teachers) to identify the cohort experiencing SEN and to examine their experiences in school relative to their peers. The remainder of this chapter presents *Growing Up in Ireland* evidence on the nature and characteristics of children with SEN, before presenting more in-depth analysis assessing the extent to which certain groups are over- or under-identified or whether school composition plays a role in SEN identification.

Prevalence of SEN

With the changing population of children in mainstream schools, assessing the size, profile and characteristics of students with SEN becomes increasingly important. Before doing so, it is crucial to fully understand how our definition of SEN has changed over time. As a consequence of broadening the definition in the *EPSEN Act*, 2004, we have changed our understanding of which students have such additional needs. Using *Growing Up in Ireland* data, a prevalence rate of 25 per cent (Banks & McCoy, 2011) has been found, based on a three-step approach combining information from teachers and parents on a range of physical, learning and emotional / behavioural difficulties (**Table 8.1**). A baseline figure of 14.1 per cent from teacher reports of four main types of SEN increases to 20 per cent with the addition of parent-reported disabilities and difficulties and a total of 25 per cent when including children scoring as 'high risk' on the SDQ social-emotional difficulties scale.

This prevalence rate largely aligns with cohort studies internationally. In the Netherlands, for example, research has found a prevalence rate of 26 per cent based on parent and teacher reports of SEN (Van der Veen *et al.*, 2010). Similarly in the UK, research concluded that teachers identified 26 per cent of children with SEN (Croll & Moses, 2003), while another study found 22 per cent of 16-year-olds had some form of SEN identified (Hills *et al.*, 2010).

It is interesting to consider the profile of the group of students with some form of SEN, in particular in terms of their gender and social background. In total, 29 per cent of boys are identified with SEN, while 21 per cent of girls fall into this category (**Figure 8.1**). Boys account for a larger share of children identified as 'high risk' on the teacher-reported scale, as well as showing greater number among those identified by teachers as having a physical disability, speech impairment, learning disability or an emotional / behavioural problem (EBD).

Table 8.1: Prevalence of Special Educational Needs among 9-year-olds

Step	Source	Domains	Incidence in population %	Additional group %	Total SEN prevalence%
			Prevalence Rate		
1	Teachers	Physical disability Speech Impairment Learning disability Emotional / behavioural problem (ADD, ADHD)	14.1	14.1	14.1
2	Parents	Learning difficulty, communication or co-ordination disorder (including dyslexia, ADHD, autism, speech and language difficulty, dyspraxia, slow progress, other)	10.6	+5.9	20.0
		Speech difficulty	1.4		
		Chronic physical or mental health problem, illness or disability hampering daily life	4.8		
3	Teachers	Emotional / psychological wellbeing / EBD (SDQ Measure): identifying a 'high risk' group	10.5	+5.0	25.0

Source: Banks & McCoy, 2011.

Figure 8.2 displays the SEN prevalence rate across social class groups. While 30 per cent of children from semi-skilled / unskilled manual backgrounds are classified as having a SEN, the prevalence rate among children from professional backgrounds is just 16 per cent. It is interesting to note that prevalence rates for the skilled manual group are significantly lower than for the semi-skilled / unskilled manual group, largely due to higher levels of reported EBD among the semi-skilled /

unskilled manual group. The picture for children from economically inactive households is distinct with much higher SEN rates: 45 per cent of children in this category are identified with a SEN, with high levels of EBD among this group.

Figure 8.1: SEN Prevalence for Boys and Girls

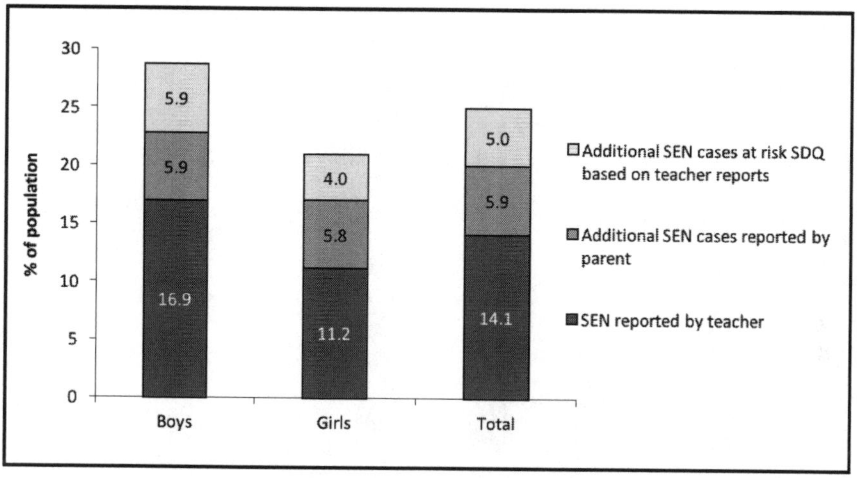

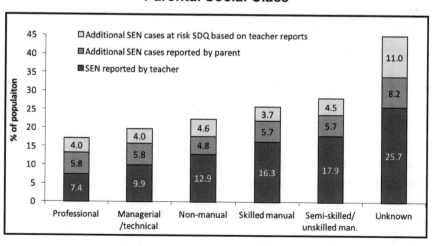

Source: Banks & McCoy (2011).

Figure 8.2: SEN Prevalence Rates, by Parental Social Class

The pattern is similar when we consider prevalence rates across household income levels (**Figure 8.3**). Significantly higher prevalence rates are reported for children in the lowest income quintile: a prevalence rate of 38 per cent among the lowest income group far exceeds rates of 23 and 18 per cent among the middle and highest income groups.

Figure 8.3: SEN Prevalence Rates, by Household Income Quintile

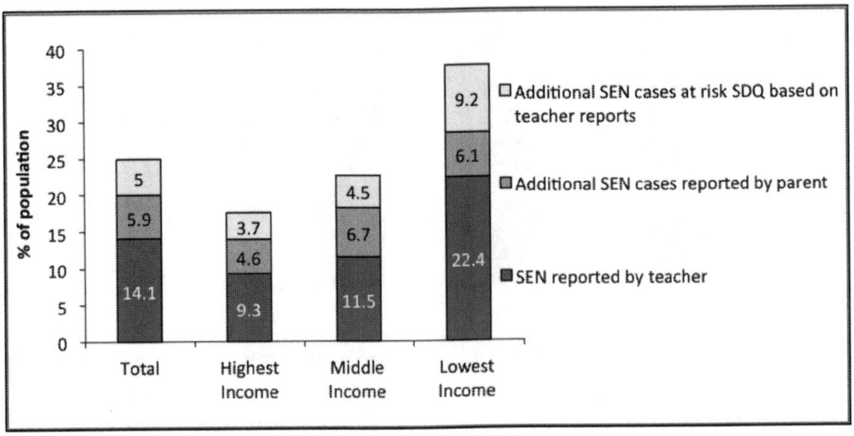

Source: Banks & McCoy (2011).

Student Wellbeing and Engagement

Inclusive education policy emphasises reducing the number of students with SEN in special education settings, with greater placement in mainstream schools. Of key interest is the extent to which the educational and social experiences of these students differ in such 'inclusive' environments. Concerns have been raised about the implications for school engagement, academic progress and peer relations among these students. In particular studies have focused on the ways in which friendships are formed between students with SEN and their peers (Cambrian & Silvestre, 2003; Koster *et al.*, 2010). The inclusion of students with SEN in mainstream environments has meant that they are frequently distinguished from their peers by both formal and informal processes involving identification and assessment that clearly differentiates them from their peers (Priestley, 2001). Some argue that, through these systems and procedures, there is a real risk that they will be viewed differently and negatively by their peers (Rose & Shevlin, 2010). As a result, research shows that children with SEN have been found to be feeling acutely aware of being treated differently by their peers and teachers (McArthur *et al.*, 2007). Studies show that students with SEN often report problems in accessing the mainstream curriculum (Dyson & Gallannuagh, 2008), are more likely than their peers to have negative teacher-student (Murray & Greenberg, 2001) and peer relations (Koster *et al.*, 2007) and there is evidence that students with SEN fail to make sufficient progress in mainstream schools (Keslair & McNally, 2009). This research is particularly relevant where children are in receipt of supports.

Figure 8.4: Proportion of 9-year-olds Indicating that They 'Never Like School', by Gender and SEN Status

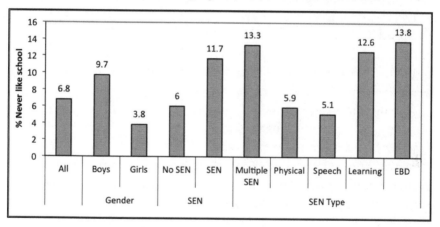

Source: McCoy & Banks (2012).

The breadth and richness of the *Growing Up in Ireland* data allow us look in depth at the school experiences of 9-year-old children in mainstream schools with and without SEN, looking at both the academic and social dimensions of school life. One important dimension of wellbeing is school engagement, which has been a relatively understudied factor (Furrer & Skinner, 2003), particularly for SEN children. Specifically, we consider children's engagement in school at age 9, as measured by their response to the question: 'What do you think about school?' to which the child could respond 'always like it', 'sometimes like it' or 'never like it'. We focus on the characteristics of children reporting that they 'never like school'. We also consider the role of social class and family income. Findings show that school experiences and overall attitudes towards school vary among children with SEN (according to the type of SEN they have). As shown in **Figure 8.4**, children with SEN are significantly more likely to indicate that they never like school: children whose teacher reported that they have some form of SEN are nearly twice as likely to never like school. When we consider the type of SEN reported, we find that children with multiple SEN, EBD and learning disabilities are much more likely to not like school.

Multivariate analysis provides further insight into patterns of school engagement within and across SEN groups, taking account of social background and other characteristics. In **Table 8.2** (see **Appendix** to this chapter), Model 1 shows that boys are more likely to never like school, as are children from economically-inactive families. The results in Model 1 also show that children with learning disabilities in isolation and those with multiple disabilities (typically learning and physical disability or learning disability and EBD) are significantly more likely to never like school than their peers without SEN.

To further examine the underlying processes, Model 2 includes measures of academic engagement and social engagement to assess whether these help to explain such disengagement from school. In common with earlier studies (Furlong & Christenson, 2008), both academic and social aspects of school life are posited to be integral for student engagement and success. Academic engagement is measured by considering whether children report liking reading and maths and their patterns of homework completion – comparing children who regularly / occasionally do not complete their homework with those who always complete their homework. Social relation and peer engagement are examined using three measures: the first considers children's attitudes towards their teacher using the question 'Do you like your teacher?' to which children could respond 'always', 'sometimes' or 'never'. The second taps into peer relationships drawing on teacher responses to the

Strengths and Difficulties Questionnaire (SDQ),[3] using the peer problems subscale where scores are divided into categories described as 'normal' and 'high risk' (Goodman, 1997). Finally, the third measure draws on the Piers-Harris Self-Concept scale, drawing on the popularity sub-scale, examining the role of child-reported friendship patterns in shaping children's enjoyment of school (see McCoy & Banks, 2012).

It is evident that all three measures of academic engagement play a role in shaping patterns of school engagement (Model 2). Children who always like maths and reading and complete their homework are less likely to dislike school. Similarly, peer and social relations play a role – those who like their teacher being less likely to be disengaged, while those who are 'high risk' on the SDQ peer sub-scale are more likely to dislike school. Of particular note, the results show that children with learning (and multiple) disabilities are no longer significantly more likely to never like school – their disengagement is largely mediated by their levels of academic engagement and the nature of their peer and social relations.

Overall, the results show that children with SEN, particularly those identified with learning disabilities, face considerable barriers to fully engage in school life. For these students, low levels of academic engagement and poor relations with their peers and teachers play a central role in understanding their low levels of school engagement. Despite efforts to broaden the range and content of learning experiences at primary level, student attitudes towards academic domains (in this case mathematics and reading) play an important role in shaping their orientation towards school and their happiness in the school setting.

---

[3]   The Strengths and Difficulties Questionnaire (SDQ) was completed by teachers in respect of each child. The SDQ is a brief mental health screening questionnaire that provides balanced coverage of children's behaviours, emotions and relations. The full measure includes items on each of five dimensions, namely conduct, emotional symptoms, hyperactivity, peer relationships and pro-social behaviour (Goodman, 1997).

SEN Identification Processes and the Role of School Context

The story thus far presents the evidence on the proportion of children with different types of SEN and how they are faring at school. But if we look more closely, the story is far more complex and more in-depth analysis throws up serious questions in relation to SEN identification. Internationally, it is increasingly argued that the identification of special educational needs is not a straightforward process and that there are tensions and complexities that must be recognised (Griffin & Shevlin, 2008). Researchers and educators are often concerned about the relationship between individual student characteristics (such as socio-economic background, gender, ethnicity) and the prevalence of specific types of SEN among certain groups of socially-marginalised children, for whom SEN identification may lead to stigmatisation and isolation (Dyson & Kozleski, 2008; NESSE, 2012). Studies have highlighted how children from working class backgrounds or those living in areas of social deprivation are much more likely to be identified as having special educational needs (Keslair & McNally, 2009). These patterns become more apparent where studies have explored the types of SEN or disabilities that are over-represented. Non-normative difficulties, in particular social, emotional and behavioural difficulties, are four times more likely to be identified in the most deprived areas compared to the least deprived (De Valenzuela *et al.*, 2006; Dyson & Gallannuagh, 2008). Furthermore, research, including Irish studies, also highlights the intersections between gender and particular types of difficulty, where boys outnumber girls in all types of difficulty; but the discrepancy is most marked in the non-normative categories such as learning disabilities (such as mild / moderate learning disabilities and specific learning disabilities) and social, emotional and behavioural difficulties, where there are also strong associations with social deprivation (Riddell *et al.*, 2006).

For the first time, *Growing Up in Ireland* data allows us to explore issues of identification and group stereotyping in an Irish context. In particular, to explore whether 'disproportionality' or over- or under-identification is at play, we examined whether emotional / behavioural disabilities as identified by teachers, or within certain schools, is matched by the child's own performance on an internationally-validated emotional and mental health self-concept measure (Piers & Hertzberg, 2002). Overall child-reported social emotional wellbeing was found to be strongly related to teachers identifying children with an emotional / behavioural disability. However, as shown in **Table 8.3** (see **Appendix** to this chapter), boys, children from economically inactive households[4] and children from one-parent families are more likely to be identified as having an emotional / behavioural disability, even after taking into account their scoring on the self-concept measure. These findings suggest that the identification of emotional / behavioural disability based on teachers' judgement results in an over-representation of certain groups of children.

The results also suggest evidence of a school context effect in the identification of emotional behavioural difficulties – with children attending the most disadvantaged school contexts[5] significantly more likely to be identified with such difficulties, even after taking into account their social background characteristics and their scoring on the internationally-recognised Piers-Harris self-concept measure (Model 3). Internationally, research is increasingly concerned with understanding patterns of SEN identification in schools by focusing on factors other than child characteristics, such as the teacher or the school. This literature focuses more broadly on the education system and a possible underlying imperative to seek homogeneity in institutional life that necessitates delineating and differentiating those who differ from the norm (Thomas & Loxley, 2001). The subjective nature of the SEN identification process, particularly for non-normative SEN such as emotional and behavioural difficulties, means that these students form part of the non-dominant culture and may be disproportionately more likely to be identified as being 'deviant' or having a SEN (Dyson & Gallannuagh, 2008). In attempting to understand this process, much of

---

[4]   Social class is measured using the European Socio-Economic Classification, a theoretically informed typology that captures key qualitative differences in employment relationships (Rose & Harrison, 2009).

[5]   The DEIS programme (Delivering Equality of Opportunity in Schools), is designed to address the educational needs of children and young people from disadvantaged communities (Department of Education and Science, 2005). The programme differentiates between Urban Band 1 schools with the most socio-economically disadvantaged intake, Urban Band 2 schools and Rural DEIS schools.

the research points to the complex interaction of student characteristics, teacher characteristics and the social composition of the school which results in higher SEN identification for particular groups of students (Van der Veen *et al.*, 2010). Furthermore, it is important to consider how teachers' judgements of ability or acceptable student behaviour are most likely based on their referent group, which naturally consists of other students in the class (Hibel *et al.*, 2010). In this way, the detection of SEN is likely to depend on what is considered normal, which will vary considerably between schools. Described as a frog-pond effect (Davis, 1966), this means that the same student appears worse when compared to higher- than to lower-performing schoolmates.

We further examine the influence of being in a DEIS school, as compared to a non-disadvantaged context, in the identification of different types of SEN. Here we differentiate between teacher-reported physical, speech, learning and emotional behavioural disabilities, as well as those identified with two or more of these disabilities.[6] We also consider the characteristics of teachers and examine whether a teacher's gender and length of teaching experience are related to the likelihood of a child being identified with (different types of) SEN, taking account of the individual characteristics of children. The results (not shown[7]) reveal important differences in the characteristics of children with different types of SEN. Social class differences emerge in relation to multiple disabilities – with semi- and unskilled manual social classes and unemployed households being at significantly greater risk of being in this group. The probability of being identified with multiple special needs is lower among less experienced teachers. It is not possible to establish whether this relates to the allocation of teachers within schools or to variations in approaches to inclusion among more and less experienced teachers. There is little variation in the incidence of physical disabilities across social class, education and income groups.[8] The incidence is higher among male teachers, which may reflect the greater

---

[6]   The group predominantly comprises children identified with a learning
      disability and an emotional behavioural problem; and children with a speech
      impairment and an emotional behavioural problem.
[7]   Full results are available in McCoy *et al.* (2012a).
[8]   Income is based on equivalised household income, divided into quintiles.

allocation of male teachers to classes comprising such children. There is similarly little variation in the prevalence of speech impairments across social class and income groups, although boys are more likely to be identified with such difficulties.

The incidence of learning disabilities is higher among children from economically-inactive households, while mother's education is also significant in the chances of being identified – with higher levels for children whose mothers have low levels of educational attainment. Highly-experienced teachers appear more likely to identify learning disabilities, but again we cannot identify whether this reflects school / class allocation processes or teacher behaviour. Children attending the most disadvantaged school contexts are less likely to be identified with a learning disability, perhaps reflecting resource constraints in such contexts. Travers (2010) found that there was no difference between the level of learning support in mathematics in designated and non-designated schools, despite a huge differential in achievement levels. The gender mix of the school is also significant – children attending co-educational and girls-only schools are more likely to be identified with a learning disability. Finally, in relation to emotional or behavioural difficulty (EBD), boys, children from economically-inactive and one-parent families are more likely to be identified with EBD. Parental education is also a strong predictor – children whose mothers have achieved third-level qualifications are much less likely to be identified. Again, it appears school context also plays a role. Children attending the most disadvantaged school contexts are substantially more likely to be identified with an EBD than children attending other school contexts.

Overall, the results provide significant evidence of a 'frog-pond' contextual effect in the most disadvantaged DEIS schools, with an under-identification of learning disabilities and an over-identification of emotional / behavioural disabilities in these contexts. The under-identification of learning disabilities may reflect greater levels of need in such disadvantaged contexts (which is not matched by comparable levels of support) with the result that only children with more severe learning disabilities are identified as having a SEN in such contexts, with more diverse learning needs identified in other school contexts. The combination of the under-identification of learning disabilities and over-identification of emotional / behavioural disabilities may mean that DEIS schools are opting for an environment of 'care' rather than 'challenge'. In any case, the findings suggest that teachers in more socio-economically disadvantaged contexts may over-identify emotional / behavioural difficulties in a context of greater levels of disciplinary problems, difficulties which take precedence over the learning difficulties students may have (McCoy *et al.*, 2012a).

Conclusion

This chapter highlights the practical implications of placing children with SEN in mainstream schools. Our findings highlight the need for discussion by policy-makers and practitioners around the definition of SEN as per the *EPSEN Act*. The rate of 25 per cent brings Ireland more in line with prevalence estimates internationally and at the same time highlights the difficulties in using government administrative data sources in cross-national comparative statistics. The true value of *Growing Up in Ireland* data, however, is in allowing us to go beyond assessing the scale and profile of children with SEN to examine the processes shaping SEN identification. In line with results internationally, evidence suggests that the identification of emotional / behavioural disabilities based on teachers' judgement is resulting in an over-representation of certain groups of children. These patterns highlight the need to re-examine existing SEN classifications systems in deciding on provision for students and point to the use of other models of classification, such as the bio-psycho-social model, which are based on the interaction between the person and the environment in order to decide on appropriate provision. Lessons can also be learned from other national contexts where SEN classification systems have been harmonised across relevant government agencies or in some instances have been removed altogether and replaced with categories based on the type of support required rather than the nature of the need.

The research also highlights how SEN identification is context specific in that the analysis has yielded evidence of a 'frog-pond' effect in socio-economically disadvantaged schools. The combination of the under-identification of learning difficulties and the over-identification of emotional / behavioural disabilities may influence the type of teaching and learning in disadvantaged schools where teachers may opt for an environment of 'care' rather than an environment of 'challenge'. Moreover, it may be that the teachers in these contexts are more likely to identify emotional / behavioural disabilities in response to greater disciplinary problems in these schools, difficulties that take precedence over the learning needs which students may have.

A natural progression from examining prevalence and processes of SEN identification is to assess how well students with SEN fare in mainstream education settings. Taking a holistic perspective, looking at both the academic and social aspects of students' lives, the evidence shows that students with SEN are less engaged in school than their peers. Although this varied by SEN type, the analysis shows that boys and children from semi- / unskilled social class backgrounds are more likely to report never liking school. It seems that despite efforts to make the Irish primary school curriculum both broader and more inclusive, its academic orientation plays a central role in influencing how children with SEN view school. By simultaneously examining the role of academic and social relations in shaping the engagement of children with SEN, the analysis provides a unique opportunity to fundamentally assess the barriers to true inclusion for children with special needs.

Appendix

Table 8.2: Probability of 'Never Liking School', as Reported by 9-year-old Children in Mainstream Schools

	Model 1 B (S.E.)	Model 2 B (S.E.)
Gender (Ref. Girls)		
Boys	1.072(0.112)***	0.877(0.119)***
Social Class (Ref. Non-manual)		
Professional	-0.253(0.189)	-0.185(0.203)
Managerial	-0.236(0.141)	-0.205(0.151)
Skilled Manual	-0.094(0.172)	-0.186(0.184)
Semi- and unskilled	0.122(0.194)	0.120(0.208)
Unknown	0.638(0.209)**	0.691(0.224)**

	Model 1	Model 2
	B (S.E.)	B (S.E.)
Household Income Quintiles (Ref. Middle income)		
Lowest	-0.396(0.200)*	-0.481(0.212)*
2nd Lowest	0.217(0.161)	0.251(0.172)
2nd highest	-0.133(0.167)	-0.196(0.178)
Highest	-0.047(0.165)	-0.057(0.176)
Unknown	0.415(0.194)*	0.430(0.208)*
SEN (Ref. no SEN)		
Multiple	0.703(0.264)**	0.245(0.290)
Physical, visual, hearing	0.425(0.379)	0.314(0.420)
Speech impairment	-0.361(0.601)	-0.771(0.632)
Learning disability	0.503(0.175)**	0.162(0.193)
EBD	0.365(0.365)	-0.440(0.437)
Academic engagement		
Liking Maths (Ref. Sometimes likes)		
Always likes Maths		-0.732(0.128)***
Never likes Maths		0.968(0.136)***
Liking Reading (Ref. Sometimes likes)		
Always likes Reading		-0.683(0.117)***
Never likes Reading		0.965(0.171)***
Homework completion (Ref. Always completes)		
Occasionally / regularly does not complete homework		0.288(0.119)**
Peer / Social Engagement		
Liking teacher (Ref. Sometimes likes)		
Always likes teacher		-0.630(0.130)***
Never likes teacher		1.471(0.142)***
SDQ Scale (Ref. Not high risk)		
Peer Sub-scale high risk score		0.262(0.179)
Piers-Harris Self-Concept Scale		
Popularity Sub-scale (low to high)		-0.070(0.022)***
Constant	-3.421(0.180)***	-2.638(0.357)***

Source: McCoy et al. (2012b); **Growing Up in Ireland** *data, 9-year-old cohort.*

***p<.001; **p<.01; *p<.05.

Table 8.3: Multilevel Logistic Regression Model for Emotional Behavioural Disability Identification: Effects of Piers-Harris Score, Gender, Social Background and School Social Mix

	Model 1	Model 2	Model 3
Constant	-0.690*	-2.412*	-2.652*
Piers Harris Score (low to high)			
Score	-0.070*	-0.066*	-0.066*
Male		1.457*	1.473*
Social Class *(Ref. Semi- / unskilled manual)*			
Professional		0.111	0.161
Managerial/Technical		0.278	0.324
Non-Manual		0.098	0.124
Skilled Manual		0.052	0.558
Unknown		0.883*	0.911*
One parent		0.590*	0.538*
Mother's education *(Ref. Lower Secondary)*			
Upper secondary		0.369	0.432*
Non-tertiary		0.115	0.186
Primary degree		-0.263	-0.197
Post-graduate		-0.940*	-0.859
School DEIS Status *(Ref. Non-DEIS)*			
Urban Band 1			0.837*
Urban Band 2			0.005
Rural DEIS			0.062
N	7,545 pupils within 850 schools		

*Source: Banks et al. (2012); **Growing Up in Ireland** data, 9 year cohort*

***p<.001; **p<.01; *p<.05

References

Banks, J. & McCoy, S. (2011). *A Study on the Prevalence of Special Educational Needs*, Trim, Co. Meath: National Council for Special Education.

Banks, J., Shevlin, M. & McCoy, S. (2012). Disproportionality in special education: Identifying children with emotional behavioural difficulties in Irish primary schools, *European Journal of Special Needs Education*, 27, 219-35.

Cambrian, C. & Silvestre, N. (2003). Students with special educational needs in the inclusive classroom: Social integration and self-concept, *European Journal of Special Needs Education, 18,* 197-208.

Carr-Fanning, K., Mc Guckin, C. & Shevlin, M. (2013). Using student voice to escape the spider's web: A methodological approach to de-victimising students with ADHD, *Trinity Education Papers, 2,* 85-112.

Commission of Inquiry on Mental Handicap (1965). *Report,* Dublin: Stationery Office.

Coolahan, J. (2007). *Irish Education: Its History and Structure,* Dublin: Institute of Public Administration.

Cosgrove, J., McKeown, C., Travers, J. Lysaght, Z., Ní Bhroin, O. & Archer, P. (2014). *Educational Experiences and Outcomes for Children with Special Educational Needs. A Secondary Analysis of Data from the Growing Up in Ireland Study,* Trim, Co. Meath: National Council for Special Education.

Croll, P. & Moses, D. (2003). Special educational needs across two decades: Survey evidence from English primary schools, *British Educational Research Journal, 29,* 731-47.

Davis, J.A. (1966). The campus as a frog pond: An application of the theory of relative deprivation to career decisions of college men, *American Journal of Sociology, 72,* 17-31.

De Valenzuela, J.S., Copeland, S.R., Huaqing Qi, C. & Park, P. (2006). Examining educational equity: Revisiting the disproportionate representation of minority students in special education, *Exceptional Children, 72,* 425-41.

Department of Education (1993). *Report of the Special Educational Review Committee (SERC),* Dublin: Stationery Office.

Department of Education and Science (2005). *DEIS: An Action Plan for Educational Inclusion,* Dublin: Stationery Office.

Department of Education and Science (2007). *Inclusion of Students with Special Educational Needs, Post-primary Guidelines,* Dublin: Stationery Office.

Department of Health (1960). *The Problem of the Mentally Handicapped: White Paper,* Dublin: Stationery Office.

Dyson, A. & Gallannuagh, F. (2008). Disproportionality in special needs education in England, *Journal of Special Education, 42,* 36-46.

Dyson, A. & Kozleski, E. (2008). Dilemmas and alternatives in the classification of children with disabilities: New perspectives, in Florian, L. & McLaughlin, M.J. (eds.), *Disability Classification in Education: Issues and Perspectives* (pp.170-90), Thousand Oaks, CA: Corwin Press.

Flood, E. (2013). *Assisting Children with Special Needs: An Irish Perspective,* Dublin: Gill and Macmillan.

Furlong, M.J. & Christenson, S.L. (2008). Engaging students at school and with learning: A relevant construct for all students, *Psychology in the Schools, 45,* 365-368.

Furrer, C. & Skinner, C. (2003). Words can hurt forever, *Educational Leadership, 60,* 18-21.

Glendenning, D. (1999). *Education and the Law,* Dublin: Butterworth Ireland.

Goodman, R. (1997). The strengths and difficulties questionnaire: A research note, *Journal of Child Psychology and Psychiatry,* 38, 581-86.

Griffin, S. & Shevlin, M. (2008). *Responding to Special Educational Needs,* Dublin: Gill and Macmillan.

Hibel, J., Farkas, G. & Morgan, P.L. (2010). Who is placed into special education?, *Sociology of Education, 83,* 312-32.

Hills, J., Brewer, M., Jenkins, S., Lister, R., Lupton, R., Machin, S., Mills, C., Modood, T., Rees, T. & Riddell, S. (2010). *An Anatomy of Economic Inequality in the UK. Report of the National Equality Panel,* London: Government Equalities Office.

Keslair, F. & McNally, S. (2009). *Special Educational Needs in England. Report to the National Equality Panel,* London: London School of Economics.

Koster, M., Pijl, S.J., van Houten, E. & Nakken, H. (2007). The social position and development of pupils with SEN in mainstream Dutch primary schools, *European Journal of Special Needs Education,* 22, 31-46.

Koster, M., Pijl, S.J., Nakken, H. & Van Houten, E. (2010). Social participation of students with special needs in regular primary education in the Netherlands, *International Journal of Disability, Development and Education 57,* 59-75.

MacGiolla Phádraig, B. (2007). Towards inclusion: The development of provision for children with special educational needs in Ireland from 1991 to 2004, *Irish Educational Studies, 26,* 289-300.

McArthur, J., Sharp, S. Kelly, B. & Gaffney, M. (2007). Disabled children negotiating school life: Agency, difference and teaching practice, *International Journal of Children's Rights, 15,* 1-22.

McCoy, S. & Banks, J. (2012). Simply academic? Why children with special educational needs don't like school, *European Journal of Special Needs Education, 27,* 81-97.

McCoy, S., Banks, J. & Shevlin, M. (2012a). School matters: How context influences the identification of different types of special educational needs, *Irish Educational Studies, 32,* 119-138.

McCoy, S., Quail, A. & Smyth, E. (2014). The effects of school social mix: Unpacking the differences, *Irish Educational Studies, 33,* 307-30.

McCoy, S., Smyth, E. & Banks, J. (2012b). *The Primary Classroom: Insights from the Growing Up in Ireland Study,* Dublin: National Council for Curriculum and Assessment / Economic and Social Research Institute.

Murray, C. & Greenberg, M.T. (2001). Relationships with teachers and bonds with school: Social emotional adjustment correlates for children with and without disabilities, *Psychology in the Schools,* 38, 25-41.

Network of Experts in Social Sciences of Education and Training (NESSE) (2012). *Education and Disability / Special Needs*, Brussels: European Commission, Directorate-General for Education and Culture.

Piers, E.V. & Hertzberg, D.S. (2002). *Piers-Harris Children's Self-Concept Scale - Second Edition Manual*, Los Angeles, CA: Western Psychological Services.

Priestley, M. (2001). *Disability and the Life Course: Global Perspectives*, Cambridge: Cambridge University Press.

Riddell, S., Tisdall, K. & Kane, J. (2006). *Literature Review of Educational Provision for Pupils with Additional Support Needs*, Edinburgh: Scottish Executive Social Research.

Rose, D. & Harrison, E. (2009). *Social Class in Europe: An Introduction to the European Socio-Economic Classification*, London: Routledge.

Rose, R. & Shevlin, S. (2010). *Count Me In: Ideas for Actively Engaging Students in Inclusive Classrooms*, London: Jessica Kingsley.

Shevlin, M. (2010). Valuing and learning from young people, in Rose, R. (ed.), *Confronting Obstacles to Inclusion: International Responses to Developing Inclusive Education* (pp.103-22), London: Routledge.

Shevlin, M. & Rose, R. (2005). Listen, hear and learn: Gaining perspectives from young people with special educational needs, in Kaikkonen, L. (ed.), *Jotain Erityistä (Something Special)* (pp.91-102), Jyväskylä: Ammattikorkeakoulu.

Stevens, P. & O'Moore, M. (2009). *Inclusion or Illusion? Educational Provision for Primary School Children with Mild General Learning Disabilities*, Dublin: Blackhall Publishing.

Swan, D. (2000). From exclusion to inclusion, *Frontline, 44*, 23 September, retrieved from: http://frontline-ireland.com/from-exclusion-to-inclusion/.

Thomas, G. & Loxley, A. (2001). *Deconstructing Special Education and Constructing Inclusion*, Milton Keynes: Open University Press.

Travers, J. (2010). Learning support policy for mathematics in Irish primary schools: Equal access but unequal needs, *Irish Educational Studies, 29*, 71-80.

United Nations (1989). *Convention on the Rights of the Child*, Geneva: United Nations.

Van der Veen, I., Smeets, E. & Derriks, M. (2010). Children with special educational needs in the Netherlands: Number, characteristics and school career, *Educational Research, 52*, 15-43.

9: THE EXPERIENCES OF MIGRANT CHILDREN IN IRELAND

Merike Darmody, Frances McGinnity &
Gillian Kingston

Introduction

One of the most dramatic changes since the 1916 Rising has been the transformation of Ireland from a largely homogenous society to one characterised by cultural, linguistic and religious diversity. Ireland has a somewhat unusual migration history from an international perspective, being a country of emigration for most of the 20th century, and then experiencing rapid and sustained growth in immigration from the 1990s onwards, triggered by the (then) economic boom. Initially, inward migration consisted to a large extent of returning Irish emigrants, attracted back by better job prospects, with a smaller number of UK and other European citizens as well as migrants from outside Europe. Following EU accession in 2004, Eastern Europeans came to dominate migrant flows to Ireland. The profile of the immigrant population in Ireland is distinctive in a number of respects:

- The fact that most immigrants arrived in the last couple of decades

- Their relatively high levels of educational qualifications (see below)

- The heterogeneous nature of the population, representing 196 different nationalities and 182 languages (Central Statistics Office, 2012).

Drawing upon *Growing Up in Ireland* data, this chapter looks at how migrant children fare in Ireland, taking academic outcomes and social interaction as indicators of their wellbeing. Academic outcomes are a crucial aspect of wellbeing, since a higher level of education means higher earnings, better health, and a longer life. Likewise, the long-term social and financial costs of educational failure are high (Dustmann & Fabbri, 2005), especially in Ireland where the Leaving Certificate acts as a channel to post-school education and where the financial returns to tertiary education are substantial. In addition, social engagement and social interaction are very important correlates of migrant integration and wellbeing, fostering a sense of belonging in the wider society (Gsir, 2014). Children's involvement in structured social and cultural activities has also been found to enhance their academic development (McCoy *et al.*, 2012). The chapter first sets the scene by taking a closer look at the families of migrant children. It then focuses specifically on how migrant children fare academically and socially, in terms of friendships and involvement in organised activities outside school. National origin is in some ways a new dimension of inequality in Ireland as some migrants or migrant groups carry forward disadvantages experienced in early life through later stages of their lives, often resulting in reduced life chances. Taken together, the indicators presented here give an insight into the academic achievement and social engagement of migrant children in Ireland.

New Irish Families

The number of immigrants tripled between 1999 and 2007 due to the open labour market policy adopted by Ireland in the context of EU accession (McGinnity *et al.*, 2012) and, by 2011, 12 per cent of the population were of a nationality other than Irish (Central Statistics Office, 2012). Reflecting the young age profile of the migrant group, the proportion of births in Ireland to non-Irish mothers also increased – from 16 per cent in 2004 to 23 per cent in 2008, largely remaining at that level since then (Healthcare Pricing Office, 2014). *Growing Up in Ireland* data provide more detailed information on the families within which migrant children are growing up. Defining migrant children is not necessarily straightforward: some studies include only children born abroad but more commonly include children whose parents are migrants (for example, OECD, 2009). For the purposes of this chapter, migrant children are defined as having a mother born outside Ireland, excluding those with Irish ethnicity.

Using this definition, migrant children make up almost 9 per cent of children surveyed at age 9 as part of *Growing Up in Ireland* (in 2008). The largest single group are from the UK (including Northern Ireland), making up over one-third of migrant children; 19 per cent are from Africa; 18 per cent from Eastern Europe; and 10 per cent from Asia. The smallest numbers are from Western Europe (6.6 per cent) and other Western / South American countries (8.8 per cent). In the analyses that follow, this last group is excluded because of its small size and diversity in terms of nationality.

Figure 9.1: Language Spoken with the Child at Home

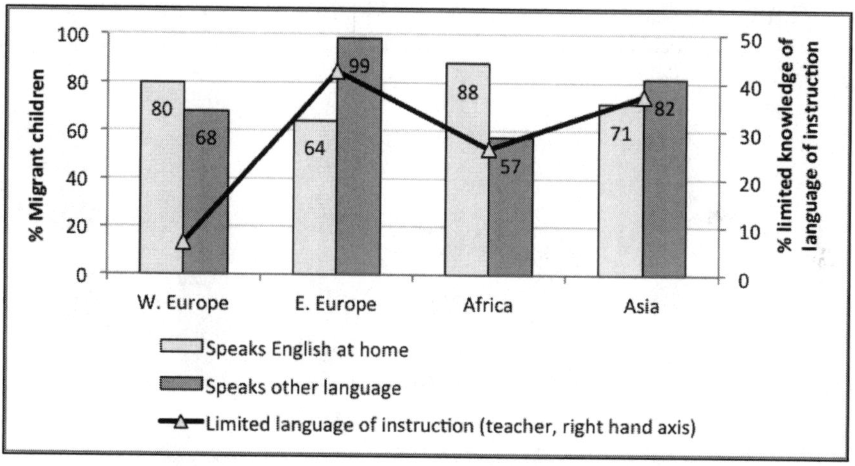

Source: *Growing Up in Ireland* Child Cohort aged 9, weighted data.

Figure 9.1 shows that most parents from outside Ireland spoke English at home to their child, at least some of the time; this was more prevalent among those from African and Western European backgrounds and least common among those from Eastern Europe. This could perhaps be explained by some parents focusing on improving the English language proficiency of their children. In addition, there are now couples of different linguistic origins, who often use English as a language of communication. In households where the mother was not born in Ireland, a range of other languages was spoken, including Polish, Lithuanian and Russian. Almost all Eastern European families spoke another language at home, with lower levels of speaking a language other than English among African families (since, in some African countries, English is an official language). Thus, most migrant families reported speaking both English and another language with their 9-year-old children. In addition, teachers were asked whether 9-year-olds experienced challenges in learning because of limited knowledge of the language of instruction. This was reported for only a small number (7 per cent) of children from Western European backgrounds but for a significant minority (42 per cent) of children of Eastern European backgrounds, in line with the Central Statistics Office (2012) findings on languages spoken in Ireland.

Figure 9.2: Educational Level of Mother, by National Group

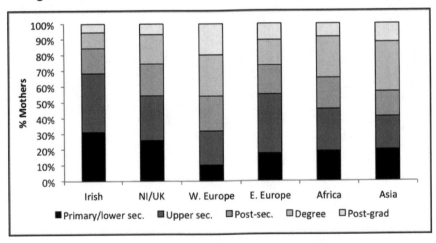

*Source: **Growing Up in Ireland** Child Cohort aged 9, weighted data.*

Mothers with a migrant background tend to be more highly educated than Irish mothers. However, levels of education vary across national groups, with newcomers from Western Europe and Asia more likely to have a degree (undergraduate or post-graduate) (see **Figure 9.2**). This pattern is not surprising, given the reliance on a work permit system for non-EU entrants, the aim of which is to attract highly-skilled workers, mostly to fill positions in sectors like ICT, engineering and medicine. Eastern European mothers tend to have lower levels of education than other migrant groups but their levels are still higher than those among Irish mothers.

Figure 9.3: Educational Expectations of Newcomer Mothers, by National Group

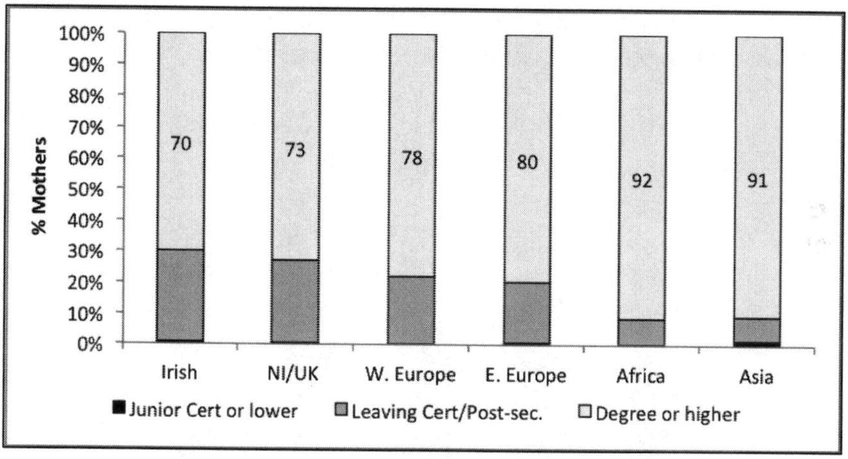

Source: *Growing Up in Ireland* Child Cohort aged 9, weighted data.

Considering the relatively high level of education among the immigrant population, it is not surprising that newcomer parents tend to have high educational expectations for their children (see also Jonsson & Rudolphi, 2011; Relikowski *et al.*, 2009). Striving for upward mobility, many see education as a key factor in achieving this goal. **Figure 9.3** shows that the majority of mothers with migrant backgrounds across all national groups expect their child to go on to third-level education and expectations among migrant mothers, especially from Africa and Asia, are somewhat higher than among Irish mothers. Existing literature has referred to the aspiration-achievement paradox, whereby many migrants with high aspirations are not able to translate it into high achievement. This can be explained, in part, by the social environment and available resources.

Despite being highly qualified, many immigrants work in occupational areas below their skill level and thus receive lower pay (O'Connell & McGinnity, 2008). **Figure 9.4** shows the household income, measured in quintiles (fifth) and adjusted for household size and composition, of migrant families comparing them to Irish households. Income levels among families from the UK are very similar to those for Irish families. Western European families tend to have higher incomes, with over a third in the top income quintile. Eastern European and Asian families tend to have lower incomes than Irish households but the lowest incomes are found among African families, with three-quarters of them in the lowest two quintiles.

Figure 9.4: Household Income (Quintiles), by National Group

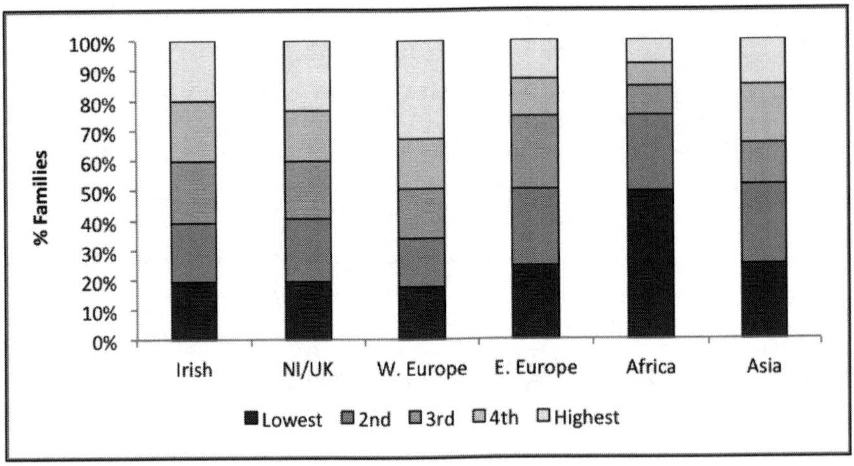

*Source: **Growing Up in Ireland** Child Cohort aged 9, weighted data.*

How Do Migrant Children Fare in Ireland?

Academic outcomes

Increased migration poses new challenges for the education systems of receiving countries. Empirical studies indicate that migrant students are disadvantaged in most educational systems (Portes & Rumbaut, 2005; Portes & Rivas, 2011; Bhattacharyya *et al.*, 2003), but also that countries vary regarding their situation (OECD, 2009). There is now a considerable body of research that focuses on the experiences of migrant children in Ireland (Devine, 2009, 2011; Kitching, 2011; Curry *et al.*, 2011; Darmody *et al.*, 2011a; 2011b). Many of these studies point towards potential institutional barriers. School enrolment policies, for example, tend to favour settled families in the immediate area so migrant students are more likely to attend large urban schools containing a concentration of students from disadvantaged backgrounds and which are less likely to be over-subscribed. Thus, one quarter (25 per cent) of African children attend the most disadvantaged schools (urban DEIS band 1), compared to 9 per cent of Irish children (McGinnity *et al.*, 2015). These schools are located in areas characterised by socio-economic disadvantage and higher levels of unemployment. While migrant students' general experience in the Irish educational system is well-addressed by existing research, very few studies have looked at the academic achievement of migrant children, as such data are not being systematically collected. In assessing their achievement, it is important to take account of the differences outlined above in terms of mother's education and income, among other factors, in order to compare like with like.

Figure 9.5: Differences in Reading Test Scores between Irish and Migrant Children, by National Group, Controlling for a Range of Other Factors

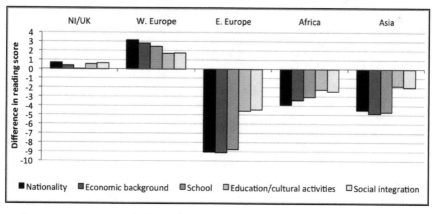

Source: McGinnity et al. *(2015).*

**Figure 9.6: Differences in Mathematics Test Scores
between Irish and Migrant Children, by National
Group, Controlling for a Range of Other Factors**

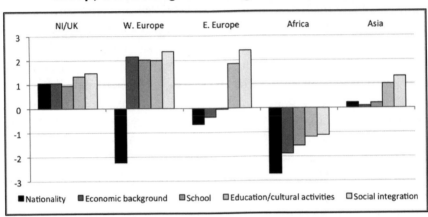

Source: McGinnity et al. (2015).

Figures 9.5 and **9.6**, derived from analyses in McGinnity *et al.* (2015), show the academic outcomes of migrant children in Irish primary schools across two dimensions: reading and mathematics. Standardised tests in English vocabulary and mathematics were administered at age 9 to all participants in the *Growing Up in Ireland* study. The tests in question are linked to the primary school curriculum. Test scores in English reading vary between national groups, though the differences are not large. There is no difference in mean English reading scores between UK and Irish 9-year-olds. For other groups, there are modest differences. The children of Western Europeans have slightly higher English reading scores but these are not significantly different from those of Irish children. Reading test scores are significantly lower among those from Eastern Europe, Asia and Africa, with the largest gap for Eastern Europeans.

Adding background characteristics (duration in Ireland, gender, mother's employment, and financial strain), migrant group differences are maintained, with little change in the scores for Eastern Europeans, which are still around 9 points lower than Irish scores (with a mean of 100). The gap between Irish students and Africans reduces slightly, after controlling for background, as this group reported the highest levels of financial strain. Children from families who have been in Ireland for six or more years tend to achieve higher test scores. The third set of columns takes account of school characteristics (such as school disadvantaged status, denomination, and gender mix). The school attended explains part of the migrant achievement gap, particularly for Africans and also Eastern Europeans. This is in line with international research, which indicates that the socio-economic profile of the school matters substantially in terms of academic achievement (Perry & McConney, 2010).

A greater role in understanding the difference between migrant and Irish children is played by cultural capital – that is, the educational resources of the family (including mother's education, educational expectations of the children, home learning environment, and language problems of the child). Taking account of these factors, the difference between African, Asian and Irish children is no longer significant, and the achievement gap for Eastern European children reduces from 8.8 to 4.6 points. This is largely driven by the prevalence of difficulties in English language proficiency across groups (see **Figure 9.1**); children with limited knowledge of English (as reported by their teacher) achieve 10 points less on average than their peers. The final set of columns takes account of social integration, which explains a small part of the Eastern European achievement gap. Children involved in structured cultural activities outside school obtain higher reading scores, while those with only one friend (or no friends) have lower scores. (These differences in social integration are discussed further in the following subsection.) Even taking account of this large set of factors, reading test scores remain significantly lower among children from Eastern European backgrounds.

Applying the same approach to mathematics performance, a slightly different pattern of results is found (**Figure 9.6**). For mathematics, there is no penalty for the children of Eastern European mothers, even before controls. Western European and Asian children do not differ from their Irish counterparts in their mathematics test scores. There is an initial modest difference between the children of African mothers and Irish children (-2.7 points with a mean of 100), but this disappears once background characteristics, including financial hardship, are taken into account. Further controls in subsequent models add measures of school disadvantage and cultural capital, but do not change this pattern of results. In sum, the evidence on mean differences suggests some differences between Irish and migrant children in English reading and mathematics at age 9, particularly for Eastern Europeans in reading and Africans in mathematics.

Social interaction and leisure participation

This subsection considers two aspects of social interaction among 9-year-old children: size of the friendship group and participation in formal leisure activities. International studies indicate that migrants are generally less likely to participate in cultural and sport activities compared to natives (Henderson & Ainsworth, 2001; Walseth & Fasting, 2003; Stodolska, 1998; Garcia, 2013; Hertting & Karlefors, 2013; Sime & Fox, 2015), although participation in leisure activities may also be a way of making new friends and developing a feeling of belonging to a new country (Kirpitchenko & Mansouri, 2014).

Figure 9.7: Number of Close Friends of the 9-year-old Child, by National Group

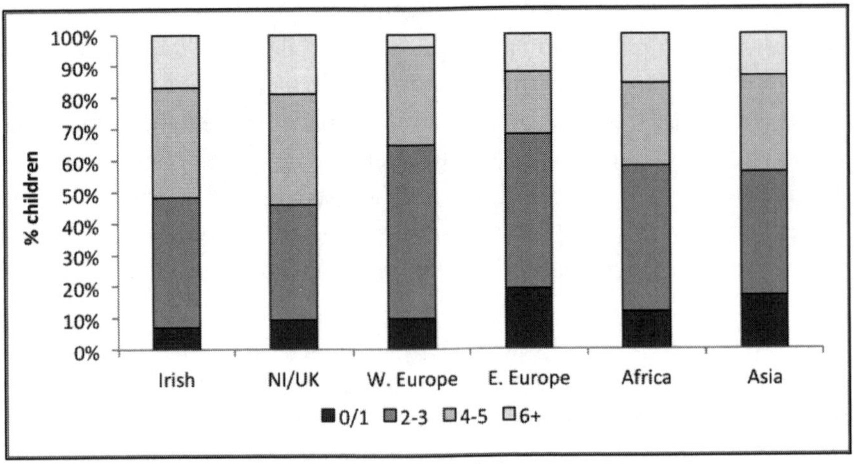

Source: *Growing Up in Ireland* Child Cohort aged 9, weighted data.

When looking at friendship patterns across national groups, the majority of children participating in the *Growing Up in Ireland* study are found to have at least some close friends. The number of close friends differs significantly by national group, with Eastern Europeans more likely than other groups to report that they have fewer friends. Asian children also tend to have fewer friends than their Irish counterparts (**Figure 9.7**). While previous research has indicated that smaller friendship networks may be explained by the lack of English language proficiency among some immigrants (see Smyth *et al.*, 2009), additional analyses indicate that differences in the number of friends by national group is not explained by having limited English. This indicates that the reasons for low participation levels may lie elsewhere.

Table 9.1: Leisure Participation, by National Group, Children Aged 9

	Ireland	NI / UK	Western Europe	Eastern Europe	Africa	Asia
Sport / fitness club	76.5%	74.8%	78.0%	40.2%	61.5%	38.5%
Cultural activities	47.8%	47.5%	62.0%	30.5%	37.8%	26.0%
Youth club	7.2%	6.1%	4.0%	0.8%	10.5%	1.3%
Scouts / Guides / Boys Brigade / Girls Brigade	13.4%	16.9%	8.0%	7.6%	7.7%	6.5%

*Source: **Growing Up in Ireland** Child Cohort aged 9, weighted data.*

Table 9.1 shows the participation levels of 9-year-old children in different organised activities and whether this varies by national group. It is evident that formal participation in sport and fitness activities is popular across all groups. However, there are significant differences by national group, with primary school children of Irish, UK and Western European origin more likely to belong to a sport or fitness club compared to Asian and Eastern European students. The sports involvement of African children is greater than that of Asian and Eastern European students but lower than for Irish children. Significant differences can also be observed in participation in cultural activities; while a considerable proportion of Western European children engage in these activities, only 26 per cent of Asians and 31 per cent of Eastern Europeans do so. Participation in groups such as Scouts shows a different pattern – participation is now led by children from the United Kingdom (17 per cent) and from Ireland (13 per cent). The lowest participation could be observed in youth clubs; this time slightly more African children (11 per cent) took part in youth club activities compared to other groups. The findings highlight differences in participation in sport and cultural activities between Eastern European and Asian children *versus* other 9-year-olds.

Figure 9.8: Frequency of Playing Sport, by National Group, Children Aged 9

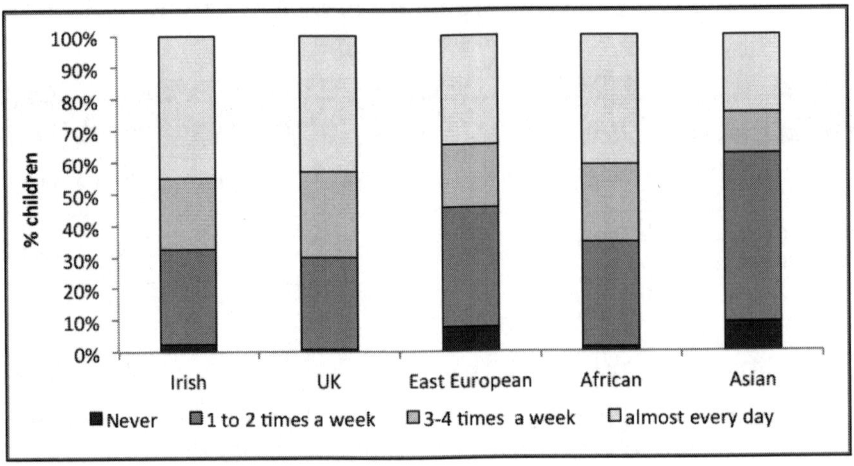

*Source: **Growing Up in Ireland** Child Cohort aged 9, weighted data.*

Taking account of all sports participation (club- and non-club-based) showed that 44 per cent of 9-year-olds play sport almost every day (**Figure 9.8**). Asian (9 per cent) and Eastern European children (8 per cent) were more likely to report never playing sport, with the highest involvement among Irish and British children. The three most frequently given reasons for not participating in sports included not liking team games (29 per cent); respondents thinking they are not good at games (18 per cent); and having no opportunities to play (16 per cent). Due to the small numbers in some groups, it was not possible to distinguish differences between national groups regarding reasons for not playing sport. It could be, however, that some migrant children face barriers to participation, such as cultural differences and lack of facilities. The fact that the majority of organised cultural and sports activities among this group require payment could also explain lower participation among lower income migrant groups.

Table 9.2: Logistic Regression Models of Participation in Sport and Cultural Activities, in Children Aged 9 (Odds Ratios)

	Model 1 (Raw differences)	Model 2 (Language and date of arrival)	Model 3 (Gender, mother's education, household income)
Sports participation *Immigrant Group* (Ref. Irish)			
UK	0.871	0.819	0.835
Western European	1.380	1.424	1.069
East European	0.250***	0.251***	0.240***
African	0.424***	0.402***	0.598*
Asian	0.210***	0.215***	0.181***
Cultural participation *Immigrant Group* (Ref. Irish)			
UK	1.015	0.911	0.804
Western European	1.331	1.496	1.364
East European	0.385***	0.444**	0.382**
African	0.691	0.659	0.647
Asian	0.435***	0.516*	0.442*

In order to compare like with like, logistic regression analysis was undertaken to examine the impact of national group on the likelihood of children participating in sport and cultural activities, taking account of other socio-demographic factors (see **Table 9.2**). Rates of participation in structured sports activities are similar for Irish, UK and Western European children. Eastern European, Asian and, to some extent, African children are much less likely to participate in sports activities than the Irish group. These differences remain even when socio-economic indicators are taken into account. Neither language spoken at home nor duration of time in Ireland is associated with sports participation and the finding may perhaps be explained by different sporting traditions across countries or by lack of awareness of local facilities.

Eastern European and Asian groups are less likely to participate in structured cultural activities than the Irish group. Children who have been resident in the country for more than six years and those whose parents speak (at least some) English with them at home are more likely to participate than others. Some of the differences in participation among Eastern European and Asian children are explained by social background. However, differences in participation remain for these national groups, even taking account of maternal education and household income. Thus, Eastern European and Asian children are less involved in structured out-of-school activities, both sports and cultural pursuits, while African children are less involved in sports.

Conclusion

In the last two decades Ireland has undergone a rapid transformation towards greater cultural and linguistic diversity. Migrants in Ireland are largely well-educated and hold high educational expectations for their children. It could be that parents with high qualifications wish their children to aim high in order to avoid downward mobility. Migrants are often positively-selected groups who are willing to migrate in order to access better opportunities for their children (Kao & Tienda, 1998). Even if the first generation of migrants does not hold high qualifications, they may hope for an improved situation for their children. Despite 'migrant optimism', children from migrant backgrounds tend to be disadvantaged by the education systems in host countries. The situation tends to vary across national groups, with some groups experiencing greater disadvantage, especially in terms of income, resources and access to facilities including schools. The disadvantage occurs, at least in part, due to the devaluation of the human, cultural and linguistic capital of the new arrivals. In fact, belonging to certain national groups could be seen to constitute a new form of inequality in Ireland. This chapter draws on *Growing Up in Ireland* data to look at two dimensions of wellbeing among migrant children – academic outcomes and social integration – factors that are key to their future life-chances.

Immigration is often driven by the wish to improve one's socio-economic situation. First-generation (voluntary) migrants expect their children to do well in host schools to ensure upward mobility. However, poor proficiency in the language of instruction may impair the academic success of even the most motivated and ambitious student. English – the language of instruction in the vast majority of Irish schools – is a mother tongue to only a minority of migrant students. The chapter has shown that the lowest levels of reading achievement among 9-year-olds are found among Eastern European children. This is in line with the figures that show that adult arrivals from some countries in Eastern Europe tend to have lower levels of English language proficiency (Central Statistics Office, 2012), compared to other migrants. African and Asian children also have lower reading scores than Irish children but this gap is accounted for by differences in educational resources and in English language difficulties (as reported by the child's teacher). In contrast, children whose mothers are from the UK or Western Europe resemble Irish children in their reading performance. International studies show mixed results in maths achievement across national groups (Hastedt, 2016). In Ireland, differences are found in maths achievement across national groups, with the lower scores found among African children accounted for by their greater levels of financial strain. While overall differences between Irish and migrant children in achievement in English reading and mathematics are relatively modest, they may lead to cumulative disadvantage as children move through the educational system (Darmody *et al.*, 2012; Darmody *et al.*, 2011a, 2011b; Jacobs, 2013). Educational achievement is a key indicator of labour market success. Yet not all children have the same chance of success. School-based and home-based efforts to support migrant children's overall academic progress are critical to supporting their later outcomes. When considering academic outcomes, it is important to remember that immigrant children differ by their country of origin and their socio-economic background. One must also be aware that not all first-generation migrants can be characterised in terms of 'migrant optimism'. The situation can be different for those undergoing involuntary migration or who arrive into a new country as unaccompanied minors.

While academic attainment is important, students spend only part of their time in schools, highlighting the importance of social integration and interactions. Social interaction provides a variety of protective functions – a sense of belonging, emotional support, and a source of information. While this is important for all individuals in society, the protective functions provided by social interaction are of particular importance for newly-arrived migrant families and their children. This may be problematic for some migrants, as migration can be transient whereby people often move from one country to another and need to adapt to new systems, networks and make new friends. In terms of close friends, Eastern Europeans have the smallest friendship networks while African and Asian children also have fewer friends than their Irish counterparts. The extent to which social contact is desired, however, may vary across groups: while some desire outward engagement as well as engagement with those from shared cultural backgrounds, for others this can be more complex, depending on their place of birth, migrant status and religion (Kirpitchenko & Mansouri, 2014). Migrant children can often find themselves as an 'out group', especially if they do not share common interests or activities with native children.

This chapter has explored how primary school children from different national groups spend their free time, an area previously under-researched in Ireland. While sport (in its generic sense) is popular across national groups, there are differences in participation rates with children from Eastern Europe, Africa and Asia less likely to engage in sport. This is in line with international studies showing lower participation in sport among some immigrant groups. The reasons behind low participation rates among migrants are varied. For adult migrants, these may include time constraints, language issues, being unfamiliar with the cultural context of the host country, insufficient access to known and desired forms of recreational activity, and experiences with discrimination. Factors that impact on the participation of Irish primary school children include parental level of education, family income and gender, but Asian, African and Eastern European children differ in their participation from Irish children, even after accounting for differences in these factors. Cultural participation shows broadly similar patterns, with lower levels of involvement among Asian and Eastern European children. Again, family background influences participation, but cross-national differences remain substantial even when this is taken into account. The findings suggest the need for further research to unpack the reasons for this variation in social engagement, especially given the role of out-of-school activities in boosting within-school learning. The longitudinal nature of the *Growing Up in Ireland* study enables future research to explore whether these differences in social engagement and academic achievement are maintained, reduced or exacerbated over time, over the transition to second-level education and beyond.

In sum, the findings point to the heterogeneity of the immigrant population in Ireland and the significant variation between national groups in child outcomes, suggesting that national background may be a new form of inequality within Irish society.

References

Bhattarcharya, G., Ison, L. & Blair, M. (2003). *Minority Ethnic Attainment and Participation in Education and Training: The Evidence*, London: Department for Education and Skills.

Central Statistics Office (2012). *Population and Migration Estimates: April 2012*, Cork: Central Statistics Office.

Curry, P., Gilligan, R., Garratt, L. & Scholtz, J. (2011). *Where To from Here? Inter-ethnic Relations among Children in Ireland*, Dublin: The Liffey Press.

Darmody, M., Byrne, D. & McGinnity, F. (2012). Cumulative disadvantage? Educational careers of migrant students in Irish secondary schools, *Race Ethnicity Education, 17*, 129-51.

Darmody, M., Smyth, E., Byrne, D. & McGinnity, F. (2011b). New school, new system: The experiences of immigrant students in Irish schools, in Bekerman, Z. & Geisen, T. (eds.), *International Handbook of Migration, Minorities and Education: Understanding Cultural and Social Differences in Processes of Learning* (pp.283-300), New York: Springer.

Darmody, M., Tyrrell, N. & Song, S. (eds.) (2011a). *The Changing Faces of Ireland: Exploring the Lives of Immigrant and Ethnic Minority Children*, Rotterdam: Sense.

Devine, D. (2009). Mobilising capitals? Migrant children's negotiation of their everyday lives in school, *British Journal of Sociology of Education, 30*, 521-35.

Devine, D. (2011). Securing migrant children's educational wellbeing: Perspective of policy and practice in Irish schools, in Darmody, M., Tyrrell, N. & Song, S. (eds.), *The Changing Faces of Ireland: Exploring the Lives of Immigrant and Ethnic Minority Children* (pp.73-88), Rotterdam: Sense.

Dustmann, C. & Fabbri, F. (2005). Immigrants in the British labour market, *Fiscal Studies, 26*, 423-70.

Garcia, R. (2013). The George Butler lecture: Social justice and leisure: The usefulness and uselessness of research, *Journal of Leisure Research, 45*, 7-22.

Gsir, S. (2014). *Social Interactions between Immigrants and Host Country Populations: A Country-of-origin Perspective*, San Domenico di Fiesole (FI) Italy: European University Institute.

Hastedt, D. (2016). *Mathematics Achievement of Immigrant Students*, Cham, Switzerland: Springer.

Healthcare Pricing Office (2014). *Perinatal Statistics Report 2013*, Dublin: Health Service Executive.

Henderson, K.A. & Ainsworth, B. (2001). Researching leisure and physical activity with women of colour: Issues and emerging questions, *Leisure Sciences, 23*, 21-23.

Hertting, K. & Karlefors, I. (2013). Sport as a context for integration: Newly-arrived immigrant children in Sweden drawing sporting experiences, *International Journal of Humanities and Social Science, 3*(18), retrieved from http://www.ijhssnet.com/journals/Vol_3_No_18_October_2013/4.pdf.

Jacobs, D. (2013). *The Educational Integration of Migrants: What Is the Role of Sending Society Actors and Is There a Transnational Educational Field?*, San Domenico di Fiesole (FI) Italy: European University Institute.

Jonsson, J.O. & Rudolphi, F. (2011). Weak performance – strong determination: School achievement and educational choice among children of immigrants in Sweden, *European Sociological Review, 27*, 487-508.

Kao, G. & Tienda, M. (1998). Educational aspirations of minority youth, *American Journal of Education, 106*, 349-84.

Kirpitchenko, L. & Mansouri, F. (2014). Social engagement among migrant youth: Attitudes and meanings, *Social Inclusion, 2*(2), 17-27.

Kitching, K. (2011). Interrogating the changing inequalities constituting 'popular', 'deviant' and 'ordinary' subjects of school / subculture in Ireland: Moments of new migrant student recognition, resistance and recuperation, *Race, Ethnicity and Education, 14*, 293-311.

McCoy, S., Quail, A. & Smyth, E. (2012). *Influences on 9-year olds' learning: Home, school and community*, Dublin: Department of Children and Youth Affairs.

McGinnity, F., Darmody, M. & Murray, A. (2015). *Academic Achievement among Immigrant Children in Irish Primary Schools*, ESRI Working Paper No. 512, Dublin: Economic and Social Research Institute.

McGinnity, F., Quinn, E., Kingston, G. & O'Connell, P. (2012). *Annual Monitoring Report on Integration 2011*, Dublin: The Integration Centre and Economic and Social Research Institute.

O'Connell, P. & McGinnity, F. (2008). *Immigrants at Work: Ethnicity and Nationality in the Irish Labour Market*, Dublin: Economic and Social Research Institute.

OECD (2009). *Reviews of Migrant Education, Ireland,* Paris: Organization for Economic Cooperation and Development.

Perry, L. & McConney, A. (2010). School socio-economic composition and student outcomes in Australia: Implications for educational policy, *Australian Journal of Education, 54,* 72-85.

Portes, A. & Rivas, A. (2011). The adaptation of migrant children, *The Future of Children,* 21(1), 219-46.

Portes, A. & Rumbaut, R.G. (2005). Introduction: The second generation and the Children of Immigrants longitudinal study, *Ethnic and Racial Studies, 28,* 983-99.

Relikowski, I., Schneider, T. & Blossfeld, H.P. (2009). Primary and secondary effects of social origin in migrant and native families at the transition to the tracked German school system, in Cherkaoui, M. & Hamilton, P. (eds.), *Raymond Boudon: A Life in Sociology* (Vol. 3, pp.149-70), Oxford: The Bardwell Press.

Sime, D. & Fox, R. (2015). Migrant children, social capital and access to services post-migration: Transitions, negotiations and complex agencies, *Children & Society, 29,* 524-34.

Smyth, E., Darmody, M., McGinnity, F. & Byrne, D. (2009). *Adapting to Diversity: Irish Schools and Newcomer Students,* Dublin: Economic and Social Research Institute.

Stodolska, M. (1998). Assimilation and leisure constraints: Dynamics of constraints on leisure in immigrant populations, *Journal of Leisure Research, 30,* 521-51.

Walseth, K. & Fasting, K. (2003). Islam's view on physical activity and sport: Egyptian women interpreting Islam, *International Review for the Sociology of Sport, 38,* 45-60.

10: SOCIAL VARIATION IN CHILD HEALTH & DEVELOPMENT: A LIFE-COURSE APPROACH

Richard Layte & Cathal McCrory

Introduction

Research has consistently shown that groups that are disadvantaged in terms of their income, occupational position or level of education tend to have poorer health and a shorter life expectancy. The distribution of health follows a distinctive pattern, with those at the bottom of the socio-economic spectrum being in the worst health, those at the top enjoying the best health, and those in the middle having better health than those at the bottom but less good health compared with those at the top. This pattern has come to be known as the social gradient in health. The gradient is apparent in early infancy and extends through childhood and adolescence into adulthood (Chen, 2004) and old age (Huisman *et al.*, 2003, 2004). Gradients are found irrespective of whether education, income, social class, race, ethnicity or a large number of other socio-economic indicators are examined, and are evident even in countries where universal healthcare coverage exists (Adler & Newman, 2002).

Indeed, so ubiquitous is the association between social position and health that it has been referred to as a 'fundamental' cause of disease (Adler & Newman, 2002; Link & Phelan, 1995) in the sense that, almost irrespective of the cause of disease or death over time and place, the socially-disadvantaged always have worse health and mortality patterns. Worryingly, despite advances in medical care and treatment, the magnitude of these differences does not appear to be reducing over time (Link & Phelan, 1995; Mackenbach *et al.*, 2015) and there is even reason to suspect that the 'Great Recession' may actually serve to amplify inequalities in health between the richest and poorest members of our society (Suhrcke & Stuckler, 2012).

Over time, research findings have increasingly suggested that adult social inequalities in health may actually reflect processes and exposures that occurred much earlier in the life-course (Kuh & Ben Shlomo, 2004; Davey-Smith, 2003), perhaps even in the womb. Adult disease may actually reflect developmental processes that shape individuals' growth and development without necessarily producing illness or overt symptoms, until old age. Nonetheless, these developmental differences can be clearly evident in the physical growth, psychological development and social and educational wellbeing of the child.

In this chapter, we first outline three different explanations that have been put forward to explain the link between social disadvantage and health. We then present evidence of social variation in children's health and development in the early years of life before setting out a number of analyses carried out using data from the *Growing Up in Ireland* Study to illustrate life-course processes.

Three Alternative Explanations

Three general models have been put forward to explain the link between social disadvantage and health. The 'critical periods' model holds that there are certain periods, during which the effects of family environment shape health, that may be particularly important. For example, the 'fetal origins' hypothesis proposes that child experience of deprivation in the womb can lead to fundamental physiological adaptations that are irreversible and may predispose to disease risk in later life (Barker, 1994).

The 'accumulation' model, on the other hand, holds that it is cumulative exposure to adverse circumstances across the life-course that is responsible for the social gradient in health outcomes in adulthood. In this model, adverse circumstances 'chip away' at the health and wellbeing of individuals, often over periods of years rather than depending upon the individual being vulnerable to change during a 'critical period'. As well as accumulation through time, the accumulation of risk can also refer to the way that risk factors tend to 'cluster' around particular individuals or groups.

This model has been formally set out by Michael Grossman (Grossman, 1972) as the concept of 'health capital', which posits a process of health capital accumulation and erosion akin to financial processes of investment and depletion, although the accumulation hypothesis literature has built up a more nuanced picture that suggests that some deficits cannot necessarily be made up for with subsequent investments. Some researchers view the social gradient in health as arising primarily from differences in resources that then influence the quality of material circumstances, producing physiological wear and tear (for example, housing quality, environmental safety, dietary quality, etc.). Meanwhile, others see the accumulation model as driven by psychosocial processes, assuming that those growing up in more disadvantaged households are exposed to a greater number of stressors over the life-course (which again results from low levels of resources), resulting in greater 'wear and tear' on physiological systems *via* a 'stress response' – specifically the hypothalamic-pituitary-adrenal (HPA) axis and the sympathetic-adrenal-medullary (SAM) axis. The HPA axis has been the subject of a great deal of research showing that the chronic activation of these systems can compromise the efficiency of function of these important signalling systems, leaving the body susceptible to disease (Dowd *et al.*, 2009).

Why Do We Care about Social Variation in Child Health and Development?

The *Growing Up in Ireland* study has the dual objective of providing a full picture of development of children in Ireland that can then be used to improve Irish public policy. Along with psychological and educational development, the study was strongly focused from the beginning on the health of children in Ireland and variations in this. For better or for worse, children vary in manifold ways and some will develop conditions, from birth or in infancy, that will have life-long consequences. Where these conditions are the consequence of genetic fate or random chance, we tend to seek solutions but accept that many are, at least at this time, unavoidable. This acceptance tends not to be the case where variation in health and wellbeing among children is related to the child's environment or other factors that are, at least in principle, modifiable, like the influence of the social and economic position of parents or the place or group to which they belong. Where inequalities appear to stem from these 'modifiable' causes, there is far less agreement that this is an acceptable situation or one that we should ignore. In fact, most people tend to believe that this situation is inequitable and that children's health and wellbeing should not depend on who their parents are, where the effect of parental background is modifiable. By identifying variations in child health and the factors associated with this, policy-makers will be in a better position to target the causes of the variation using the public policy tools available both to improve quality of life and to reduce inequality.

The third and final model exploring the link between social disadvantage and health is the 'health selection' model. Although evidence suggests that children from poorer families are more likely to experience poor health and that early disadvantage may prime the body for chronic illness in adulthood, research tends to assume that the direction of causality is from social status and material conditions to health rather than the reverse. Another body of evidence, generally referred to as 'health selection', reverses the direction of causality and explores the influence of poor health on later socio-economic status. There are two variants of this literature. The first, often referred to as 'drift', posits that those in poor health move from more to less advantaged social positions as poor health impacts on labour force participation, income and living standards (Case et al., 2005; Haas, 2008). The second variant, often known as 'stunting', argues that poor health and wellbeing in childhood and adolescence can adversely impact on cognitive and educational development and the child's accumulation of human capital, thereby lowering their socio-economic trajectory into adulthood (Palloni & Milesi, 2006; Palloni et al., 2009). The process of health selection can be straightforward but it can also operate recursively through feedback loops, with poor early health leading to the accumulation of fewer resources / exposure to adverse conditions and this then leading to the development of further unhealthy states.

Cohort studies like *Growing Up in Ireland* have proven to have a number of advantages when studying these life-course processes. Cohort studies are well suited to establishing the prevalence and the natural course of disease as the temporal sequence linking cause and effect can be explicitly tested and competing explanations ruled out. Indeed, part of the motivation and rationale for prospective studies is that they shed light on longitudinal processes (sensitive periods, transitions, accumulation and trajectories) that are not possible when using cross-sectional or case control designs. Cohort studies also tend to be broad and omnibus in nature, collecting information at the social, behavioural, biological, and increasingly, the genetic level; this lets researchers look at the complex interactions between factors, how they are affected by, and in turn may affect, social and economic position and health over time.

Social Inequalities in Health among Irish Children

Data from the *Growing Up in Ireland* study show that Ireland, just like other countries, has a great deal of variation in child health across groups defined by the occupational position, income or education of the parents. For example, **Figure 10.1** shows the proportion of children at age 3 and age 9 whose parents report that they have a long-standing illness (a chronic condition), grouped according to the household's income group from highest to lowest. This shows that reported chronic illness is lower at age 9 across the groups. This is a common pattern as children tend to grow out of many early acute and chronic illnesses as they enter middle childhood leading to less healthcare use, although the pattern is somewhat reversed as children enter adolescence. For both age groups, children in the lowest income group have the highest rates of chronic illness and the extent of the relationship appears to increase between age 3 and age 9.[9] This latter finding of increasing inequalities as the child ages is a common finding in health research among children

---

[9]   We do not show this breakdown by child sex but research shows that the social variation in reported illness is stronger for girls than for boys.

and is one hint that the accumulation model of life-course inequalities in health has some veracity. It also reflects greater sensitivity to, and thus reporting of, chronic disease among higher income / educated parents early in the child's life.

Figure 10.1: Proportion of Parents Reporting Child Has a 'Long-standing' Health Condition at Age 3 and Age 9, by Household Income Group

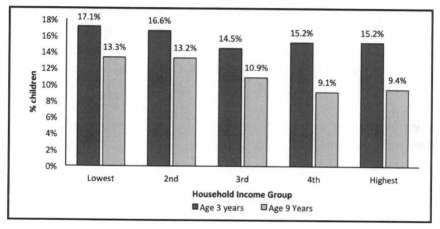

Figure 10.2: Proportion of Children with 'Low Birth Weight' (<2500g), by Household Income Group

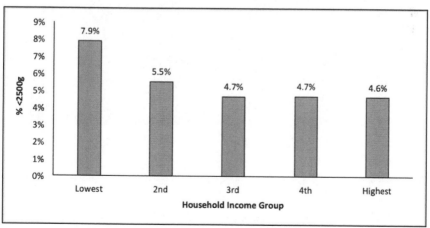

Another stark example of health inequalities relates to social variation in the child's birth weight. As **Figure 10.2** shows, the risk that children will have a very low birth weight (<2500g) falls as household income increases. Children born to mothers in the lowest income group are 42 per cent more likely to be born light compared to those in the highest income group.

Low birth weight may not be a problem if the child grows quickly, catches up with the weight of their peers who were heavier and shows no lasting impact. Whilst evidence shows that the children do catch up in terms of weight status, **Figure 10.3** shows that low birth weight does have consequences for the child. Low birth weight children are five times more likely to fail the developmental tests for communication and gross motor skills when measured at age 9 months. If such deficits subsequently diminish later in childhood, this may not be a serious issue but *Growing Up in Ireland* data also show that, even at age 9, children who were born light score significantly lower on standardised reading and maths tests (Layte & McCrory, 2012).

Figure 10.3: Proportion of Children Failing the 'Ages and Stages Questionnaire' (ASQ) Developmental Tests at Age 9 Months, by Child Birth Weight and ASQ Domain

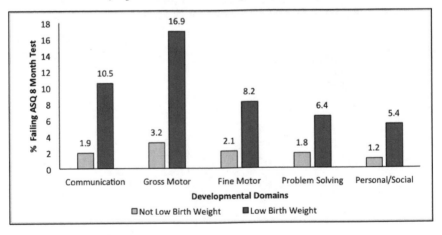

Analysis of the younger cohort of children in the *Growing Up in Ireland* study at age 9 months shows that the most important determinant of birth weight, and particularly low birth weight, was the extent to which the mother smoked in pregnancy. Comparison of exposure to smoke during pregnancy for the younger and older cohorts showed that the prevalence of smoking had fallen dramatically over time from 28 per cent in the late 1990s to 18 per cent in 2007. Yet, whilst the prevalence of smoking in pregnancy fell in the last decade for all groups, low income women remained almost 8 times more likely to smoke during pregnancy (and after) than their high income peers (Layte & McCrory, 2015). Why should this be so? Often smoking is perceived as a 'lifestyle choice' but analysis of the *Growing Up in Ireland* data shows, in line with research from other countries, that smoking in pregnancy is strongly associated with maternal depression and anxiety as well as markers of deprivation and social isolation (Layte & McCrory, 2015). It appears that smoking among mothers in the *Growing Up in Ireland* study should be explained more by the mental health of the woman rather than as a proactive lifestyle choice or personal indulgence.

Smoking in Pregnancy – A 'Critical Period' Effect on Child Development?

Smoking in pregnancy is the most important determinant of low birth weight in developed countries but there is now increasing evidence that it is also associated with the child's longer-term physical and behavioural development. A number of international studies also now suggest that smoking in pregnancy is associated with an increased risk of childhood behavioural problems, particularly conduct problems and attention deficit and hyperactivity disorder. Evidence has already shown that exposure to nicotine leads to heightened tremors and startles and to more irritability in early infancy. Results from the Millennium Cohort Study in the UK (Hutchinson *et al.*, 2010) and the Early Childhood Longitudinal Study in the US (Boutwell & Beaver, 2010) have also found that foetal exposure to cigarette smoke is associated with a significantly higher risk of behavioural problems in later childhood. Animal experiments show that exposure to cigarette smoke can alter brain development during early pregnancy and studies comparing brain scans of children who were or were not exposed to cigarette smoke in pregnancy have confirmed this relationship (Jauniaux & Burton, 2007). This suggests that exposure to smoke during pregnancy has an effect on the brain during a 'critical period' of development, which then has longer-term effects on the child and their behaviour.

However, as noted above, smoking during pregnancy is also strongly associated with maternal social disadvantage and deprivation, which are themselves independently associated with behavioural problems among children through other processes (Conger *et al.*, 1992). **Figure 10.4** shows the relationship between smoking in pregnancy and the prevalence of child behavioural problems by social class as found in the *Growing Up in Ireland* study for children aged 9 in the first wave of the Child Cohort.

Figure 10.4: Proportion Defined as 'Having Child Behavioural Problem' at Age 9, by Social Class Group and Maternal Smoking in Pregnancy

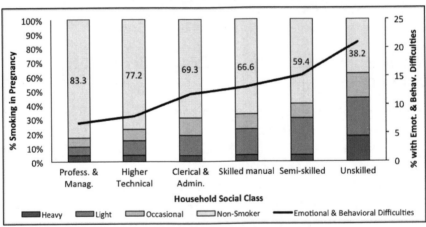

The problem of separating the direct, causal impact of exposure to tobacco smoke *in utero* from the correlated, but actually unrelated, impact of deprivation on child behaviour presents a real challenge for researchers. It would not be ethical to use what is considered the 'gold standard' approach to such analytical problems in scientific research: to construct an experiment where children are randomly allocated to an intervention (which here is exposure to smoke *in utero*) or not so that the two groups of children are identical apart from the fact that one group received the intervention and the other did not. Instead we adopt an analytical strategy based on comparing children's behaviours (reported by both parents and teachers) between women who are matched on a large number of different factors, including measures of deprivation, but who differ in terms of whether they smoked in pregnancy. Importantly, *Growing Up in Ireland* collected information on the mother's *level* of smoking in pregnancy and this provides us with an important additional tool with which to corroborate the causal relationship between exposure to cigarette smoke in the womb and behavioural problems at age 9. If the strength of the relationship between smoking and behavioural problems increases with the level of maternal smoking, this is more persuasive than a simple association (it provides what is known as a 'dose-response' relationship). The full outcome of this study can be found in McCrory & Layte (2012).

Figure 10.5: Mean Difference in the Percentage of 9-year-olds Scoring above the 90th Percentile on 'Conduct Problems' and 'Attention Problems' (SDQ), by Level of Maternal Smoking During Pregnancy (Teachers' Report), Adjusting for Other Factors

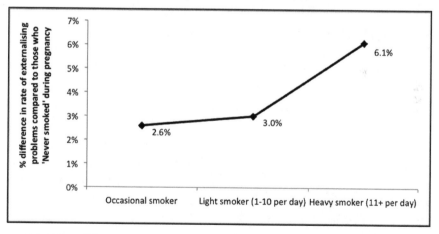

Note: Mean difference between exposed and non-exposed children (see McCrory & Layte, 2012, for details).

As **Figure 10.5** shows, the difference in the risk of the child having behavioural problems (such as overly emotional reactions, conduct disorder or hyperactivity) between children whose mothers smoked and those who did not increases as the number of cigarettes that the mother smoked on a daily basis increased. This is very persuasive evidence that maternal smoking during a critical period of brain development influences the child's behaviour. Moreover, it also provides a partial explanation for the higher rates of behavioural problems among children from more disadvantaged households found from ages 3 upward in a number of studies, including the Millennium Cohort (from the UK) and *Growing Up in Ireland*.

This study is also a good example of the broader importance of critical period effects in shaping subsequent health and wellbeing, often across the life-course. In the *Growing Up in Ireland* study we are currently able to follow children to age 13 but we will have to wait a number of years before we can see whether these 'critical period' factors continue to affect the child into adulthood. This need for data on the same children over an extended period is one of the reasons why there have been comparatively few studies of life-course effects until recently. However, some studies based on records gathered in the past have begun to show the life-long consequence of early life exposure to disadvantage. For example, Dutch researchers (see Roseboom *et al.*, 2006, 2011) have followed the health of the cohort of children who were conceived at the time of, or shortly before, the 'Dutch Hunger Winter' of 1944. During this period, the retreating German army cut off food supplies to the Netherlands, leading to widespread famine and increased mortality. Official daily rations for the adult population were 1,000 calories per day during the crisis, and although pregnant women were entitled to some additional provision, at the peak of the famine these additional calories could no longer be guaranteed (Roseboom *et al.*, 2011). Women who were exposed to these famine conditions were in different trimesters of their pregnancy at the time so this natural experiment afforded researchers the opportunity to examine trimester-specific effects of foetal malnutrition on the subsequent health and development of affected children when they were followed up in later life. Subsequent research has shown that children exposed to this famine in the womb were more likely to develop glucose intolerance, more coronary heart disease, high blood pressure and worse cognitive decline in older age than individuals born both before and after, even though the famine ended in early 1945 and these people became part of one of the most affluent societies in the world (Roseboom *et al.*, 2006; de Rooij *et al.*, 2010). This is clear evidence that, irrespective of later experience, particular experiences at a crucial time in development can have consequences much later in life.

Accumulating Risks for Obesity and Overweight

There is now strong evidence that the prevalence of overweight and obesity among children in Ireland has increased in recent decades. Obesity is one of the leading causes of preventable morbidity and mortality and evidence suggests that obese children are very likely to become obese adults with all of the attendant health risks that this brings. When measured in 2007, one-quarter of children aged 9 in the *Growing Up in Ireland* study were overweight and about 5 per cent obese. Worryingly, when measured in 2010, around the same proportions were overweight and obese among a younger cohort of children aged 3.

The last section showed that exposure to a risk factor at a particular point in a child's development can have long-term consequences, even if the exposure stops shortly afterwards. On the other hand, risk factors can accumulate over time to produce poor health later in life, sometimes in adulthood. A good example of this is the individual's risk of overweight and obesity. Simplistically, a person's weight is the result of the balance of energy inputs in the form of food and drink and energy outputs in terms of level of physical exercise. Some individuals will use energy and store excess energy (as fat) more efficiently than others for a range of reasons and these processes will vary for the same individual over time. Even for individuals who are predisposed to weight gain, however, change does not occur overnight and the emergence of obesity tends to be the result of behaviours over an extended period, often a period of years. In this sense, the development of obesity is the result of an 'accumulation process' where the 'drip, drip, drip' of excess energy intake leads to the accumulation of excess weight. As suggested earlier, accumulation of risk can also occur because of the clustering of different risk factors around the same individual. Whilst one risk factor may not produce a poor outcome, the cumulative effect of the clustered risks does produce poor health outcomes overall. The *Growing Up in Ireland* study provides us with an opportunity to study these processes in children, as it includes a measure of the child's height and weight from birth plus repeated measures of important risk factors.

As is often the case with health risks, a child's risk of overweight and obesity is related to the socio-economic position of their parents. The children of unskilled manual parents are 65 per cent more likely to be obese at age 3 than the children of professional parents. We have already seen that children from more disadvantaged households are lighter at birth, on average, than other children, so it is rather surprising that these children grow to have a higher overall risk of child obesity. **Figure 10.6** gives the absolute difference in weight between the children of professional parents and other groups from birth to age 3. It shows clearly how the children of manual working class and 'unclassified' group parents are lighter at birth (the solid black line representing the weight of children from professional parents); yet their weight increases much quicker than their more advantaged peers so that by age 9 months, these children are now heavier than the children of non-manual and professional families (on the right, above the black line). By age 3, the children are significantly heavier, whilst at the same time being slightly shorter in stature, leading to a higher prevalence of overweight and obesity.

Figure 10.6: Average Difference in Weight Between the Children of Professional Parents and All Other Classes at Birth, Age 9 Months and Age 3

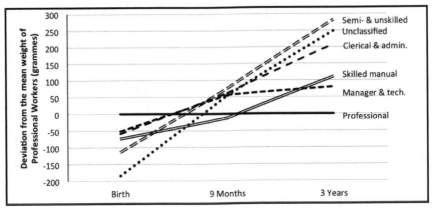

What makes these children more likely to put on weight so much more quickly from such a young age? We were particularly interested in the way that different risk factors combine together to shape the difference in risk of child obesity at age 3 between different social class groups and so analysed how a range of different factors related to child weight gain from birth (Layte *et al.*, 2014).

Past research has identified a number of different factors that may influence the young child's weight gain and thus their risk of subsequent obesity. These include birth weight, extent of breastfeeding, age at weaning, maternal smoking in pregnancy, consumption of alcohol in pregnancy, parental weight status, maternal weight gain in pregnancy, child's dietary quality and child physical exercise. As with smoking and child behaviour, it is possible that some of the risks above may be 'critical period' effects. For example, being born light clearly has effects on other bodily systems and so it is logical to expect that the same is true for weight gain. In fact, analysis shows that, whilst children born light do put on weight more quickly (in a process known as 'catch-up growth'), most will converge with the growth path of their peers and grow more normally by age 6 months. On the other hand, some children born a normal weight continue to grow more quickly and this may be related to other factors to which these children are exposed.

What became apparent was that children from lower working class groups tended to be exposed to a number of different risk factors for child obesity. For example, both lack of breastfeeding and early weaning onto solid foods (before age 6 months) have been suggested as possible contributors to rapid child weight gain and obesity risk. **Figure 10.7** shows that both of these risk factors are more common for the children of manual working class and unclassified groups. Other analyses (not shown here) showed that lack of breastfeeding and early weaning exerted an independent and positive influence on the risk that the child would be measured as obese at age 3. Similarly, when weaned, children in the working class and unclassified groups were also more likely to receive a diet classified as 'low quality', which contained a higher proportion of high calorie foods containing fats and sugars and to have a lower activity level that included more hours watching television and playing computer games. This then exerted an independent effect on the child's growth trajectory, leading to a higher risk of rapid weight gain from birth to age

3. Importantly, this above average weight gain was accompanied by below average height gain, accelerating the risk of subsequent overweight and obesity (which are measured as height squared divided by weight). Together, the lower level of breastfeeding and earlier weaning among children from working class households accounted for over one-third of the difference in overall obesity risk at age 3 relative to children whose parents had professional occupations. Once we added in information on the child's diet and lifestyle (types of food consumed and level of physical exercise), we could account for over 92 per cent of the differential risk of child obesity at age 3 between the children of semi- / unskilled working class households and professional households (Layte *et al.*, 2014).

Figure 10.7: Proportion of Children Breastfed and Proportion Weaned onto Solid Foods after Age 5 Months, by Social Class

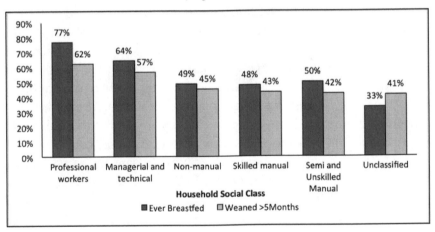

These results show that a number of different factors can accumulate to produce the worse health outcomes that we observe in the children of low social class, income and education groups.

The Role of 'Health Selection'

The models and evidence that we have presented so far show how environmental exposures, influenced by the social position of parents, shape the child's health either during a period when the child's body and mind are particularly vulnerable to influence (during a critical period) or more generally over a period of time (accumulation). Thus, social position precedes the risk exposure and causes the long-term damage to health (a process known as social causation). Yet it is also possible that health can have an impact on social position, a process known as 'health selection'. Researchers seeking to explain the positive association between social position and health have always been concerned about the impact that health may have on level of income or occupational position through the impact of health on the person's ability to work, although repeated studies all show that 'social causation' accounts for more variation in health than downward 'drift' caused by the influence of health on social and economic life.

On the other hand, research looking at the effect of childhood health on later educational and occupational attainment has found a strong association (Palloni & Milesi, 2006; Palloni *et al.*, 2009; Case *et al.*, 2005; Haas, 2008). This model, often referred to as 'stunting', argues that poor health and wellbeing in childhood and adolescence adversely impact on the child's cognitive and educational development and accumulation of human capital, lowering the child's socio-economic trajectory into adulthood (Palloni & Milesi, 2006; Palloni *et al.*, 2009). The process of health selection can be straightforward but it can also operate recursively through feedback loops, with poor early health leading to the accumulation of fewer resources / exposure to adverse conditions and this then leading to the development of further unhealthy states. Notice that this model does not exclude the possibility that parental social position may itself influence the child's risk of developmental 'stunting' and in so doing reproduce both lower social position and a poorer health profile across generations.

We used data from the *Growing Up in Ireland* study to investigate the health selection mechanism by looking at the mediating mechanisms that lead children with a chronic illness to have worse educational outcomes. This is now a well-established pattern in the research literature, with most analysts attributing the harmful effect of chronic illness on education to the frequent absences from school that these children experience. However, our analyses showed that children with a chronic illness were unusually prone to emotional and behavioural problems and this suggested another mechanism that may link chronic illness and educational development: poor home and classroom behaviour. As mentioned earlier in this chapter, child chronic illness brings psychological distress for both parents and children, which often results in poor child behaviour and strained family relationships, sometimes exacerbated by poor family finances (Cadman *et al.*, 1987; Hysing *et al.*, 2009). Our research, which can be found in Layte & McCrory (2012), found that just over 10 per cent of parents reported that their child had a long-standing illness or condition. Asthma accounted for around half of this chronic ill-health, with mental and behavioural conditions such as ADHD and autism spectrum disorder the next highest group at around one-sixth of the sample. As we have already seen, children in lower income and social class groups are more likely to experience chronic health conditions so our hypothesis was that parental social position may impact on educational development through child chronic illness as well as through other mechanisms.

Figure 10.8: 'Drumcondra' Reading and Maths Test Scores by Child Chronic Illness or Disability with Extent of the Mean Emotional and Behavioural Difficulties

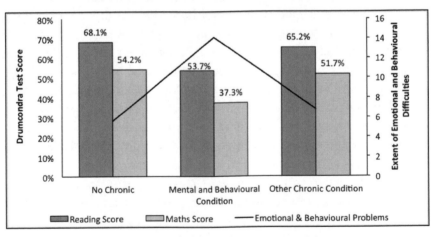

Note: Mental and behavioural condition is measured as the child being in the top 10 per cent using the Strengths and Difficulties Questionnaire (SDQ).

As shown in **Figure 10.8**, children with a chronic illness have lower test scores in reading and maths than children with no chronic illness as well as higher levels of emotional and behavioural difficulties as measured using the Strengths and Difficulties Questionnaire (SDQ). Moreover, statistical analysis showed that almost all of the effect of non-mental and behavioural chronic illness on educational test scores was the result of the more frequent emotional and behavioural problems among these children (Layte & McCrory, 2012).

These results show that health selection can shape the educational development of children. Should this effect influence the child's success in academic exams and educational transitions, it will then have influenced the pathways through which the child moves through the life-course. Ultimately, this could shape the child's chance of getting a good job, putting them at a greater risk of unemployment and low income and, in so doing, expose the child to poorer health and wellbeing. This is just one illustration of the importance of different social pathways in human development.

Conclusion

There are marked differences in the health of children in Ireland by parental social position. The child's developmental trajectory is shaped by the complex interaction of physical and psycho-social environment with internal sources of resilience and vulnerability that together dictate the child's ability to acquire knowledge and specific skills, establish relationships and self-regulate their emotions. The child's environment literally shapes their very physiology and this interaction of biology and social environment is key to understanding variation across children in terms of physical growth, health and readiness to learn. Robust evidence from different countries now shows that socio-economic gradients are reflected in both the cognitive and behavioural development of children, with direct effects for school performance and long-term occupational attainment. This chapter has discussed how childhood environment can influence health across the life-course through a number of different mechanisms and processes. The chapter has also used evidence from the *Growing Up in Ireland* study to show that these theories are not mutually exclusive and that each may play a role in explaining child inequalities in health and wellbeing.

The findings from this chapter and elsewhere have important implications for government policy because they show, without doubt, that early environment is crucial in shaping the future life chances of the child. Indeed, it has been estimated that if all children had the same outcome as the most socially advantaged, this would lead to reductions of:

- 24 per cent in the incidence of low birth weight
- 41 per cent in longstanding illness or disability
- 27 per cent in asthma prevalence
- 54 per cent in conduct disorders (Spencer, 2010).

Socio-economic inequalities in child health are not only inequitable but are also economically short-sighted, given the short- and long-term costs that they create in terms of health and social care expenditure as well as the waste of potential talent that they represent. This suggests that government should consider the underlying processes that produce these pronounced inequalities in the general policy formation process.

The work discussed in this chapter also suggests that early intervention rather than subsequent amelioration of problems would both be more effective and cost-effective in improving outcomes for children. Evidence supporting this line of argument has now been published in a large number of government reports from the UK, US and Ireland, including the recent report from the Department of Children and Youth Affairs in Ireland, *Better Outcomes, Brighter Futures: The National Policy Framework for Children and Young People* (Department of Children and Youth Affairs, 2014). As well as setting out the argument for early and coordinated intervention to improve outcomes for all children, this report also remarked that:

> *[A]cross OECD countries, expenditure on early childhood education accounts for, on average, 0.5 per cent of the overall GDP. However, in Ireland less than 0.1 per cent of GDP is spent on early childhood educational institutions.* (Department of Children and Youth Affairs, 2014, p.15)

We now have a good understanding of the reasons for inequalities in child development and a suite of policy responses. As Ireland emerges from austerity and its economy grows stronger, it may be the ideal time to begin the process of making equality of opportunity among children in Ireland a reality.

References

Adler, N.E. & Newman, K. (2002). Socio-economic disparities in health: Pathways and policies, *Health Affairs, 21*, 60-76.

Barker, D. (1994). The fetal origins of adult disease, *Fetal and Maternal Medicine Review, 6*, 71-80.

Boutwell, B.B. & Beaver, K.M. (2010). Maternal cigarette smoking during pregnancy and offspring externalising behavioural problems: A propensity score matching analysis, *International Journal of Environmental Research and Public Health, 7*, 146-63.

Cadman, D., Boyle, P., Szatmari, P. & Offord, D. (1987). Chronic illness, disability and mental and social wellbeing: Findings of the Ontario Child Health Study, *Pediatrics, 79*, 805-13.

Case, A., Fertig, A. & Paxson, C. (2005). The lasting impact of childhood health and circumstance, *Journal of Health Economics, 24*, 365-89.

Chen, E. (2004). Why socio-economic status affects the health of children, *Current Directions in Psychological Science, 13*, 112-15.

Conger, R.D., Conger, K.J., Elder, G.H.J., Lorenz, F.O., Simons, R.L. & Whitbeck, L.B. (1992). A family process model of economic hardship and adjustment of early adolescent boys, *Child Development, 63*, 526-41.

Davey-Smith, G. (2003). *Health Inequalities: Life-course Approaches*, Bristol: Policy Press.

de Rooij, S.R, Wouters, H., Yonker, J.E, Painter, R.C. & Roseboom, T.J. (2010). Prenatal undernutrition and cognitive function in late adulthood, *Proceedings of the National Academy of Sciences of the United States of America, 107*(39), 16881-86.

Department of Children and Youth Affairs (2014). *Better Outcomes, Brighter Futures: The National Policy Framework for Children and Young People*, Dublin: Stationery Office.

Dowd, J.B., Simanek, A.M. & Aiello, A.E. (2009). Socio-economic status, cortisol and allostatic load: A review of the literature, *International Journal of Epidemiology, 38*, 1297-309.

Grossman, M. (1972). On the concept of health capital and the demand for health, *The Journal of Political Economy, 80*, 223-55.

Haas, S.A. (2008). Trajectories of functional health: The 'Long Arm' of childhood health and socio-economic factors, *Social Science & Medicine, 66*, 849-61.

Huisman, M., Kunst, A.E. & Mackenbach, J.P. (2003). Socio-economic inequalities in morbidity among the elderly: A European overview, *Social Science & Medicine, 57*, 861-73.

Huisman, M., Kunst, A.E., Andersen, O., Bopp, M., Borgan, J.K., & Borrell, C. (2004). Socio-economic inequalities in mortality among elderly people in 11 European populations, *Journal of Epidemiology and Community Health, 58*, 468-75.

Hutchinson, J., Pickett, K.E., Green, J., & Wakschlag, L.S. (2010). Smoking in pregnancy and disruptive behaviour in 3-year-old boys and girls: An analysis of the UK Millennium Cohort Study, *Journal of Epidemiological and Community Health, 64,* 82-88.

Hysing, M., Elgen, I., Gillberg, C. & Lundervold, A.J. (2009). Emotional and behavioural problems in subgroups of children with chronic illness: Results from a large-scale population study, *Child: Health, Care and Development, 35,* 527-33.

Jauniaux, E., & Burton, G. J. (2007). Morphological and biological effects of maternal exposure to tobacco smoke on the fetoplacental unit, *Early Human Development, 83,* 699-706.

Kuh, D. & Ben Shlomo, Y. (eds.) (2004). *A Life-course Approach to Chronic Diseases Epidemiology,* Oxford, UK: Oxford University Press.

Layte, R. & McCrory, C. (2012). Pediatric chronic illness and educational failure: The role of emotional and behavioural problems, *Social Psychiatry and Psychiatric Epidemiology, 48,* 1307-16.

Layte, R. & McCrory, C. (2015). *Maternal Health Behaviours and Child Growth in Infancy,* Dublin: Department of Children and Youth Affairs.

Layte, R., Bennett, A., McCrory, C. & Kearney, J. (2014). Social class variation in the predictors of rapid growth in infancy and obesity at age 3 years, *International Journal of Obesity, 38,* 82-90.

Link, B.G. & Phelan, J. (1995). Social conditions as fundamental causes of disease, *Journal of Health and Social Behavior, 35,* 80-94.

Mackenbach, J.P., Kulhánová, I. & Menvielle, G. (2015). Trends in inequalities in premature mortality: A study of 3.2 million deaths in 13 European countries, *Journal of Epidemiology and Community Health, 69,* 207-17.

McCrory, C. & Layte, R. (2012). Prenatal exposure to maternal smoking and childhood behavioural problems: A quasi-experimental approach, *Journal of Abnormal Child Psychology, 40,* 1277-88.

Palloni, A. & Milesi, C. (2006). Economic achievement, inequalities and health disparities: The intervening role of early health status, *Research in Social Stratification and Mobility, 24,* 21-40.

Palloni, A., Milesi, C., White, R.G. & Turner, A. (2009). Early childhood health, reproduction of economic inequalities and the persistence of health and mortality differentials, *Social Science & Medicine, 68,* 1574-82.

Roseboom, T.J., Painter, R.C, van Abeelen, A.F.M., Veenendaal, M.V.E, de RooijHungry, S.R. (2011). Hungry in the womb: What are the consequences? Lessons from the Dutch famine, *Maturitas, 70*(2), 141-145.

Roseboom, R., de Rooij, S. & Painter, R. (2006). The Dutch Famine and its long-term consequences for adult health, *Early Human Development, 82,* 485-91.

Spencer, N. (2010). Child health inequities, *Paediatrics and Child Health, 20,* 157-62.

Suhrcke, M. & Stuckler, D. (2012). Will the recession be bad for our health? It depends, *Social Science & Medicine, 74,* 647-53.

11: CHILD ACCESS TO GP SERVICES IN IRELAND: DO USER FEES MATTER?

Anne Nolan & Richard Layte

Introduction

If we compare current healthcare provision in Ireland to that which existed nearly a century ago at the foundation of the State, it is clear that much has changed. In spending terms, Ireland has the health system of a rich nation, although there is much discussion about the performance of the system and its ranking among developed countries on various health outcomes. Yet despite the changes that have occurred in healthcare delivery and population health since the foundation of the State, the manner in which healthcare is financed in Ireland still bears remarkable similarities to the situation in the 1920s. Then, the State only provided healthcare free at the point of delivery to a minority of the population who were deemed incapable of paying for it themselves, a principle that persists to this day. In the 1920s this was through the dispensaries and poor law hospitals, whereas now the mechanism is *via* the means-tested medical card system under the General Medical Services Scheme. In the 1920s, many healthcare services were provided privately by general practitioners (GPs), medical consultants and private hospitals (Barrington, 1987). This public / private mix in the delivery and financing of healthcare in Ireland continues to this day, although now private healthcare is financed by private health insurance as well as out-of-pocket charges. Now, as in the 1920s, there is a large group of Irish citizens who have neither access to a medical card nor private health insurance, who must pay for healthcare as they receive it and for whom the financial consequences of ill-health can often be substantial.

Although the size of the various entitlement groups has changed through time, this basic differentiation between those with medical cards, private health insurance and neither a medical card nor private health insurance still structures patterns of healthcare use in Ireland. As a result, many have voiced doubts about whether healthcare use in Ireland reflects the level of health need, or in part also the financing mechanism that delivers it. All healthcare needs to be paid for, but research suggests that the pattern of healthcare received better reflects the level of need in countries where healthcare is free at the point of delivery (and financed *via* taxation, social health insurance or other pre-paid mechanisms). While current Irish health policy contains a commitment to 'universal healthcare', it is not yet clear how it will be financed.

Why should we be particularly concerned about inequalities in access to healthcare services among children? International evidence demonstrates that unequal access to healthcare among children is an important contributor to inequalities in child health outcomes. In turn, poor childhood health has detrimental consequences not only for adult health, but also for other life outcomes such as education, employment and financial security. *Better Outcomes, Brighter Futures*, which sets out the national policy framework for children and young people in Ireland, highlights the importance of early intervention and prevention for improving child health outcomes, noting that what happens early in life affects health and wellbeing in later life (Department of Children and Youth Affairs, 2014).

A key commitment of *Better Outcomes, Brighter Futures* is the introduction of universal general practitioner (GP) services. This reflects the fact that the majority of the Irish population face the full cost of GP services, a situation that marks Ireland apart from most other European countries. Most individuals first come into contact with the health system *via* their GP, and GPs in Ireland act as gatekeepers for access to secondary care services. Therefore, GPs play a pivotal role in providing a wide range of primary care services to the population, and by extension, reducing reliance on more costly acute hospital services. Steps to reducing financial barriers to accessing GP services are already underway, with universal free GP care extended to all children under age 6 and all those aged 70+ in 2015, and a further extension planned for all children under age 18.

In this context, it is important to understand the extent to which the current system of healthcare financing in Ireland leads to differences in patterns of use of GP services by children that are not predicted by their need for healthcare. This analysis may also help to assess the demand implications of future policy proposals around extending free GP care to further cohorts of children. In the next section we examine the complex system of healthcare financing and associated entitlements in Ireland and profile the types of children in the various entitlement groups. We then examine the extent to which the observed pattern of GP use is the result of differences in the need for healthcare across children in Ireland or whether it also reflects in part the ability of their families to pay for it. Data from the *Growing Up in Ireland* study are used. In the final section of the chapter we draw out some of the implications of our work for the development of health policy with regard to children in Ireland.

Money, Healthcare and Health

System of healthcare financing and entitlements in Ireland

Most developed countries use a mixture of public (taxation, social health insurance) and private (private health insurance, out-of-pocket payments) methods to finance healthcare services. The current Irish system of healthcare financing relies predominately on taxation, with smaller contributions from private health insurance and direct out-of-pocket payments by individuals. However, while the proportion of overall out-of-pocket contributions to total healthcare financing is comparable with other EU countries, for certain services such as GP care they are much more significant than is the case elsewhere. This reflects the way in which entitlements to free or heavily-subsidised healthcare are structured at present in Ireland.

Currently, there are two main categories of entitlements to public health services. Those in Category I (full medical cardholders) are entitled to free public health services (including inpatient and outpatient hospital care, GP care and other primary and community care services), but must pay a co-payment of €2.50 per prescription item, up to a maximum of €25 per family per month. Those in Category II are entitled to subsidised public hospital services and prescription medicines (the latter up to a monthly deductible of €144 per family), but must pay the full cost of GP services (and other primary and community care services). In October 2005, the GP visit card was introduced; GP visit cardholders have the same entitlements to free GP care as Category I individuals, but the same entitlements to all other public health services (including prescription medicines) as Category II individuals.

Eligibility for a full medical / GP visit card is assessed primarily on the basis of an income means test. The income thresholds for the GP visit card are 50 per cent higher than for the full medical card. In a small number of cases, individuals who are otherwise ineligible for a full medical / GP visit card may be granted a card on a 'discretionary' basis, if they have particular health needs that would cause them undue hardship.

There are some additional primary care services that are provided free of charge to children, even if their parents do not have a full medical or GP visit card. These services are generally provided as part of maternity and infant welfare services (two free postnatal GP visits), health services for pre-school children (home visits by public health nurses, and a full developmental check at age 9 months) and school health services (free vision, dental and hearing examinations and treatment). Children are also entitled to vaccination and immunisation services free of charge.

A further layer of complexity is added to the Irish system by the existence of private health insurance. Approximately 46 per cent of the population currently have private health insurance, which mainly provides cover for private or semi-private acute hospital services (which may be delivered in public hospitals), but which increasingly offers partial reimbursement of certain primary care expenses (for example, GP visits, routine dental care, physiotherapy, etc.). Full medical card and GP visit cardholders may take out private health insurance if they wish, although the numbers doing so are generally small.

Distribution of healthcare entitlements among children in Ireland

In terms of prices for GP services, a useful way of categorising the population is to think in terms of five broad categories of entitlement, as set out in **Table 11.1**. As noted, in 2015, GP visit cards were extended to all children under age 6, regardless of family income. The analysis in this chapter reflects the situation prior to the introduction of this policy change, using data from *Growing Up in Ireland* over the period 2007-2012. A 2010 survey found that the average GP fee was €51, with a range of €35 to €70 observed across the country. A minority of GPs surveyed reported that they charged lower fees for children, although more respondents reported that they used discretion in applying fees for children and / or had a 'family rate' (National Consumer Agency, 2010).

Table 11.1: Healthcare Entitlement Groups and GP User Fees

Entitlement Group	GP User Fee
Full medical card only	Free
GP visit card only	Free
Private health insurance with GP cover	Full cost with full / partial reimbursement from private health insurance plan
Private health insurance with no GP cover	Full cost
No cover, i.e., no medical/GP visit card or private health insurance	Full cost

The crucial question is whether this complex mix of public and private financing of healthcare, with some people having to pay for their child's GP care as they receive it and others not, has an impact on the patterns of GP use that we actually observe. Before considering this question in detail, we describe the types of children in Ireland who fall into each of these entitlement groups.

Figure 11.1 shows how public healthcare entitlement status varies across the children in *Growing Up in Ireland*, surveyed at 9 months, age 3, age 9 and age 13. For the children in the Infant Cohort, surveyed for the first time in 2008-2009 at age 9 months, nearly 30 per cent have either a full medical or GP visit card, with a further 52 per cent having some form of private health insurance cover, and just over 18 per cent having neither a full medical / GP visit card nor private health insurance (which we term 'no cover' for GP care in this chapter). By 2010-2011, when the Infant Cohort was surveyed again at age 3, the proportion with a full medical or GP visit card had increased to 38 per cent, reflecting general economic conditions (rising unemployment, falling household incomes, etc.) over this period. The proportion with private health insurance fell to just over 46 per cent, again a reflection of the continued deterioration in family finances over this period.

Figure 11.1: Healthcare Entitlement Groups, by Cohort and Age

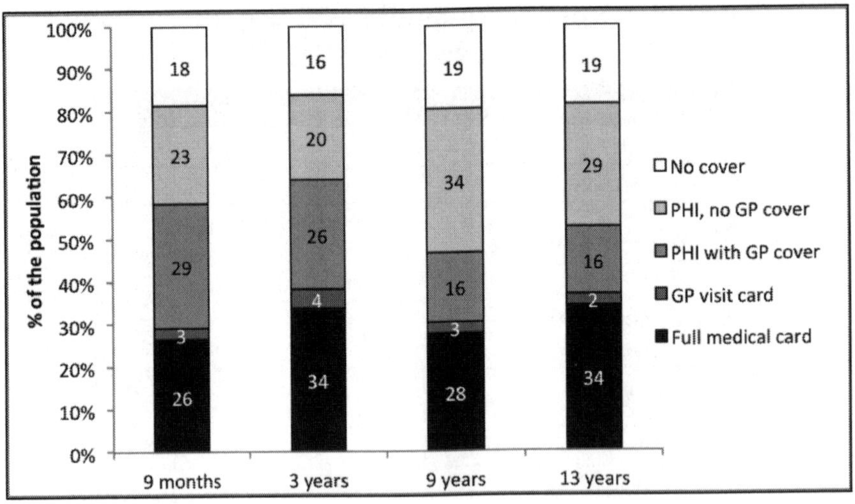

Notes: Population weights are employed. PHI = private health insurance.

Similar trends over time are evident for the Child Cohort. When first surveyed at age 9 in 2007-2008, 31 per cent had access to a full medical or GP visit card, and this proportion had increased to 36 per cent in 2011-2012, when the children were surveyed again at age 13. Private health insurance cover fell from 50 per cent to 45 per cent over the period for this cohort.

Characteristics of children across entitlement groups

As full medical and GP visit card eligibility is assessed primarily on the basis of an income means test, it is not surprising that average family income levels are lowest for full medical cardholder children, and highest for children whose families have private health insurance with cover for GP expenses. For example, in 2008-2009, the average equivalised family income of a 9-month-old child in the Infant Cohort with a full medical card was €12,507 *per annum*, in comparison with €28,020 *per annum* for a child covered by private health insurance with GP cover (**Figure 11.2**). Other indicators of socio-economic position are also similarly distributed across the various entitlement groups. **Figure 11.3** illustrates the proportion of children in each entitlement group whose mothers have a third level qualification, with substantially higher rates of third level education among the mothers of children with private health insurance than among those with full medical or GP visit cards.

Figure 11.2: Average Annual Household Income, by Entitlement Group, Cohort and Age

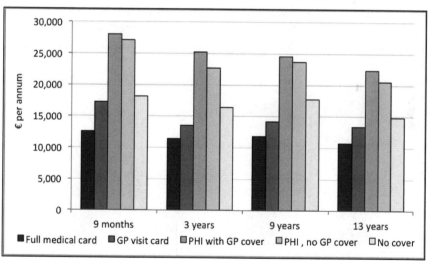

Notes: Population weights are employed. Household income is adjusted for household composition using equivalence scales. PHI = private health insurance.

Figure 11.3: Proportion of Mothers with a Third Level Qualification, by Entitlement Group, Cohort and Age

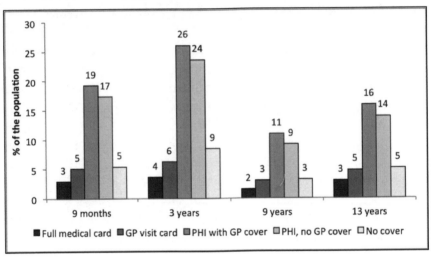

Notes: Population weights are employed. PHI = private health insurance.

Figure 11.4: Proportion of 'Very Healthy' Children, by Entitlement Group, Cohort and Age

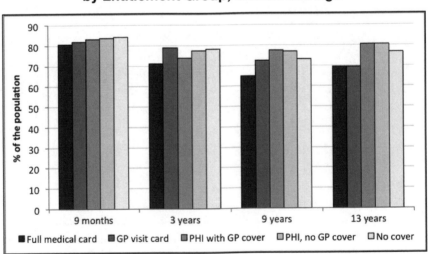

Notes: Population weights are employed. The data refer to the proportion of children who are classified as 'very healthy, no problems' by their parents when asked to rate their child's current general health status. PHI = private health insurance.

Socio-economic position and health are closely related, and this is reflected in the distribution of child health status across the various entitlement groups. As illustrated in **Figure 11.4**, while the vast majority of children are reported to be in very good health, there is evidence of a gradient in child health, with those entitled to full medical cards demonstrating poorer health than those with private health insurance and / or no cover. For example, among the Child Cohort at age 9, 65 per cent of children with a full medical card are classified as 'very healthy, no problems'; the corresponding proportion for children with private health insurance including GP cover is 77 per cent.

The Pattern of GP Service Use among Children

The descriptive patterns presented above highlight a key challenge in identifying the role of healthcare entitlement structures in explaining inequalities in access to healthcare services – that is, children who have the greatest need for healthcare are also more likely to be poorer, and therefore entitled to free public healthcare. In the Irish context for example, simply comparing the utilisation levels of children with and without medical cards would be misleading: any difference in use of GP services could be because of medical cards, or it could occur because children in the different entitlement groups may have very different health risks and other characteristics. Later in the chapter we attempt to disentangle the multitude of factors that may explain variation in the use of GP services across children in Ireland, including healthcare entitlements, health need and other family characteristics such as mother's level of education. Before doing so, however, we provide an overview of GP visiting rates among children in Ireland, and how they vary across these key characteristics.

Information on use of GP services in *Growing Up in Ireland* is reported by the child's primary caregiver, which in the vast majority of cases is the child's mother. Mothers are asked to record the number of times the child visited their GP in the previous 12 months (since birth, in the case of the Infant Cohort at age 9 months). Information is also collected in *Growing Up in Ireland* on other types of healthcare use, such as emergency department (ED) visits, outpatient visits, public health nurse visits, inpatient nights in hospital, etc. but is not examined here as the focus is on GP services.

Figure 11.5: Average Number of GP Visits *per annum,* by Cohort and Age

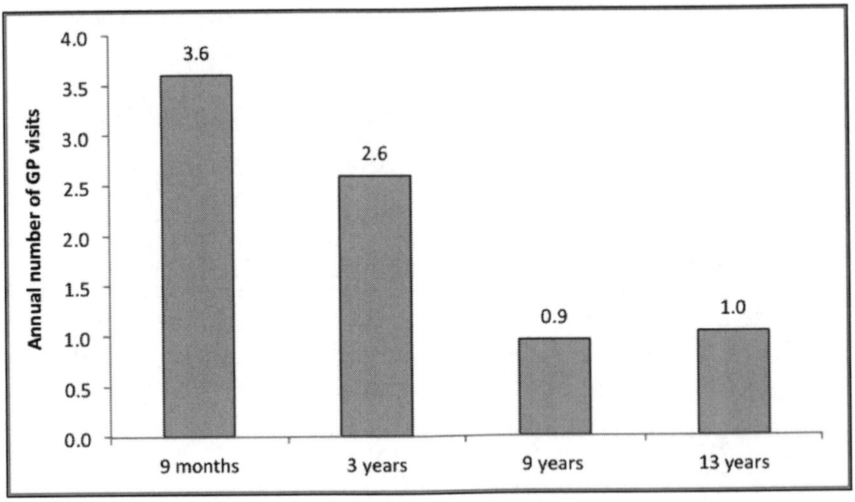

Notes: *Population weights are employed. GP visiting rates for the 9-month-olds are adjusted to reflect the annual level of GP visiting for this group.*

As illustrated in **Figure 11.5**, the average annual number of GP visits for 9-month-old children is 3.6; by the time the children are age 3, this falls to 2.6. For the older cohort, the average number of GP visits at age 9 is 0.9, and 1.0 at age 13. This is consistent with patterns observed in other countries where healthcare use (and spending) falls after the first few years of life.

Patterns of GP service use

We now examine whether the distribution of GP service use among children reflects need for healthcare, or does it also partly reflect the prices that parents have to pay for GP services for their children? **Figure 11.6** shows how the number of GP services varies across the five entitlement categories defined earlier.

Figure 11.6: Average Number of GP Visits *per annum*, by Entitlement Group, Cohort and Age

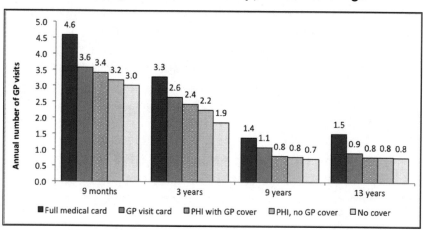

Notes: *Population weights are employed. PHI = private health insurance.*

The patterns we observe in **Figure 11.6** are consistent with what we would expect, given the different prices that these groups face in accessing GP care; the average number of GP visits *per annum* is highest for full medical card holders, and lowest for those with no cover. Across all age groups, children with full medical cards have approximately 1.5 to 2 times the number of GP visits *per annum* compared to children with 'no cover'. In some cases, there are also differences across groups that have to pay out-of-pocket for GP care; for example, 3-year-old children with private health insurance and full / partial cover for GP care have 2.4 GP visits *per annum*, in comparison with their counterparts with no cover who visit 1.9 times *per annum*.

Looking at the patterns in **Figure 11.6**, it would be easy to conclude that the difference in the rate of visiting is entirely due to the fact that the different groups face different monetary disincentives to visit (see also **Table 11.1**). However, these groups also differ according to a large number of other characteristics that also have a bearing on their GP use. **Figures 11.2, 11.3** and **11.4** demonstrated that these entitlement groups differ considerably in terms of other characteristics such as socio-economic and health status. As we show now, these characteristics are in turn associated with differing needs for GP care. For example, children with worse health will require more GP care as shown clearly in **Figure 11.7**, where we show how the number of GP services varies with parental assessments of the child's health status. Although we may have concerns that the parental report of child health status may be subject to some inaccuracies, international studies of adults show that self-assessed health status is a good predictor of the person's likelihood of death and use of healthcare over the following year. As expected, **Figure 11.7** shows a clear gradient in GP visiting by parental-assessed child health, with children in poorer health having a higher number of GP visits.

Figure 11.7: Average Number of GP Visits *per annum*, by Child Health Status, Cohort and Age

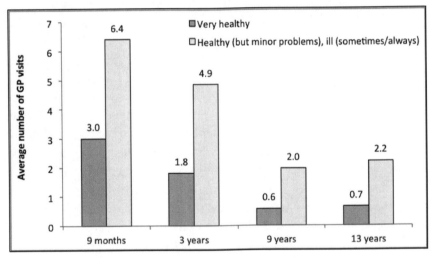

Notes: *Population weights are employed.*

GP visiting rates may also be affected by other socio-economic characteristics, such as mother's level of education (**Figure 11.8**) and early life behaviours such as mother's smoking behaviour during pregnancy (**Figure 11.9**). While there is little difference in GP visiting rates by mother's level of education for 9-month-old children, in general, the children of mothers with a lower level of education have a higher annual number of GP visits.

Figure 11.8: Average Number of GP Visits *per annum*, by Mother's Education, Cohort and Age

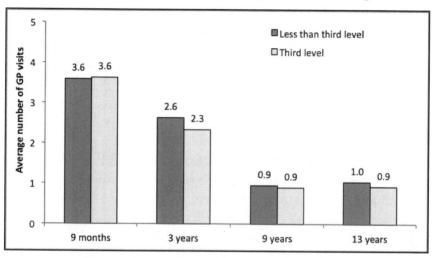

Notes: Population weights are employed.

Figure 11.9: Average Number of GP Visits *per annum*, by Mother's Smoking Behaviour during Pregnancy, by Cohort and Age

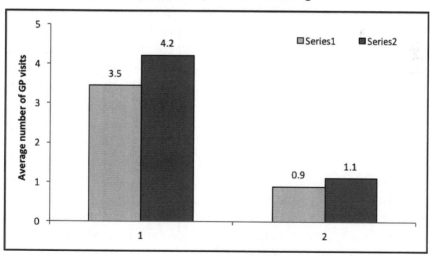

Notes: Population weights are employed. The question about smoking behaviour in pregnancy is asked in wave 1 for each Cohort only (at age 9 months for the Infant Cohort, and at age 9 for the Child Cohort).

The data for maternal smoking during pregnancy are much clearer. Across the two cohorts, the children of mothers who smoked occasionally or daily in pregnancy have approximately 1.2 times the number of GP visits *per annum* than those whose mothers did not smoke in pregnancy. It is important to highlight the differing socio-economic profile of the two cohorts, reflecting wider changes in Irish society over the 2000s. Increasing levels of parental education, and reductions in smoking prevalence are evident when we compare the children of the Infant Cohort (born in 2008) with the children of the Child Cohort (born in 1998).

Disentangling the relative contribution of healthcare entitlements and these other socio-economic and behavioural factors to variation in GP visiting patterns across children is difficult, as many of the predictors of GP visiting rates are related to each other (for example, **Figure 11.7** clearly shows that those with poorer health have a higher number of GP visits *per annum*, yet a higher proportion of those with poorer health have a full medical card as illustrated in **Figure 11.4**). In other words, it could be the case that part of the differential we observe in GP visiting patterns across the five entitlement groups could be due to the fact that children from lower income families also have a greater need for healthcare. It is therefore important to control for these factors using multivariate statistical analysis to determine the net effect of healthcare entitlements on GP visiting. Using this approach we can hold the child's health status (and other family characteristics) constant whilst looking specifically at the effect of public healthcare entitlements. We present the results of this analysis in **Figure 11.10**. Consistent with the descriptive patterns presented in **Figure 11.6**, we find that healthcare entitlement status exerts a significant effect on GP visiting rates, even after controlling for other potential determinants of child GP visiting such as health, mother's education and behaviours during pregnancy. For example, we find that children at age 9 months whose families have a full medical card have approximately 1.2 extra GP visits *per annum* compared to those with no cover. At the same age, families with a GP only card or private health insurance have between 0.6 and 0.7 extra GP visits *per annum*, compared to those with no cover. The average effects are smaller for the Child Cohort, but it must be remembered that the average level of GP visits *per annum* is smaller for the Child Cohort (see **Figure 11.5**).

Figure 11.10: Number of Additional GP Visits *per annum*, by Entitlement Group, Cohort and Age

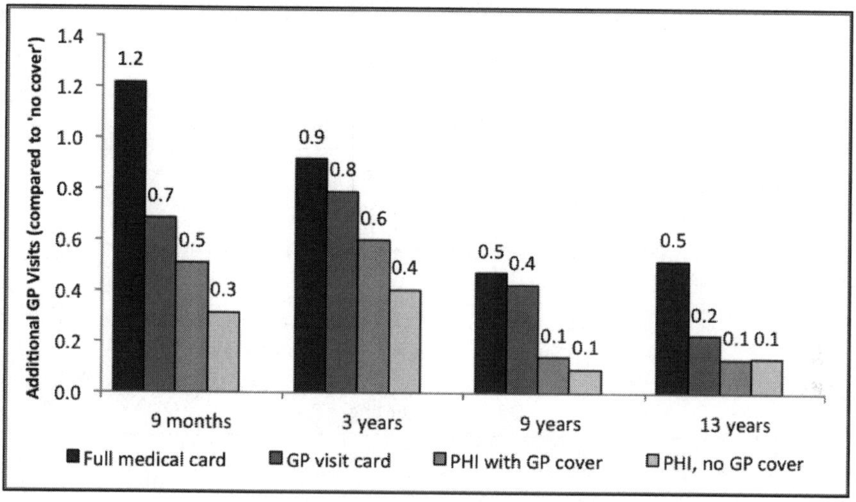

Notes: The bars represent the additional visits over and above those observed for the no cover group. For example, 9-month-old children with a full medical card have approximately 1.2 extra GP visits per annum in comparison with 9-month-old children with no cover, while 9-month-old children with a GP visit card have approximately 0.7 extra GP visits per annum in comparison with the no cover group.

The Pattern of GP Service Use among Private Patients

In this section, we focus in greater detail on the situation of children whose family income makes them ineligible for a full medical or GP visit card. The current net weekly income threshold for a GP visit card is €514 for a family of two adults and two children under the age of 16 years. An average GP fee of €50 for one family member therefore amounts to nearly 10 per cent of net weekly family income for a family just above that threshold, a significant outlay before any associated prescription medicine costs are taken into account. There are, therefore, very real concerns that those on low, but not the lowest, incomes face particular hardship in accessing GP services (and indeed this was part of the motivation for the introduction of the GP visit card in 2005).

Figure 11.11: Average Number of GP Visits *per annum,* by Equivalised Family Income, Cohort and Age (Private Patients)

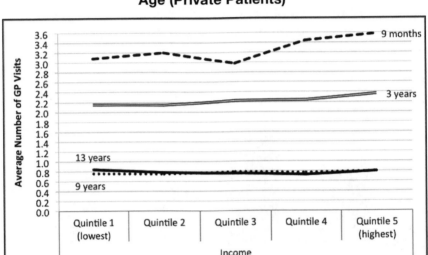

Notes: Population weights are employed.

Figure 11.11 classifies children in each cohort and age group based on their family income, and illustrates how GP visiting rates differ by family income (divided into five equally-sized groups, or quintiles). The data indicate a clear gradient in GP visiting by family income for 9-month-olds, whereby children from higher income families have higher GP visiting rates. For the other age groups, there are smaller differences in GP visiting rates as one moves up the distribution of family income, and indeed for the 13-year-old children, there is some evidence that children from lower income families have higher levels of GP visiting than children from higher income families.

However, this does not take into account other differences in characteristics across these children that might also influence their use of GP services. We therefore ran a multivariate model that adjusts for these other factors to isolate the effect of family income on GP visiting rates among children who are not eligible for a full medical or GP visit card. If the cost of a GP consultation is indeed a substantial burden for children whose families are just above the income threshold for a GP visit card, it would be expected that GP visiting increases as we move further up the income distribution, adjusting for all other influences on GP visiting such as health status. In **Figure 11.12** we show that the results indicate that, for the children of the Infant Cohort at age 9 months, there is a significant difference in GP visiting rates by family income, indicating that children from better-off families visit their GP more often than children from less well-off families, even after controlling for other determinants of GP visiting rates such as child health need, mother's education, mother's employment status, etc. However, by the time these children reach age 3, there is no significant difference in GP visiting rates by family income. In addition, for the children of the Child Cohort (at age 9 and again at age 13), there are few significant differences across family income, although where they exist, those in lower income quintiles have fewer visits than those in the highest income quintile.

Figure 11.12: Number of Additional GP Visits *per annum*, by Family Income, Cohort and Age (Private Patients)

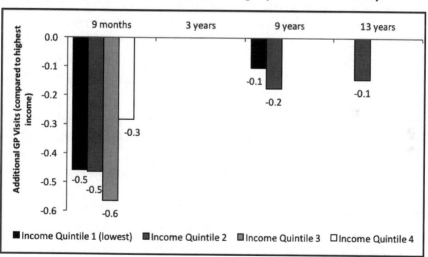

Notes: The bars represent the additional visits over and above those observed for the highest income quintile group (statistically significant results are shown only). For example, 9-month-old children without a full medical or GP visit card in the lowest income quintile have approximately 0.5 fewer GP visits per annum than 9-month-old children without a full medical or GP visit card in the highest income quintile.

Conclusion

Equity of access to healthcare is regarded as a key objective of national and international health policy. The current Irish system of healthcare financing and public healthcare entitlements is unusual internationally, with the requirement for a large proportion of the population to pay the full cost of GP care at the point of use a particular concern. A major reform of this financing system and associated public healthcare entitlement structure was outlined in the Fine Gael / Labour Programme for Government in 2011. It was proposed there that a system of universal health insurance be introduced that guaranteed equal access to care for all. The second main pillar of the reform was the introduction of free GP care at the point of use for all. In summer 2015, the first phase (for under 6s, and over 70s) was implemented. The Government Budget of 2015 contained a commitment to extend free GP care to all children aged under 12, and the Programme for Government of the minority Government formed in May 2016 commits to an extension of free GP care to all children aged under 18. In the context of the proposed phased introduction of universal free GP care, it is crucial to understand current patterns of healthcare use, not only for highlighting the extent to which the current system leads to financial barriers to accessing healthcare services, but also for forecasting the likely implications of the new policy proposals.

The analyses summarised in this chapter demonstrate that eligibility for free GP care *via* a full medical card or GP only card is associated with a higher number of GP visits, even adjusting for a range of other factors including detailed measures of the child's health status. Given the patterns we observe, a key question concerns the extent to which those with a full medical card / GP visit card may be visiting their GP 'unnecessarily' and / or the extent to which those with private health insurance with no cover for GP expenses, and those with no cover, may be deterring 'necessary' GP visits due to the cost. However, distinguishing between 'necessary' or 'effective' and 'unnecessary' or 'ineffective' healthcare is very difficult, and requires much more detailed data on diagnoses, length of consultation, etc. Taking antibiotics for a viral infection such as a head cold is often considered an example of 'ineffective' healthcare use. However, previous research from other settings has highlighted the negative effects of user fees on healthcare access – user fees deter both 'necessary' as well as 'unnecessary' care (Robinson, 2002; Baicker & Goldman, 2011; Lohr *et al.*, 1986). In this context, large differences in GP visiting behaviour between different segments of the population are a concern, as they suggest that access may be granted partly on the basis of ability to pay, rather than health need alone.

Despite the commitments towards the removal of user fees for GP care for children in current Irish health policy, user fees for other services (for example, prescription drugs) have been introduced (and subsequently increased) in recent years. Patient cost-sharing has been a key method of healthcare expenditure control in many countries because it assumes that people will value what they pay for, and as a result will reduce their use of 'unnecessary' or 'ineffective' healthcare when they are required to pay for it. However, healthcare is not a usual consumer good, and the presence of uncertainty and information asymmetry means that, as noted above, there is now a considerable body of evidence from a variety of settings demonstrating that user fees reduce both 'necessary' as well as 'unnecessary' healthcare use. However, that is not to say that patient cost-sharing should never be used in healthcare settings; there is increasing attention now on value-based pricing – adjusting user fees to reflect the value of care rather than applying user fees to broad categories of care (for example, eliminating cost-sharing for childhood immunisations) (Chernew & Newhouse, 2008; Evetovits *et al.*, 2012; Swartz, 2010).

Focusing in particular on private patients (children whose family income is higher than the income thresholds for a full medical or GP visit card), we find some evidence that higher income children without full medical or GP visit cards visit their GP more often than their counterparts on lower incomes, even after adjusting for other determinants of use such as health need. This suggests that user fees acted as a barrier to access for children from low, but not the lowest, income families in Ireland. The absence of any significant effect for the children at age 3 (in comparison to the significant effects for the same children at age 9 months) may be due to the timing of the data collection for the two waves. The Wave 1 data of the Infant Cohort were collected between September 2008 and April 2009 when the recession was just beginning, while the Wave 2 data were collected between January and August 2011, when the recession was in its fourth year. In Wave 1, 71 per cent of the sample was private patients, while the corresponding proportion in Wave 2 was 62 per cent (see also **Figure 11.1**). It is therefore possible that enhanced access to the full medical and GP visit cards (as a result of falling household incomes and increased unemployment) resulted in those who previously faced particular barriers in accessing GP services becoming eligible for free GP care.

While we may be interested in the patterning of healthcare use from an equity perspective, the ultimate question is whether the current system of healthcare entitlements has an impact on health outcomes. It may be that timely treatment in primary care may also be more cost-effective in the long-run if lack of treatment leads to worse health and more expensive (possibly hospital) treatment at a later date. For children, lack of treatment in childhood may also mean a lifetime of subsequent treatment as well as a lower quality of life. Studies from other countries have demonstrated significant effects of enhanced access to healthcare among children on child health outcomes; for example, a number of studies from the US have shown that enhanced access to Medicaid (which grants entitlement to free healthcare to those on low incomes in the US) has had beneficial effects on child health outcomes such as mortality, as well as later life health outcomes (Currie, 1995; Currie *et al.*, 2008; Lin, 2009). As further waves of *Growing Up in Ireland* data become available, these complex questions about the relationship between entitlements, use and health can be investigated further.

References

Baicker, K. & Goldman, D. (2011). Patient cost-sharing and healthcare spending growth, *Journal of Economic Perspectives, 25,* 47-68.

Barrington, R. (1987). *Health, Medicine and Politics in Ireland: 1900-1970,* Dublin: Institute of Public Administration.

Chernew, M. & Newhouse, J. (2008). What does the RAND Health Insurance Experiment tell us about the impact of patient cost-sharing on health outcomes?, *American Journal of Managed Care, 14,* 412-14.

Currie, J. (1995). Socio-economic status and child health: Does public insurance narrow the gap?, *Scandinavian Journal of Economics, 97,* 603-20.

Currie, J., Decker, S. & Lin, W. (2008). Has public insurance for older children reduced disparities in access to care and health outcomes?, *Journal of Health Economics, 27,* 1567-81.

Department of Children and Youth Affairs (2014). *Better Outcomes, Brighter Future: The National Policy Framework for Children and Young People*, Dublin: Stationery Office.

Evetovits, T., Figueras, J., Jowett, M., Mladovsky, P., Nolan, A., Normand, C. & Thomson, S. (2012). *Health System Responses to Financial Pressures in Ireland: Policy Options in an International Context*, Brussels: European Observatory on Health Systems and Policies.

Lin, W. (2009). Why has the health inequality among infants in the US declined? Accounting for the shrinking gap, *Health Economics, 18*, 823-41.

Lohr, K., Brook, R., Kamberg, C., Goldberg, G., Leibowitz, A., Keesey, J., Reboussin, D. & Newhouse, J. (1986). *Use of Medical Care in the RAND Health Insurance Experiment: Diagnosis- and Service-specific Analyses in a Randomised Control Trial*, Santa Monica: RAND.

National Consumer Agency (2010). *Doctor and Dentists Survey: May 2010*, Dublin: National Consumer Agency.

Robinson, R. (2002). User charges for healthcare, in Mossialos, E., Dixon, A., Figueras, J. & Kutzin, J. (eds.), *Funding Healthcare: Options for Europe* (pp.161-83), Milton Keynes, UK: Open University Press.

Swartz, K. (2010). *Cost-sharing: Effects on Spending and Outcomes*, Princeton: The Robert Wood Johnson Foundation.

12: ANTI-SOCIAL BEHAVIOUR AT AGE 13

Maeve Thornton & James Williams

Introduction

This chapter is concerned with the prevalence of anti-social behaviour in the early teenage years and how this varies from one group of young people to another. In particular, the relationship between anti-social behaviour and social disadvantage is investigated.

There is really no information that can be used to compare what would be generally accepted today as anti-social behaviour with the situation in 1916. Reformatory and Industrial Schools were set up in the latter half of the 19th century to care for 'neglected, orphaned and abandoned children'. The 1916 *Annual Report* of the Chief Inspector of such schools notes that there were five Reformatory Schools in Ireland at that time, containing 597 boys and 67 girls under a detention order. Of the 179 children committed to Reformatory Schools in 1916 the majority were found guilty of 'Larcency and Petty Theft' (102), followed by 'Housebreaking, Shopbreaking etc.' (38) and 'Wilful Damage and other Malicious Offences' (12). On 31 December 1916 a total of 7,922 children were on the rolls of Industrial Schools, with 822 having been committed in 1916 (Chief Inspector, 1917). The grounds for committal are summarised in **Table 12.1**.

**Table 12.1: Grounds for Committal of Boys and
Girls to Industrial Schools, 1916**

Grounds for committal	Boys	Girls	Total
Begging	55	67	**122**
Wandering	201	168	**369**
Destitute orphan, or destitute parent, or parents in prison	47	47	**94**
Parent or guardian of drunken or criminal habits	39	61	**100**
Father convicted under Sec. 4 or 5 of *Criminal Law Amendment Act, 1885*	0	1	**1**
Frequenting the company of reputed thieves or prostitutes	4	3	**7**
Residing in a brothel	1	5	**6**
Charged with offences punishable in the case of adults with penal servitude etc. (being under 12 years of age)	74	4	**78**
Charged with offences punishable in the case of adults with penal servitude etc. (being above age 12 but under 14)	28	7	**35**
Uncontrollable by parents	3	1	**4**
Refractory pauper	2	0	**2**
Non-compliance with Attendance Orders (*Education Act* cases)	3	1	**4**
Total	**457**	**365**	**822**

Source: Chief Inspector (1917).

It is clear that conceptualising and defining anti-social behaviour in Ireland (and elsewhere) is very different today compared to 1916, as are the supports and programs in place to address it. The Garda Juvenile Diversion Programme has steered young people who are involved in anti-social and criminal activity in Ireland away from the courts since 1963, when the programme began on a relatively informal basis. It was not until the introduction of the *Children Act, 2001*,[10] however, that this was finally put on a statutory footing with a focus on prevention, diversion from the criminal justice system and the rehabilitation of children, rather than the use of detention. In 2007 a number of specific

---

[10] http://www.iyjs.ie/en/IYJS/Pages/WP08000061#About_the_Diversion
_Programme.

measures to address anti-social behaviour by children, were introduced to offer alternative ways of dealing with children meaning that the vast bulk of anti-social behaviour as it is now defined is not processed through the courts system. For example, a series of stages are now required before an anti-social behaviour order (ASBO) can be sought, including a warning, a good behaviour contract and referral to the Garda Diversion Programme.

In terms of research, apart from the very extensive work on the reform of the criminal justice system by, for example, O'Mahony (1997), the general lack of relevant data and research on youth anti-social behaviour in Ireland continues to be a real challenge to the present day. What we do know (largely from the international literature) is that most teens who participate in anti-social behaviour tend to do so by committing non-violent offences, only once or a few times, and only during adolescence. For some, however, these types of behaviour may lead to less trivial acts more clearly falling within the definition of crime, such as shoplifting. In fact, research indicates that theft (including shoplifting) is the most prevalent initial crime and one of the most common offences committed by adolescents (Barry, 2006; Cunneen & White, 2002; Rutter *et al.*, 1998).

The international literature draws a distinction between anti-social behaviour that is limited to adolescence and that which persists (for example, Stattin & Magnusson, 1991; Fergusson *et al.*, 2000; Eklund & af Klinteberg, 2006). Recent analysis of data from Ireland (Irish Youth Justice Service, 2013) also shows that while most young people grow out of anti-social behaviour, a small number persist. In fact a national average of 5 per cent of young people are referred to the Garda Diversion Programme each year, although this percentage varies significantly from the overall average in some local communities. While relatively small in number, these young people nonetheless demand considerable attention in terms of understanding the specific contexts that influence and sustain offending behaviour. Furthermore, for those young people who consistently participate in problematic behaviour, the effects have been found to be wide-ranging and associated with high social, interpersonal and financial costs, not only to affected families and communities but across society (National Institute for Health & Care Excellence, 2013). Simply put, anti-social behaviour poses a significant challenge to the social equality of those who become involved in it, as well as those around them.

Influences on Anti-social Behaviour

The specific aim of the chapter is to identify the extent to which anti-social behaviour is associated with socially-disadvantaged and potentially more marginalised children, their individual characteristics, family structure and processes, and peer factors.

Anti-social behaviour is described in terms of property-related (theft and vandalism) and person-related activity (violent behaviour). These are explored separately, as previous research has demonstrated that different types of behaviour are associated to an extent with different risk factors (Sprott *et al.*, 2000; Burt *et al.*, 2011; Elliot, 1994; Loeber *et al.*, 1998; Thornberry & Krohn, 2003).

Socio-economic influences

There is consistent cross-national support for the notion that economic and social disparities result in inequality in education, quality of life and socio-emotional and behavioural development. There is also evidence that these differences have become relatively greater in most Western countries in recent years (Neckerman & Torche, 2007).

Socio-economic status matters for anti-social behaviour because of differential access to resources and / or exposure to stressful situations. A recent analysis of multiple studies (Piotrowska *et al.*, 2015) showed that lower family socio-economic status was associated with higher levels of anti-social behaviour, the strength of the relationship depending on the specific nature of the behaviour under investigation.

The Family Stress Model (FSM) is especially relevant to our understanding of how socio-economic factors can influence social, emotional and behavioural outcomes at adolescence (Conger & Conger, 2002). This theoretical model takes the broad ideas of ecological systems theory, which essentially explores how a child's development is influenced by the interaction between their own inherent qualities and the characteristics of the external environment in which they live, and applies them to a focussed concept of how economic difficulties can influence adolescent outcomes. The FSM predicts that economic problems may lead to deterioration in couple relationships and increased risk of relationship instability. This in turn may result in less effective parenting – possibly through insufficient monitoring, lack of control over the child's behaviour, lack of warmth and support, and higher levels of conflict (McLeod & Shanahan, 1993). In this case parenting is an intervening, or mediating, variable explaining the impact of disadvantage on child development, while also highlighting how different styles of parenting might operate in different ways (for example, McLoyd, 1990).

Gender of child

Significant gender differences in anti-social behaviour have been consistently reported in the literature (Lahey *et al.*, 2000; Maughan *et al.*, 2004; Odgers *et al.*, 2008). For example, Stanger *et al.* (1997) found that boys tended to be more likely than girls to be associated with anti-social behaviour, especially in aggressive or violent behaviours. Two major studies (the Dunedin and Christchurch Studies) both found higher scores for boys in anti-social behaviour from ages 5 to 21 (Moffitt *et al.*, 2001) and offending trajectories for girls to be half that of boys from ages 8 to 20 (Fergusson & Horwood, 2002).

Studying the developmental trajectory of physical aggression (particularly chronic aggression) in six longitudinal studies, Broidy *et al.* (2003) found that girls showed less physical aggression than boys. While it is well-established that males engage in more delinquent and criminal acts than females (see review by Dodge *et al.*, 2006), some believe that the gender gap may be decreasing, with girls becoming more frequent and possibly more aggressive in their offences (Snyder, 2004). There is as yet little evidence that this change is occurring on a significant scale and the evidence from different studies is often contradictory.

Family structure

Evidence from the literature indicates that children who live with one parent only are more prone to anti-social behaviour and drug use (for example, Amato, 2005; Cairney *et al.*, 2003), although it is not clear if these effects are a direct result of household composition. Amato's review in 2005 concluded that children and adolescents who grow up with two continuously-married parents were less likely to experience a wide range of emotional and social problems, including anti-social behaviour. However, the precise mediating factors of family structure are hard to identify. It may be that non-traditional family forms are not problematic for children *per se*, but that these particular family types tend to co-occur with other risk factors, such as lower income, parental depression, or parental conflict (which often occurs around separation or divorce). It may be that it is these co-occurring characteristics, rather than family structure, that influence important outcomes, including aggression and anti-social behaviour (Barrett & Turner, 2006).

More recent research in this area has also demonstrated the importance of family instability and change, rather than structure *per se* (McLanahan & Garfinkel, 2012). Beck *et al.* (2010) found that the effect of family instability on mothers' parenting may differ depending on her education and the types of parenting under examination. Some researchers (for example, Fomby & Cherlin, 2007) suggest that multiple parental relationship transitions increases risk for children's behaviour problems. However, it may be that the correlation between relationship transitions and anti-social behaviour in children is confounded by risk factors for parental relationship transitions that also increase risk for anti-social behaviour. For example, some studies of divorce indicate that risk for relationship dissolution is associated with unemployment, lack of education, poverty, and parental anti-social behaviour (for example, Cherlin, 2010).

Other Factors Related to Anti-social Behaviour

Parenting style

Regardless of family structure, many researchers regard the quality of parenting as one of the best predictors of child and adolescent socio-emotional and behavioural wellbeing, including anti-social behaviour (Baumrind, 1978, 1991; Demaray & Malecki, 2002; Musitu *et al.*, 2007), as well as being an important protective factor (for example, Criss *et al.*, 2003).

Research also suggests that parents who systematically monitor their children's behaviour result in adolescents being less likely to engage in anti-social behaviour (Pettit *et al.*, 2001; Roche *et al.*, 2005).

Furthermore, research also suggests that adolescent disclosure may be an even stronger predictor of both parental knowledge and adolescent adjustment than parents' active efforts at monitoring their children (Stattin & Kerr, 2000). This precedence of adolescent disclosure over certain parenting behaviours has been found to hold for problems like anti-social behaviour, as well as others like low self-esteem and depressed mood.

Self-concept / esteem

Drawing on the results of three studies, Donnellan *et al.* (2005) found a strong relationship between low self-esteem and anti-social behaviour. Other findings, using prospective data from the Dunedin Multidisciplinary Health and Development Study birth cohort, showed that adolescents with low self-esteem had poorer mental and physical health, worse economic prospects, and higher levels of criminal behaviour during adulthood, compared to adolescents with high self-esteem (Trzesniewski *et al.*, 2006).

One argument proposed for the mechanism by which self-esteem works is that people who think they are worthless have no self-esteem to lose from any negativity they might attract through anti-social behaviour. Kaplan (1980) argues the case for 'esteem enhancement', where children want to think well of themselves and go about making efforts to enhance their esteem if it is low. According to this theory, anti-social behaviour follows low self-esteem because it provides a means of raising esteem.

Peer influences

Regardless of its size, the influence of the peer group varies in the overall rate of anti-social behaviour; however, if one member of a group engages in problem behaviour, there is a high probability that other members will do the same (Dishion *et al.*, 1995), and with larger friendship networks the chances of this become more likely.

Hanging out with older peers has also been associated with anti-social behaviour, with some authors suggesting that at-risk children may be more likely to *choose* older peers because they believe these older children can provide them with some kind of protection or affirmation. However, because later adolescence is also associated with higher levels of anti-social behaviour, then by definition hanging out with older peers is often likely to be more risky.

The Prevalence of Anti-social Behaviour

The measure of anti-social behaviour used here is based on nine items that were self-reported by 13-year-olds in the *Growing Up in Ireland* study. The 13-year-old respondents recorded how often s/he had been engaged in the activity 'in the last year': *Never, Once, 2-5 times, 6 or more times*. Three broad categories of anti-social behaviour are considered: theft; vandalism; and interpersonal violence. The measure of **theft** (or acquisitive anti-social behaviour) included the following four items: 'stolen from a shop'; 'stolen or ridden in a stolen car'; 'burgled'; 'broken into a car'. The measure of **vandalism** included two items: 'damaged or destroyed property that didn't belong to you'; 'committed arson'. Finally, the measure of **violent behaviour** included three items: 'used force or threats'; 'involvement in a fight resulting in injury to someone'; 'carried a knife or a weapon'. For the purposes of the analysis presented here, if the young person had *ever* committed any of these acts they were categorised accordingly (to the particular subgroup of behaviour).

Figure 12.1: Percentage of 13-year-olds Committing Anti-social Behaviour at least Once

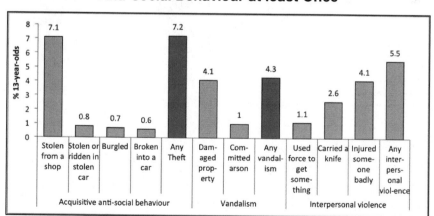

Figure 12.1 gives an overall breakdown of the prevalence of different property- and person-related anti-social behaviour self-reported by 13-year-olds in *Growing Up in Ireland*. It indicates, for example, that 7 per cent of 13-year-olds recorded having stolen from a shop at least once in the previous year; 4 per cent having damaged property; 3 per cent having carried a knife; and 4 per cent having injured someone badly.

Social disadvantage

With a view to understanding the extent to which social and economic advantage or disadvantage was associated with different anti-social behaviour, a four-fold classification of family social class (based on the occupation of the 13-year-old's main caregiver at age 9) was used. The categories range from 'Professional / Managerial' to 'Class Unknown'. The latter category refers to young people whose main caregivers have no recorded occupational or work history and are, in general, from the most disadvantaged group of families.

Figure 12.2: Percentage of Adolescents in Each Social Class Committing Anti-social Behaviour

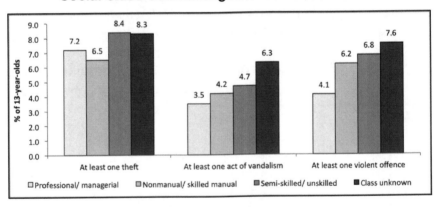

Figure 12.2 illustrates important and significant differences between the least and most disadvantaged social groups in terms of self-reported vandalism or violent behaviour – 4 per cent of 13-year-olds from the most advantaged group recorded having committed at least one act of vandalism compared to 6 per cent among the most disadvantaged. Similarly, 4 per cent of the most advantaged 13-year-olds recorded

having committed at least one act of violent behaviour, compared with 8 per cent among young teenagers from the most socially-disadvantaged group. For theft however, there was no statistical difference between the two groups.

Individual characteristics and anti-social behaviour

Figure 12.3 shows differences in prevalence levels between boys and girls. It is clear that boys were much more likely than girls to report all types of anti-social behaviour, with 10 per cent reporting theft (compared to 5 per cent of girls), 6 per cent reporting vandalism (compared to 2 per cent of girls) and 8 per cent reporting violent behaviour (compared to 3 per cent of girls). These trends strongly reflect findings from the international literature.

Further analysis (not shown here), and also in keeping with research in this area in other countries, indicates that the 13-year-old's self-concept was linked to behaviour. A detailed measure of self-concept (known as the Piers-Harris II scale) was used to measure self-esteem. This scale is based on 60 questions that are self-completed by the young person. We find that 13-year-olds with below average self-esteem were more likely than their counterparts with significantly higher levels of self-esteem to report involvement in all types of anti-social behaviour: theft – 12 per cent compared to 5 per cent; vandalism – 7 per cent compared to 3 per cent; and violent behaviour – 10 per cent compared to 4 per cent.

Figure 12.3: Percentage of Boys and Girls Committing Anti-social Behaviour

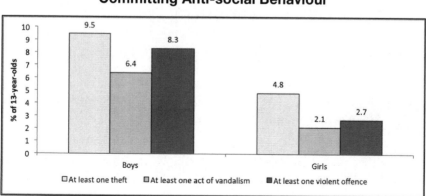

When the young person was interviewed at age 9, his / her main caregiver was asked to complete a detailed 25-item inventory of questions on their child's socio-emotional and behavioural wellbeing. (This detailed inventory is known as the Strengths and Difficulties Questionnaire – the SDQ – and is very widely used in studies in Ireland and elsewhere). Based on their main caregiver's responses to the five questions contained in the conduct subscale of the SDQ questionnaire, one can classify a child as being in a 'potentially problematic' range in terms of their conduct or behaviour – that is, being among the children in the top decile of scores on this subscale. Significant associations were found between self-reported anti-social behaviour at age 13 and whether the child was classified as being in the 'potentially problematic' range of the SDQ conduct subscale four years earlier, at age 9. This was found for all three types of anti-social behaviour: theft – 12 per cent among those in the 'potentially problematic' behavioural range at age 9 compared to 7 per cent for other children; vandalism – 8 per cent compared to 4 per cent; and violent behaviour – 11 per cent compared to 5 per cent.

Family characteristics and anti-social behaviour

Information recorded on family composition at both age 9 and age 13 was used to classify children in terms of *stability* of family structure over the previous four years of the child's life. A four-fold classification was used:

- Children who had remained in *stable one-parent families over the period*
- Children in *stable two-parent families*
- Children who had transitioned from *one- to two-parent families*
- Children who had transitioned from *two- to one-parent families*.

This type of classification gives us an opportunity to explore relationships between anti-social behaviour and family transitions, rather than just static family structures.

Figure 12.4 illustrates that family stability was also linked to lower levels of anti-social behaviour, this being particularly true of children in stable two-parent families. This group was the least likely to report involvement in violent behaviour (5 per cent), while those in families where a new partner had joined the household since the time of the previous interview at age 9 were the most likely (13 per cent). Vandalism was also least likely to be reported by those in stable two-parent homes (4 per cent) and most likely to be reported by those where a partner had left the household since age 9 (9 per cent). Theft was also most common among those where either a parent had left the household (9 per cent) or a new parent had joined (10 per cent), compared to those in stable two-parent families (7 per cent).

Figure 12.4: Percentage of Anti-social Behaviours, by Family Stability

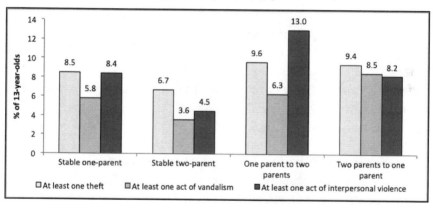

Figure 12.5: Social Class Groups, by Family Stability

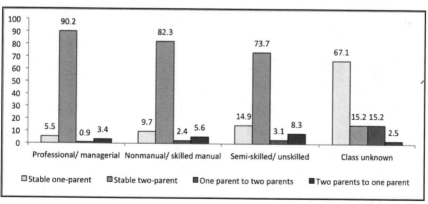

In interpreting these figures it should also be noted that the stability of family structure between ages 9 and 13 is itself socially structured. Nine out of 10 children in the professional / managerial social class were in stable two-parent families, while the largest proportions of those in unstable families (new partner or partner left) came from the two most-disadvantaged social groups (**Figure 12.5**). The relationship between family stability and anti-social behaviour, net of socio-economic disadvantage, will be explored in further detail below.

Figure 12.6 highlights other family processes (such as parent-child conflict and parental responsiveness and autonomy-granting) that were associated with anti-social behaviour. The chart classifies the 13-year-olds in terms of high and low levels of parent-child conflict; parental responsiveness and parental autonomy-granting. 'High' levels in each refer to 13-year-olds in the top tertile (or third) of the distribution, 'low' levels to those in the bottom tertile. The chart indicates that more positive aspects of the parent-child relationship (top tertiles of both parental responsiveness and autonomy-granting) had small but significant associations with lower levels of anti-social behaviour. Contrary to this, higher levels of parent-child conflict (top tertile) were significantly associated with more involvement in anti-social behaviour.

Figure 12.6: Levels of Anti-social Behaviour among 13-year-olds in the Top and Bottom Thirds of Parent-child Conflict, Parental Responsiveness and Parental Autonomy-granting

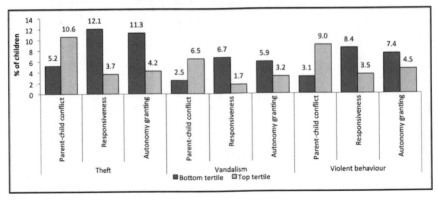

High levels of child disclosure and parental control were also significantly associated with lower risk of all anti-social behaviours, although in the current analysis higher levels of monitoring were not significantly associated with any of the anti-social behaviours examined.

Analysis of other family context indices indicated that children whose parents had themselves reported in the course of their *Growing Up in Ireland* interview that they had been in trouble with the Gardaí were significantly more likely to report involvement in theft (15 per cent) than those who did not (7 per cent). There was no significant difference, however, between 13-year-olds who had self-reported having either vandalised property or having been involved in violent behaviour.

Peer groups

Teenagers with larger groups of friends were more likely to report anti-social behaviour, especially theft and vandalism. For instance, those who normally hung out in groups of 10 or more were more likely to report theft or vandalism – 12 per cent and 15 per cent respectively – compared to those with between one and five friends, of whom 8 per cent and 5 per cent reported these behaviours.

The age of peers was also important. In keeping with the literature, the findings showed that spending time with mostly older friends was associated with a greater chance of involvement in anti-social behaviour, particularly when compared to those who had no older friends. So, 17 per cent of young people with mostly older friends reported theft, 15 per cent reported vandalism and 12 per cent reported violent behaviour, compared to 7 per cent, 5 per cent, and 3 per cent (respectively) of those with no older friends.

Disentangling Different Influences on Anti-social Behaviour

It is difficult to disentangle different influences on anti-social behaviour. For instance, we saw that social class and family stability were associated (with each other) and that both were associated with anti-social behaviour. Adopting a statistical modelling approach known as logistic regression can help us to identify whether there are any additional differences in anti-social behaviour by social class, apart, for example, from those linked to family instability. By including the variables in groups or 'blocks', we are able to explore first the independent effect of social class (as the base model), and then the extent to which this is changed by:

- The **individual characteristics of the child** (gender, self-esteem, previous conduct problems)

- **Family processes** (family stability, parent-child conflict, parenting style, parental monitoring and control, child disclosure, life events (for example, parental conflict, alcoholism or mental disorder in immediate family), parental contact with the Criminal Justice System)

- **Peer characteristics** (group size and age).

Figure 12.7: Odds Ratios from Logistic Regressions for Social Class and Anti-social Behaviours, Comparing the Most Disadvantaged to the Most Advantaged Young People

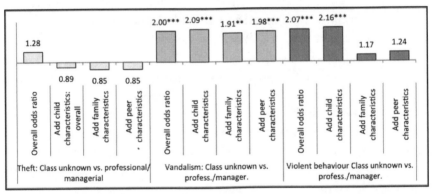

Note: The (control) variables referred to in the models are: **child characteristics**: gender, self-esteem, previous conduct problems; **family processes**: family stability, parent-child conflict, parenting style, parental monitoring and control, child disclosure, life events, parental contact with CJS; **peer characteristics**: group size and age. The vertical axis is on a logarithmic scale to give a better indication of the magnitude of the effects.

Figure 12.7 illustrates the effect of each 'block' of variables as they are added to the models. While the impact of individual variables is not included in the graph, they are described in detail below. Since our main focus is on social equality, the results are presented in order to compare the most disadvantaged social group (social class unknown) to the most advantaged social group (professional / managerial).

The three types of anti-social behaviour (theft, vandalism and violence) are examined in separate models and the results for each are presented as odds ratios. An odds ratio greater than 1 indicates a higher rate of anti-social behaviour compared to the reference group, while a ratio less than 1 indicates a lower rate. In each case, what we are looking at in **Figure 12.7** is the odds ratio of a 13-year-old in the most socially-disadvantaged social group ('Class unknown') being engaged in the respective types of anti-social behaviour compared to their counterparts in the most socially-advantaged group. The first model includes social class alone, with no controls for other characteristics; the second model controls for child characteristics; the third model controls for family characteristics; and the fourth further controls for peer characteristics.

Results of the Models

Social class

As the main marker for the social and economic circumstances of the family, social class was used in our base models to allow us to explore the associations between social background and anti-social behaviour separately before including any other variables in the models. Differential findings emerged depending on the particular behaviour examined. One such finding, illustrated in **Figure 12.7**, shows that being in the most-disadvantaged group was associated with significantly higher odds of vandalism (OR, 2.0) and violent behaviour (OR, 2.07), although there was no significant relationship found for theft, indicating that this behaviour was not socially-structured. However, as we will see in later results other factors were associated with theft.

Child characteristics

As a next step we added those variables measuring certain child characteristics to the models. As with the descriptive findings outlined earlier, gender was independently linked to all of the behaviours under discussion, boys having significantly higher odds than girls of being involved. For example, the bivariate odds indicated that they had around 2.5 times the odds of being involved in theft (OR, 2.41), almost 5 times the odds of reporting vandalism (OR, 4.94), and 4.8 times the odds of being involved in violent behaviour (not shown separately in **Figure 12.7**).

Other child characteristics linked to anti-social behaviour in the current models were self-esteem and previous problematic behaviour. Having lower than average self-esteem was linked to significantly higher odds of being involved in all types of anti-social behaviour, including theft. This group was more than twice as likely to have stolen something (OR, 2.06) or been involved in vandalism (OR, 2.09) and was over 3 times more likely to report committing a violent act (OR, 3.12) compared to those with average or above self-esteem. According to the bivariate odds ratios (not shown here) being in the 'potentially problematic' group for conduct problems at age 9 (measured by the Strengths and Difficulties Questionnaire (SDQ)) was associated with higher odds of all behaviours but was only significant for theft (OR, 1.38) at age 13.

Figure 12.7 also illustrates that the addition of these child characteristics to our models actually strengthened the association between social class and anti-social behaviours involving vandalism and violence, but not theft. The chart shows that when the additional controls for child characteristics were added to the models the odds of someone in the most socially-disadvantaged group being involved in vandalism were not reduced.

Family characteristics

At the third stage of the models we included variables relating to family processes, which also included family stability. As discussed above, family stability can be linked to the social class of the household, although distinct and direct links between family structure and anti-social behaviour also emerged. Vandalism was more evident among 13-year-olds who had experienced the departure of a parent (or parent figure) in the last four years (OR, 2.29) compared to those in stable two-parent families. On the other hand, violent behaviour was significantly associated with living in either a stable lone-parent household (OR, 1.58) or in a household where a new partner had joined, where the odds ratio was over 3 times higher than for those in stable two-parent families (OR, 3.13) (not shown here).

Furthermore, the odds ratios for some of the different aspects of the parent-child relationship and parenting showed that higher levels of parental control (essentially a form of behavioural regulation) were associated with significantly lower odds of all three subtypes of anti-social behaviour (theft – OR, 0.65; vandalism – OR, 0.65; violence – OR, 0.67). Spontaneous disclosure between child and parent was also significantly and negatively associated with a roughly 50 per cent lower odds of reporting violent behaviour (OR, 0.51). Contrary to expectations though, in the current models we found higher levels of parental monitoring to be associated with significantly higher levels of theft and vandalism. One explanation may be that this is an example of child behaviour impacting parenting behaviour, where knowledge of poor conduct is linked to parents employing more monitoring behaviours (not shown here).

Responsive parenting, engendered by high levels of warmth, was also associated with significantly lower levels of all the behaviour under discussion, and supports the widely-held notion of this as a protective factor in terms of negative behavioural outcomes (theft – OR, 0.91; vandalism – OR, 0.91; violence – OR, 0.96). Autonomy-granting (parental trust) was associated with lower odds of theft (OR, 0.93), but not vandalism or violent behaviour, while parent-child conflict was associated with increased odds for all behaviours (theft – OR, 1.16; vandalism – OR, 1.42; violence – OR, 1.43) (Not shown here).

While the findings illustrate how different aspects of parenting are related to different behaviour, it was also clear from the findings that, in general, negative aspects of parenting were linked to more anti-social behaviour, while positive parenting was linked to less anti-social behaviour. However, as the findings on parental monitoring indicate, there may be more than an element of bi-directionality in this relationship, where bad behaviour may elicit higher levels of monitoring, and indeed good behaviour may be driving higher levels of parental warmth and child disclosure (not shown here).

In relation to the other family context variables, it was also found that certain adverse 'life events', including the 13-year-old's experience of drug / alcohol misuse in the immediate family was associated with theft (OR, 2.31), as was parent behaviour (being in trouble with the Gardaí – OR, 1.64), while mental disorder in the child's immediate family was associated with higher odds of violent behaviour among our sample (OR, 3.02), as was parental conflict witnessed by the child (OR, 1.52).

In sum, the addition of these particular variables related to family characteristics reduced the effect of social class on vandalism only very slightly, whereas they completely attenuated the association between social class and violent behaviour, which became non-significant at this stage.

Peer characteristics

In the final stages of the models the information on peer groups was added, namely, peer network size and age of peers. The findings showed that peer characteristics were independently associated with anti-social behaviours. Hanging out in large peer groups (more than 10) was associated with higher odds of theft (OR, 2.41), vandalism (OR, 3.56) and violent behaviour (OR, 1.80) among 13-year-olds, compared to hanging out in smaller groups of five or less. Furthermore, having some or mostly older friends (compared to none) was also associated with increased odds of involvement in all anti-social behaviour subtypes. We found that 13-year-olds with some older friends were more likely to be involved in theft (OR,1.64), vandalism (OR, 1.68) and violent behaviour (OR, 2.44), while these odds were even higher for those hanging out with mostly older friends (theft – OR, 2.31; vandalism – OR, 1.86; violence – OR, 3.19). (not shown here).

In the final models, when peer characteristics were included as controls as well as the child and family characteristics, social disadvantage remained significantly associated with vandalism among the current sample (OR, 1.98), and non-significant for violent behaviour and theft.

Conclusion

The current chapter focused on some of the main factors associated with youth anti-social behaviour in Ireland, with a particular focus on the social and economic characteristics of the family, here principally indexed by household social class. While it is important to note that anti-social behaviour is a relatively rare event among this age group, nonetheless some interesting and important findings came to light, although these also highlighted the complexity of the issue.

For example, we found that, at a basic level (looking at no other variables), social disadvantage was associated with both vandalism and violence, but not theft. However, in our final models we also found that vandalism was related to social disadvantage, even when we accounted for child, family and peer characteristics. Violent behaviour was slightly different, in that there was a significant relationship with social disadvantage even when we controlled for child characteristics but this relationship was explained away when family and peer characteristics were taken into consideration.

Furthermore, while links were found between social disadvantage and vandalism, and, to a certain extent, violence, all anti-social behaviour, including theft, was associated with many other factors including family stability, family relationships and parenting, peer relationships, and the child's own characteristics. Some of these variables also emerged as being highly salient in the current findings, further indicating the extent to which anti-social behaviour is truly multi-determined.

For instance, the finding that gender was such a strong correlate of anti-social behaviour in the current models suggests that gender may interact with social class to impact the likelihood of (some) anti-social behaviour. Some recent studies have suggested that gender may moderate the relationship between socio-economic status and anti-social behaviour (Letourneau et al., 2013), although evidence of this effect is scarce and inconsistent. Some research has found a significant effect of social disadvantage in increasing the likelihood of anti-social behaviour among boys but not girls (Veenstra et al., 2006), but also among girls and not boys (Henninger & Luze, 2013). This issue will be the subject of future work by the current authors.

Another example was family structure. Instability in family structure in particular can often impact parenting skills, as has been highlighted in the existing literature. One such finding suggests that mothers often give more attention to a new partner who joins the household, possibly to the detriment of the existing relationship with her child (King, 2009). It is recognised, however, that other factors such as recency of change in family structure, as well as the number of previous transitions, socio-economic circumstances, and prior relationship with mother, etc. are all likely to influence this association. While stability of family structure is linked to the social class of the household, its distinct links with (all) anti-social behaviour were evident in the current findings, even when other family factors were accounted for. This may suggest that there are particular effects associated with family transition, rather than with the family structure *per se*.

The current findings also pointed to the importance of parent-child relationships, indicating that conflict was associated with involvement in anti-social behaviour, and this was particularly true for both vandalism and violent behaviour. In addition, high levels of child disclosure and parental responsiveness (warmth) were associated with less anti-social behaviour in general, although caution should be exercised in assigning causality here. Furthermore, links between parental behaviour (contact with the criminal justice system) and child behavioural outcomes indicate that some of this behaviour may be learnt by the child in the family setting. However, while parent criminality may affect the development of anti-social child behaviour, its influence is also likely mediated by the extent to which it disrupts day-to-day parenting practices.

The current work adds to the existing research, and recognises the importance of the social milieu, in particular social disadvantage, as being highly salient in certain aspects of anti-social behaviour, although not all. However, it also draws attention to the importance of other factors that have been less well-researched in Ireland to date, including (relatively) new phenomena such as changing family structures, as well as other important family processes. We recognise the need for further work to try to pinpoint the most salient mechanisms and processes that facilitate or impede, not only the development of adolescent anti-social behaviour, but also, as we have seen here, the different types of anti-social behaviour and their potential for affecting social equality. For example, what particular aspects of the family and parenting are the most important in mediating the relationship between social disadvantage and anti-social behaviour? And, if gender is moderating the relationship between disadvantage and (some) anti-social behaviours, why? And what are the mechanisms involved? Future waves of *Growing Up in Ireland* data will help us to further untangle some of these relationships as well as helping to identify transient and persistent offenders, and critically allow for bespoke interventions to help those who need them.

References

Amato, P.R. (2005). Parenting through family transitions, *New Zealand Journal of Social Policy, 23*, 31-44.

Barrett, A.E. & Turner, R.J. (2006). Family structure and substance use problems in adolescence and early adulthood: Examining explanations for the relationship, *Addiction, 101*, 109-20.

Barry, M. (2006). *Youth Offending in Transition: The Search for Social Recognition*, New York, NY: Routledge.

Baumrind, D. (1978). Parental disciplinary patterns and social competence in children, *Youth and Society, 9*, 238-76.

Baumrind, D. (1991). The influence of parenting styles on adolescent competence and substance use, *Journal of Early Adolescence, 11*, 56-95.

Beck, A.N., Cooper C.E., McLanahan S. & Brooks-Gunn, J. (2010). Partnership transitions and maternal parenting, *Journal of Marriage and the Family, 72*, 219-33.

Broidy, L.M., Nagin, D.S., Tremblay, R.E., Bates, J.E., Brame, B., Dodge, K.A. *et al.* (2003). Developmental trajectories of childhood disruptive behaviours and adolescent delinquency: A six-site, crossnational study, *Developmental Psychology, 39*, 222-45.

Burt, S.A., Donnellan, M.B., Iacono, W.G. & McGue, M. (2011). Age-of-onset or behavioural sub-types? A prospective comparison of two approaches to characterizing the heterogeneity within anti-social behaviour, *Journal of Abnormal Child Psychology, 39*, 633-44.

Cairney, J., Boyle, M., Offord, D.R. & Racine, Y. (2003). Stress, social support, and depression in single and married mothers, *Social Psychiatry and Psychiatric Epidemiology, 38*, 442-49.

Cherlin, A. (2010). Demographic trends in the United States: A review of research in the 2000s, *Journal of Marriage and the Family, 72*, 403-19.

Chief Inspector (1917). *Fifty-fifth Report of the Chief Inspector Appointed to Visit the Reformatory and Industrial Schools in Ireland for the Year Ended 31 December 1916*, Dublin: Her Majesty's Stationery Office.

Conger, R.D. & Conger, K.J. (2002). Resilience in Midwestern families: Selected findings from the first decade of a prospective, longitudinal study, *Journal of Marriage and Family, 64*, 361-73.

Criss, M.M., Shaw, D.S. & Ingoldsby, E.M. (2003). Mother-son positive synchrony in middle childhood: Relation to anti-social behaviour, *Social Development, 12*, 379-400.

Cunneen, C. & White, R. (2002). *Juvenile Justice: Youth and Crime in Australia* (2nd ed.), Melbourne: Oxford University Press.

Demaray, M.K., & Malecki, C.K. (2002). Critical levels of perceived social support associated with student adjustment, *School Psychology Quarterly, 17*, 3213-41.

Dishion, T.J., Andrews, D.W., & Crosby, L. (1995). Anti-social boys and their friends in early adolescence: Relationship characteristics, quality, and interactional process, *Child Development, 66*, 139-51.

Dodge, K., Coie, J., & Lynam, D. (2006). Aggression and anti-social behavior in youth, in Damon, W. & Lerner, R. (series eds.) & Eisenberg, N. (vol. ed.), *Handbook of Child Psychology*: Vol. 3. *Social, Emotional and Personality Development* (6th ed., pp.719-88), New York: Wiley.

Donnellan, M.B., Trzesniewski, K.H., Robins, R.W., Moffitt, T.E. & Caspi, A. (2005). Low self-esteem is related to aggression, anti-social behaviour and delinquency, *Psychological Science, 16*, 328-35.

Eklund, J.M. & af Klinteberg, B. (2006). Stability and change in criminal behavior: A prospective study of young male lawbreakers and controls, *International Journal of Forensic Mental Health, 5*, 83-95.

Elliott, D.S. (1994). Serious violent offenders: Onset, developmental course and termination, The American Society of Criminology 1993 presidential address, *Criminology, 32*, 1-21.

Fergusson, D.M. & Horwood, L.J. (2002). Male and female offending trajectories, *Development and Psychopathology, 14*, 159-177.

Fergusson, D.M., Horwood, L.J. & Woodward, L.J. (2000). The stability of child abuse reports: A longitudinal study of young adults, *Psychological Medicine, 30*, 529-44.

Fomby P. & Cherlin, A.J. (2007). Family instability and child wellbeing, *American Sociological Review, 72*, 181-204.

Henninger, W.R. & Luze, G. (2013). Moderating effects of gender on the relationship between poverty and children's externalizing behaviours, *Journal of Child Healthcare, 17*, 72-81.

Irish Youth Justice Service (2013). *Tackling Youth Crime – Youth Justice Action Plan 2014-2018*, Dublin: Department of Justice and Equality.

Kaplan, H. (1980). *Self-attitudes and Deviant Behaviour*, Santa Monica, CA: Goodyear.

King, V. (2009). Stepfamily formation: Implications for adolescent ties to mothers, nonresident fathers, and stepfathers, *Journal of Marriage and Family, 71*, 954-68.

Lahey, B.B., Schwab-Stone, M., Goodman, S.H., Waldman I.D., Canino, G., Rathouz, P.J., Miller, T.L., Dennis, K.D., Bird, H. & Jensen, P.S. (2000). Age and gender differences in oppositional behaviour and conduct problems: A cross-sectional household study of middle childhood and adolescence, *Journal of Abnormal Psychology, 109*, 488-503.

Letourneau, N.L., Duffet-Leger, L., Levac, L., Watson, B. & Young-Morris, C. (2013). Socio-economic status and child development: A meta-analysis, *Journal of Emotional and Behavioural Disorders, 21,* 211-24.

Loeber, R., Farrington, D.P., Stouthamer-Loeber, M. & Van Kammen, W.B. (1998). *Anti-social Behaviour and Mental Health Problems: Explanatory Factors in Childhood and Adolescence,* Mahwah, NJ: Lawrence Erlbaum.

Maughan, B., Rowe, R., Messer, J., Goodman, R. & Meltzer, H. (2004). Conduct disorder and oppositional defiant disorder in a national sample: Developmental epidemiology, *Journal of Child Psychology and Psychiatry, 45,* 609-21.

McLanahan, S. & Garfinkel, I. (2012). Fragile families: Debates, facts and solutions, in Scott, E. & Garrison, M. (eds.), *Marriage at the Crossroads* (pp.142-69), Cambridge, UK: Cambridge University Press.

McLeod, J.D., & Shanahan, M.J. (1993). Poverty, parenting, and children's mental health, *American Sociological Review, 58,* 351-66.

McLoyd, V. (1990). The impact of economic hardship on black families and children: Psychological distress, parenting, and socio-emotional development, *Child Development, 61,* 311-46.

Moffitt, T.E., Caspi, A., Rutter, M. & Silva, P.A. (2001). *Sex Differences in Anti-social Behaviour: Conduct Disorder, Delinquency and Violence in the Dunedin Longitudinal Study,* Cambridge University Press.

Musitu, G., Estévez, E. & Emler, N. (2007). Adjustment problems in the family and school contexts, attitude towards authority and violent behaviour at school in adolescence, *Adolescence, 42,* 779-94.

National Institute for Health and Care Excellence (2013). *Anti-social Behaviour and Conduct Disorders in Children and Young People: Recognition, Intervention and Management,* London: Royal College of Psychiatrists / Leicester: British Psychological Society.

Neckerman, K. & Torche, F. (2007). Inequality: Causes and consequences, *Annual Review of Sociology, 33,* 335-57.

O'Mahony, P. (1997). *Mountjoy Prisoners: A Sociological and Criminological Profile,* Dublin: Stationery Office.

Odgers, C.L., Moffitt, T.E., Broadbent, J.M., Dickson, N., Hancox, R.J., Harrington, H., Poulton, R., Sears, M.R., Thomson, W.M. & Caspi, A. (2008). Female and male anti-social trajectories: From childhood origins to adult outcomes, *Development and Psychopathology, 20,* 673-716.

Pettit, G.S., Laird, R.D., Dodge, K.A., Bates, J.E. & Criss, M.M. (2001). Antecedents and behaviour-problem outcomes of parental monitoring and psychological control in early adolescence, *Child Development, 72,* 583-98.

Piotrowska, P.J., Stride, C.B., Croft, S.E. & Rowe, R. (2015). Socio-economic status and anti-social behaviour among children and adolescents: A systematic review and meta-analysis, *Clinical Psychology Review, 35,* 47-55.

Roche, K.M., Ellen, J. & Astone, N.M. (2005). Effects of out-of-school care on early sex initiation in low-income, central city neighbourhoods, *Archives of Pediatrics and Adolescent Medicine, 159,* 68-73.

Rutter, M. & The English and Romanian Adoptees (ERA) study team (1998). Developmental catch-up, and deficit, following adoption after severe global early privation, *Journal of Child Psychology and Psychiatry, 39,* 465-76.

Snyder H. (2004). *Juvenile arrests 2002,* Washington, DC: Office of Juvenile Justice and Delinquency Prevention.

Sprott, J.B., Jenkins, J.M. & Doob, A.N. (2000). *Early Offending: Understanding the Risk and Protective Factors of Delinquency,* Hull, Quebec: Applied Research Branch, Strategic Policy: Human Resources Development Canada.

Stanger, C., Achenbach, T.M. & Verhulst, F.C. (1997). Accelerated longitudinal comparisons of aggressive *versus* delinquent syndromes, *Developmental Psychopathology, 9,* 43-58.

Stattin, H. & Kerr, M. (2000). Parental monitoring: A reinterpretation, *Child Development, 71,* 1072-85.

Stattin, H. & Magnusson, D. (1991). Stability and change in criminal behaviour up to age 30, *The British Journal of Criminology, 31,* 327-46.

Thornberry, T.P. & Krohn, M.D. (2003). *Taking Stock of Delinquency: An Overview of Findings from Contemporary Longitudinal Studies,* New York, NY: Kluwer / Plenum.

Trzesniewski, K.H., Donnellan, M.B., Moffitt, T.E., Robins, R.W., Poulton, R. & Caspi, A. (2006). Low self-esteem during adolescence predicts poor health, criminal behaviour, and limited economic prospects during adulthood, *Developmental Psychology, 42,* 381-90.

Veenstra, R.S., Lindenberg, S., Oldehinkel, A.J., De Winter, A.F. & Ormel, J. (2006). Temperament, environment, and anti-social behaviour in a population sample of pre-adolescent boys and girls, *International Journal of Behavioural Development, 30,* 422-32.

13: CHILD ECONOMIC VULNERABILITY DYNAMICS IN THE RECESSION

*Dorothy Watson, Bertrand Maître,
Christopher T. Whelan & James Williams*

Introduction

Poverty and economic disadvantage have a range of negative effects on children, including on their physical and mental health, educational achievement, and emotional and behavioural outcomes. While the lives of children in Ireland may have improved in many respects since 1916, as discussed in **Chapter 2**, inequalities remain in the circumstances of children and these inequalities have consequences for child development. A great deal of work on disadvantage in childhood has followed Heckman's (2011) argument that the highest rate of return in terms of investment in children comes from investing as early as possible, from birth through to age 5. While not seeking to contradict this claim, this chapter shows that the impact of even a short-term deterioration in the circumstances of children matters for child development. Furthermore, in demonstrating the manner in which the costs of the recession at later stages of childhood are unequally distributed across socio-economic groups, it brings into focus that fact that it is necessary to balance efficiency concerns with equity considerations in seeking to redress the negative impacts of the economic crisis. A failure to do so will increase the likelihood of the emergence of processes of cumulative disadvantage in which those most 'scarred' by the recession become least able to take advantage of the upturn.

We make use of the first and second waves of the 2008 (Infant) and 1998 (Child) cohorts of the *Growing Up in Ireland* study to examine the impact on families and children in Ireland of the 'Great Recession'. The availability of data for two waves for each cohort allows us to compare the pre- and post-recession situations of families with infant children (age 9 months and age 3) and children in middle childhood (age 9 and age 13).

Ireland has seen quite remarkable macroeconomic fluctuations over the past two decades, with the fastest economic growth rate in the Organisation for Economic Co-operation and Development (OECD) during the so-called 'Celtic Tiger' boom being followed by a recession that had a more negative impact on national output in Ireland than in any other OECD country. The decade of exceptionally rapid growth from the mid-1990s saw the numbers employed expand dramatically and unemployment reduced to 4 per cent, but included an unsustainable credit-fuelled expansion in the construction sector and an unbridled property price boom. Recession from 2008 onwards went together with a bursting of the property bubble and related tax revenues, a collapse in asset values, a banking crisis of unprecedented proportions and a ballooning fiscal deficit. This combination meant that, by late 2010, despite substantial increases in taxation and expenditure cuts, the Irish government had to avail itself of a 'bail-out' from the Troika (Whelan, 2010). The impact of the recession involved an unprecedented decline of 13 per cent in GDP between 2007 and 2011 and a rise in unemployment from 4 to 14 per cent, despite substantial net emigration (Whelan, 2010). The percentage of children in jobless households rose from 12 per cent in 2007 to 20 per cent from 2010 to 2012 (Watson *et al.*, 2015).

Previous Research

Research has indicated that poverty and deprivation have serious consequences for the development of children in a range of areas, including socio-emotional development, academic achievement and health (Bolger *et al.*, 1995; Brooks-Gunn & Duncan, 1997; Department for Work and Pensions, 2007; Duncan *et al.*, 1994; Duncan *et al.*, 2007; Duncan *et al.*, 2012; Holzer *et al.*, 2007; Jarjoura *et al.*, 2002; McLeod & Shanahan, 1996; Williams & Whelan, 2011; Williams *et al.*, 2009). An increasing focus on child poverty is related to the United Nations' demands that, having ratified the *Convention on the Rights of the Child* (United Nations, 1989), countries monitor trends in the living conditions of children. As Mood & Jonsson (2014) note, this has led to the development of a range of relevant welfare indices with access to basic goods and services featuring as a central indicator of children's wellbeing (Bradshaw *et al.*, 2006; Bradshaw & Richardson, 2009; Fanjul, 2007).

There is clear evidence that children born into poverty are more likely to have poorer health outcomes, such as a lower birth weight, higher infant mortality and poorer health than better-off children (Department for Work and Pensions, 2007). Focusing on developmental issues, Duncan *et al.* (1994) found that low income and poverty were good predictors of cognitive development and behavioural measures at age 5, even controlling for factors such as family structure and maternal education. Other research also points to the importance of the early childhood years for learning self-regulation skills such as regulating attention (Duncan *et al.*, 2007; Holzer *et al.*, 2007; but see NICHHD, 2005, which suggests that later poverty may be more detrimental for behaviour in middle childhood). Many studies have found that long-term exposure to poverty is associated with behavioural problems at school, low self-esteem, problems in peer relations (Bolger *et al.*, 1995), and depression and anti-social behaviour (McLeod & Shanahan, 1996; Jarjoura *et al.*, 2002). In fact, a study by the NICHHD (2005) finds that the persistence of poverty is more important than its timing for cognitive development and behaviour in middle childhood.

Research from the ***Growing Up in Ireland*** study on the 1998 cohort at age 9 has already established the concurrent association between childhood poverty and child outcomes, including achievement in maths and reading, social adjustment, behavioural problems and health (Williams & Whelan, 2011). For instance, 9-year-old children from the lowest income quintile were more likely to have emotional and conduct difficulties, as well as problems with hyperactivity and peer relationships. These children also had higher levels of absences from school, higher rates of non-completion of homework and their mothers were more likely to have literacy and numeracy difficulties (Williams *et al.*, 2009). The present chapter goes beyond this analysis in examining the link between economic vulnerability at age 9 and later socio-emotional wellbeing at age 13 and conducting a similar exercise for the 2008 (Infant) cohort.

Child economic vulnerability is a concern not only because of its immediate consequences for the wellbeing of children but also because it has potentially long-term negative consequences that persist into adulthood. Duncan *et al.* (2012) summarise a range of evidence from the US relating to the consequences of early childhood poverty for adult labour market outcome. Longitudinal research, particularly in the United States, has shown that poverty in childhood is associated with reduced life opportunities and a greater risk of experiencing poverty during adulthood. A review by Brooks-Gunn & Duncan (1997) found that family income seems to be even more strongly related to children's ability and achievement-related outcomes than to emotional outcomes. The evidence drawn from the literature affirms not only the long-term damaging impact of poverty on children's personal outcomes, but also the enduring costs to society associated with these negative outcomes – encompassing health problems, crime, low educational achievement and welfare dependence (Duncan *et al.*, 2012; Waldfogel, 2013). The fact that childhood economic disadvantage can have long-lasting consequences has been demonstrated in the Irish longitudinal study on ageing (TILDA), a study of adults aged 50 and over that includes retrospective information on childhood experiences. This research has found that growing up in poor households increased the risk of a number of health problems in later life, including cardiovascular disease, lung disease and mental health issues (McCrory *et al.*, 2015).

The persistence of poverty over several years is particularly harmful and the timing of poverty is also important. In particular, income poverty experienced in the early years of childhood can be more consequential for adult employment outcomes than income poverty experienced in later childhood (Duncan *et al.*, 2012). Low household income during the early childhood years was also associated with lower rates of high-school completion and high neighbourhood poverty and poor quality schooling may exacerbate this effect (Brooks-Gunn & Duncan, 1997).

Earlier research on the *Growing Up in Ireland* data has found that family type is associated with the risk of disadvantage, with lone-parent and cohabiting families at higher risk (Fahey *et al.*, 2012; Hannan & Halpin, 2014). Results reported by Fahey *et al.* (2012) indicate that poverty and low levels of maternal education are important in accounting for the lower wellbeing of children in one-parent families. Hannan & Halpin (2014), similarly, point to the significance of socio-economic differences between family types, in accounting for the disadvantage in health and self-concept faced by children in lone-parent or cohabiting families.

Research Questions

In this chapter we focus on socio-emotional outcomes among children because these are important aspects of child wellbeing. We also have an indicator that is measured in a similar way for the older and younger cohorts so that we can compare the impact of inequality at different stages. We examine four main questions in this chapter:

- How did the recession affect the material circumstances of families?
- Does the impact of poverty on child socio-emotional development differ for younger and older cohorts of children?
- Is persistent poverty more harmful than transient poverty?
- Are there factors that protect children in the context of poverty?

Methodology

Data

In this chapter, data from the first two waves of both cohorts of *Growing Up in Ireland* are used, when the children in the 2008 (Infant) Cohort were aged 9 months and subsequently age 3 and those in the 1998 (Child) Cohort were age 9 and subsequently age 13. The present analysis includes the 9,793 families who responded in both waves of the

2008 cohort and the 7,423 families who responded in both waves for
the 1998 cohort.

The timing of the *Growing Up in Ireland* surveys in relation to the
onset of the 'Great Recession' is important in interpreting change over
time. The first wave of the 1998 cohort was conducted with the families
of the 9-year-olds between August 2007 and June 2008, slightly before
the major shocks of the recession began later that year. The second wave,
when the children were aged 13, took place between August 2011 and
March 2012 (**Figure 13.1**). This corresponded to the deepest point of the
recession, before any growth in employment was evident. The first wave
of the 2008 cohort, when the children were aged 9 months, occurred a
little later: between September 2008 and March 2009, right at the start of
the recession when unemployment was rising most sharply. The second
wave, when the children were age 3, was from December 2010 to July
2011. At this stage, unemployment was still increasing and GNP was still
falling but at a much slower rate (**Figure 13.1**).

**Figure 13.1: Timing of *Growing Up in Ireland*
Fieldwork and Unemployment Rate**

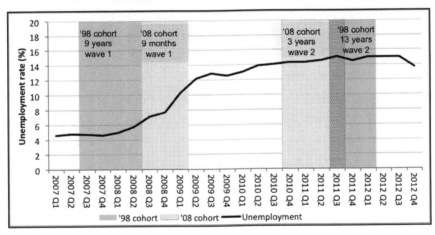

Given the timing of the fieldwork, we would expect that the families of
the 2008 cohort would already be affected by the recession in the first
wave. As a result, the impact of the recession would be seen most
clearly in the 1998 cohort since the interviewing was completed before
the very steep rise in unemployment in the fourth quarter of 2008.

Identifying economically vulnerable groups

It has been known for some time that it is not enough to rely on income to identify those who are economically disadvantaged. This has resulted in a focus on poverty and social exclusion as multi-dimensional (Grusky & Weeden, 2007; Nolan & Whelan, 2007, 2010). Focusing on purely relative income poverty gives a particularly partial picture in periods of economic boom and crisis where there are significant changes in absolute living standards across the population as a whole. However, a focus purely on absolute standards also has limitations, since it neglects issues relating to inequality. When the focus is on trends, conclusions can be crucially influenced by the choice of start and end points. One example of the difficulties involved in making such decisions is the recent UNICEF report (Fanjul, 2014). An analysis of child poverty in a range of countries, including Ireland, the change in poverty rates was calculated by using a poverty line fixed at 60 per cent of median income in 2008. Using the same poverty line in 2012, adjusted for inflation, the rate is computed and the difference in the two rates is taken as the change in the poverty rate. While this undoubtedly captures the unprecedented decline in real incomes during the recession, it tells us little about trends in inequality and provides a very limited basis for evaluating the impact of policy changes. It also ignores the fact that the economic crisis in Ireland was preceded by an equally unprecedented boom, involving a dramatic increase in real income levels. Thus the choice of a slightly earlier reference point would substantially alter conclusions.

These concerns have led to the emergence of a focus on 'vulnerability'. Vulnerability is a broader concept than current disadvantage as it also includes insecurity and exposure to risk of deprivation. Vulnerability may remain latent until families are challenged by critical events or the depletion of limited resources. The basic notion is that there are underlying processes that result in distinct clusters of individuals with similar risk profiles.

There has been a great deal of debate regarding the range of dimensions that should be covered in measures of childhood poverty or deprivation. Rather than attempting to capture the full range of deprivation experienced by children, our approach was to develop a multidimensional, but necessarily restricted, indicator of economic vulnerability, where the emphasis is on identifying economically-vulnerable families rather than characterising the nature of their deprivation. In other words, our emphasis was on *identifying* those children exposed to economic vulnerability and analysing risk factors and consequences of this vulnerability rather than a complete enumeration of the goods, services and activities that these children lack.

Table 13.1: Indicators of Economic Vulnerability

Income level	Income quartile of family calculated separately for each cohort in each period. One quarter of each cohort in each wave is found in each quartile, so the bottom quartile contains the one quarter of families with the lowest incomes.
Economic stress	Whether the family has 'great difficulty' or 'difficulty' in making ends meet.
Household joblessness ('very low work intensity')	The working-age adults in the household are currently in employment for less than one fifth of the available hours. Working-age adults are aged 18 to 59, excluding full-time students under age 25. The percentage of available time worked is calculated as a percentage of 35 hours (capped at 100 per cent), which is regarded as full-time for this purpose. Note: hours worked are available for the primary and secondary caregivers only. We include any other adults at work but assume that any work is full-time.

*Source: **Growing up in Ireland** study, Waves 1 and 2 for the 1998 and 2008 cohorts.*

The indicators used to identify the vulnerable group in this study were income level, economic stress and household joblessness (see **Table 13.1**). They encompass relative and absolute aspects of the household's experience and objective and subjective facets. The indicators were employed to distinguish a 'vulnerable' and 'non-vulnerable' group for each cohort and wave, using latent class analysis. The details of the latent class analysis and construction of the indicator are provided elsewhere and will not be repeated here (Watson *et al.*, 2015). In what follows, each family is assigned to the class (vulnerable or not vulnerable) to which it has the highest probability of belonging, based on their income, economic stress and household joblessness status. In interpreting the results of the vulnerability analysis, we stress the importance of taking into account the timing of data collection.

Socio-emotional problems

Socio-emotional problems are measured using four subscales of the Strengths and Difficulties Questionnaire (SDQ, Goodman, 1997), a widely-used scale designed to assess emotional health and problem behaviours among children and young people. Using the questionnaire completed by the mother in the second wave, we calculate a Total Difficulties score based on 4 sub-scales: emotional symptoms, conduct problems, hyperactivity / inattention and peer relationship problems. The scores ranged from 0 to 40, with higher scores indicating a greater level of difficulty. The distributions of SDQ scores (based on parent report) are summarised in Watson *et al.* (2015). We take the top 10 per cent of the distribution for both cohorts as indicating potential socio-emotional problems.

Protective factors

As well as the level of education of the mother, which can be regarded as a human capital resource, we examine two other factors that may protect children from the negative effects of socio-emotional problems: the quality of the relationship between parents in a couple household and the emotional wellbeing of the mother. Both of these have been found to be important to the socio-emotional wellbeing of 9-year-olds (Nixon, 2012).

Partner satisfaction is an important factor in family functioning and the manner in which parents interact is crucial for child outcomes. For example, partner satisfaction has been highlighted as not only important in impacting on the child's wellbeing (Nixon, 2012), but also on the parents' wellbeing, as it is seen as a component of adult life satisfaction (Bradbury *et al.*, 2000). The quality of parental relationships was based on the mother's responses to the 7-item dyadic adjustment scale (DAS; Spanier, 1976; Sharpley & Rogers, 1984). This scale provides an assessment of dyadic satisfaction based on participants' self-report of partner agreement on issues, time spent doing things together and relationship satisfaction. This was used as a means of categorising partner relationships as either distressed or adjusted. The analysis also examined the association between the psychological distress of the mother at Wave 1 and child socio-emotional outcomes. Information on parental experience of depression is particularly important in the light of research showing that not only is depression a prevalent condition but that depression in a parent can also impact on child outcomes (for example, Beardslee *et al.*, 1996; Nixon, 2012). *Growing Up in Ireland* used the short (8-item) version of the CES-D, a widely used self-report measure that was developed specifically as a screening instrument for depression in the general population. The CES-D has been shown to discriminate depressive disorders from other forms of psychopathology (for example, Roberts *et al.*, 1990), as well as correlating highly with other measures of depression, thereby supporting its validity. Total scores on the CES-D range from 0 to 24. Respondents were categorised according to the recommended criterion for depression, with composite scores of 7 or more being classified as depressed.

Results

Changes in economic vulnerability

Figure 13.2 shows the level of economic vulnerability for the two cohorts of children in the first and second waves. As expected, there was a sizeable increase in the level of vulnerability for both groups, with a larger rise for the 1998 cohort. As noted earlier, this difference between the two cohorts was expected because the recession had already begun in the first wave for the 2008 cohort. As a result, the level of vulnerability in Wave 1 was higher for the 2008 cohort at 19 per cent compared to 15 per cent for the 1998 cohort. By the second wave, mid-recession, the level of economic vulnerability was 25 per cent for both groups of families.

The size of the vulnerable groups increased for both cohorts, but more so for the older 1998 one. Over time, members of the vulnerable group remained sharply distinguished from the non-vulnerable but trends varied across the dimensions of vulnerability. Over time, vulnerability became significantly more widely distributed across the income distribution as the impact of the recession led to a more pervasive distribution of economic stress (Whelan & Maître, 2014).

Figure 13.2: Level of Economic Vulnerability in Wave 1 and Wave 2 for Both Cohorts

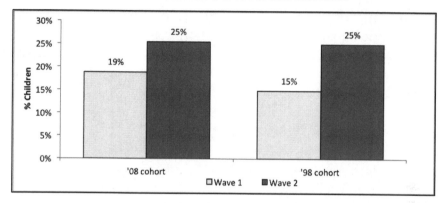

*Source: **Growing up in Ireland** study, Waves 1 and 2 for the 1998 and 2008 cohorts.*

Figure 13.3: Economic Vulnerability Dynamics for Both Cohorts

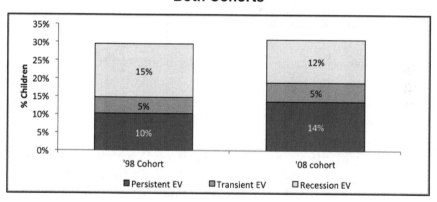

*Source: **Growing up in Ireland** study, Waves 1 and 2 for the 1998 and 2008 cohorts.*

Figure 13.3 shows the dynamic profile for both groups: the percentage of families economically-vulnerable in Wave 1 only (transient vulnerability), in Wave 2 only (recession vulnerability) or in both waves (persistent vulnerability). For both cohorts, the group of families who were vulnerable in both periods account for a sizeable proportion of total vulnerability in the period. Persistent vulnerability is higher in the 2008 cohort at 14 per cent compared to 10 per cent for the 1998 cohort, but this is likely to be because of the timing of the Wave 1 fieldwork after the start of the recession for this group. As a consequence, the group of families becoming economically vulnerable between the two waves is smaller for the 2008 cohort (12 per cent compared to 15 per cent). For both cohorts, only 5 per cent of families moved out of economic vulnerability between waves. The fact that this group is smaller than the number of families moving into economic vulnerability is due to the impact of the recession.

Impact of economic vulnerability on socio-emotional development

At this point we examine the consequences of economic vulnerability for the socio-emotional development of children. To do this, we estimate a statistical model. The purpose of the statistical models is to disentangle the influences of different related factors. For instance, lone parents tend to have lower levels of education than parents who are partnered. The statistical model allows us to separate the impact of living in a lone-parent family from the impact of having a mother with a lower level of education. We use logistic regression, a well-established method for carrying out multiple regression analysis on models with categorical outcomes, such as having an SDQ score in the top 10 per cent. One disadvantage of this approach is that it is somewhat more difficult to explain the results of logistic regressions than simpler regression techniques. In order to facilitate the interpretation of the results, we use the models to estimate the percentage of people expected to have the characteristic of interest, with other factors held constant. These are the 'average marginal effects' as discussed by Williams (2012). For example, we use the models to calculate the percentage of children of lone parents we would expect to have socio-emotional problems, if they were similar to the 'average' child terms of their current age, level of education of the mother and so on. We refer to these as 'adjusted percentages' to distinguish them from the observed percentages.

Most of the characteristics of the child and family are measured at the first wave (family type, mother's education, age of mother at birth of child). We also include some characteristics measured at the second wave, however, such as economic vulnerability, which is assessed in both waves, whether there was a change in family size and whether there was a change in who was acting as the main caregiver.

Figure 13.4: Adjusted Risk of Socio-Emotional Problems, by Characteristics of Child and Family

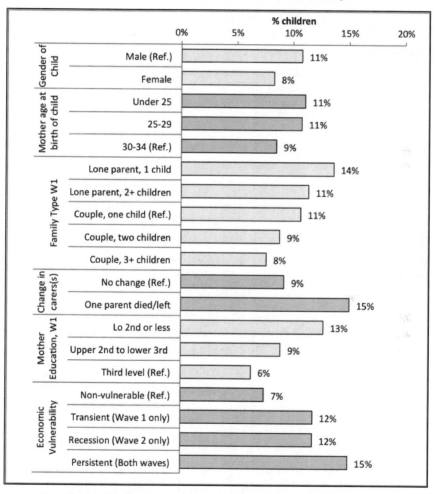

Source: **Growing Up in Ireland** Research Microdata Files for the 2008 and 1998 cohorts; analysis by authors.

Note: Calculated from Model 1 in **Table 13.2**.
**p<0.01; *p<0.05.

Figure 13.4 shows the adjusted percentages for those characteristics of the child and family that had a significant association with socio-emotional development. As noted in the methodology section, our focus is on the chances that a child will be in the top 10 per cent – the group most likely to have social-emotional problems. So the overall risk of having socio-emotional problems, according to this measure, is 10 per cent.

Turning first to economic vulnerability, we can see that the risk of socio-emotional problems is higher for children in economically vulnerable families at 12 per cent for those economically vulnerable in one of the two periods and 15 per cent for those who were persistently vulnerable compared to 7 per cent for those economically vulnerable in neither wave. Persistent vulnerability – being vulnerable in both periods – has a stronger effect than recession vulnerability (becoming vulnerable in the second wave).

Other large differences are associated with family type, a caregiver / parent leaving or dying, and the education of the primary caregiver who is usually the mother. The risk of socio-emotional problems is higher for lone-parent families, with an estimated risk of 14 per cent for lone-parent families with one child and 11 per cent for lone-parent families with two or more children compared to 8 to 9 per cent for couples with two or more children. Couples with just one child do not differ significantly from lone-parent families, however, with an adjusted risk of socio-emotional problems at 11 per cent. Lone parents with two or more children differ significantly only from couples with three or more children.

Where one of the caregivers left or died between waves, the risk of socio-emotional problems also increases to an estimated 15 per cent. The adjusted risk was 13 per cent where the mother had less than full second-level education. Other significant differences were associated with the age of the mother at the child's birth and child gender. Where the mother was under age 30 at the child's birth, the risk of socio-emotional problems was estimated at 11 per cent. The risk was also higher for boys at 11 per cent than for girls at 8 per cent.

Figure 13.4 does not show the patterns that were not statistically significant (see **Table 13.1** in the **Appendix** to this chapter). There was no significant difference between the 1998 and the 2008 cohorts, between married and cohabiting couples or by whether the number of children in the family increased between Wave 1 and Wave 2.

We checked whether economic vulnerability had a greater effect on the socio-emotional development of younger children by testing an interaction between economic vulnerability and cohort (Model 2 in **Table 13.1**). The interaction was not statistically significant, indicating that the impact of economic vulnerability was broadly similar for the younger and the older cohorts of children. This is consistent with findings from the NICHHD (2005) and – at least for socio-emotional problems – is contrary to other findings suggesting that poverty in early childhood may be more detrimental than poverty later in childhood (for example, Duncan *et al.*, 2007; Holzer *et al.*, 2007).

Socio-emotional development and protective factors

At this point we consider the fourth research question, which asked whether there were protective factors, such as parental education, the quality of the relationship between parents and parental emotional wellbeing that helped to ameliorate the negative effects of economic vulnerability on the socio-emotional development of children. We estimated a simplified version of the model shown in **Figure 13.5**.

We distinguished between families who were vulnerable in either wave and the non-vulnerable and examined interactions between economic vulnerability and parental education, couple relationship quality and mother's depression. Since the relationship between parents was only assessed where both parents were resident, we distinguish between couples with 'good' and 'poor' relationships, keeping lone parents as a separate category. The full model is shown in **Table 13.2** in the **Appendix** to this chapter. Here we focus on the results for the interaction between economic vulnerability and the potentially protective factors (**Figure 13.5**).

In **Figure 13.5** the patterns that are similar for both vulnerable and non-vulnerable families are shown at the top of the chart. Those that differed for economically vulnerable and non-vulnerable children are shown in the lower part of the chart with the darker shading used for economically-vulnerable children and the lighter shade used for the non-economically-vulnerable children. From the figure we can see that the quality of the relationship between the parents, whether the parents are married or cohabiting, the level of education and the emotional wellbeing of the mother all matter for the socio-emotional development of the child. Further, apart from the emotional wellbeing of the mother, the extent to which these factors matter differs depending on whether the family is economically-vulnerable.

Figure 13.5: Adjusted Risk of Socio-Emotional Problems, by Characteristics of Child and Family and Protective Factors

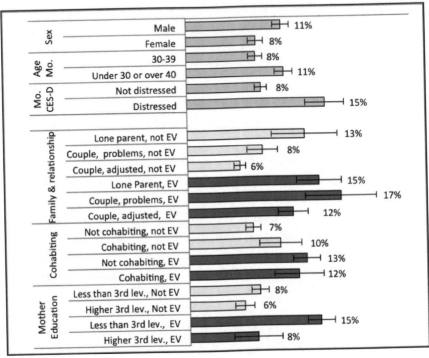

*Source: **Growing Up in Ireland** Research Microdata Files for the 2008 and 1998 cohorts; analysis by authors.*

*Note: 'EV' = economically vulnerable. Includes cases for whom CES-D is available and includes couples where DAS is available. Calculated from Model 3 in **Table 13.3**. Error bars show the 95 per cent confidence interval for the adjusted percentages.*

Considering first the quality of relationships between parent in families that are not economically-vulnerable, we see from the light-coloured bars that children are least likely to show signs of socio-emotional problems in couple families where the couple relationship is good (6 per cent), followed by couple families where the relationship has problems (8 per cent) and finally in lone-parent families (13 per cent). In the context of economic vulnerability, however, the advantage enjoyed by couples over lone parents is a good deal less. In fact couples with problems have children with a higher risk of socio-emotional problems than lone parents (17 per cent compared to 15 per cent). For couples without such problems, the risk level is only marginally lower at 12 per cent. Thus the relative advantage enjoyed by couples, whether with or without problems, is eroded by the experience of economic vulnerability.

There are parallels in the contrast between cohabiting couples and married couples, with a significant difference found where the family is not economically vulnerable, but no significant difference in the context of economic vulnerability. Among non-vulnerable married couple families, the adjusted percentage of children showing socio-emotional problems is 7 per cent compared to 10 per cent of their cohabiting counterparts. In the context of economic vulnerability, the respective figures are not significantly different between married and cohabiting couples at 12 to 13 per cent.

The level of education of the mother has a significant association with the risk of children showing socio-emotional problems whether the family is economically-vulnerable or not economically-vulnerable. In fact, the level of education of the mother makes significantly more of a difference in economically-vulnerable families. In non-vulnerable families, the adjusted percentage of children with socio-emotional problems is 8 per cent where the mother does not have a third-level degree and 6 per cent where she has a degree. The corresponding figures for economically-vulnerable families are 15 per cent and 8 per cent. As a result, the gap between vulnerable and non-vulnerable families is larger where the mother has lower levels of education than where the mother has a third-level degree.

Conclusion

In this chapter our focus was on the consequences of economic inequality for children's socio-emotional development. Drawing on the *Growing Up in Ireland* data that spanned the recession, we found that the level of economic vulnerability, as measured by low income, economic stress and household joblessness, increased for both cohorts of families compared to the first wave, reaching 25 per cent by the second wave.

Using a statistical model, we estimated the proportion of children we would expect to see with socio-emotional problems, based on having a high SDQ score. The statistical analysis took account of child's gender, age of mother at birth, family type and family change, level of education of the mother and cohort. The results were presented as adjusted percentages: the percentage we would expect to have a high SDQ score with other characteristics held constant.

The literature in general pointed to the negative impact of economic vulnerability on child outcomes, but with some mixed results on whether persistent economic disadvantage differed from transient disadvantage. Our results indicated that persistent economic vulnerability was the most detrimental: the highest adjusted percentage with socio-emotional problems was for children in families that were economically vulnerable in both waves (15 per cent), compared to 12 per cent where the family had been economically vulnerable in either wave and only 7 per cent where the family had been economically vulnerable in neither wave. Persistent economic vulnerability has a stronger impact on socio-emotional development than economic vulnerability at just one point. Nevertheless, even economic vulnerability in one wave (but not both) had negative consequences for child socio-emotional development.

Other characteristics of the child and family also mattered. The risk of socio-emotional problems was also higher where the mother was under age 30 at the time of the child's birth, in lone-parent families, where the parents were cohabiting rather than married, in cases of relationship breakdown, and where the mother's education was low. The risk was also significantly higher for boys than girls (11 per cent and 8 per cent, respectively).

Given the emphasis on the importance of early childhood experiences to the development of children, we asked whether there was evidence that the socio-emotional wellbeing of younger children may be more affected by economic vulnerability than that of older children. However, we found that there was no difference in the impact of economic vulnerability when we compared the experiences of children at ages 9 to 13 to those of children at age 9 months to age 3. Of course, it is possible that the impact of early childhood economic vulnerability may cumulate over a longer period of time and later waves of the *Growing Up in Ireland* data will allow us to examine this. What the findings here suggest is that economic vulnerability matters at all stages of childhood and that poverty does not have to be persistent to have negative consequences.

The analysis identified certain family characteristics that appeared to be 'protective' in that they were associated with a reduced risk of socio-emotional problems. These included the mother having third-level education; both parents being present in the household; parents being married rather than cohabiting, and the mother being aged 30 to 39 at the child's birth. We then investigated whether this protective effect was present for children who were economically-vulnerable as well as for those who were not economically-vulnerable. We found that some protective factors operate in a similar way for children in both vulnerable and non-vulnerable families. This was true of mother's age at the time of the child's birth and the absence of mother's emotional distress.

Three factors appeared to operate differently for economically-vulnerable and non-vulnerable families: the nature and quality of the parental relationship, whether the couple was married or cohabiting and the mother having third-level education. In non-vulnerable families, children benefit from the presence of both parents and benefit further from a good relationship between the parents. However, in economically-vulnerable families, the socio-emotional outcomes for children are no different in lone-parent than in couple families and the quality of the relationship between parents makes less of a difference. In other words, the impact of economic vulnerability on child outcomes overshadows any effect of living in a lone-parent household or of a poor quality relationship between the parents.

Similarly, in couple families, the risk of socio-emotional problems among children is lower where the parents are married than where they are cohabiting but this difference is only found in non-economically-vulnerable families. Again, the impact of vulnerability washes out any difference based on whether the parents are cohabiting or married.

On the other hand, the level of education of the mother matters even more in economically-vulnerable families than in non-vulnerable families. As a result, the gap between vulnerable and non-vulnerable families is larger where the mother has lower levels of education than where the mother has a third-level degree.

Appendix

Table 13.2: Relative Risk Ratios for Potentially Problematic SDQ in Wave 2, by Characteristics of Child and Family and by Cohort

		Model 1	Model 2	
			Main Effects	Interaction (1998 cohort)
Gender of Child	Male	(Ref)	(Ref)	(Ref)
	Female	0.738**	0.651**	1.314
Age of mother at birth of child	Under 25	1.485**	1.782**	0.775
	25-29	1.437**	1.570**	0.860
	30-34	1.096	1.126	0.942
	35-39	(Ref)	(Ref)	(Ref)
	40+	1.403	1.09	1.776
Household Type W1	Lone parent, 1 child	1.334	1.205	1.672
	Lone parent, 2+ children	1.077	1.074	1.372
	Couple, one child	(Ref)	(Ref)	(Ref)
	Couple, two children	0.801*	0.724**	1.676*
	Couple, 3+ children	0.680**	0.788	1.121
Cohabiting W1?	No	(Ref)	(Ref)	(Ref)
	Yes, cohabiting W1	1.101	0.930	1.694*
Change in carers(s)	No change	(Ref)	(Ref)	(Ref)
	New carer joins	1.122	0.667	2.882**
	One parent died/left	1.795**	1.587*	1.239
More children W2?	No	(Ref)	(Ref)	(Ref)
	Yes, more children	1.049	1.107	0.699
Mother Education, W1	Lo 2nd or less	2.225**	1.990**	1.238
	Upper 2nd to lower 3rd	1.473**	1.512**	0.975
	Third level	(Ref)	(Ref)	(Ref)
Economic	Neither wave	(Ref)	(Ref)	(Ref)

		Model 1	Model 2	
			Main Effects	Interaction (1998 cohort)
Vulnerability	Wave 1 only	1.682**	2.032**	0.629
	Wave 2 only	1.678**	1.641**	1.029
	Both waves	2.227**	2.124**	1.116
Cohort	2008	(Ref)	(Ref)	(Ref)
	1998	1.149	0.688	
Constant		0.050**	0.054**	
Observations		17,079	17,079	

Source: **Growing Up in Ireland** Research Microdata Files for the 2008 and 1998 cohorts; analysis by authors.

Note: The models were run in Stata using the svy prefix to provide correct standard errors when analysing weighted data from a cluster sample (the 1998 cohort was clustered at the level of school).
$**p<0.01$; $*p<0.05$.

Table 13.3: Odds Ratios for Potentially Problematic SDQ in Wave 2, by Characteristics of Child and Family, including Protective Factors

	Model 1	Model 2	Model 3
Female vs. Male	0.703**	0.692**	0.700**
Mother in 30s at birth of child vs. 20s or 40s	0.665**	0.755**	0.675**
Couple, relationship difficulties vs. Lone parent	0.902	0.576**	0.599*
Couple with no relationship difficulties vs. lone parent	0.545**	0.388**	0.405**
Cohabiting W1 vs. not	1.271*	1.541**	1.491**
Mother has higher third-level education	0.653**	0.746**	0.761**
Economic vulnerability in any wave	2.026**	1.338	1.323
1998 (child) cohort vs. 2008 (infant) cohort	1.019	1.011	1.032
Mother CESD W1: distressed vs. not		1.985**	2.085**
Interactions with economic vulnerability			
Female vs. Male		1.025	
Mother in 30s at birth of child vs. 20s or 40s		0.780	
Couple, relationship difficulties vs. lone parent		2.195**	2.023**
Couple, no relationship difficulties vs. lone parent		2.051**	1.892**

	Model 1	Model 2	Model 3
Cohabiting W1 vs. not cohabiting		0.576**	0.616*
Mother has higher third-level education		0.641	0.618*
1998 (child) cohort vs. 2008 (infant) cohort		1.046	
Mother CESD W1: distressed vs. not		1.072	
Constant	0.174**	0.197**	0.198**
Number Observations	15,922	15,922	15,922

Source: **Growing Up in Ireland** *Research Microdata Files for the 2008 and 1998 cohorts; analysis by authors.*

Note: Includes cases for whom we have information on the CESD depression score and the Dyadic Adjustment Scale measuring relationship difficulties. The models were run in Stata using the svy prefix to provide correct standard errors when analysing weighted data from a cluster sample (the 1998 cohort was clustered at the level of school). Model 2 adds interactions to Model 1. Model 3 drops the non-significant interaction terms.

**p<0.01; *p<0.05.

References

Beardslee, W.R., Keller, M.B., Seifer, R., Podorefsky, D., Staley, J., Lavori, P. W. & Shera, D. (1996). Prediction of adolescent affective disorder: Effects of prior parental affective disorders and child psychopathology, *Journal of the American Academy of Child and Adolescent Psychiatry, 35*, 279-88.

Bolger, K.E., Patterson, C.J., Thompson, W.W. & Kupersmidt, J.B. (1995). Psychosocial adjustment among children experiencing persistent and intermittent family economic hardship, *Child Development, 66*, 1107-29.

Bradbury, T.N., Fincham, F.D., & Beach, S.R.H. (2000). Research on the nature and determinants of marital satisfaction: A decade in review, *Journal of Marriage and the Family, 62*, 964-80.

Bradshaw, J. & Richardson, D. (2009). An index of child wellbeing in Europe, *Child Indicators Research, 2*, 319-51.

Bradshaw, J., Hoelscher, P. & Richardson, D. (2006). *Comparing Child Wellbeing in OECD Countries: Concepts and Methods*, Innocenti Working Paper IWP-2006-03, Florence: UNICEF Innocenti Research Centre.

Brooks-Gunn, J. & Duncan, G. J. (1997). The effects of poverty on children, *The Future of Children, 7*(2), 55-71.

Department for Work and Pensions (2007). *Opportunity for All*, London: Department for Work and Pensions.

Duncan, G.J., Brooks-Gunn, J. & Klebanov, P.K. (1994). Economic deprivation and early childhood development, *Child Development, 65*, 296-318.

Duncan, G.J., Ludwig, J. & Magnuson, K. (2007). Reducing poverty through pre-school interventions, *The Future of Children, 17*(2), 143-60.

Duncan, G.J., Magnuson, K., Kalil, A. & Ziol-Guest, K. (2012). The importance of early childhood poverty, *Social Indicators Research, 108,* 87-98.

Fahey, T., Keilthy, P. & Polek, E. (2012). *Family Relationships and Family Wellbeing: A Study of the Families of Nine-Year-Olds in Ireland*, Dublin: University College Dublin / Family Support Agency.

Fanjul, G. (2014). *Children of the Recession: The Impact of the Economic Crisis on Child Wellbeing in Rich Countries*, Florence: UNICEF Innocenti Research Centre.

Goodman, R. (1997). The strengths and difficulties questionnaire: A research note, *Journal of Child Psychology and Psychiatry, 38,* 581-86.

Grusky, D.B. & Weeden, K.A. (2007). Measuring poverty: The case for a sociological approach, in Kakawani, N. & Silber, J. (eds.), *The Many Dimensions of Poverty* (pp.20-35), Basingstoke: Palgrave Macmillan.

Hannan, C. & Halpin, B. (2014). The influence of family structure on child outcomes: Evidence for Ireland, *Economic and Social Review, 45,* 1-24.

Heckman, J.J. (2011). The economics of inequality: The value of early childhood education, *American Educator, Spring,* 31-47.

Holzer, H.J., Duncan, G.J., & Ludwig, J. (2007). *The Economic Costs of Poverty in the United States: Subsequent Effects of Children Growing Up Poor*, Madison, WI: Institute for Research on Poverty.

Jarjoura, G.R., Triplett, R.A. & Brinker, G.P. (2002). Growing up poor: Examining the link between persistent childhood poverty and delinquency, *Journal of Quantitative Criminology, 18,* 159-87.

McCrory, C., Dooley, C., Layte, R. & Kenny, R.A. (2015). The lasting legacy of childhood adversity for disease risk in later life, *Health Psychology, 34,* 687-96.

McLeod, J.D. & Shanahan, M.J. (1996). Trajectories of poverty and children's mental health, *Journal of Health and Social Behaviour, 37,* 207-22.

Mood, C. & Jonsson, J. (2014). *Poverty and Welfare among Children and Their Families 1968-2010*, Stockholm: Institute for Future Studies.

National Institute of Child Health and Human Development Early Childcare Research Network (NICHHD) (2005). Duration and developmental timing of poverty and children's cognitive and social development from birth through third grade, *Child Development, 76,* 795-810.

Nixon, E. (2012). *How Families Matter for the Social and Emotional Development of Nine-year-old Children*, Dublin: Department of Children and Youth Affairs.

Nolan, B. & Whelan, C.T. (2007). On the multidimensionality of poverty and social exclusion, in Micklewright, J. & Jenkins, S. (eds.), *Poverty and Inequality: New Directions* (pp.146-65), Oxford University Press, Oxford.

Nolan, B. & Whelan, C.T. (2010). Using non-monetary deprivation indicators to analyse poverty and social exclusion in rich countries: Lessons from Europe?, *Journal of Policy Analysis and Management, 29,* 305-23.

Roberts, R.E., Andrews, J.A., Lewinsohn, P.M. & Hops, H. (1990). Assessment of depression in adolescents using the Center of Epidemiologic Studies Depression Scale, *Journal of Consulting and Clinical Psychology, 2,* 122-28.

Sharpley, C.F. & Rogers, H.J. (1984). Preliminary validation of the abbreviated Spanier Dyadic Adjustment Scale: Some psychometric data regarding a screening test of marital adjustment, *Educational and Psychological Measurement, 44,* 1045-49.

Spanier, G.B. (1976). Measuring dyadic adjustment: New scales for assessing the quality of marriage and similar dyads, *Journal of Marriage and the Family, 38,* 15-28.

StataCorp (2013a). *Stata: Release 13. Statistical Software*, College Station, TX: StataCorp LP.

StataCorp (2013b). *Stata Survey Data Reference Manual, Release 13*, College Station, TX: StataCorp LP.

UNICEF (2007). *Child Poverty in Perspective: An Overview of Child Wellbeing in Rich Countries*, Report Card 7, Florence: UNICEF Innocenti Research Centre.

United Nations (1989). *Convention on the Rights of the Child*, Geneva: United Nations.

Waldfogel, J. (2013). Socio-economic inequality in childhood and beyond: An overview of challenges and findings from comparative analyses of cohort studies, *Longitudinal and Life Course Studies, 4,* 268-75.

Watson, D., Maître, B. & Russell, H. (2015). *Transitions into and out of Household Joblessness, 2004 to 2014: An Analysis of the Central Statistics Office (CSO) Quarterly National Household Survey (QNHS)*, Dublin: Department of Social Protection and the Economic and Social Research Institute.

Whelan, C.T. & Maître, B. (2014). The Great Recession and the changing distribution of economic vulnerability by social class: The Irish case, *Journal of European Social Policy, 24,* 470-85.

Whelan, K. (2010). Policy lessons from Ireland's latest depression, *Economic and Social Review, 41,* 225-54.

Williams, J. & Whelan, C.T. (2011). *Prevalence of Relative Income Poverty and Its Effect on Outcomes among Nine-year-olds*, paper presented at Growing Up in Ireland Annual Conference, Dublin, December.

Williams, J., Greene, S., Doyle, E., Harris, E., Layte, R., McCoy, S., McCrory, C., Murray, A., Nixon, E., O'Dowd, T., O'Moore, M., Quail, A., Smyth, E., Swords, L. & Thornton, M. (2009). *Growing Up in Ireland: The Lives of Nine-Year-Olds*, Dublin: Office of the Minister for Children and Youth Affairs.

Williams, R. (2012). Using the margins command to estimate and interpret adjusted predictions and marginal effects, *The Stata Journal, 12,* 308-31.

14: CONCLUDING OBSERVATIONS

James Williams, Elizabeth Nixon, Emer Smyth & Dorothy Watson

Introduction

In this book we set out to investigate equality in outcomes among children living in 21st century Ireland. As noted in **Chapter 1**, the *Proclamation of Independence* of 1916 aspired to '... cherishing all of the nation's children equally ...', albeit the metaphorical (rather than actual) children of 'Mother Ireland'. The book has considered the extent to which this aspiration has been achieved over the last 100 years.

There can be little doubt that the Ireland of 2016 would be unrecognisable to Pádraig Pearse and his contemporaries. Economic and demographic structures, as well as social values and mores, have been transformed over the century. Life in Ireland has changed completely for everyone, not just for children.

The way we think about children and conceptualise their childhood has been dramatically reshaped over the last 100 years, generally for the better. We have seen a gradual (although, at times, a somewhat grudging) acceptance of the rights of the individual child and their personhood. The early years of state policy focused on the family, not children in their own right. **Chapter 2** notes that the 1937 *Constitution* placed a higher value on the parent than on the child. Ireland's ratification of United Nation's *Convention on the Rights of the Child* in 1992 was a significant step in the development of children's rights in Ireland. Not until April 2015 (following a referendum in 2012), however, did we implement the *31ˢᵗ Amendment to the Constitution* with the insertion of Article 42A, which notes that:

> ... *the State recognises and affirms the natural and imprescriptible rights of all children and shall, as far as practicable, by its laws protect and vindicate those rights.*

One aspect of this amendment was that the rights of all children (regardless of the marital status of their parents) would be equal under the *Constitution*.

Dimensions of Inequality among Children in 21ˢᵗ century Ireland

In examining equality in the more salient aspects of children's lives, the book explored whether systematic trends and patterns are evident in the factors associated with child outcomes. Principally using data from the *Growing Up in Ireland* project, consideration was given to the size and structure of families, their socio-demographic background, their economic, cultural and social resources, and, most importantly, to how these characteristics were associated with how well children and young people were faring in modern Ireland. Children's educational development, their physical and socio-emotional health and their families' economic well-being were explored.

Family size and structures

We saw in **Chapter 3** that substantial changes have taken place in family size and structure over the last century. The important distinction was made between measuring family size from the perspective of women's completed fertility, on the one hand, and from the perspective of the child on the other. When viewed from the woman's perspective, family size in Ireland, averaged across all women, has fallen dramatically in the last century. From the child's perspective, what matters is the number of siblings in their own family, referred to as 'sibsize'. This measure shows that Ireland's family size has fallen, but less dramatically than might be thought to have been the case. By 2011, for example, just over one-third of children were still living in families of four or more children. In this respect, contemporary Ireland could perhaps be better referred to as a country of moderately-sized, rather than small, families.

Some quite spectacular changes in other aspects of family structure have taken place over the last century. The notion of the family in Ireland has traditionally been based on marriage, a perspective that was enshrined in the *Constitution*. An indicator of change in attitudes and practice in this regard is the substantial growth in recent decades in the percentage of children born outside marriage. This has increased from less than 5 per cent annually up to the early 1980s to a current level of approximately 35 per cent. This increase in non-marital births reflects changes in traditional attitudes regarding children who are born outside marriage. It was not, for example, until the *Status of Children Act, 1987* that discrimination in succession rights for non-marital children was abolished.

The factors associated with family disruption also have changed over the century. In 1916, the main form of disruption was premature death of parents. By 2016, divorce, unstable cohabitation, relationship dissolution and the formation of new relationships have radically affected family structures and resulted in the decline of hitherto traditional family forms, with a resulting increase in the proportion of one-parent and blended families.

The impact of changing family form on children's development was considered in **Chapter 4**. This indicated a consistent pattern of disadvantage for children living in one-parent families, including in terms of their socio-emotional development. For example, even accounting for variations in the levels of human and social capital (measured in terms of family income, maternal education, maternal depression and parent-child conflict), children in one-parent families were still at a significant disadvantage in terms of their risk of experiencing socio-emotional and behavioural difficulties.

Cognitive and educational development

Differences in children's cognitive and learning outcomes according to family socio-economic status were explored in **Chapter 5**. Here, we illustrated that the development of language skills in early childhood was strongly associated with the economic and educational resources available to a child in the home.

Chapter 6 considered equality of access to early care and education. Historically, Ireland had very low levels of provision and take-up of formal care for pre-school children. Changes in female labour force participation (since the mid-1970s, but even more dramatically during the economic boom of the early 2000s), along with state investment in early care and education, have changed this landscape markedly. Socio-economic advantage, mother's employment status and family income were associated not just with higher use of care, but also with type of care. Care by non-relatives (almost always paid for) was most common among more socially-advantaged families, with care by relatives dominating among families with lower levels of income and education. The introduction of the universal Free Pre-school Year scheme made a very big difference in the proportion of children attending centre-based care settings. Participation in the Free Pre-school Year scheme is high among all social groups, though slightly higher among advantaged groups. Most notably, the scheme provided access to pre-school among disadvantaged groups, who would not otherwise have been able to avail of it. The medium- to long-term impact of access to non-parental childcare must await further rounds of data collection by the *Growing Up in Ireland* study. In the interim, the levelling of access to pre-school care and education within regulated centres as a result of an initiative such as the Free Pre-school Year is clearly to be welcomed.

Ease of transition and integration into the school system are key to positive development for children including, of course, in terms of direct educational outcomes. The evidence presented in **Chapter 7** suggested that ease of transition to primary school does not vary markedly by social class, maternal education or income but is, at least in part, related to the home-learning environment as well as exposure to non-parental childcare and pre-school. Despite these patterns, the language and communication skills children bring to the school setting do differ significantly by the educational and social resources of their family and thus may have longer term implications for inequalities in their educational outcomes.

Children's attitudes to school and development of language skills are also related to their experience of Special Educational Needs (SEN) or disability. **Chapter 8** highlighted an active and important debate around the most appropriate definition of SEN in establishing prevalence levels and planning for the provision of the necessary supports. The possible over-identification of emotional / behavioural disabilities and under-identification of learning difficulties may result in a misrepresentation of certain groups of children in the relevant classifications. Notwithstanding on-going debates in this area and the need to re-consider traditionally-used models of classification, children who have a SEN are more likely to be in the 'at risk' group than others. Children with SEN (especially those with multiple SEN, learning or socio-emotional difficulties) thus face considerably more barriers in engaging fully with school than their peers.

With increased immigration over the last 20 years – especially during the so-called 'Celtic Tiger' years – Irish society has become progressively characterised by cultural, linguistic and religious diversity. This is reflected in over one-quarter of annual births now being to mothers who were themselves not born in Ireland. This increased pluralism is a sign of a very healthy and vibrant society. It is important, however, to consider how migrant children are faring in Ireland relative to their Irish-born peers. **Chapter 9** compared aspects of the academic and social integration of migrant and non-migrant children. The children of migrant parents may be at an immediate disadvantage if English (the principal language of instruction in schools in Ireland) is not their mother tongue, a pattern that is reflected in lower reading and maths scores at age 9 than are found among children born in Ireland. An important feature of Irish immigration is the heterogeneity of profile of immigrants in terms of national background and language of origin. The analyses in **Chapter 9** point to important differences between national groups in child outcomes. Taking account of family characteristics, Eastern European children in particular, but also those from African and Asian families, are at the greatest relative disadvantage in terms of reading scores compared to children born in Ireland. In contrast, children whose mother is from the UK or Western European countries are on par with those born in

Ireland. Although the differences in academic performance between Irish-born and migrant children are relatively modest when account is taken of background characteristics, one should note that these differences may lead to greater disadvantage as the children move through the education system.

Whilst academic performance is an important aspect of integration for children (migrant and others), equally important is their more broadly-based social integration. It is essential that all children have a sense of belonging, of emotional support and of being part of Irish society on an equal footing with their peers. We noted in **Chapter 9** that children from Eastern European, African and Asian families had fewer friends than their Irish counterparts – though one must also acknowledge potential variations in the extent of desired outward engagement across national groups. Participation in structured sports and cultural activities also varied among children from different national backgrounds, some of which was related to family background and other characteristics. Cross-national variations in participation persisted, however, even accounting for such differences.

Health

A key indicator of disadvantage (particularly among children) is their health and physical well-being. **Chapter 10** examined differences in physical health, using both cohorts in *Growing Up in Ireland*. Some differences in health outcomes were apparent from birth. Low birth weight (often an indicator of long-term health problems) and the proportion of children with a long-standing 'chronic' health condition are both strongly associated with a range of measures of social disadvantage. For example, we saw that low birth-weight children are five times more likely to fail developmental tests for gross motor and communications skills at age 9 months, and four times more likely to fail tests for fine motor skills. The proportion of children who were ever breastfed (clearly identified with long-term healthier outcomes for the child over the life course) is strongly related to social advantage – 77 per cent of children from professional families are breastfed compared to only 33 per cent of children from families in the most socially disadvantaged groups.

In line with international trends in the developed world, overweight and obesity in Ireland are becoming the modern form of malnutrition, with over one-quarter of our children classified as overweight or obese. Substantial social variations in the risk of childhood weight problems were identified – the children of unskilled manual parents are 65 per cent more likely to be obese at age 3 than are the children of professional parents.

Some of our children are exposed more than others to health-compromising behaviours, many of which have lasting negative effects on their well-being. For example, low income mothers are eight times more likely to smoke during pregnancy than others. This has been identified (in *Growing Up in Ireland* data, as elsewhere) to be one of the more important determinants of low birth weight. It must be noted, however, that smoking in pregnancy is strongly related to maternal depression and anxiety, as well as deprivation and social isolation, and so must be interpreted as much more than a proactive lifestyle choice or a personal indulgence.

Equity in terms of access to healthcare was also explored. We saw in **Chapter 11** that access to free GP care *via* a full medical card was associated with more GP visits, even adjusting for a range of other factors, including underlying health conditions of the child. Issues of 'necessary' and 'unnecessary' visits are very difficult to untangle, especially without access to detailed data on diagnosis and length of consultation, etc. The fear is, however, that those who are not covered by a medical card (for healthcare generally or GP visits in particular) may be discouraged from accessing primary care due to cost. When focusing on children whose family income was higher than the income thresholds for a full medical or GP visit card, we found some evidence to indicate that children from higher income families without full medical card or GP visit cards attended their GP more frequently than their peers from lower income families, even after adjusting for other determinants of use, including health need or condition.

Anti-social behaviour

Antisocial behaviour in adolescence is important not only in its own right but also as an early indicator of subsequent behavioural problems in later life. Some studies indicate that the risk of such behaviour is higher in more socially-disadvantaged families, which may result in cumulative disadvantage and increased inequities among the vulnerable young people in question into adolescence and beyond. Prevalence and factors associated with anti-social behaviour among 13-year-olds were therefore considered in **Chapter 12**. As one would expect, overall prevalence levels were relatively low. The social structuring of such behaviours was found to be complex. Social disadvantage was associated with the incidence of both vandalism and violence, but not theft. There were, however, also strong variations in the prevalence of anti-social behaviours with other factors and characteristics, including gender, family stability, family relationships, parenting, peer networks and peer relationships. In general, prevalence among boys was much higher than among girls. Violent inter-personal behaviour was highest in situations of changing family structures, especially where the changes were from one- to two-parent family structures, possibly reflecting adjustment issues for the teenager. The overall story told by the *Growing Up in Ireland* data in this area suggests that, although social environment is a component in understanding the prevalence and drivers of anti-social behaviour, the issue is a particularly complex one in which other characteristics of the young person and his / her family also play an important role.

Economic vulnerability

Poverty and economic disadvantage have a range of direct and indirect effects on children, including on their physical and mental health, educational achievement, and emotional and behavioural outcomes. **Chapter 13** examined the changing prevalence and nature of economic vulnerability in Ireland. Economic vulnerability is understood in terms of having an increased risk of low income, household joblessness or economic stress, or some combination of these. As would be expected, this analysis found that the risk and levels of economic vulnerability increased for children in both cohorts in the wake of the recession of 2008, reaching approximately 25 per cent by the second wave of interviewing. The chapter also examined the consequences of economic inequality for children's socio-emotional well-being. Overall, economic vulnerability had negative consequences for socio-emotional well-being, especially where it was experienced on a consistent basis over two rounds of interviews with the family. Other family characteristics and processes also mattered. Risks of socio-emotional problems were higher for boys and where the child had a younger mother, in a one-parent family, where the parents were co-habiting rather than married and where the mother had lower levels of educational attainment. Most importantly, the impact of vulnerability on child outcomes overshadows the effects of living in a lone-parent household or one in which there is a poor quality of relationship between the parents. Equally, the impact of economic vulnerability appears to wash out the effect of whether the parents in two-parent families are married or co-habiting. Finally, the level of mother's education matters more in economically-vulnerable than non-vulnerable families.

The Importance of a Longitudinal Child Cohort Study

Ireland is extremely lucky to have a national longitudinal study of children like *Growing Up in Ireland* and the State's commitment of resources to a project focusing on the lives of children throughout the deepest recession in Ireland's history is to be welcomed. The study offers a unique scientific framework for informing research, policy and practice communities on an enormous range of topics in the lives of children and young people. It facilities the development of a 'whole child' perspective and (from an early age) gives the children themselves a direct voice in the identification and articulation of the issues and challenges facing them in their lives. From an applied perspective, the project greatly supports the government's main policy document on children, *Better Outcomes Brighter Futures* (Department of Children and Youth Affairs, 2014). This has established an integrated, cross-government approach to ensuring that the lives of children, young people and their families are researched, developed and understood and that such research feeds into policy development and service provision.

Data from the *Growing Up in Ireland* study were the principal source used throughout the book. The range of topics addressed throughout the book illustrates the versatility of the project in delivering analysis across numerous areas of the lives of children and young people at different ages and stages of development.

No single study, however, can encompass all children or all aspects of their well-being. The ***Growing Up in Ireland*** project is a general population study, which is representative of the totality of children in its relevant age cohorts. Children were recruited into the study in proportion to their representation in the overall population. Children from two disadvantaged subgroups of the population are not included – those living in homeless families and those in families in direct provision for asylum seekers. Although these children face a substantially higher risk of disadvantage than their peers in other groups, they are relatively small in number. It is estimated, for example, that there are approximately 2,206 homeless children in Ireland (Department of the Environment, Community and Local Government, 2016) and 1,212 in direct provision (Reception and Integration Agency, 2015). If one wishes to examine their lives and circumstances or the extent to which they are treated equitably within Irish society, one would have to adopt a different design to that used in the ***Growing Up in Ireland*** project. ***Growing Up in Ireland*** can, of course, play an important role in that process by providing a national benchmark against which to compare the welfare and well-being of children in the minority subgroups in question.

Cherishing All the Children Equally?

Before concluding, we must attempt to provide an overall answer to the question posed in the title and introductory chapter of the book. Have we reached a position in the Ireland of 2016 which suggests that we do, in fact, "... cherish all of the children equally ..."? On the basis of the evidence presented throughout the book, it would appear, regrettably, that the answer must be "No". Much progress has been made over the last 100 years (particularly since the late 1970s) in the ways in which we think about children and view them as holding rights. Much progress has been made in the way in which we legislate to support their more equitable treatment than heretofore. Ireland has become a much more pluralist and tolerant society than was the case 100 years ago. As noted throughout the book, new models of the family have gained much wider acceptance over recent decades, notably in regard to one-parent and blended family structures. Overall, levels of education and health have improved dramatically, as have supports for children and families under stress and in need of assistance – financial or otherwise. Nonetheless, it is unfortunately the case that much of the evidence presented in the series of essays in this book indicates that a great deal remains to be done to address some marked inequalities in child outcomes. In many aspects of their lives (albeit different to those of 1916), the outcomes and wellbeing of children and young people continue to be shaped, and indeed limited, by the circumstances of the family into which they are born.

We saw in the chapters of this book that many of these inequalities may be related to family type or instability. Much of the variation in child outcomes may be associated with a family's economic, educational and social resources, with migrant status, with a child's SEN or a disability. The holy grail of policy or other overarching interventions to address the challenges and problems facing children and their families is particularly elusive. The multi-dimensional nature of the problems and the range of factors associated with those problems mean that, in reality, it is not possible to put in place a single solution or suite of solutions. Some of the factors involved are more amenable to interventions than others. For example, parent's age, a child's temperament, family type and so on as are not readily susceptible to policy or other interventions. However, inequalities in economic and other resources can be more easily mitigated (at least partially) through State policies and interventions. It is crucial that these policy effects be viewed over the longer term, as inequality shapes conditions and outcomes over generations.

The importance of research of the sort presented throughout this book (and more generally from the *Growing Up in Ireland* study) largely lies in the extent to which it assists in identifying the nature of problems and inequities, as well as informing evidence-based policies and interventions on several (often parallel) fronts. As noted in the *Foreword*, our children are our greatest national asset and deserve that, at a minimum, we strive towards establishing a greater understanding of their development and the supports they and their families need to ensure a brighter future. If this book adds in any measure to enhancing that understanding and achieving that goal, we might consider it to be at least a minor success.

References

Department of Children and Youth Affairs (2014). *Better Outcomes, Brighter Future: The National Policy Framework for Children and Young People*, Dublin: Stationery Office.

Department of the Environment, Community and Local Government (2016). *Homelessness Report January 2016*, retrieved from http://www.environ.ie/sites/default/files/publications/files/homelessness_report _january_2016_0.pdf.

Reception and Integration Agency (2015). *Reception and Integration Agency, Monthly Statistics: December*, retrieved from http://www.ria.gov.ie/en/ RIA/RMR2015December.pdf/Files/RMR2015December.pdf.

BIBLIOGRAPHY

Acock, A. & Demo, D.H. (1994). *Family Diversity and Wellbeing*, Thousand Oaks, CA: Sage.

Adamson, P. (2008). *The Childcare Transition: A League Table of Early Childhood Education and Care in Economically Advanced Countries*, Report Card 8, Florence: UNICEF Innocenti Research Centre.

Adler, N.E. & Newman, K. (2002). Socio-economic disparities in health: Pathways and policies, *Health Affairs, 21*, 60-76.

Amato, P.R. (1995). Single-parent households as settings for children's development, wellbeing and attainment: A social network / resources perspective, *Sociological Studies of Children, 7*, 19-47.

Amato, P.R. (2001). Children of divorce in the 1990s: An update of the Amato & Keith (1991) meta-analysis, *Journal of Family Psychology, 15*, 355-70.

Amato, P.R. (2005). Parenting through family transitions, *New Zealand Journal of Social Policy, 23*, 31-44.

Amato, P.R. & Keith, B. (1991). Parental divorce and the wellbeing of children: A meta-analysis, *Psychological Bulletin, 110*, 26-46.

Andrabi, T., Das, J. & Khwaja, A.I. (2011). What did you do all day?' Maternal education and child outcomes, *The Journal of Human Resources, 47*, 873-912.

Angold, A., Costello, E.J., Messer, S.C., Pickles, A., Winder, F. & Silver, D. (1995). The development of a short questionnaire for use in epidemiological studies of depression in children and adolescents, *International Journal of Methods in Psychiatric Research, 5*, 237-49.

Area Development Management (2002). *National Childcare Census Report: Baseline Data 1999-2000*, Dublin: Area Development Management / Department of Justice, Equality and Law Reform.

Arensberg, C. & Kimball, S.T. (1940). *Family and Community in Ireland*, Cambridge, MA: Harvard University Press.

Aries, P. (1960). *Centuries of Childhood: A Social History of Family Life*, New York: Vintage.

Armsden, G.C. & Greenberg, M.T. (1987). The inventory of parent and peer attachment: Relationships to wellbeing in adolescence, *Journal of Youth & Adolescence, 16,* 427-54.

Arriaga, R.J., Fenson, L., Cronan, T. & Pethick, S.J. (1998). Scores on the MacArthur Communicative Development: Inventory of children from low- and middle-income families, *Applied Psycholinguistics, 19,* 209-23.

Augustine, J.M., Cavanagh, S.E. & Crosnoe, R. (2009). Maternal education, early childcare and the reproduction of advantage, *Social Forces, 88,* 1-29.

Baicker, K. & Goldman, D. (2011). Patient cost-sharing and healthcare spending growth, *Journal of Economic Perspectives, 25,* 47-68.

Banks, J. & McCoy, S. (2011). *A Study on the Prevalence of Special Educational Needs,* Trim, Co. Meath: National Council for Special Education.

Banks, J., Shevlin, M. & McCoy, S. (2012). Disproportionality in special education: Identifying children with emotional behavioural difficulties in Irish primary schools, *European Journal of Special Needs Education, 27,* 219-35.

Barker, D. (1994). The fetal origins of adult disease, *Fetal and Maternal Medicine Review, 6,* 71-80.

Barrett, A.E. & Turner, R.J. (2006). Family structure and substance use problems in adolescence and early adulthood: Examining explanations for the relationship, *Addiction, 101,* 109-20.

Barrington, R. (1987). *Health, Medicine and Politics in Ireland: 1900-1970,* Dublin: Institute of Public Administration.

Barry, M. (2006). *Youth Offending in Transition: The Search for Social Recognition,* New York, NY: Routledge.

Baumrind, D. (1978). Parental disciplinary patterns and social competence in children, *Youth and Society, 9,* 238-76.

Baumrind, D. (1991). The influence of parenting styles on adolescent competence and substance use, *Journal of Early Adolescence, 11,* 56-95.

Beardslee, W.R., Keller, M.B., Seifer, R., Podorefsky, D., Staley, J., Lavori, P. W. & Shera, D. (1996). Prediction of adolescent affective disorder: Effects of prior parental affective disorders and child psychopathology, *Journal of the American Academy of Child and Adolescent Psychiatry, 35,* 279-88.

Beck, A.N., Cooper C.E., McLanahan S. & Brooks-Gunn, J. (2010). Partnership transitions and maternal parenting, *Journal of Marriage and the Family, 72,* 219-33.

Bennett, J. (2007). Values and primary school textbooks in Ireland 1900-1999, in Shine Thompson, M. & Coghlan, V. (eds.), *Studies in Children's Literature: Divided Worlds* (pp.170-85), Dublin: Four Courts Press.

Bhattarcharya, G., Ison, L. & Blair, M. (2003). *Minority Ethnic Attainment and Participation in Education and Training: The Evidence,* London: Department for Education and Skills.

Bianchi, S.M. & Robinson, J.P. (1997). 'What did you do today?' Children's use of time, family composition, and the acquisition of social capital, *Journal of Marriage and the Family*, 59, 332-44.

Blanden, J. (2006). *Bucking the Trend – What Enables Those Who Are Disadvantaged in Childhood to Succeed Later in Life?*, London: Department for Work and Pensions.

Bolger, K.E., Patterson, C.J., Thompson, W.W. & Kupersmidt, J.B. (1995). Psychosocial adjustment among children experiencing persistent and intermittent family economic hardship, *Child Development*, 66, 1107-29.

Bornstein, M.H. & Bradley, R.H. (eds.) (2003). *Socio-economic Status, Parenting, and Child Development*, Mahwah, NJ: Erlbaum.

Bornstein, M.H., Hahn, C.S., Suwalsky, J. & Haynes, O.M. (2003). Socio-economic status, parenting, and child development: The Hollingshead Four-Factor Index of Social Status and The Socio-economic Index of Occupations, in Bornstein, M.H. & Bradley, R.H. (eds.), *Socio-economic Status, Parenting, and Child Development* (pp.29-82), Mahwah, NJ: Erlbaum.

Boutwell, B.B. & Beaver, K.M. (2010). Maternal cigarette smoking during pregnancy and offspring externalising behavioural problems: A propensity score matching analysis, *International Journal of Environmental Research and Public Health*, 7, 146-63.

Bradbury, B., Corak, M., Waldfogel, J. & Washbrook, E. (2012). Inequality in early childhood outcomes, in Ermisch, J., Jantti, M. & Smeeding, T. (eds.), *From Parents to Children: The Intergenerational Transmission of Advantage* (pp.87-119), New York: Russell Sage Foundation.

Bradbury, T.N., Fincham, F.D., & Beach, S.R.H. (2000). Research on the nature and determinants of marital satisfaction: A decade in review, *Journal of Marriage and the Family*, 62, 964-80.

Bradley, R.H. & Corwyn, R.F. (2002). Socio-economic status and child development, *Annual Review of Psychology*, 53, 371-99.

Bradley, R.H., Corwyn, R.F., McAdoo, H.P. & Garcia Coll, C. (2001). The home environments of children in the United States Part I: Variations by age, ethnicity, and poverty status, *Child Development*, 72, 1844-67.

Bradshaw, J. & Richardson, D. (2009). An index of child wellbeing in Europe, *Child Indicators Research*, 2, 319-51.

Bradshaw, J., Hoelscher, P. & Richardson, D. (2006). *Comparing Child Wellbeing in OECD Countries: Concepts and Methods*, Innocenti Working Paper IWP-2006-03, Florence: UNICEF Innocenti Research Centre.

Breen, R. (1983). Farm servanthood in Ireland, 1900-1940, *Economic History Review* 36, 87-102.

Brody, H. (1973). *Inishkillane: Change and Decline in the West of Ireland*, London: Faber & Faber.

Broidy, L.M., Nagin, D.S., Tremblay, R.E., Bates, J.E., Brame, B., Dodge, K.A. *et al.* (2003). Developmental trajectories of childhood disruptive behaviours and adolescent delinquency: A six-site, crossnational study, *Developmental Psychology, 39*, 222-45.

Bronfenbrenner, U. (1979). *The Ecology of Human Development: Experiment by Nature and Design*, Cambridge, MA: Harvard University Press.

Bronfenbrenner, U. (1995). Developmental ecology through space and time: A future perspective, in Moen, P., Elder, G.H. & Luscher, K. (eds.), *Examining Lives in Context: Perspectives on the Ecology of Human Development* (pp.619-47), Washington DC: American Psychological Association.

Bronfenbrenner, U. (2001). The bioecological theory of human development, in Smelser, N.J. & Baltes, P.B. (eds.), *International Encyclopedia of the Social and Behavioural Sciences* (Vol. 10, pp.6963-70), New York: Elsevier.

Bronfenbrenner, U. & Morris, P.A. (2006). The bioecological model of human development, in Damon, W. & Lerner, R.M. (series eds.) & Lerner, R.M. (vol. ed.), *Handbook of Child Psychology: Vol. 1. Theoretical Models of Human Development* (6th ed., pp.793-828), New York: Wiley.

Bronfenbrenner, U., McClelland, P., Wetherington, E., Moen, P. & Ceci, S.J. (1996). *The State of Americans: This Generation and the Next*, New York: The Free Press.

Brooks-Gunn, J. & Duncan, G. J. (1997). The effects of poverty on children, *The Future of Children, 7*(2), 55-71.

Bumpass, L. & Lu, H. (2000). Trends in cohabitation and implications for children's family contexts in the United States, *Population Studies, 54*, 29-41.

Burger, K. (2010). How does early childhood care and education affect cognitive development?, *Early Childhood Research Quarterly, 25*, 140-65.

Burt, S.A., Donnellan, M.B., Iacono, W.G. & McGue, M. (2011). Age-of-onset or behavioural sub-types? A prospective comparison of two approaches to characterizing the heterogeneity within anti-social behaviour, *Journal of Abnormal Child Psychology, 39*, 633-44.

Burton, P., Phipps, S. & Zhang, L. (2012). From parent to child: Emerging inequality in outcomes for children in Canada and the US, *Child Indicators Research, 6*, 1-38.

Byrne, D. & O'Toole, C. (2015). The influence of childcare arrangements on child wellbeing from infancy to middle childhood. A report for TUSLA, Maynooth: Maynooth University.

Cadman, D., Boyle, P., Szatmari, P. & Offord, D. (1987). Chronic illness, disability and mental and social wellbeing: Findings of the Ontario Child Health Study, *Pediatrics, 79*, 805-13.

Cairney, J., Boyle, M., Offord, D.R. & Racine, Y. (2003). Stress, social support, and depression in single and married mothers, *Social Psychiatry and Psychiatric Epidemiology, 38*, 442-49.

Cambrian, C. & Silvestre, N. (2003). Students with special educational needs in the inclusive classroom: Social integration and self-concept, *European Journal of Special Needs Education, 18*, 197-208.

Canavan, J. (2012). Family and family change in Ireland, *Journal of Family Issues, 33,* 10-28.

Carr-Fanning, K., Mc Guckin, C. & Shevlin, M. (2013). Using student voice to escape the spider's web: A methodological approach to de-victimising students with ADHD, *Trinity Education Papers, 2,* 85-112.

Case, A., Fertig, A. & Paxson, C. (2005). The lasting impact of childhood health and circumstance, *Journal of Health Economics, 24,* 365-89.

Central Statistics Office (1961). *Census,* Dublin: Stationery Office.

Central Statistics Office (2010). *Survey on Income and Living Conditions 2009,* Dublin: Stationery Office.

Central Statistics Office (2012). *Census 2011,* Dublin: Stationery Office.

Central Statistics Office (2012). *Population and Migration Estimates: April 2012,* Dublin: Stationery Office.

Central Statistics Office (2012). *Statistical Yearbook of Ireland, 2012,* Dublin: Stationery Office.

Central Statistics Office (2012). *This is Ireland: Highlights from Census 2011,* Dublin: Stationery Office.

Central Statistics Office (2014). *Vital Statistics: Yearly Summary 2014,* Dublin: Stationery Office.

Central Statistics Office (2015). *Irish Life Tables No. 16, 2010-12,* Dublin: Stationery Office.

Central Statistics Office (2015). *Survey of Income and Living Conditions 2014,* Dublin: Stationery Office.

Central Statistics Office (2015). *Survey on Income and Living Conditions, 2013,* Dublin: Stationery Office.

Central Statistics Office (2016a). *Marriages and Civil Partnerships, 2015,* Statistical Release, 15 April, Dublin: Stationery Office, available at http://www.cso.ie/en/releasesandpublications/er/mcp/ marriagesandcivilpartnerships2015/.

Central Statistics Office (2016b). *Life in 1916 Ireland: Stories from Statistics,* retrieved from http://www.cso.ie/en/statistics/ lifein1916irelandstoriesfromstatistics/

Chapple, S. (2009). *Child Wellbeing and Sole Parent Family Structure in the OECD: An Analysis,* OECD Social, Employment and Migration Working Papers No. 82, Paris: Organization for Economic Cooperation and Development.

Chen, E. (2004). Why socio-economic status affects the health of children, *Current Directions in Psychological Science, 13,* 112-15.

Cherlin, A. (2010). Demographic trends in the United States: A review of research in the 2000s, *Journal of Marriage and the Family, 72,* 403-19.

Chernew, M. & Newhouse, J. (2008). What does the RAND Health Insurance Experiment tell us about the impact of patient cost-sharing on health outcomes?, *American Journal of Managed Care, 14,* 412-14.

Chief Inspector (1917). *Fifty-fifth Report of the Chief Inspector Appointed to Visit the Reformatory and Industrial Schools in Ireland for the Year Ended 31 December 1916*, Dublin: Her Majesty's Stationery Office.

Children's Rights Alliance (2015). *Briefing Note on the Children and Family Relationships Bill, 2015*, Dublin: Children's Rights Alliance.

Children's Rights Alliance (2016). *Report Card 2016*, Dublin: Children's Rights Alliance, available from http://www.childrensrights.ie/content/report-card-2016.

Coleman, D.A. (1992). The demographic transition in Ireland in international context, *Proceedings of the British Academy*, 79, 53-77.

Commission of Inquiry on Mental Handicap (1965). *Report*, Dublin: Stationery Office.

Commission to Inquire into Child Abuse (2009). *Report of the Commission to Inquire into Child Abuse, vols. I-V*, Dublin: Stationery Office.

Conger, R.D. & Conger, K.J. (2002). Resilience in Midwestern families: Selected findings from the first decade of a prospective, longitudinal study, *Journal of Marriage and Family*, 64, 361-73.

Conger, R.D., Conger, K.J., Elder, G.H.J., Lorenz, F.O., Simons, R.L. & Whitbeck, L.B. (1992). A family process model of economic hardship and adjustment of early adolescent boys, *Child Development*, 63, 526-41.

Conti-Ramsden, G. & Botting, N. (2004). Social difficulties and victimisation in children with SLI at 11 years of age, *Journal of Speech, Language, and Hearing Research*, 47, 145-61.

Coolahan, J. (2007). *Irish Education: Its History and Structure*, Dublin: Institute of Public Administration.

Cosgrove, J. & Creaven, A.M. (2013). Understanding achievement in PIRLS and TIMSS 2011, in Eivers, E. & Clerkin, A. (eds.), *National Schools, International Contexts: Beyond the PIRLS and TIMSS Test Results* (pp.201-239), Dublin: Educational Research Centre.

Cosgrove, J., McKeown, C., Travers, J. Lysaght, Z., Ní Bhroin, O. & Archer, P. (2014). *Educational Experiences and Outcomes for Children with Special Educational Needs. A Secondary Analysis of Data from the Growing Up in Ireland Study*, Trim, Co. Meath: National Council for Special Education.

Criss, M.M., Shaw, D.S. & Ingoldsby, E.M. (2003). Mother-son positive synchrony in middle childhood: Relation to anti-social behaviour, *Social Development*, 12, 379-400.

Croll, P. & Moses, D. (2003). Special educational needs across two decades: Survey evidence from English primary schools, *British Educational Research Journal*, 29, 731-47.

Crossman, V. (2009). Cribbed, contained and confined? The care of children under the Irish Poor Law, 1850-1920, *Eire-Ireland*, 44, 1 & 2, 37-61.

Cunneen, C. & White, R. (2002). *Juvenile Justice: Youth and Crime in Australia* (2nd ed.), Melbourne: Oxford University Press.

Currie, J. (1995). Socio-economic status and child health: Does public insurance narrow the gap?, *Scandinavian Journal of Economics, 97*, 603-20.

Currie, J., Decker, S. & Lin, W. (2008). Has public insurance for older children reduced disparities in access to care and health outcomes?, *Journal of Health Economics, 27*, 1567-81.

Curry, P., Gilligan, R., Garratt, L. & Scholtz, J. (2011). *Where To from Here? Inter-ethnic Relations among Children in Ireland*, Dublin: Liffey Press.

Daly, M. E. (2006). Marriage, fertility and women's lives in 20th century Ireland, *Women's History Review, 15*, 571-85.

Darmody, M., Byrne, D. & McGinnity, F. (2012). Cumulative disadvantage? Educational careers of migrant students in Irish secondary schools, *Race Ethnicity Education, 17*, 129-51.

Darmody, M., Smyth, E., Byrne, D. & McGinnity, F. (2011b). New school, new system: The experiences of immigrant students in Irish schools, in Bekerman, Z. & Geisen, T. (eds.), *International Handbook of Migration, Minorities and Education: Understanding Cultural and Social Differences in Processes of Learning* (pp.283-300), New York: Springer.

Darmody, M., Tyrrell, N. & Song, S. (eds.) (2011a). *The Changing Faces of Ireland: Exploring the Lives of Immigrant and Ethnic Minority Children*, Rotterdam: Sense.

Davey-Smith, G. (2003). *Health Inequalities: Life-course Approaches*, Bristol: Policy Press.

Davis, J.A. (1966). The campus as a frog pond: An application of the theory of relative deprivation to career decisions of college men, *American Journal of Sociology, 72*, 17-31.

de Rooij, S.R, Wouters, H., Yonker, J.E, Painter, R.C. & Roseboom, T.J. (2010). Prenatal undernutrition and cognitive function in late adulthood, *Proceedings of the National Academy of Sciences of the United States of America, 107*(39), 16881-86.

De Valenzuela, J.S., Copeland, S.R., Huaqing Qi, C. & Park, P. (2006). Examining educational equity: Revisiting the disproportionate representation of minority students in special education, *Exceptional Children, 72*, 425-41.

Demaray, M.K., & Malecki, C.K. (2002). Critical levels of perceived social support associated with student adjustment, *School Psychology Quarterly, 17*, 3213-41.

Department for Work and Pensions (2007). *Opportunity for All*, London: Department for Work and Pensions.

Department of Children and Youth Affairs (2006-2014). *State of the Nation's Children*, biennial reports, accessible at http://www.dcya.gov.ie/viewdoc.asp?fn=/documents/Research/StateoftheNationReport.htm.

Department of Children and Youth Affairs (2014). *Better Outcomes, Brighter Future: The National Policy Framework for Children and Young People*, Dublin: Stationery Office.

Department of Children and Youth Affairs (2015). *National Strategy on Children's and Young People's Participation in Decision-making, 2015-2020*, Dublin: Stationery Office.

Department of Education (1928). *Report of the Department of Education for the School Years 1925-26-27 and the Financial and Administrative Year 1926-27*, Dublin: Stationery Office. Available at http://www.education.ie/en/Publications/Statistics/stats_statistical_report_1926_1927.pdf.

Department of Education and Science (1993). *Report of the Special Educational Review Committee (SERC)*, Dublin: Stationery Office.

Department of Education and Science (2004). *A Brief Description of the Irish Education System*. Dublin: Communications Unit, Department of Education and Science, available https://www.education.ie/en/Publications/Education-Reports/A-Brief-Description-of-the-Irish-Education-System.pdf.

Department of Education and Science (2005). *DEIS: An Action Plan for Educational Inclusion*, Dublin: Stationery Office.

Department of Education and Science (2007). *Inclusion of Students with Special Educational Needs, Post-primary Guidelines*, Dublin: Stationery Office.

Department of Education and Skills (2015). *Retention Rates of Pupils in Second-level Schools: 2008 Entry Cohort*, Dublin: Stationery Office.

Department of Health (1960). *The Problem of the Mentally Handicapped: White Paper*, Dublin: Stationery Office.

Department of Health and Children, National Children's Office (2000). *Our Children, Their Lives: National Children's Strategy*, Dublin: Stationery Office.

Department of Industry and Commerce, Statistics Branch (1926). *Census of Population*, Dublin: Stationery Office.

Department of Industry and Commerce, Statistics Branch (1946). *Census of Population*, Dublin: Stationery Office.

Department of Social Protection (2015). *Social Inclusion Monitor 2013*, Dublin: Stationery Office.

Department of the Environment, Community and Local Government (2016). *Homelessness Report January 2016*, retrieved from http://www.environ.ie/sites/default/files/publications/files/homelessness_report_january_2016_0.pdf.

Devine, D. (2009). Mobilising capitals? Migrant children's negotiation of their everyday lives in school, *British Journal of Sociology of Education, 30*, 521-35.

Devine, D. (2011). Securing migrant children's educational wellbeing: Perspective of policy and practice in Irish schools, in Darmody, M., Tyrrell, N. & Song, S. (eds.), *The Changing Faces of Ireland: Exploring the Lives of Immigrant and Ethnic Minority Children* (pp.73-88), Rotterdam: Sense.

Dishion, T.J., Andrews, D.W., & Crosby, L. (1995). Anti-social boys and their friends in early adolescence: Relationship characteristics, quality, and interactional process, *Child Development, 66*, 139-51.

Dodge, K., Coie, J., & Lynam, D. (2006). Aggression and anti-social behavior in youth, in Damon, W. & Lerner, R. (series eds.) & Eisenberg, N. (vol. ed.),

Handbook of Child Psychology: Vol. 3. *Social, Emotional and Personality Development* (6th ed., pp.719-88), New York: Wiley.

Donnellan, M.B., Trzesniewski, K.H., Robins, R.W., Moffitt, T.E. & Caspi, A. (2005). Low self-esteem is related to aggression, anti-social behaviour and delinquency, *Psychological Science, 16,* 328-35.

Dowd, J.B., Simanek, A.M. & Aiello, A.E. (2009). Socio-economic status, cortisol and allostatic load: A review of the literature, *International Journal of Epidemiology, 38,* 1297-309.

Downey, D.B. & Condron, D.J. (2016). Fifty years since the Coleman Report: Rethinking the relationship between schools and inequality, *Sociology of Education, 89,* 207-20.

Duffy, J. (2015). *Children of the Rising: The Untold Story of the Young Lives Lost during Easter 1916,* Dublin: Hachette Books Ireland.

Duncan, G.J. & Brooks-Gunn, J. (eds.) (1997). *Consequences of Growing Up Poor,* New York: Russell Sage Foundation.

Duncan, G.J. & Magnuson, K. (2003). Off with Hollingshead: Socio-economic resources, parenting and child development, in Bornstein, M.H. & Bradley, R.H. (eds.), *Socio-economic Status, Parenting, and Child Development* (pp.83-106), Mahwah, NJ: Erlbaum.

Duncan, G.J. & Murnane, R.J. (2011). The American dream: Then and now, in Duncan, G.J. & Murnane, R.J. (eds.), *Whither Opportunity? Rising Inequality, Schools and Children's Life Chances* (pp.3-23), New York, NY: Russell Sage Foundation / Spencer Foundation.

Duncan, G.J., Brooks-Gunn, J. & Klebanov, P.K. (1994). Economic deprivation and early childhood development, *Child Development, 65,* 296-318.

Duncan, G.J., Brooks-Gunn, J., Yeung, J. & Smith, J. (1998). How much does childhood poverty affect the life chances of children?, *American Sociological Review, 63,* 406-23.

Duncan, G.J., Ludwig, J. & Magnuson, K. (2007). Reducing poverty through pre-school interventions, *The Future of Children, 17*(2), 143-60.

Duncan, G.J., Magnuson, K., Kalil, A. & Ziol-Guest, K. (2012). The importance of early childhood poverty, *Social Indicators Research, 108,* 87-98.

Dustmann, C. & Fabbri, F. (2005). Immigrants in the British labour market, *Fiscal Studies, 26,* 423-70.

Dyson, A. & Gallannuagh, F. (2008). Disproportionality in special needs education in England, *Journal of Special Education, 42,* 36-46.

Dyson, A. & Kozleski, E. (2008). Dilemmas and alternatives in the classification of children with disabilities: New perspectives, in Florian, L. & McLaughlin, M.J. (eds.), *Disability Classification in Education: Issues and Perspectives* (pp.170-90), Thousand Oaks, CA: Corwin Press.

Eivers, E., Clerkin, A., Millar, D. & Close, S. (2010). *The 2009 National Assessments Technical Report,* Dublin: Educational Research Centre.

Eklund, J.M. & af Klinteberg, B. (2006). Stability and change in criminal behavior: A prospective study of young male lawbreakers and controls, *International Journal of Forensic Mental Health*, 5, 83-95.

Elliott, D.S. (1994). Serious violent offenders: Onset, developmental course and termination, American Society of Criminology 1993 presidential address, *Criminology*, 32, 1-21.

Entwisle, D.R. & Astone, N.M. (1994). Some practical guidelines for measuring youth's race / ethnicity and socio-economic status, *Child Development*, 65, 1521-40.

Epplé, C. (2007). 'Wild Irish with a vengeance': Definitions of Irishness in Kathleen Tynan's children's literature, in Shine Thompson, M. and Coghlan, V. (eds.), *Studies in Children's Literature: Divided Worlds* (pp.32-40), Dublin: Four Courts Press.

Evetovits, T., Figueras, J., Jowett, M., Mladovsky, P., Nolan, A., Normand, C. & Thomson, S. (2012). *Health System Responses to Financial Pressures in Ireland: Policy Options in an International Context*, Brussels: European Observatory on Health Systems and Policies.

Fahey, T. (1990). Measuring the female labour supply: Conceptual and procedural problems in Irish official statistics, *The Economic and Social Review*, 21, 163-91.

Fahey, T. (1992). State, family and compulsory schooling in Ireland, *Economic and Social Review*, 23, 369-96.

Fahey, T. (1998). Family policy in Ireland: A strategic overview, in Commission on the Family, *Strengthening Families for Life: Final Report of the Commission on the Family* (pp.384-403), Dublin: Stationery Office.

Fahey, T. (2012). Small bang? The impact of divorce legislation on marital breakdown in Ireland, *International Journal of Law, Policy and the Family* 26, 242-58.

Fahey, T. (2014). Divorce patterns and trends: An overview, in Eekelaar, J. & George, R. (eds.), *Routledge Handbook of Family Law and Policy* (pp.96-110), London: Routledge.

Fahey, T. (2015). The family in Ireland in the new millennium, in Connolly, L. (ed.), *The 'Irish' Family* (pp.54-69), London: Routledge.

Fahey, T. & Field, C.A. (2008). *Families in Ireland: An Analysis of Patterns and Trends*, Dublin: Stationery Office.

Fahey, T. & Nixon, E. (2013). Family policy in Ireland, in Robila, M. (ed.), *Family Policies across the Globe* (pp.125-36), New York: Springer.

Fahey, T. & Russell, H. (2001). *Family Formation in Ireland*, Dublin: Economic and Social Research Institute.

Fahey, T. & Russell, H. (2006). Childcare, in Morgenroth, E. & Fitzgerald, J. (eds.), *Ex-ante Evaluation of the Investment Priorities for the National Development Plan* 2007-2013 (pp.290-303), Dublin: Economic and Social Research Institute.

Fahey, T., Keilthy, P. & Polek, E. (2012). *Family Relationships and Family Wellbeing: A Study of the Families of Nine-year-olds in Ireland*, Dublin: University College Dublin / Family Support Agency.

Fahey, T., Russell, H. & Smyth, E. (2000). Gender equality, fertility decline and labour market patterns among women in Ireland, in Nolan, B., O'Connell, J. & Whelan, C.T. (eds.), *Bust to Boom? The Irish Experience of Growth and Inequality* (pp.244-67), Dublin: Institute of Public Administration.

Fallon, J. (ed.) (n.d.). *Early Childhood in Ireland: Evidence and Perspectives*, Dublin: Centre for Early Childhood Development and Education, retrieved from http://siolta.ie/media/pdfs/03_early_childhood_in_ireland.pdf.

Fanjul, G. (2014). *Children of the Recession: The Impact of the Economic Crisis on Child Wellbeing in Rich Countries, Report Card 12*, Florence: UNICEF Innocenti Research Centre.

Farmar, T. (1995). *Ordinary Lives*, Dublin: A & A Farmar.

Fenson, L., Dale, P., Reznick, J., Bates, E., Thal, D. & Pethick, J. (1994). Variability in early communication development, *Monographs of the Society for Research in Child Development, 59*(5), Ann Arbor, MI: Society for Research in Child Development.

Fergusson, D.M. & Horwood, L.J. (2002). Male and female offending trajectories, *Development and Psychopathology, 14,* 159-177.

Fergusson, D.M., Horwood, L.J. & Woodward, L.J. (2000). The stability of child abuse reports: A longitudinal study of young adults, *Psychological Medicine, 30,* 529-44.

Fine-Davis, M. (1983). Annex 1: Complete Report of Nationwide Survey of Mothers' Attitudes toward Child Care and Employment, in Working Party on Childcare Facilities for Working Parents (1983), *Report to the Minister for Labour*, Dublin: Stationery Office.

Fine-Davis, M. (2011). *Attitudes to Family Formation in Ireland: Findings from the Nationwide Study*, Dublin: Family Support Agency.

Flood, E. (2013). *Assisting Children with Special Needs: An Irish Perspective*, Dublin: Gill and Macmillan.

Fomby P. & Cherlin, A.J. (2007). Family instability and child wellbeing, *American Sociological Review, 72,* 181-204.

Fuller, B., Holloway, S. & Liang, X. (1996). Family selection of childcare centers: The influence of household support, ethnicity, and parental practices, *Child Development, 67,* 3320-37.

Furlong, M.J. & Christenson, S.L. (2008). Engaging students at school and with learning: A relevant construct for all students, *Psychology in the Schools, 45,* 365-368.

Furrer, C. & Skinner, C. (2003). Words can hurt forever, *Educational Leadership, 60,* 18-21.

Gambaro, L., Stewart, K. & Waldfogel, J. (eds.) (2014). *An Equal Start? Providing Quality Early Education and Care for Disadvantaged Children*, Bristol: Policy Press.

Garcia, R. (2013). The George Butler lecture: Social justice and leisure: The usefulness and uselessness of research, *Journal of Leisure Research, 45,* 7-22.

Geraghty, R., Gray, J. & Ralph, D. (2015). 'One of the best members of the family': Continuity and change in young children's relationships with their grandparents, in Connelly, L. (ed.), *The Irish Family*, Oxford: Routledge.

Gillis, J. (2009). Transitions to modernity, in Qvortrup, J., Corsaro, W.A. & Honig, M.S. (eds.), *The Palgrave Handbook of Childhood Studies* (pp.114-26), Basingstoke: Palgrave Macmillan.

Ginsborg, J. (2006). The effects of socio-economic status on children's language acquisition and use, in Clegg, J. & Ginsborg, J. (eds.), *Language and Social Disadvantage: Theory into Practice* (pp.9-27), London: Wiley.

Glass, D.V. (1968). Fertility trends in Europe since the Second World War, *Population Studies 22,* 103-46.

Glendenning, D. (1999). *Education and the Law*, Dublin: Butterworth Ireland.

Goodman, R. (1997). The strengths and difficulties questionnaire: A research note, *Journal of Child Psychology and Psychiatry, 38,* 581-86.

Government of Ireland (1937/2012). *Bunreacht na hÉireann (Irish Constitution)*, Dublin: Stationery Office.

Gray, J. (2014). The circulation of children in rural Ireland during the first half of the 20th century, *Continuity and Change 29,* 399-421.

Greene, S. (in press). Nine-year-old boys and girls: On different paths?, in Ryan-Flood, R. (ed.), *Gender, Intimacy and Contemporary Ireland*, London: Routledge.

Greene, S. & Moane, G. (2000). Growing up Irish: Changing children in a changing society, *Irish Journal of Psychology*, 21, 122-37.

Greene, S., Williams, J., Doyle, E., Harris, E., McCrory, C., Murray, A., Quail, A., Swords, L., Thornton, M., Layte, R., O'Dowd, T. & Whelan, C.T. (2010b). *Growing Up in Ireland: Review of the Literature Pertaining to the First Wave of Data Collection with the Child Cohort at 9 years*, Dublin: Department of Health and Children.

Greene, S., Williams, J., Layte, R. Doyle, E., Harris, E., McCrory, C., Murray, A., O'Dowd, T., Quail, A., Swords, L., Thornton, M. & Whelan, C.T. (2010a). *Growing Up in Ireland: Background and Conceptual Framework*, Dublin: Department of Health and Children.

Gregory, Lady A. (1910/1999). *Irish Myths and Legends*, Philadelphia, PA: Running Press.

Griffin, S. & Shevlin, M. (2008). *Responding to Special Educational Needs*, Dublin: Gill and Macmillan.

Grossman, M. (1972). On the concept of health capital and the demand for health, *The Journal of Political Economy, 80,* 223-55.

Growing Up in Ireland Study Team (2013). Transition to school among five-year-olds, *Key Finding No. 1, Infant Cohort at Five Years*, Dublin: Economic and Social Research Institute / Department of Children and Youth Affairs.

Grusky, D.B. & Weeden, K.A. (2007). Measuring poverty: The case for a sociological approach, in Kakawani, N. & Silber, J. (eds.), *The Many Dimensions of Poverty* (pp.20-35), Basingstoke: Palgrave Macmillan.

Gsir, S. (2014). *Social Interactions between Immigrants and Host Country Populations: A Country-of-origin Perspective*, San Domenico di Fiesole (FI) Italy: European University Institute.

Guinnane, T.W. (1997). *The Vanishing Irish: Households, Migration and the Rural Economy in Ireland*, Princeton: Princeton University Press.

Guo, G. & Harris, K.M. (2000). The mechanisms mediating the effects of poverty on children's intellectual development, *Demography, 37*, 431-47.

Guryan, J., Hurst, E. & Kearney, M. (2008). Parental education and parental time with children, *Journal of Economic Perspectives, 22*, 23-46.

Haas, S.A. (2008). Trajectories of functional health: The 'Long Arm' of childhood health and socio-economic factors, *Social Science & Medicine, 66*, 849-61.

Hajnal, J. (1982). Two kinds of pre-industrial household formation system, *Population and Development Review, 8*, 449-94.

Halle, T., Forry, N., Hair, E., Perper, K., Wandner, L., Wessel, J. & Vick, J. (2009). *Disparities in early learning and development: Lessons from the early childhood longitudinal study – Birth Cohort (ECLS)*, Washington, DC: Child Trends.

Halpenny, A.M., Greene, S., Hogan, D. & McGee, H. (2001). *Homeless Mothers and Their Children*, Dublin: Children's Research Centre / Royal College of Surgeons in Ireland.

Hannan, C. (2015). Marriage, fertility and social class in 20th century Ireland, in Connolly, L. (ed.), *The 'Irish' Family* (pp.39-53), London: Routledge.

Hannan, C. & Halpin, B. (2014). The influence of family structure on child outcomes: Evidence for Ireland, *Economic and Social Review, 45*, 1-24.

Hannan, C., Halpin, B. & Coleman, C. (2013). *Growing Up in a One-parent Family: Family Structure and Child Outcomes*, Dublin: Family Support Agency.

Hannan, D.F. (1979). *Displacement and Development: Class, Kinship and Social Change in Irish Rural Communities*, Dublin: Economic and Social Research Institute.

Hannan, D.F. & Katsiaouni, L.A. (1977). *Traditional Families? From Culturally-prescribed Roles to Negotiated Roles in Farm Families*, Dublin: Economic and Social Research Institute

Hannan, D.F., Smyth, E., McCullagh, J., O'Leary, R. & McMahon, D. (1996). *Coeducation and Gender Equality*, Dublin: Oak Tree Press.

Hansen, K. & Jones, E.M. (2008). Foundation stage profile and devolved teacher administration survey, in Hansen, K. & Joshi, H. (eds.), *Millennium Cohort Study Third Survey: A User's Guide to Initial Findings* (pp.98-117), London: Institute of Education.

Harrison, L.J., McLeod, S., Berthelsen, D. & Walker, S. (2009). Literacy, numeracy, and learning in school-aged children identified as having speech and language impairment in early childhood, *International Journal of Speech-Language Pathology, 11*, 392-403.

Hart, B. & Risley, T. (1995). *Meaningful Differences in the Everyday Experience of Young American Children*, Baltimore, MD: Paul H. Brookes.

Hastedt, D. (2016). *Mathematics Achievement of Immigrant Students*, Cham, Switzerland: Springer.

Haveman, R. & Wolfe, B. (1995). The determinants of children's attainments: A review of methods and findings, *Journal of Economic Literature, 33*, 1829-78.

Hayes, N. & Bradley, S. (2006). A decade of reflection: Early childhood care and education in Ireland 1996-2006, *Proceedings of Centre for Social and Educational Research Early Childhood Care and Education Seminar Series, Dublin*, November, retrieved from http://arrow.dit.ie/csercon/1/.

Health Information and Quality Authority (2015). *Report on Inspection of the Child Protection and Welfare Services Provided to Children Living in Direct Provision Accommodation under the National Standards for the Protection and Welfare of Children, and Section 8(1)(c) of the Health Act 2007*, Dublin, Health Information and Quality Authority.

Healthcare Pricing Office (2014). *Perinatal Statistics Report 2013*, Dublin: Health Service Executive.

Heckman, J.J. (2002). Skill formation and the economics of investing in disadvantaged children, *Science, 312*, 1900-02.

Heckman, J.J. (2011). The economics of inequality: The value of early childhood education, *American Educator, Spring*, 31-47.

Henderson, K.A. & Ainsworth, B. (2001). Researching leisure and physical activity with women of colour: Issues and emerging questions, *Leisure Sciences, 23*, 21-23.

Hendrick, H. (1997). *Children, Childhood and English Society*, Cambridge: Cambridge University Press.

Hendrick, H. (2009). The evolution of childhood in Western Europe *c.*1400-1750, in Qvortrup, J., Corsaro, W.A. & Honig, M.S. (eds.), *The Palgrave Handbook of Childhood Studies* (pp.99-113), Basingstoke: Palgrave Macmillan.

Henninger, W.R. & Luze, G. (2013). Moderating effects of gender on the relationship between poverty and children's externalizing behaviours, *Journal of Child Healthcare, 17*, 72-81.

Hertting, K. & Karlefors, I. (2013). Sport as a context for integration: Newly-arrived immigrant children in Sweden drawing sporting experiences, *International Journal of Humanities and Social Science, 3*(18), retrieved from http://www.ijhssnet.com/journals/Vol_3_No_18_October_2013/4.pdf.

Hetherington, E.M. (1989). Coping with family transitions: Winners, losers and survivors, *Child Development, 60*, 1-14.

Hibel, J., Farkas, G. & Morgan, P.L. (2010). Who is placed into special education?, *Sociology of Education, 83*, 312-32.

Hills, J., Brewer, M., Jenkins, S., Lister, R., Lupton, R., Machin, S., Mills, C., Modood, T., Rees, T. & Riddell, S. (2010). *An Anatomy of Economic Inequality in the UK. Report of the National Equality Panel*, London: Government Equalities Office.

Hoff-Ginsberg, E. (1991). Mother-child conversation in different social classes and communicative settings, *Child Development, 62,* 782-96.

Hoff, E. (2003). The specificity of environmental influence: Socio-economic status affects early vocabulary development *via* maternal speech, *Child Development, 74,* 1368-78.

Hofferth, S.L. (2006). Residential father family type and child wellbeing: Investment *versus* selection, *Demography, 43,* 53-77.

Holzer, H.J., Duncan, G.J., & Ludwig, J. (2007). *The Economic Costs of Poverty in the United States: Subsequent Effects of Children Growing Up Poor*, Madison, WI: Institute for Research on Poverty.

Huisman, M., Kunst, A.E. & Mackenbach, J.P. (2003). Socio-economic inequalities in morbidity among the elderly: A European overview, *Social Science & Medicine, 57,* 861-73.

Huisman, M., Kunst, A.E., Andersen, O., Bopp, M., Borgan, J.K., & Borrell, C. (2004). Socio-economic inequalities in mortality among elderly people in 11 European populations, *Journal of Epidemiology and Community Health, 58,* 468-75.

Humphreys, A.J. (1966). *New Dubliners,* London: Routledge.

Huston, A.C., Duncan, G.J., McLoyd, V.C., Crosby, D.A., Ripke, M.N., Weisner, T.S. & Eldred, C.A. (2005). Impacts on children of a policy to promote employment and reduce poverty for low-income parents: New Hope after 5 years, *Developmental Psychology, 41,* 902-18.

Hutchinson, J., Pickett, K.E., Green, J., & Wakschlag, L.S. (2010). Smoking in pregnancy and disruptive behaviour in 3-year-old boys and girls: An analysis of the UK Millennium Cohort Study, *Journal of Epidemiological and Community Health, 64,* 82-88.

Huttenlocher, J., Haight, W., Bryk, A., Seltzer, M. & Lyons, T. (1991). Vocabulary growth: Relation to language input and gender, *Developmental Psychology, 27,* 236-48.

Huttenlocher, J., Vasilyeva, M., Cymerman, E. & Levine, S.C. (2002). Language input at home and at school: Relation to syntax, *Cognitive Psychology, 45*(3), 337-74.

Huttenlocher, J., Waterfall, H., Vasilyeva, M., Vevea, J. & Hedges, L. (2010). Sources of variability in children's language growth, *Cognitive Psychology, 61,* 343-65.

Hysing, M., Elgen, I., Gillberg, C. & Lundervold, A.J. (2009). Emotional and behavioural problems in subgroups of children with chronic illness: Results from a large-scale population study, *Child: Health, Care and Development, 35,* 527-33.

Inglis, T. (2011). Mapping changes in Irish childhood, *Eire-Ireland, 46 (Fall/Winter)*, 63-83.

Irish Youth Justice Service (2013). *Tackling Youth Crime – Youth Justice Action Plan 2014-2018*, Dublin: Department of Justice and Equality.

Iruka, I., Dotterer, A.M., & Pungello, E. (2014). Ethnic variations of pathways linking socio-economic status, parenting, and pre-academic skills in a national representative sample, *Early Education and Development, 25*, 973-94.

Jacob, J.I. (2009). The socio-emotional effects of non-maternal childcare on children in the USA: A critical review of recent studies, *Early Childhood Development and Care, 179*, 559-70.

Jacobs, D. (2013). *The Educational Integration of Migrants: What Is the Role of Sending Society Actors and Is There a Transnational Educational Field?*, San Domenico di Fiesole (FI) Italy: European University Institute.

Jarjoura, G.R., Triplett, R.A. & Brinker, G.P. (2002). Growing up poor: Examining the link between persistent childhood poverty and delinquency, *Journal of Quantitative Criminology, 18*, 159-87.

Jauniaux, E., & Burton, G. J. (2007). Morphological and biological effects of maternal exposure to tobacco smoke on the fetoplacental unit, *Early Human Development, 83*, 699-706.

Jonsson, J.O. & Rudolphi, F. (2011). Weak performance – strong determination: School achievement and educational choice among children of immigrants in Sweden, *European Sociological Review, 27*, 487-508.

Kaga, Y., Bennett, J. & Moss, P. (2010). *Caring and Learning Together: A Cross-national Study on the Integration of Early Childhood Care and Education within Education*, Paris: UNESCO.

Kalil, A., Ryan, R. & Corey, M. (2012). Diverging destinies: Maternal education and the developmental gradient in time with children, *Demography, 49*, 1361-83.

Kao, G. & Tienda, M. (1998). Educational aspirations of minority youth, *American Journal of Education, 106*, 349-84.

Kaplan, H. (1980). *Self-attitudes and Deviant Behaviour*, Santa Monica: Goodyear.

Keating, D.P. & Hertzman, C. (1999). Modernity's Paradox, in Keating, D.P. & Hertzman, C. (eds.), *Developmental Health and the Wealth of Nations*, New York: Guilford Press.

Kelleghan, T. (1977). *The Evaluation of an Intervention Programme for Disadvantaged Children*, Windsor: NFER Publishing Co.

Kelleher, C. (2010). *All-Ireland Traveller Health Survey: Our Geels. Summary of Findings*, Dublin: School of Public Health, Physiotherapy and Population Science, University College Dublin.

Kelloggs (2015). *Is the Food Divide Getting Bigger?*, May, retrieved from http://www.kelloggs.ie/en_IE/news-center.html.

Kendig, S.M. & Bianchi, S.M. (2008). Single, cohabiting and married mothers' time with children, *Journal of Marriage and Family, 70*, 1228-40.

Kennedy, F. (2001). *Cottage to Crèche: Family Change in Ireland*, Dublin: Institute of Public Administration.

Keslair, F. & McNally, S. (2009). Special Educational Needs in England. Report to the National Equality Panel, London: London School of Economics.

Key, E. (1900/1909). *The Century of the Child*, London & New York: G.P. Putnam's Sons.

Kiberd, D. (2007). Literature, childhood and Ireland, in Bradford, C. & Coghlan, V. (eds.), *Expectations and Experience: Children, Childhood and Children's Literature* (pp.13-28), Lichfield: Pied Piper Publishing Ltd.

Kiernan, K. & Mensah, F. (2010). Partnership trajectories, parent and child wellbeing, in Hansen, K., Joshi, H. & Dex, S. (eds.), *Children of the 21st Century: The First Five Years* (pp.77-94), Bristol: Policy Press.

King, V. (2009). Stepfamily formation: Implications for adolescent ties to mothers, nonresident fathers, and stepfathers, *Journal of Marriage and Family, 71,* 954-68.

Kirpitchenko, L. & Mansouri, F. (2014). Social engagement among migrant youth: Attitudes and meanings, *Social Inclusion, 2*(2), 17-27.

Kitching, K. (2011). Interrogating the changing inequalities constituting 'popular', 'deviant' and 'ordinary' subjects of school / subculture in Ireland: Moments of new migrant student recognition, resistance and recuperation, *Race, Ethnicity and Education, 14,* 293-311.

Koster, M., Pijl, S.J., van Houten, E. & Nakken, H. (2007). The social position and development of pupils with SEN in mainstream Dutch primary schools, *European Journal of Special Needs Education, 22,* 31-46.

Koster, M., Pijl, S.J., Nakken, H. & Van Houten, E. (2010). Social participation of students with special needs in regular primary education in the Netherlands, *International Journal of Disability, Development and Education 57,* 59-75.

Kuh, D. & Ben Shlomo, Y. (eds.) (2004). *A Life-course Approach to Chronic Diseases Epidemiology,* Oxford, UK: Oxford University Press.

Küntay, A. (2013). Learning to Talk about Chairs (and Other Things: Emergence and Development of Language-and-Communication in Children), Inaugural address 22 May, University of Utrecht.

Lahey, B.B., Schwab-Stone, M., Goodman, S.H., Waldman I.D., Canino, G., Rathouz, P.J., Miller, T.L., Dennis, K.D., Bird, H. & Jensen, P.S. (2000). Age and gender differences in oppositional behaviour and conduct problems: A cross-sectional household study of middle childhood and adolescence, *Journal of Abnormal Psychology, 109,* 488-503.

Laosa, L.H. (1980). Parent education, cultural pluralism, and public policy: The uncertain connections, *Research Report Series, 1,* 1-22.

Layte, R. & McCrory, C. (2012). Pediatric chronic illness and educational failure: The role of emotional and behavioural problems, *Social Psychiatry and Psychiatric Epidemiology, 48,* 1307-16.

Layte, R. & McCrory, C. (2015). *Maternal Health Behaviours and Child Growth in Infancy,* Dublin: Department of Children and Youth Affairs.

Layte, R., Bennett, A., McCrory, C. & Kearney, J. (2014). Social class variation in the predictors of rapid growth in infancy and obesity at age 3 years, *International Journal of Obesity*, 38, 82-90.

Lesthaeghe, R. (2010). The unfolding story of the second demographic transition, *Population and Development Review*, 36, 211-51.

Letourneau, N.L., Duffet-Leger, L., Levac, L., Watson, B. & Young-Morris, C. (2013). Socio-economic status and child development: A meta-analysis, *Journal of Emotional and Behavioural Disorders*, 21, 211-24.

Leventhal, T., Fauth, R.C. & Brooks-Gunn, J. (2005). Neighborhood poverty and public policy: A 5-year follow-up of children's educational outcomes in the New York City Moving to Opportunity Demonstration, *Developmental Psychology*, 41, 933-52.

Li, J., McMurray, A. & Stanley, F. (2008). Modernity's paradox and the structural determinants of child health and wellbeing, *Health Sociology Review*, 17, 64-77.

Liberatos, P., Link, B.G. & Kelsey, J.L. (1988). The measurement of social class in epidemiology, *Epidemiological Review*, 10, 87-121.

Lin, W. (2009). Why has the health inequality among infants in the US declined? Accounting for the shrinking gap, *Health Economics*, 18, 823-41.

Link, B.G. & Phelan, J. (1995). Social conditions as fundamental causes of disease, *Journal of Health and Social Behavior*, 35, 80-94.

Linver, M.R., Brooks-Gunn, J. & Kohen, D.E. (2002). Family processes as pathways from income to young children's development, *Developmental Psychology*, 38, 719-34.

Loeber, R., Farrington, D.P., Stouthamer-Loeber, M. & Van Kammen, W.B. (1998). *Anti-social Behaviour and Mental Health Problems: Explanatory Factors in Childhood and Adolescence*, Mahwah, NJ: Lawrence Erlbaum.

Lohr, K., Brook, R., Kamberg, C., Goldberg, G., Leibowitz, A., Keesey, J., Reboussin, D. & Newhouse, J. (1986). Use of Medical Care in the RAND Health Insurance Experiment: Diagnosis- and Service-specific Analyses in a Randomised Control Trial, Santa Monica, CA: RAND.

Luddy, M. (2011). Unmarried mothers in Ireland, *Women's History Review*, 20, 109-26.

Luddy, M. (2014). The early years of the NSPCC in Ireland, in Luddy, M. & Smith, J. (eds.), *Children, Childhood and Irish Society, 1500 to the Present* (pp.100-20), Dublin: Four Courts Press.

Luddy, M. & Smith, J. (eds.) (2014). *Children, Childhood and Irish Society, 1500 to the Present*, Dublin: Four Courts Press.

Lunn, P. & Fahey, T. (2011). *Households and Family Structures in Ireland: A Detailed Statistical Analysis of Census 2006*, Dublin: Family Support Agency / Economic and Social Research Institute.

Lunn, P., Fahey, T. & Hannan, C. (2009). *Family Figures: Family Dynamics and Family Types in Ireland, 1986-2006*, Dublin: Family Support Agency / Economic and Social Research Institute.

MacGill, P. (1914). *Children of the Dead End: Autobiography of a Navvy*, London: Herbert Jenkins Limited.

MacGiolla Phádraig, B. (2007). Towards inclusion: The development of provision for children with special educational needs in Ireland from 1991 to 2004, *Irish Educational Studies, 26*, 289-300.

Mackenbach, J.P., Kulhánová, I. & Menvielle, G. (2015). Trends in inequalities in premature mortality: A study of 3.2 million deaths in 13 European countries, *Journal of Epidemiology and Community Health, 69*, 207-17.

Magnuson, K.A., Sexton, H.R., Davis-Kean, P.E. & Huston, A.C. (2009). Increases in maternal education and young children's language skills, *Merrill-Palmer Quarterly, 55*, 319-50.

Magnusson, K.A. & Waldfogel, J. (2005). Early childhood care and education: Effects on ethnic and racial gaps in school readiness, *The Future of Children, 15*(1), 169-96.

Maguire, M. & Ó Cinnéide, S. (2005). 'A good beating never hurt anyone': The punishment and abuse of children in 20th century Ireland, *Journal of Social History, 38*, 635-52.

Maughan, B., Rowe, R., Messer, J., Goodman, R. & Meltzer, H. (2004). Conduct disorder and oppositional defiant disorder in a national sample: Developmental epidemiology, *Journal of Child Psychology and Psychiatry, 45*, 609-21.

Mayer, S. (1997). *What Money Can't Buy: Family Income and Children's Life Chances*, Cambridge, MA: Harvard University Press.

McArthur, J., Sharp, S. Kelly, B. & Gaffney, M. (2007). Disabled children negotiating school life: Agency, difference and teaching practice, *International Journal of Children's Rights, 15*, 1-22.

McCoy, S. & Banks, J. (2012). Simply academic? Why children with special educational needs don't like school, *European Journal of Special Needs Education, 27*, 81-97.

McCoy, S., Banks, J. & Shevlin, M. (2012a). School matters: How context influences the identification of different types of special educational needs, *Irish Educational Studies, 32*, 119-138.

McCoy, S., Quail, A. & Smyth, E. (2012). *Influences on 9-year olds' learning: Home, school and community,* Dublin: Department of Children and Youth Affairs.

McCoy, S., Quail, A. & Smyth, E. (2014a). The effects of school social mix: Unpacking the differences, *Irish Educational Studies, 33*, 307-30.

McCoy, S., Smyth, E. & Banks, J. (2012b). *The Primary Classroom: Insights from the Growing Up in Ireland Study*, Dublin: National Council for Curriculum and Assessment / Economic and Social Research Institute.

McCoy, S., Smyth, E., Watson, D. & Darmody, M. (2014a). *Leaving School in Ireland: A Longitudinal Study of Post-School Transitions*, Research Series 36, Dublin: Economic and Social Research Institute.

McCrory, C. & Layte, R. (2012). Prenatal exposure to maternal smoking and childhood behavioural problems: A quasi-experimental approach, *Journal of Abnormal Child Psychology, 40,* 1277-88.

McCrory, C., Dooley, C., Layte, R. & Kenny, R.A. (2015). The lasting legacy of childhood adversity for disease risk in later life, *Health Psychology, 34,* 687-96.

McGinnity, F., Darmody, M. & Murray, A. (2015). *Academic Achievement among Immigrant Children in Irish Primary Schools,* ESRI Working Paper No. 512, Dublin: Economic and Social Research Institute.

McGinnity, F., Murray, A. & McNally, S. (2013). *Mothers' Return to Work and Childcare Choices for Infants in Ireland,* Dublin: Department of Children and Youth Affairs.

McGinnity, F., Murray, A. & Russell H. (2015). *Non-parental Childcare and Child Cognitive Outcomes at Age 5: Results from the Growing Up in Ireland Infant Cohort,* Dublin: Department of Children and Youth Affairs.

McGinnity, F., Quinn, E., Kingston, G. & O'Connell, P. (2012). *Annual Monitoring Report on Integration 2011,* Dublin: The Integration Centre / Economic and Social Research Institute.

McGinnity, F., Russell, H. & Murray, A. (2015). *Non-parental Childcare and Child Cognitive Outcomes at Age 5,* Dublin: Department of Children and Youth Affairs.

McLanahan, S. & Garfinkel, I. (2012). Fragile families: Debates, facts and solutions, in Scott, E. & Garrison, M. (eds.), *Marriage at the Crossroads* (pp.142-69), Cambridge, UK: Cambridge University Press.

McLanahan, S. & Sandefur, G. (1994). *Growing Up with a Single Parent: What Hurts, What Helps,* Cambridge, MA: Harvard University Press.

McLeod, J.D. & Shanahan, M.J. (1996). Trajectories of poverty and children's mental health, *Journal of Health and Social Behaviour, 37,* 207-22.

McLeod, J.D., & Shanahan, M.J. (1993). Poverty, parenting, and children's mental health, *American Sociological Review, 58,* 351-66.

McLoyd, V. (1990). The impact of economic hardship on black families and children: Psychological distress, parenting, and socio-emotional development, *Child Development, 61,* 311-46.

McLoyd, V.C. (1998). Socio-economic disadvantage and child development, *American Psychologist, 53,* 185-204.

McNally, S. & Quigley, J. (2014). An Irish cohort study of risk and protective factors for infant language development at 9 months, *Infant and Child Development, 23,* 634-49.

Meadows, S.O., McLanahan, S.S. & Brooks-Gunn, J. (2008). Stability and change in family structure and mental health trajectories, *American Sociological Review, 73,* 314-34.

Minnesota Population Center (2015). *Integrated Public Use Microdata Series, International: Version 6.4* [machine-readable database], Minneapolis: University of Minnesota.

Mirowsky, J. & Ross, C.E. (2003). *Education, Social Status and Health*, NJ: Aldine Transaction.

Moffitt, T.E., Caspi, A., Rutter, M. & Silva, P.A. (2001). *Sex Differences in Anti-social Behaviour: Conduct Disorder, Delinquency and Violence in the Dunedin Longitudinal Study*, Cambridge: Cambridge University Press.

Mood, C. & Jonsson, J. (2014). *Poverty and Welfare among Children and Their Families 1968-2010*, Stockholm: Institute for Future Studies.

Moore, Q. & Schmidt, L. (2004). *Do Maternal Investments in Human Capital Affect Children's' Academic Achievement?*, Department of Economics Working Papers 13, Williamstown, MA: Department of Economics, Williams College.

Morris, P., Duncan, G. & Clark-Kauffman, E. (2005). Child wellbeing in an era of welfare reform: The sensitivity of transitions in development to policy change, *Developmental Psychology, 41*, 919-32.

Murray, C. & Greenberg, M.T. (2001). Relationships with teachers and bonds with school: Social emotional adjustment correlates for children with and without disabilities, *Psychology in the Schools*, 38, 25-41.

Musitu, G., Estévez, E. & Emler, N. (2007). Adjustment problems in the family and school contexts, attitude towards authority and violent behaviour at school in adolescence, *Adolescence, 42*, 779-94.

National Consumer Agency (2010). *Doctor and Dentists Survey: May 2010*, Dublin: National Consumer Agency.

National Institute for Health and Care Excellence (2013). *Anti-social Behaviour and Conduct Disorders in Children and Young People: Recognition, Intervention and Management*, London: Royal College of Psychiatrists / Leicester: British Psychological Society.

National Institute of Child Health and Human Development Early Childcare Research Network (NICHHD) (2005). Duration and developmental timing of poverty and children's cognitive and social development from birth through third grade, *Child Development, 76*, 795-810.

Neckerman, K. & Torche, F. (2007). Inequality: Causes and consequences, *Annual Review of Sociology, 33*, 335-57.

Network of Experts in Social Sciences of Education and Training (NESSE) (2012). *Education and Disability / Special Needs*, Brussels: European Commission's Directorate-General for Education and Culture.

Nic Congáil, R. (2009). 'Fiction, amusement, instruction': The Irish Fireside Club and the educational ideology of the Gaelic League, in Luddy, M. & Smith, J. (eds.), *Children, Childhood and Irish Society, 1500 to the Present* (pp.164-83), Dublin: Four Courts Press.

Nixon, E. (2012). *How Families Matter for the Social and Emotional Development of Nine-year-old Children*, Dublin: Department of Children and Youth Affairs.

Nixon, E., Halpenny, A.M. & Watson, D. (2009). *Parents' and Children's Perspectives on Parenting Styles and Discipline in Ireland*, Dublin: Stationery Office.

Noble, K.G. (2014). Rich man, poor man: Socio-economic adversity and brain development, *Cerebrum*, May, retrieved from http://www.dana.org/Cerebrum/2014/Rich_Man,_Poor_Man__Socioeconomic_ Adversity_and_Brain_Development/.

Noble, K.G., Norman, M.F. & Farah, M.J. (2005). The neurocognitive correlates of socio-economic status in kindergarten children, *Developmental Science, 8,* 74-87.

Nolan, B. & Whelan, C.T. (2007). On the multidimensionality of poverty and social exclusion, in Micklewright, J. & Jenkins, S. (eds.), *Poverty and Inequality: New Directions* (pp.146-65), Oxford: Oxford University Press.

Nolan, B. & Whelan, C.T. (2010). Using non-monetary deprivation indicators to analyse poverty and social exclusion in rich countries: Lessons from Europe?, *Journal of Policy Analysis and Management, 29,* 305-23.

Nolan, B., Layte, R., Whelan, C.T. & Maître, B. (2006). *Day In, Day Out: Understanding the Dynamics of Child Poverty in Ireland*, Dublin: Institute of Public Administration / Combat Poverty Agency.

Ó Buachalla, S. (1988). *Education Policy in 20th Century Ireland*, Dublin: Wolfhound Press.

O'Connell, P. & McGinnity, F. (2008). *Immigrants at Work: Ethnicity and Nationality in the Irish Labour Market,* Dublin: Economic and Social Research Institute.

O'Connor, A. (2012). *Small Lives 1860-1970*, Dublin: Gill and Macmillan.

O'Connor, M. (2010). *The Development of Infant Education in Ireland, 1838-1948: Epochs and Eras*, Oxford / Bern: Peter Lang.

O'Dannachair, C. (1962). The family in Irish tradition, *Christus Rex, XVI(3)*, 185-96.

O'Higgins, K. (1974). *Marital Desertion in Dublin: An Exploratory Study*, Broadsheet No. 9, Dublin: Economic and Social Research Institute.

O'Mahony, E. (2011). *Practice and Belief among Catholics in the Republic of Ireland*, Dublin: Irish Catholic Bishops Conference.

O'Mahony, P. (1997). *Mountjoy Prisoners: A Sociological and Criminological Profile*, Dublin: Stationery Office.

Odgers, C.L., Moffitt, T.E., Broadbent, J.M., Dickson, N., Hancox, R.J., Harrington, H., Poulton, R., Sears, M.R., Thomson, W.M. & Caspi, A. (2008). Female and male anti-social trajectories: From childhood origins to adult outcomes, *Development and Psychopathology, 20,* 673-716.

OECD (2009). *Reviews of Migrant Education, Ireland,* Paris: Organization for Economic Cooperation and Development.

OECD (2010a). *Doing Better for Children*, Paris: Organization for Economic Cooperation and Development.

OECD (2010b). *A Family Affair: Intergenerational Social Mobility across OECD Countries,* Paris: Organization for Economic Cooperation and Development.

OECD (2016). *Family Database*, Paris: Organization for Economic Cooperation and Development.

OECD / Department of Education (1966). *Investment in Education*, Dublin: Stationery Office.

Oireachtas Library & Research Service (2012). *Early Childhood Education and Care*, Spotlight Series, No. 4, April 2012. Retrieved from https://www.oireachtas.ie/parliament/media/housesoftheoireachtas/libraryresearch/spotlights/spotEarlyEd180412.pdf, 22 August 2016.

One Family (2015). *One Family Pre-Budget Submission 2015*, retrieved from http://www.onefamily.ie/policy/one-family-pre-budget-submission-2015.

Palloni, A. & Milesi, C. (2006). Economic achievement, inequalities and health disparities: The intervening role of early health status, *Research in Social Stratification and Mobility*, 24, 21-40.

Palloni, A., Milesi, C., White, R.G. & Turner, A. (2009). Early childhood health, reproduction of economic inequalities and the persistence of health and mortality differentials, *Social Science & Medicine*, 68, 1574-82.

Pan, B.A., Rowe, M.L., Singer, J.D. & Snow, C.E. (2005). Maternal correlates of growth in toddler vocabulary production in low-income families, *Child Development*, 76, 763-82.

Pearse, P., Ireland (Provisional Government, 1916) & Dolmen Press (1975). *The Easter Proclamation of the Irish Republic, 1916*, Dublin: Dolmen Press.

Perry, L. & McConney, A. (2010). School socio-economic composition and student outcomes in Australia: Implications for educational policy, *Australian Journal of Education*, 54, 72-85.

Petrill, S.A., Pike, A., Price, T. & Plomin, R. (2004). Chaos in the home and socio-economic status are associated with cognitive development in early childhood: Environmental mediators identified in a genetic design, *Intelligence*, 32, 445-60.

Pettit, G.S., Laird, R.D., Dodge, K.A., Bates, J.E. & Criss, M.M. (2001). Antecedents and behaviour-problem outcomes of parental monitoring and psychological control in early adolescence, *Child Development*, 72, 583-98.

Pianta, R., Egeland, B. & Sroufe, L.A. (1990). Maternal stress and children's development: Prediction of school outcomes and identification of protective factors, in Rolf, J.E., Masten, A., Cicchetti, D., Nuechterlein, K. & Weintraub, S. (eds.), *Risk and Protective Factors in the Development of Psychopathology* (pp.215-35), Cambridge: Cambridge University Press.

Pianta, R.C. (1992). *Child-parent Relationship Scale*, Virginia: University of Virginia.

Piers, E.V. & Herzberg, D.S. (2002). *Piers-Harris Children's Self-Concept Scale – Second Edition Manual*, Los Angeles, CA: Western Psychological Services.

Piotrowska, P.J., Stride, C.B., Croft, S.E. & Rowe, R. (2015). Socio-economic status and anti-social behaviour among children and adolescents: A systematic review and meta-analysis, *Clinical Psychology Review*, 35, 47-55.

Pobal (2015). *Annual Early Years Sector Survey Report 2014*, Dublin: Pobal / Department of Children and Youth Affairs.

Portes, A. & Rivas, A. (2011). The adaptation of migrant children, *The Future of Children*, 21(1), 219-46.

Portes, A. & Rumbaut, R.G. (2005). Introduction: The second generation and the Children of Immigrants longitudinal study, *Ethnic and Racial Studies, 28,* 983-99.

Preston, S. (1976). Family sizes of children and family sizes of women, *Demography, 13,* 105-14.

Priestley, M. (2001). *Disability and the Life Course: Global Perspectives,* Cambridge: Cambridge University Press.

Pryor, J. & Rodgers, B. (2001). *Children in Changing Families,* Oxford: Blackwell.

Purcell-Gates, V. (2000). *Now We Read, Now We Speak,* Hillsdale, NJ: Erlbaum.

Radloff, L.S. (1977). The CES-D scale: A self-report depression scale for research in the general population, *Applied Psychological Measurement, 1,* 385-401.

Raftery, M. & O'Sullivan, E. (1999). *Suffer the Little Children: The Inside Story of Ireland's Industrial Schools,* Dublin: New Island.

Raley, R.K. & Wildsmith, E. (2004). Cohabitation and children's family instability, *Journal of Marriage and the Family, 66,* 210-19.

Ramsden, E. (2008). Eugenics from the New Deal to the Great Society: Genetics, demography and population quality, *Studies in History and Philosophy of Biological and Biomedical Sciences* 39(4), 391-406.

Reardon, S.F. (2013). The widening income achievement gap, *Educational Leadership, 70,* 10-16.

Reception and Integration Agency (2015). *Reception and Integration Agency, Monthly Statistics: December,* retrieved from http://www.ria.gov.ie/en/RIA/RMR2015December.pdf/Files/RMR2015December.pdf.

Registrar General of Births, Deaths and Marriages (1901). *Census of Population,* Dublin: Stationery Office.

Registrar General of Births, Deaths and Marriages (1911). *Census of Population,* Dublin: Stationery Office.

Reher, D.S. (2011). Economic and social implications of demographic transition, *Population and Development Review, 37 (Supplement),* 11-33.

Relikowski, I., Schneider, T. & Blossfeld, H.P. (2009). Primary and secondary effects of social origin in migrant and native families at the transition to the tracked German school system, in Cherkaoui, M. & Hamilton, P. (eds.), *Raymond Boudon: A Life in Sociology* (Vol. 3, pp.149-70), Oxford: Bardwell Press.

Richman, A.L., Miller, P.M. & LeVine, R.A. (1992). Cultural and educational variations in maternal responsiveness, *Developmental Psychology, 28,* 614-21.

Riddell, S., Tisdall, K. & Kane, J. (2006). *Literature Review of Educational Provision for Pupils with Additional Support Needs,* Edinburgh: Scottish Executive Social Research.

Roberts, R.E., Andrews, J.A., Lewinsohn, P.M. & Hops, H. (1990). Assessment of depression in adolescents using the Center of Epidemiologic Studies Depression Scale, *Journal of Consulting and Clinical Psychology, 2,* 122-28.

Robinson, R. (2002). User charges for healthcare, in Mossialos, E., Dixon, A., Figueras, J. & Kutzin, J. (eds.), *Funding Healthcare: Options for Europe* (pp.161-83), Milton Keynes, UK: Open University Press.

Roche, K.M., Ellen, J. & Astone, N.M. (2005). Effects of out-of-school care on early sex initiation in low-income, central city neighbourhoods, *Archives of Pediatrics and Adolescent Medicine, 159,* 68-73.

Rose, D. & Harrison, E. (2009). *Social Class in Europe: An Introduction to the European Socio-Economic Classification*, London: Routledge.

Rose, N. (1989). *Governing the Soul*, London: Routledge.

Rose, R. & Shevlin, S. (2010). *Count Me In: Ideas for Actively Engaging Students in Inclusive Classrooms*, London: Jessica Kingsley.

Roseboom, T.J., Painter, R.C, van Abeelen, A.F.M., Veenendaal, M.V.E, de RooijHungry, S.R. (2011). Hungry in the womb: What are the consequences? Lessons from the Dutch famine, *Maturitas, 70*(2), 141-145.

Roseboom, R., de Rooij, S. & Painter, R. (2006). The Dutch Famine and its long-term consequences for adult health, *Early Human Development, 82,* 485-91.

Russell, H., McGinnity, F., Callan, T. & Keane, C. (2009). *A Woman's Place? Female Participation in the Paid Labour Market*, Dublin: Equality Authority / Economic and Social Research Institute.

Rutter, M. (2002). Nature, nurture and development: From evangelism through science toward policy and practice, *Child Development, 73,* 1-21.

Rutter, M. & Smith, D.J. (1995). *Psychosocial Disorders in Young People: Time Trends and Their Causes*, Chichester: Wiley.

Rutter, M. & The English and Romanian Adoptees (ERA) study team (1998). Developmental catch-up, and deficit, following adoption after severe global early privation, *Journal of Child Psychology and Psychiatry, 39,* 465-76.

Sandberg, J.F., & Hofferth, S.L. (2001). Changes in children's time with parents, U.S. 1981-1997, *Demography, 38,* 423-36.

Sharpley, C.F. & Rogers, H.J. (1984). Preliminary validation of the abbreviated Spanier Dyadic Adjustment Scale: Some psychometric data regarding a screening test of marital adjustment, *Educational and Psychological Measurement, 44,* 1045-49.

Sheehy, J.S. (1909). The need of an Irish 'boys' paper, *The College Chronicle, Castleknock 24,* 32.

Shevlin, M. (2010). Valuing and learning from young people, in Rose, R. (ed.), *Confronting Obstacles to Inclusion: International Responses to Developing Inclusive Education* (pp.103-22), London: Routledge.

Shevlin, M. & Rose, R. (2005). Listen, hear and learn: Gaining perspectives from young people with special educational needs, in Kaikkonen, L. (ed.), Jotain *Erityistä (Something Special)* (pp.91-102), Jyväskylä: Ammattikorkeakoulu.

Shkolnikov, V.M., Andreev, E.M., Houle, R. & Vaupel, J.W. (2007). The concentration of reproduction in cohorts of women in Europe and the United States, *Population and Development Review, 33,* 67-99.

Shonkoff , J.P. & Phillips, D.A. (2000) (eds.). *From Neurons to Neighbourhoods: The Science of Early Childhood Development*, National Academy Press: Washington, DC.

Sime, D. & Fox, R. (2015). Migrant children, social capital and access to services post-migration: Transitions, negotiations and complex agencies, *Children & Society, 29*, 524-34.

Simons, R.L. & Associates (1996). *Understanding the Differences between Divorced and Intact Families: Stress, Interaction and Child Outcome*, Thousand Oaks, CA: Sage.

Smeeding, T. (2013). *On the Relationship between Income Inequality and Intergenerational Mobility*, AIAS, GINI Discussion Paper 89.

Smith, C. & Greene, S. (2014). *Key Thinkers in Childhood Studies*, Bristol: Policy Press.

Smyth, E. (1999). *Do Schools Differ?*, Dublin: Oak Tree Press.

Smyth, E. (2008). Just a phase? Youth unemployment in the Republic of Ireland, *Journal of Youth Studies, 11*, 313-329.

Smyth, E. & McCoy, S. (2009). *Investing in Education: Combating Educational Disadvantage*, Dublin: Barnardo's / Economic and Social Research Institute.

Smyth, E., Banks, J. & Calvert, E. (2011). *From Leaving Certificate to Leaving School: A Longitudinal Study of Sixth Year Students*, Dublin: Liffey Press.

Smyth, E., Darmody, M., McGinnity, F. & Byrne, D. (2009). *Adapting to Diversity: Irish Schools and Newcomer Students*, Dublin: Economic and Social Research Institute.

Smyth, E., McCoy, S. & Darmody, M. (2004). *Moving Up: The Experiences of First Year Students in Post-primary Education*, Dublin: Liffey Press.

Smyth, E., Whelan, C.T., McCoy, S., Quail, A. & Doyle, E. (2010). Understanding parental influence on educational outcomes among 9-year-old children in Ireland, *Child Indicators Research, 3*, 85-104.

Snow, C., Burns, S. & Griffin, P. (eds.). (1998). *Preventing Reading Difficulties in Young Children*, Washington, DC: National Academy Press.

Snyder H. (2004). *Juvenile arrests 2002*, Washington, DC: Office of Juvenile Justice and Delinquency Prevention.

South Eastern Health Board (1993). *Kilkenny Incest Investigation*, Dublin: Stationery Office.

Spanier, G.B. (1976). Measuring dyadic adjustment: New scales for assessing the quality of marriage and similar dyads, *Journal of Marriage and the Family, 38*, 15-28.

Spencer, N. (2010). Child health inequities, *Paediatrics and Child Health, 20*, 157-62.

Sprott, J.B., Jenkins, J.M. & Doob, A.N. (2000). *Early Offending: Understanding the Risk and Protective Factors of Delinquency*, Hull, Quebec: Applied Research Branch, Strategic Policy: Human Resources Development Canada.

Stanger, C., Achenbach, T.M. & Verhulst, F.C. (1997). Accelerated longitudinal comparisons of aggressive *versus* delinquent syndromes, *Developmental Psychopathology, 9,* 43-58.

Start Strong (2014a). *The Double Dividend: Childcare That's Affordable and High Quality*, Dublin: Start Strong.

Start Strong (2014b). *'Childcare': Business or Profession?*, Dublin: Start Strong.

StataCorp (2013a). *Stata: Release 13. Statistical Software*, College Station, TX: StataCorp LP.

StataCorp (2013b). *Stata Survey Data Reference Manual, Release 13*, College Station, TX: StataCorp LP.

Stattin, H. & Kerr, M. (2000). Parental monitoring: A reinterpretation, *Child Development, 71,* 1072-85.

Stattin, H. & Magnusson, D. (1991). Stability and change in criminal behaviour up to age 30, *The British Journal of Criminology, 31,* 327-46.

Stevens, J.A. (2007). The little big house: Somerville and Ross's works for children, in Shine Thompson, M. & Coghlan, V. (eds.), *Studies in Children's Literature: Divided Worlds* (pp.41-49), Dublin: Four Courts Press.

Stevens, P. & O'Moore, M. (2009). *Inclusion or Illusion? Educational Provision for Primary School Children with Mild General Learning Disabilities*, Dublin: Blackhall Publishing.

Stodolska, M. (1998). Assimilation and leisure constraints: Dynamics of constraints on leisure in immigrant populations, *Journal of Leisure Research, 30,* 521-51.

Suhrcke, M. & Stuckler, D. (2012). Will the recession be bad for our health? It depends, *Social Science & Medicine, 74,* 647-53.

Swan, D. (2000). From exclusion to inclusion, *Frontline, 44,* 23 September, retrieved from: http://frontline-ireland.com/from-exclusion-to-inclusion/.

Swartz, K. (2010). *Cost-sharing: Effects on Spending and Outcomes*, Princeton: The Robert Wood Johnson Foundation.

Sylva, K., Melhuish, E., Sammons, P., Siraj-Blatchford, I. & Taggart, B. (2010). *Early Childhood Matters*, London: Routledge.

Taylor, C.L., Christensen, D., Lawrence, D., Mitrou, F. & Zubrick, S.R. (2013). Risk factors for children's receptive vocabulary development from four to eight years in the Longitudinal Study of Australian Children, *PLoS ONE* 8(9): e73046.

Teddlie, C. & Reynolds, D. (eds.) (2000). *The International Handbook of School Effectiveness Research*, London: Falmer Press.

Tein, J., Sandler, I.N. & Zautra, A.J. (2000). Stressful life events, psychological distress, coping and parenting of divorced mothers: A longitudinal study, *Journal of Family Psychology, 14,* 27-41.

Therborn, G. (2004). *Between Sex and Power: Family in the World, 1900-2000*, London: Routledge.

Thomas, G. & Loxley, A. (2001). *Deconstructing Special Education and Constructing Inclusion*, Milton Keynes: Open University Press.

Thomas, M.S., Forrester, N.A. & Ronald, A. (2013). Modeling socio-economic status effects on language development, *Developmental Psychology, 49*, 2325-43.

Thornberry, T.P. & Krohn, M.D. (2003). *Taking Stock of Delinquency: An Overview of Findings from Contemporary Longitudinal Studies*, New York, NY: Kluwer / Plenum.

Tracey, D.H. & Young, J.W. (2002). Mothers' helping behaviours during children's at-home oral-reading practice: Effects of children's reading ability, children's gender, and mothers' educational level, *Journal of Educational Psychology, 94*, 729-37.

Travers, J. (2010). Learning support policy for mathematics in Irish primary schools: Equal access but unequal needs, *Irish Educational Studies, 29*, 71-80.

Trzesniewski, K.H., Donnellan, M.B., Moffitt, T.E., Robins, R.W., Poulton, R. & Caspi, A. (2006). Low self-esteem during adolescence predicts poor health, criminal behaviour, and limited economic prospects during adulthood, *Developmental Psychology, 42*, 381-90.

Tucker-Drob, E.M, Rhemtulla, M., Harden, K.P, Turkheimer, E. & Fask, D. (2011). Emergence of a gene X socio-economic status interaction on infant mental ability between 10 months and 2 years, *Psychological Science, 22*, 125-33.

Tucker-Drob, E.M. (2013). How many pathways underlie socio-economic differences in the development of cognition and achievement?, *Learning and Individual Differences, 25*, 12-20.

Turkheimer, E., Haley, A., Waldron, M., D'Onofrio, B. & Gottesman, I.I. (2003). Socio-economic status modifies heritability of IQ in young children, *Psychological Science, 14*, 623-28.

Tussing, D. (1978). *Irish Educational Expenditure – Past, Present and Future*, Dublin: Economic and Social Research Institute.

UNICEF (2007). *Child Poverty in Perspective: An Overview of Child Wellbeing in Rich Countries, Report Card 7*, Florence: UNICEF Innocenti Research Centre.

United Nations (1989). *Convention on the Rights of the Child*, Geneva: United Nations.

van Bavel, J. (2010). Subreplacement fertility in the West before the baby boom: Past and current perspectives, *Population Studies, 64*, 1-18.

Van der Veen, I., Smeets, E. & Derriks, M. (2010). Children with special educational needs in the Netherlands: Number, characteristics and school career, *Educational Research, 52*, 15-43.

Veenstra, R.S., Lindenberg, S., Oldehinkel, A.J., De Winter, A.F. & Ormel, J. (2006). Temperament, environment, and anti-social behaviour in a population sample of pre-adolescent boys and girls, *International Journal of Behavioural Development, 30*, 422-32.

Waldfogel, J. (2013). Socio-economic inequality in childhood and beyond: An overview of challenges and findings from comparative analyses of cohort studies, *Longitudinal and Life Course Studies, 4*, 268-75.

Walseth, K. & Fasting, K. (2003). Islam's view on physical activity and sport: Egyptian women interpreting Islam, *International Review for the Sociology of Sport, 38*, 45-60.

Watson, D., Maître, B. & Russell, H. (2015). *Transitions into and out of Household Joblessness, 2004 to 2014: An Analysis of the Central Statistics Office (CSO) Quarterly National Household Survey (QNHS)*, Dublin: Department of Social Protection / Economic and Social Research Institute.

Whelan, C.T. & Maître, B. (2014). The Great Recession and the changing distribution of economic vulnerability by social class: The Irish case, *Journal of European Social Policy, 24*, 470-85.

Whelan, K. (2010). Policy lessons from Ireland's latest depression, *Economic and Social Review, 41*, 225-54.

Whitehurst, G.J., Arnold, D.S., Epstein, J.N., Angell, A.L., Smith, M. & Fischel, J.E. (1994). A picture book reading intervention in day-care and home for children from low-income families, *Developmental Psychology, 30*, 679-89.

Williams, J. & Collins, C. (1998). Childcare arrangements in Ireland: A report to the Commission on the Family, in Commission on the Family (eds.), *Strengthening Families for Life* (pp.460-504), Dublin: Stationery Office.

Williams, J. & Whelan, C.T. (2011). *Prevalence of Relative Income Poverty and Its Effect on Outcomes among Nine-year-olds*, paper presented at Growing Up in Ireland Annual Conference, Dublin, December.

Williams, J., Greene, S., Doyle, E., Harris, E., Layte, R., McCoy, S., McCrory, C., Murray, A., Nixon, E., O'Dowd, T., O'Moore, M., Quail, A., Smyth, E., Swords, L. & Thornton, M. (2009). *Growing Up in Ireland: The Lives of Nine-year-olds*, Dublin: Office of the Minister for Children and Youth Affairs.

Williams, R. (2012). Using the margins command to estimate and interpret adjusted predictions and marginal effects, *The Stata Journal, 12*, 308-31.

Wolfe, T., O'Donoghue-Hynes, B. & Hayes, N. (2013). Rapid change without transformation: The dominance of a national policy paradigm over international influences on ECEC development in Ireland 1995-2012, *International Journal of Early Childhood, 45*,191-205.

Working Party on Childcare Facilities for Working Parents (1983). *Report to the Minister for Labour,* Dublin: Stationery Office.

Yeung, W.J., Linver, M.R. & Brooks-Gunn, J. (2002). How money matters for young children's development: Parental investment and family processes, *Child Development, 73*, 1861-79.

Yoshikawa, H., Aber, J.L. & Beardslee, W.R. (2012). The effects of poverty on the mental, emotional and behavioural health of children and youth: Implications for prevention, *American Psychologist, 67*, 272-84.

OAK TREE PRESS

Oak Tree Press develops and delivers information, advice and resources for entrepreneurs and managers. It is Ireland's leading business book publisher, with an unrivalled reputation for quality titles across business, management, HR, law, marketing and enterprise topics. NuBooks is its ebooks-only imprint, publishing short, focused ebooks for busy entrepreneurs and managers.

In addition, Oak Tree Press occupies a unique position in start-up and small business support in Ireland through its standard-setting titles, as well training courses, mentoring and advisory services.

Oak Tree Press is comfortable across a range of communication media – print, web and training, focusing always on the effective communication of business information.

OAK TREE PRESS
E: info@oaktreepress.com
W: www.oaktreepress.com / www.SuccessStore.com.